Time, Ignorance, and Uncertainty in Economic Models

Time, Ignorance, and Uncertainty in Economic Models

Donald W. Katzner

Ann Arbor

THE UNIVERSITY OF MICHIGAN PRESS

Copyright © by the University of Michigan 1998
All rights reserved
Published in the United States of America by
The University of Michigan Press
Manufactured in the United States of America
♾ Printed on acid-free paper

2001   2000   1999   1998   4   3   2   1

A CIP catalog record for this book is available from the British Library.

Library of Congress Cataloging-in-Publication Data applied for
ISBN 0-472-10938-3

to Ruth,

with love

Contents

PART IV: Theory and Observation

Preface

Time, wrote Alfred Marshall, is ". . . the source of many of the greatest difficulties in economics."[1] To which, one might argue, he subsequently added uncertainty and, at least by implication, ignorance.[2] Over the years, these elements have, by and large, found expression, somewhat contrary to the meanings Marshall originally gave to them, in terms of the grand equilibrium paradigm that gradually, during the twentieth century, overtook the bulk of economic theorizing. Thus, time came to be represented abstractly as a subscript, t, in a periodic equation, or as the independent variable with respect to which numerical magnitudes would modify continuously in a differential equation. And uncertainty and ignorance were captured by the language of probability. But, even as it developed, there has always been an uneasiness with this state of affairs. For along with the acceptance of the equilibrium paradigm has been an undercurrent of thought reflecting the ideas, implicit in Marshall, that the time humans actually experience, and in which they live, that is, historical time, is not reasonably approximated by the time that structures the equilibrium paradigm, and that, due to the ignorance humans actually face (which arises, in part, from the reality of historical time), the epistemological basis underlying the construction

---

[1] A. Marshall, *Principles of Economics*, 8th ed. (New York: Macmillan, 1948), p. 48.

[2] *Ibid.*, p. 347.

of probability might not, in the end, hold up.[3] The question arises, then, of what contours and features economic analysis might exhibit if the equilibrium paradigm were discarded and historical time, nonprobabilistic uncertainty, and ignorance were fully taken into account.

However, with one major exception, not much progress has been made in developing models that would give concrete illustrations of the nature of economic analysis under such conditions. The one exception is the model of decision making in ignorance introduced by G. L. S. Shackle.[4] Shackle not only argued eloquently that, for the reasons suggested above, the equilibrium paradigm is wanting in its relevance to reality,[5] but his model, a modified version of which will be examined in detail in Section 4.3 below, represents, in spite of its flaws, a remarkably original attempt to introduce historical time, nonprobabilistic uncertainty, and ignorance into the analytical texture of decision making. But Shackle's work in general, and this model in particular, while enjoying some resonance in the economics literature,[6] seem, nevertheless, to have largely been dismissed as ". . . an exercise in the economics of pure chaos or . . . an elegant nihilism of no practical relevance."[7] Even

---

[3] E.g., Marshall, op. cit.; F. H. Knight, Risk, Uncertainty and Profit (Boston: Houghton Mifflin, 1921); J. M. Keynes, "The General Theory of Employment," Quarterly Journal of Economics 51 (1937), pp. 209-223; G. L. S. Shackle, Epistemics and Economics (Cambridge: Cambridge University Press, 1972); and J. R. Hicks, "Some Questions of Time in Economics," in Evolution, Welfare, and Time in Economics, A. M. Tang, F. M. Westfield, and J. S. Worley, eds. (Lexington: D. C. Heath, 1976), pp. 135-151.

[4] Decision, Order and Time in Human Affairs, 2nd ed. (Cambridge: Cambridge University Press, 1969).

[5] E.g., op. cit. See also G. L. S. Shackle, Keynesian Kaleidics (Edinburgh: Edinburgh University Press, 1974).

[6] E.g., B. Loasby, Choice, Complexity and Ignorance (Cambridge: Cambridge University Press, 1976); D. Vickers, Financial Markets in the Capitalist Process (Philadelphia: University of Pennsylvania Press, 1978), Part 3; and D. Vickers, "On Relational Structures and Non-Equilibrium in Economic Theory," Eastern Economic Journal 11 (1985), pp. 384-403.

[7] C. Rogers, Money, Interest and Capital (Cambridge: Cambridge University Press, 1989), p. 234. Rogers is actually dissenting from such claims. See also A. Coddington, Keynesian Economics: The Search for First Principles (London: George Allen & Unwin, 1983), p. 61; S. A. Ozga, Expectations in Economic Theory (London: Weidenfeld and Nicolson, 1965), p. 223; and G. Winston, The Timing of Economic Activities (Cambridge: Cambridge University Press, 1982), p. 15.

the incorporation of nonprobabilistic uncertainty itself into economics has been set aside on the grounds that it would ". . . deprive economic analysis of all definite content. . . ."[8] Part of the problem may be that, although it has both been improved[9] and inspired offshoots,[10] Shackle's model has not yet been subjected to an analytical workout on the order of that comparable to the hoops through which standard models in the economics literature are currently propelled. Another possibility might be that the model has not yet been explicitly extended and applied as the basis for rigorous models of the general microeconomy and its components, or for the microfoundations of models of the macroeconomy. That is to say, the Shacklean model has not yet been pushed, in a formal sense, to the same heights as traditional models of decision making under certainty and probabilistic uncertainty, and thus the analytical potential of the Shacklean approach to economics in general is, to a considerable extent, uncharted and murky.

The central concern of the present volume relates, in the manner just described as lacking, to the character of formal economic analysis when historical time, nonprobabilistic uncertainty, and ignorance are fully integrated into its fabric or, in other words, when that analysis is pursued from the Shacklean perspective. What, under these latter conditions, would economic models look like? What kinds of epistemological, methodological, and analytical problems would have to be dealt with to build them? How could rigorous analysis within their frameworks proceed? In short, if the equilibrium paradigm and all that springs from it is to be rejected, what might be put in its place? The book addresses these questions by first exploring a modified version of Shackle's model in considerable analytical detail, and then employing it to construct models of the firm, the consumer, and the micro- and

---

[8]M. Milgate and J. Eatwell, "Unemployment and the Market Mechanism," in *Keynes's Economics and the Theory of Value and Distribution*, J. Eatwell and M. Milgate, eds. (New York: Oxford University Press, 1983), p. 279. See also J. Hirschleifer and J. G. Riley, *The Analytics of Uncertainty and Information* (Cambridge: Cambridge University Press, 1992), p. 10; and R. E. Lucas, Jr., *Studies in Business-Cycle Theory* (Cambridge: MIT Press, 1981), p. 224.

[9]*E.g.*, D. Vickers, *Money Capital in the Theory of the Firm* (Cambridge: Cambridge University Press, 1987), Ch. 12.

[10]*E.g.*, J. L. Ford, *Economic Choice under Uncertainty: A Perspective Theory Approach* (New York: St. Martin's, 1987).

macroeconomies. By investigating the above questions in the process of constructing and exploring particular models, the emphasis of subsequent chapters is more on the actual doing of economic analysis in the context of historical time, nonprobabilistic uncertainty, and ignorance than on methodologically discussing how to go about doing it. Hopefully a better comprehension of the kind of theorizing that might be produced from the Shacklean vantage point will emerge. That approach, clearly, will never receive acceptance, or even a sympathetic hearing, until we first fully understand exactly what it can do.

It is important to emphasize that the ensuing offering attempts to present something rather different from traditional economic inquiry. Indeed, in moving to an analytical environment of historical time, nonprobabilistic uncertainty, and ignorance, a clean methodological break is made with that tradition. This is not to say that nothing in traditional theory is relevant for, or appropriate to, the Shacklean approach. For, in point of fact, a number of ideas on the pages that follow are borrowed directly from traditional investigations. But it does raise a potential obstacle for the reader. People, after all, come to works they read with a given mind-set (*i.e.*, they read in historical time). That mind-set is determined by their own historical backgrounds and it colors their understandings of what they read. They are conditioned to expect certain things and often, and quite naturally, read those things into what they see on the printed page, even if it was not the author's intention to put them there. Thus it can be difficult, when submitting a radically different perspective for a reader's consideration, to present it in a manner that enables him to escape from his existing mind-set and take off in a new direction. In writing this book, although I have been aware of the problem, I cannot say that, even with substantial effort, I have been able to overcome it.

As is common these days, the level of discourse throughout the volume includes the use of mathematical symbolism and reasoning. I see this as an appropriate means of analytical expression, the application of which in economics has been given numerous justifications dating at least to Cournot.[11] However, to aid readers who prefer to avoid detailed

---

[11]See D. W. Katzner, "In Defense of Formalization in Economics," *Methodus* 3, no. 1 (June 1991), pp. 17-24.

mathematical argument where possible, I have identified material that can be skipped without seriously impairing their ability to understand what is going on. It should also be noted that, due to the broad spectrum of topical coverage, it has not been possible to develop a system of notation in which each symbol always appears with the same meaning everywhere from one end of the investigation to the other. Only within chapters, and occasionally across successive chapters, is such symbolic consistency maintained. In each chapter, then, all symbols are defined where they are introduced. Moreover, the theorem-proof style of exposition is employed where convenient.

It was Douglas Vickers who, some years ago, suggested that I take up an inquiry into the effect on economic modeling of introducing historical time, nonprobabilistic uncertainty, and ignorance. With two exceptions, the following chapters appear in the same order in which I engaged the issues they address. Each of these chapters was initially written and, in all cases but two (not the same two as the aforementioned exceptions), published as an independent paper.[12] In this process, Vickers played a major role. The following pattern, with some variation here and there, repeated itself over and over again: after preliminary discussions with him concerning the kinds of issues to be entertained and the means by which those issues might be faced in a given paper (chapter), I would work out a way of dealing with the subject (*e.g.*, build a particular model) and write a draft of the paper. Next Vickers would comment on the draft, pointing out errors, weaknesses, omissions, and alternatives. Then it would be back to the drawing board to rethink and rewrite. Further commentary by Vickers with each instance succeeded by my rewriting would ensue. Sometimes a result that we were both happy with would emerge after two or three tries. Occasionally, as many as a dozen or more iterations were required. (Often Vickers would write his own paper on the same subject and, in discussions of it, our roles would reverse.) A similar procedure was used in reworking and combining these papers into the present book. (Vickers wrote his own book too.)[13] Thus, at all stages, Vick-

---

[12]Publication of the original version of Chapter 10, however, has been delayed.

[13]D. Vickers, *Economics and the Antagonism of Time: Time, Uncertainty, and Choice in Economic Theory* (Ann Arbor: University of Michigan Press, 1994).

ers has been a driving force and a significant contributor. Not many authors are fortunate enough to have this kind of support and I am deeply grateful for it. I can only absolve him of the responsibility for any errors that have survived, and hope that the final result is worthy of such effort.

Numerous other individuals have also given their time and energy to various parts of the manuscript at various stages of its development. The help of some has already been acknowledged in the previously published versions of those chapters heretofore in print. Although the limitations of space do not permit the listing of all who remain, I would especially like to thank Andy B. Anderson, Philippe De Ville, David J. Foulis, and Frank Wattenberg for their assistance. Of course, my intellectual debt to G. L. S. Shackle is both, at the same time, rather heavy and quite obvious. Thanks are also due to the *Eastern Economic Journal*, Edward Arnold, M. E. Sharpe, Routledge, and Springer Verlag for their permission, explicitly acknowledged later on, to freely use published materials below. Finally, I would like to thank George E. Zinsmeister for help with the preparation of the diagrams.

CHAPTER 1

Introduction: Alternatives to Equilibrium Analysis

> *Here is Edward Bear, coming downstairs now,*
> *bump, bump, bump, on the back of his head,*
> *behind Christopher Robin. It is, as far as*
> *he knows, the only way of coming downstairs,*
> *but sometimes he feels that there really is*
> *another way, if only he could stop bumping*
> *for a moment and think of it.*
> A. A. Milne, *Winnie-the-Pooh*

Economists, too, often seem to yearn for another way. It is not only the uneasy feeling that assumptions may be "unrealistic," or techniques "inadequate" or "improper," but sometimes even the approach itself can appear to be a straitjacket that lacks the necessary flexibility to deal appropriately with the problems at hand. The evidence of discontent is considerable and growing: numerous articles and books have been written that detail complaints.[1] Numerous sessions at conventions take up these questions.[2] Thus, for example, Georgescu-Roegen [8, p. 319] sees

---

[1]*E.g.*, Katouzian [18], Klamer and McCloskey [22], McCloskey [26], [27], Ward [41], Woo [44], and the collections of essays edited by Bell and Kristol [4] and Wiles and Routh [42].

[2]*E.g.*, "Has Formalization in Economics Gone Too Far?" *Methodus* 3 (June 1991), pp. 6-31.

This chapter is reproduced, with considerable additions, corrections, and other modifications, from my "Alternatives to Equilibrium Analysis," *Eastern Economic Journal* 11 (1985), pp. 404-421.

the economic "method," largely transferred from classical mechanics, as the primary source of a malaise in Economic Science. Hicks, in addition to repudiating received theory (including his own work) by changing his name [13, p. 365], laments that much of economic theorizing is, to its detriment, "out of time" [14]. And Hutchison [15, p. 88] speaks of a "crisis of abstraction" brought on by assumptions that oversimplify and result in analysis that is irrelevant for interpreting economic reality. To understand many of the issues involved, it is necessary to introduce some concepts.

1.1   Preliminaries

In the present context, the *purpose* of analysis is to explain or make sense of what is happening in the world. This notion of analytical objective is meant to be sweeping, intentionally including such possibilities as the exploration of hypothetical policy options and prediction. Moreover, regardless of whether explicitly stated, each analysis comes fully equipped with both methodological and epistemological supports. The *methodology* of an analysis is the conceptual means by which the analysis is put together. Its *epistemology* elucidates how the analysis does its explaining or, in other words, how it is able to produce knowledge.

Traditionally, epistemology has been based on the presumption of a dichotomy between observations of reality and thoughts about those observations. From the *rationalist* perspective (Descartes), knowledge is gained by first thinking or theorizing about reality and then fitting what is seen into the thoughts or theories already secured (reality is made to correspond to thoughts). Alternatively, the *empiricist* (Locke) would argue that one obtains knowledge by looking first, and then building thoughts and theories to understand what has been seen (thoughts are made to correspond to reality). Thus these approaches dichotomize thinking and seeing, and produce knowledge or truth by taking one to be the "cause" or "essence" of the other. In this sense, traditional epistemology may be called *essentialistic (reductionistic)*.

There is, however, an alternative epistemology that does not recognize the dichotomy between observation and thinking.[3] Unlike ratio-

---

[3]Resnick and Wolff [31] and Rorty [34].

nalism or empiricism, no single unique procedure generates knowledge. Knowledge, rather, comes from discourse that recognizes the interrelatedness of observation and thinking, and hence the nonunique and *nonessentialistic* character of truth. On this view, the ability to organize and understand the patterns of happenings in the world rests on deeply penetrating interdependencies. Here the challenge to economists is to consider whether and how such a pervasive interaction between events and contemplations of them impinges on established modes of economic analysis.

The notion of essentialism also arises with respect to methodology. A methodology is *essentialistic* if explanation obtained through its use elucidates the conceptual phenomenon in question as the outcome of a single cause or set of causes, that is, in terms of an "essence." Contrariwise, a *nonessentialistic* or *nonreductionistic* methodology bases explanation on the idea that each and every conceptual phenomenon exists only as the combined result of the interactions of all other conceptual entities. Conceptual phenomena, then, cannot be said to have single causes since they are understood to codetermine each other. They are distinct but not independent.

The mainstay of the current approach to economic analysis is, of course, the notion of equilibrium. In its static form, equilibrium is simply the outcome of the timeless interaction of forces, the resolution of simultaneity. In dynamic contexts, it appears in the guise of either the stationary or the steady state. Most contemporary economic theorizing, henceforth referred to as *equilibrium analysis*, takes place through the construction of (usually mathematical) models in which equilibrium, in one of these forms, is studied. And most empirical investigations are propped up by such a construct. Thus the methodology of today's equilibrium analysis is the essentialistic methodology of model building in which all variables and relations among them are assumed to be (at least probabilistically) known and stable over time. And, though rarely mentioned in specific applications, the epistemology of current equilibrium analysis is either rationalism (*e.g.*, Robbins [32]) or empiricism (*e.g.*, Friedman [7]).

Economists searching for another way, then, may be uneasy with equilibrium analysis for (among other possibilities) one of the following three reasons. First, they might believe that the methodology and epistemology of equilibrium analysis are sound, but that the emphasis on equilibrium is misplaced. Second, they may be uncomfortable with the essentialistic nature of both the methodology and epistemology on which equilibrium analysis rests. And finally, while subscribing to either rationalism or empiricism and to essentialism in methodology, they may feel that the particular essentialistic methodology of equilibrium analysis is flawed.

But what are the options if equilibrium analysis is rejected? Under such conditions, how might economic inquiry proceed? There are, of course, other ways of looking at the world and, therefore, other analytic structures and paradigms within which to understand it. But, not surprisingly, the worldview adopted, and the paradigmatic framework invoked as a result, can imply an analysis based on very different axiomatic foundations from those that inform the equilibrium approach. Thus, in order to establish a background and perspective from which the argument of subsequent chapters can be evaluated and compared, it will be useful at this point to present, in briefest outline, the general nature of some alternatives. Without attempting to be exhaustive, then, the remainder of this chapter compares and contrasts three substitutes, each of which responds, respectively, to the dissatisfaction of those economists who reject equilibrium analysis for one of the three reasons listed above. After an initial description of the workings of typical equilibrium analysis, discussion turns to so-called *disequilibrium analysis* in which both the essentialistic methodology and epistemologies of equilibrium analysis are retained, but in which interest concentrates on out-of-equilibrium situations. Next to be taken up is an approach, identified as *mutually interactive analysis*, that is based on a nonessentialistic methodology and epistemology focusing on the mutually interactive character of all aspects of reality, including the analysis of reality itself. Finally, a perspective is presented whose epistemologies are identical to those of equilibrium analysis, and whose methodology, though still essentialistic, emerges from the notions that (i) the nature of time is "historical," as opposed to the "logical" time required in the methodology of equilibrium analysis, and (ii) human beings investigate issues, and make and attempt to execute decisions, under conditions of sufficient ignorance that they are unable to even calculate the probabilities normally required in many traditional approaches. This last analytical vision is referred to as *nonequilibrium analysis* and is the center of attention in the remaining chapters of the present volume.

Before proceeding, however, it is well to be clear about the distinction between logical and historical time. Since more will be said about these concepts later on, only a brief introductory discussion is presented here. Following Winston [43, pp. 32-38], who uses the adjectives "analytical" and "perspective" in place of, respectively, "logical" and "historical," the difference between these concepts has to do with the way in which time is perceived to order events. When pairwise comparisons of events are made such that any one event, regardless of whether it is considered to occur in the past, present, or future, is said to take place before, after, or simultaneously with any other, time is expressed in its *logical* form. Logical time, then, is not a manifestation of the real time in which human beings live. Rather, it provides only a means for the sequencing of events through time without regard to the actual experiencing of them as past events, present events, or future events. It is because one may move back and forth through a sequence of such timed or dated events hypothetically, but never experientially, that Hicks [14] invoked the previously cited phrase "out of time," meaning "out of actually experienced time," to describe analysis placed in logical time. In the *historical* approach to time, however, all events are placed in one of the three categories of past events, present events, and future events. Here time orders sets containing many events at once, rather than sets having only single events, and the basis of that ordering is solely experiential: past events come before present events, and present events come before future events. For this reason, historical time is sometimes called "real" time and analysis based upon it was referred to by Hicks [14] as analysis "in time."

At a fundamental level, the significance of the distinction between logical and historical time is related to, though not necessarily completely dependent on, the assumed ontological status of mankind. Generally speaking, there are two different interpretations of human existence. On the one hand, individuals may be perceived as being totally constituted by the material pieces (*e.g.*, neurons and other cells, molecules, atoms, etc.) of which they are made up. From this vantage point, to be referred to here as *philosophical materialism,* if enough were known about the properties of these material pieces (including the ways they interact with other material pieces both within and outside of the individual), then a person's behavior in any situation could be determined with a high degree of accuracy from a careful examination of his material characteristics and his environment. A parallel assertion could be made with respect to the behavior of an institution that is, from the perspective of philosophical materialism, fully comprised of the people who form it. Thus, accepting philosophical materialism, there may be little necessity to recognize the importance for the analysis of human behavior of the movement of historical time. In that case, however, a residual difficulty in the explanation of human behavior may arise from the impact on historical reality of haphazard shocks and unanticipatable developments.

On the other hand, it may be thought that human beings have cognitive capacities that go beyond, and are not solely determined by, their material parts. That is, knowing all of the material facts about an individual (and his environment) is not sufficient to be able to explain his behavior. This implies that, in relation to the world in which human beings live and act, only the experiencing of things and events can directly interact with those extra-material cognitive capacities since the material pieces cannot go that far. Of course, due to the individual's continually changing knowledge and circumstances, the interactions with respect to things and events can happen in any particular way only once, only when the individual makes intellectual contact with them, and only in the order in which those contacts actually occur. All mental processes, regardless of whether they relate to material or nonmaterial elements, together with whatever knowledge has been accumulated, necessarily contribute to the making of an individual's decisions. It follows that experience and its orderly interaction with the extra-material capacities become of major significance in the generation of human behavior. And the latter, clearly, can only be properly accounted for in the context of historical time. Thus, although it is possible to remain agnostic in analytical outlook about philosophical materialism and still hold to the assumption of logical time, adherence to historical time as the setting in which human action occurs necessarily requires the rejection of philosophical materialism. That rejection could also be seen to be implied in the previous acknowledgment of the difficulties introduced to explanation by the possibility of unforeseen and unforeseeable shocks and external events.

There are three differences between logical time and historical time that are important for present purposes. First, as suggested above, time in the logical sense can be controlled. For example, an investigator may move backward through a sequence of timed events, restart his analytical clock, and, if nothing else is changed analytically, repeat the same sequence of events over again. Neither the values of the variables he employs nor the explanatory edifice he constructs are subject to variation simply by virtue of their existence at different actual (historical) time dates. Thus the outcomes produced by his system emerge from the resolution of a fixed, often mathematical, structure having the same analytical properties at all dates. Logical time is, in other words, reversible. But the investigator has no such control of time in the historical sense. For historical time locks him in the present. As previously indicated, the events of each moment can be experienced only once; although their effects may linger, after these events are experienced they are forever past. In that case, restarting his analytical clock, if that notion has any meaning at all, necessarily leads to an entirely different analysis and a totally new sequence of events. This is because, under the conditions implicit in the passing of historical time, the possibility of re-experiencing past events, in the same precise way and in terms of the same structural relations with respect to which they previously occurred, is precluded. What is experientially new or novel after the clock has been restarted determines human behavior. Second, although each moment in logical time has the same status as any other, in historical time past, present, and future moments have their own unique statuses. That is because all action takes place in the present, all actions of the future are yet to come, and all actions of the past are history. Thus the moment of the present has a different significance and meaning than either past moments or future moments. Third, since the individual actor under investigation can be thought of as an investigator himself, and since the assumption of logical time permits the investigator to wander back and forth across sequences of timed events, the actor in logical time necessarily knows everything that exists and is relevant to know about the past, present, and future. His knowledge is therefore *complete* or *perfect*, even if it is only expressed probabilistically. But in historical time, although the actor may be able to make some intelligent guesses, it is not possible for him to know anything at all about the future. Knowledge of future events, even probabilistic knowledge, is not only unknown, but also unknowable until the events are past. (Under the conditions of historical time and ingorance invoked with respect to nonequilibrium analysis as described in Section 1.5 below, knowledge of the past and present, too, is incomplete and imperfect.) The question of the applicability of probability concepts under conditions of historical time and ignorance is taken up again in Sections 1.5 and 2.4.

One more word about conventions concerning time, logical or historical, will avoid confusion later on. The irreducible unit of time can be taken to be either the "moment" or "period." In the latter case, that period cannot be subsequently split up into subperiods, nor can moments within it be separated out and considered independently of the whole. To do so destroys the original analysis and creates a new one. If the moment is taken as the base unit, all simultaneous behaviors or actions of that moment, as well as their interactions, occur simultaneously at that moment and cannot be stretched out across any period containing that moment. Time is referred to as *continuous* when the moment is the base unit; with the period as the base unit, it is *discrete*. Any dynamic mathematical model has equivalent expressions in continuous and discrete time, the former in the guise of differential equations and the latter as difference or periodic equations.

The term "period" is also employed in a more informal sense in which it is capable of being broken up into subperiods and from which individual moments can be extracted as foci of attention. But such a notion of period is quite distinct from the irreducible unit of time that forms the basis of a mathematical construction. In addition, both the words "moment" and "period" may be used to describe the present. The former usage is clearly in reference to continuous time, while the latter invokes discrete time.

1.2   Equilibrium Analysis

The following paragraphs are intended not so much to deal with methodological and epistemological questions (although implicit and some explicit reference to them is unavoidable) as to present a recipe that shows how to do traditional equilibrium analysis. The game-theoretic version of equilibrium analysis is ignored. Hereafter, the phrase "equilibrium analysis" is understood to mean the construction and examination of a micro- or macroequilibrium-type model of the sort described below, along with the standard methodological and epistemological baggage (described above) that usually accompanies such a model.

Static equilibrium analysis requires a model such as, for example,

$$x_j = f^j(x_1, \ldots, x_{j-1}, x_{j+1}, \ldots, x_I, \rho), \quad j = 1, \ldots, J, \quad (1.2\text{-}1)$$

where x_i is a scalar variable for $i = 1, \ldots, I$, the f^j denote single-valued functions for $j = 1, \ldots, J$, and ρ represents a vector of parameters. Time does not appear. A very common assumption in this model is that $I = J$, or that the number of variables and equations is the same. Given a value for ρ, an equilibrium (solution) of (1.2-1) is a vector $x = (x_1, \ldots, x_I)$, which satisfies all equations of (1.2-1) simultaneously. Thus at equilibrium, all forces "balance out" and the system is "at rest." It is often possible to solve (1.2-1) so as to secure equilibrium as a function of the values of ρ.

Dynamic equilibrium analysis, as suggested above, can be expressed in the language of either continuous or discrete time. Although at a sufficiently abstract level there is no formal difference between them, the distinction is still worth maintaining here. To pursue dynamic equilibrium analysis in continuous time necessitates the specifications of a system of first-order differential equations such as

$$\frac{dz_k}{dt} = g^k(z, \rho, t), \quad k = 1, \ldots, K, \quad (1.2\text{-}2)$$

where $t \geq 0$ varies over real numbers representing (scalar) time, ρ remains a vector of parameters, $z = (z_1, \ldots, z_K)$ is a vector of scalar variables z_k, and the g^k are functions of z, ρ, and t. Frequently (1.2-2) is abbreviated to

$$\frac{dz}{dt} = g(z, \rho, t), \quad (1.2\text{-}3)$$

where $dz/dt = (dz_1/dt, \ldots, dz_K/dt)$ and $g = (g^1, \ldots, g^K)$. The counterpart of (1.2-2) in discrete time is the system of first-order periodic equations

$$z_k^t = g^k(z^{t-1}, \rho), \quad k = 1, \ldots, K, \qquad (1.2\text{-}4)$$

where t now assumes as values only the positive integers, z_k^t denotes the value of z_k at time t, $z^{t-1} = (z_1^{t-1}, \ldots, z_K^{t-1})$, and the functions g^k are defined in terms of z^{t-1} and the parameter vector ρ. The shortened form of (1.2-4) is

$$z^t = g(z^{t-1}, \rho), \qquad (1.2\text{-}5)$$

where $z^t = (z_1^t, \ldots, z_K^t)$ and $g = (g^1, \ldots, g^K)$. Note that it is not necessary here to consider higher order systems of differential or periodic equations since they all may be reduced to larger, equivalent systems of the first order.

Given the value for ρ, a *time-path* (*solution*) of (1.2-3) starting at z^0 is a function

$$z = \theta(z^0, \rho, t), \qquad (1.2\text{-}6)$$

which satisfies (1.2-3), that is,

$$\frac{d\theta(z^0, \rho, t)}{dt} = g(\theta(z^0, \rho, t), \rho, t),$$

for all $t > 0$, and which passes through the starting point so that $z^0 = \theta(z^0, \rho, t)$. Observe that the symbolism in (1.2-6) is a truncation of

$$z_k = \theta^k(z^0, \rho, t), \quad k = 1, \ldots, K,$$

with $\theta = (\theta^1, \ldots, \theta^K)$. By contrast, a *time-path* of (1.2-5) starting at z^0 (for fixed ρ) is a sequence of points $\{z^t\}$, one for each $t = 1, 2, \ldots$, generated by starting (1.2-5) at z^0:

$$
\begin{aligned}
&z^0, \\
&z^1 = g(z^0, \rho), \\
&z^2 = g(g(z^0, \rho), \rho), \\
&\quad \cdot \\
&\quad \cdot \\
&\quad \cdot
\end{aligned}
\qquad (1.2\text{-}7)
$$

Implicit in the way these time-paths are used in dynamic equilibrium analysis is the concept of logical or clock time through which "machines" (1.2-3) and (1.2-5) run as they crank out (1.2-6) and (1.2-7). Either machine may be started over and over again at z^0, and in every case the same time-paths result as long as ρ does not shift. The machines themselves, that is, the functions g, are definitionally independent of time, although, of course, they are still functions of t for all t.

With ρ fixed, a time-path starting at z^0 is *stationary*, or a *stationary state* or an *equilibrium path*, when none of the values of the variables along that time-path are changing. For continuous time, stationary states are defined in terms of (1.2-6) by the equation

$$z^0 = \theta(z^0, \rho, t)$$

for all t. In the case of discrete time, a time-path from (1.2-7) is a stationary state provided that

$$z^t = z^0$$

for all t. With either continuous or discrete time, variation in ρ alters the stationary state.

Whereas stationarity is characterized by variables that do not change as time passes, the concept of steady state permits these same variables to increase at set rates over time. Thus constancy in the steady state occurs with respect to the growth rates of the variables rather than with respect to the variables themselves, and the stationary state is the special steady state in which all growth rates are zero. Once again, let ρ be fixed. A continuous time-path (1.2-6) starting at z^0 is a *steady state* if and only if

$$\theta^k(z^0, \rho, t) = z_k^0 e^{\psi^k(\rho)t}, \quad k = 1, \ldots, K, \tag{1.2-8}$$

for all t and some functions ψ^k of ρ. Since (1.2-8) implies

$$\frac{dz_k}{dt} \frac{1}{z_k} = \psi^k(\rho), \quad k = 1, \ldots, K,$$

along the steady state each variable z_k is growing at the constant rate $\psi^k(\rho)$. For the discrete time-path (1.2-7) starting at z^0 to be a *steady state*, it is necessary and sufficient that

$$z_k^t = z^0 \left[1 + \psi^k(\rho)\right]^t, \quad k = 1, \ldots, K, \tag{1.2-9}$$

for all t. Using (1.2-9) with $t \geq 1$,

$$\frac{z_k^t}{z_k^{t-1}} = 1 + \psi^k(\rho), \quad k = 1, \ldots, K,$$

whence, as before, each z_k grows at the constant rate $\psi^k(\rho)$. In either case, changes in ρ modify the steady state.

Equilibrium analysis – static or dynamic – presumes an underlying vision of the way the world operates in terms of the models described above. Although sightings in actuality are epistemologically distinct from conceptualized equilibria (which lie in the realm of thinking as opposed to seeing), the creation of explanation (knowledge) proceeds by linking them in either a rationalist or empiricist union. In the static case, the observations of reality are identified with unique equilibria in the model. Therefore the thrust of static equilibrium analysis is to explain what is seen as determined by simultaneously interacting forces like those described in (1.2-1). From a dynamic perspective, observations can be interpreted either as lying on one or more unique stationary or steady state time-paths or as falling on not necessarily unique time-paths that are converging to unique stationary or steady states. Thus what appears in reality is understood as the outcome of dynamic processes such as those of (1.2-3) or (1.2-5), which, if not initially placing the world in a stationary or steady state, are at least pushing it toward one. Furthermore, since the methodology of equilibrium analysis takes (1.2-1), (1.2-3), or (1.2-5) to be stable over time, formal predictions of future observations may be made by extrapolating along the time-path currently pursued or by adjusting that time-path for expected parameter changes. Note that if all sightings of the world are taken to be observations of, say, unique stationary states, then it is not possible to watch empirically the dynamic processes at work that force convergence. Regardless, for both static and dynamic equilibrium analysis the role of equilibrium is central: from both rationalist and empiricist points of view, equilibrium is the organizing concept through which observations of, and thoughts about, reality derive their meaning. Of course, the relevant form of equilibrium must exist uniquely and, when appropriate, be (locally or globally) stable in models (1.2-1), (1.2-3), or (1.2-5) if an equilibrium analysis based on any one of them is to have genuine explanatory significance.

Another aspect of dynamic equilibrium analysis has to do with movements from one equilibrium position to another. Suppose, for example, the world is understood to be at some unique stationary state. Let an exogenous change in the parameter vector ρ occur, which results in an altered, but still unique, stationary state. Then subsequent development is taken to follow a time-path, called a *traverse*, which converges to the new stationary state.[4] The laws of motion governing the traverse (say, [1.2-3] or [1.2-5]) provide an explanation of how reality progresses from a position of being in the old stationary state to a location at the new stationary state. Once again, if all real world sightings are interpreted as lying on unique stationary state time-paths, then the traverse cannot be seen. In that case, observations made after successive changes in ρ yield pictures of one stationary state after another.

It frequently happens in equilibrium analysis that one or more of the x_i or z_k in (1.2-1), (1.2-3), or (1.2-5) are thought of as random variables, each with a definable probability distribution. Under such specification, the standard approach is to use the probability distributions to sum or integrate out all random variation. The result is expectational systems of equations that are formally similar to (1.2-1), (1.2-3), and (1.2-5). Definitions of the various forms of equilibrium remain as before, and both static and dynamic equilibrium analysis proceeds as depicted above. The introduction of randomness, then, complicates but does not really change the character of equilibrium analysis.

Also worthy of mention is the fact that equilibrium analysis does not depend on an ability to measure the variables involved. Although differential equations like (1.2-3) and steady state time-paths like (1.2-8) and (1.2-9) surely require numbers for their coherent expression, little else does. The static model (1.2-1), the periodic model (1.2-5) and its time-path (1.2-7), the specification of unique equilibrium for (1.2-1) and of unique stationarity for (1.2-5), and the notion of convergence in the case of (1.2-5), are all meaningful in the absence of measurement.[5] Therefore, static and dynamic equilibrium analysis may be applied as described earlier to explain and understand qualitative, nonnumerical

---

[4]Hicks [12, pp. 81-82].
[5]Katzner [19, Ch. 5].

phenomena.

Returning to the numerical world, perhaps the most common example in economics of static equilibrium analysis is the determination of (short-run) observed market price and quantity through the forces of supply and demand. A second illustration is the IS-LM model of macroeconomic theory, and a third is provided by any of the so-called (macro)models of income distribution. The market supply-demand model is extended in static Walrasian microeconomics to explain observations of outputs produced and inputs hired by firms, final outputs consumed and factors supplied by individuals, the relative prices of all goods, and the distribution of income, in terms of profit maximization by firms, constrained utility maximization by individuals, and the simultaneous interaction of supply and demand in all markets. The latter model also serves as the basis for dynamic equilibrium analysis of the perfectly competitive microeconomy by adding dynamic rules of the form of (1.2-3) or (1.2-5), which make the above static equilibrium correspond to the stationary state and explain how prices adjust when the system is out of equilibrium.[6] Note further that the Walrasian construction rests on the assumption that all individual decision makers have complete or perfect knowledge of the past, present, and future, as described earlier, about all relevant economic matters. Regardless, observations of the actual economy are now interpreted either as located on unique stationary states or as placed on time-paths that converge to unique stationary states. In both cases, sufficient assumptions are imposed so that the time-path along which observations are assumed to lie exists within the model. An alternative example of dynamic equilibrium analysis is the investigation of convergent and steady-state time-paths in models of economic growth.

It is also clear that models in which equilibrium is thought of as "temporary" fall within the realm of equilibrium analysis too. For, with the current, temporary, equilibrium state of the economy (z_t) depending on individual decision makers' forecasts of the next period's equilibrium state, and with those latter forecasts depending on what is presently happening (z_t) and what has happened in the past ($z_{t-1}, z_{t-2}, \ldots, z_0$), a periodic equation is obtained in which, in principle, the current equilib-

---

[6]*E.g.*, Katzner [20, pp. 15-18 and Ch. 9].

rium state is determined by past equilibrium states.[7] Its higher order notwithstanding, this equation has a similar conceptual basis and is similar in form to (1.2-5).

Those economists who employ equilibrium analysis with a rationalist epistemology are likely to accept the statement that economic inquiry requires ". . . an equilibrium notion to make precise the limits of economics. . . ."[8] For them, economic knowledge is obtained through the construction of models in which equilibrium exists and gives meaning to economic reality. By contrast, the equilibrium analyst with an empiricist bent would assert that "Only factual evidence can show whether [equilibrium analysis] is 'right' or 'wrong'. . . ."[9] But regardless of epistemological orientation, there are economists (as suggested earlier) who consider equilibrium analysis to be seriously defective. Some[10] take the position that, although there is nothing wrong with models such as (1.2-1), (1.2-3), and (1.2-5), with the equilibrium methodology, and with an essentialist epistemology, the real world either has too many structural and institutional barriers preventing the attainment of equilibrium or is in such rapid structural and institutional flux that the notion of equilibrium is irrelevant. Thus the focus in models (1.2-1), (1.2-3), and (1.2-5) should be on out-of-equilibrium positions or on either time-paths that do not converge to stationary or steady states or converging time-paths along which, for some reason, convergence is blocked. Others[11] reject the essentialism in both methodology and epistemology of equilibrium analysis. In their view, knowledge of the economy derives from discourse in which the interrelated complexities of actuality are not reduced to a single set of causes and which does not recognize a dichotomy between observations and thoughts about them. Still others[12] accept the essentialist epistemologies of equilibrium analysis and its essentialism in methodology but argue that its methodology is inappropriate. The particular usage of functions and probability distributions, and the notion of logical time

---

[7]*E.g.*, Grandmont [9, pp. xiv-xvi].

[8]Hahn [10, p. 38].

[9]Friedman [7, p. 8].

[10]*E.g.*, Benassy [5, p. 9].

[11]*E.g.*, Amariglio [2], Resnick and Wolff [31], and Ruccio [35].

[12]*E.g.*, Bausor [3], Shackle [37], and Vickers [39].

employed, renders impossible in equilibrium analysis the taking into account of certain facts of life considered to be fundamental, namely, that time is irreversible, that novelty is unpredictable, and that human beings live in ignorance of, and hence with nonprobabilistic uncertainty about, much of the past and present, and all of the future. Moreover, the models of equilibrium analysis abstract too far from the actual institutional environments in which the phenomena they are to explain are set, and are not themselves sufficiently stable over time to permit their use for more than the immediate moment of analysis, and certainly never in prediction. Thus knowledge of the real economy gleaned from equilibrium analysis is faulty because its methodology is blemished. Analysis reflecting a different essentialistic methodological flavor, one imbued with historical time and human ignorance, is required.

The alternatives to which each of the above groups subscribes are now considered in turn.

1.3   Disequilibrium Analysis

What is usually referred to as disequilibrium analysis in the economics literature generally employs the same essentialist epistemologies, the same essentialist methodology, and the same kind of models as those used in equilibrium analysis. But the question of the existence of the relevant form of unique equilibrium is no longer of major consequence since analysis here proceeds from the construction of the model to an explanation within it of what is seen in the real world, often without explicit reference to equilibrium at all.

Consider the static case first. Suppose a unique equilibrium exists in a system such as (1.2-1) but certain independent "outside" forces prevent the attainment of that equilibrium. For example, (1.2-1) could represent the typical supply and demand equations (invariant with respect to government policy) of an isolated market in which the government has imposed a minimum price above the equilibrium price (*e.g.*, minimum wage laws) or a maximum price below the equilibrium price (*e.g.*, price controls designed to stop inflation). Alternatively, the pressures encapsulated by (1.2-1) could be insufficient by themselves to ensure the existence of a unique equilibrium. In the isolated market example, supply and demand curves might be coincident, distinct but parallel, or, if extended beyond their usual domain, might intersect only at a negative price and (or) quantity. In all of these situations, to explain happenings in the real world (market), it is necessary to add outside (nonmarket) elements that, together with (1.2-1), determine a unique vector of variables in the model. Such unique vectors must then be identified with actual observations either rationalistically or empiricistically. Only then can static disequilibrium analysis provide an explanation of what is seen.

Similarly, disequilibrium analysis frequently ignores stationary and steady states in its construction and study of models like (1.2-3) and (1.2-5), even when present.[13] It locates all sightings of reality on non-stationary, non-steady-state time-paths that do not converge to stationary or steady states. Divergent and constant oscillatory time-paths are two possibilities. It might also permit consideration of time-paths that would normally converge to stationary or steady states but for which convergence is either too slow to have any "practical" meaning or is prevented from occurring by certain outside forces. Prediction proceeds as in equilibrium analysis. In such circumstances as these, disequilibrium analysis has to discern the nature of the actual time-path along which the real world is moving, for otherwise it cannot furnish much understanding of reality.

Examination of nonconvergent time-paths for prices and quantities in a cobweb model of an isolated market with unchanging demand and supply curves is an example of dynamic disequilibrium analysis. As a second example, consider the dynamic version of the model of the Walrasian microeconomy described earlier in which trading transpires before stationarity is reached. For expositional purposes, let there be a traditional auctioneer who guides the economy in the usual way. In this particular case, then, after the auctioneer announces a set of prices, trades take place regardless of whether the prices are equilibrium prices or not. These trades affect initial endowments in the next round, which begins with the auctioneer announcing a new set of prices. Disequilibrium analysis would involve the working out of this process for not necessarily convergent time-paths and the identification of each such

---

[13]See, for example, Allen [1, pp. 76-77] and Benassy [5].

time-path with actual behavior in the economy.

Although the proponents of each approach may believe that theirs is the only correct way, it is clear that, in many respects, equilibrium and disequilibrium analysis are quite similar. In addition to relying on identical methodological and epistemological foundations, the concept of equilibrium can be (though it not always is) defined in either case. The primary difference between them is that equilibrium analysis interprets reality in relation to equilibrium in these models, while disequilibrium analysis elucidates it with respect to ideas having little to do directly with equilibrium, even when a unique equilibrium may be available. However, static disequilibrium analysis may still be viewed as "equilibrium analysis" with an altered system of equations, since, in order to explain observations, new relations must be added to or substituted in (1.2-1), and the unique solution of the modified system (*i.e.*, its "equilibrium") can then be identified or related to the seen thing. Likewise, dynamic disequilibrium analysis might be thought of as "equilibrium analysis" with respect to nonequilibrium and nonconvergent time-paths. By contrast, the remaining forms of analysis discussed below make a clean methodological and (or) epistemological break with equilibrium analysis. Not only do the models employed have a different meaning and applicability, but the notion of equilibrium as defined in Section 1.2 cannot arise in exactly the same way within their frameworks.

1.4   Mutually Interactive Analysis

The second substitute approach presented here, namely, mutually interactive analysis, denies the possibility of analyzing any one piece of reality in isolation from any other piece or collection of pieces.[14] Everything in actuality – physical, social, mental, etc. – is assumed to interact in a mutually constitutive manner with everything else. Each entity, that is to say, exists only as the result of the combined effects on it of all other entities. This perspective clearly requires a different methodology from those described earlier. Moreover, the assertion

---

[14]The ideas of this section are elaborated by Amariglio [2, Ch. 1], Resnick and Wolff [30], [31], and Ruccio [35].

that such interdependence or mutually constitutive determinations extend to the intellectual as well as the material and social is the point
at which the proponents of this approach depart from epistemological
tradition and formulate their own distinctive epistemology. Because of
these interdependencies, no single event can be understood by detach-
ing it from the milieu of all events. No phenomenon can be described
as the outcome of independently construed (static or dynamic) forces.
(An "economy," for example, cannot be conceived except as in relation
to all cultural, social, political, psychological, and, of course, economic
factors of which it is comprised.) Furthermore, mental constructs such
as concepts, variables, functions, and analyses (also a part of reality
in the present sense) cannot exist apart from all other concepts, variables, functions, and analyses, nor can an analysis be disentangled from
that which it purports to analyze. Thus there is no dichotomy between
observations of the real world and thoughts about those observations,
and it is not possible to explain a particular observation as the outcome of a single set of causes or an essence such as the solution of a
simultaneous-equation system. Evidently the methodology and epistemology of mutually interactive analysis are nonessentialistic.

At the moment at which a mutually interactive study is begun,
the investigator has a specific meaning of the idea of an "analysis" in
mind. His particular meaning has been developed over time in relation
to his past experiences, including his interactions with other scholars
and their work, and his interactions with previous investigations in
which he himself has engaged. In addition to having an idea of what
an analysis is, he must also determine what language he will use and
what rules of reasoning he will follow. Due to the mutually interactive nature of the elements upon which the analysis operates, neither
deductive nor inductive logic can be applied. Rather, the investigator
establishes and employs his own standard or logic of mutually interactive analysis indicating how to proceed from one sentence to the next.
These principles set his guidelines for identifying what he considers to
be "correct" reasoning as opposed to that which is "incorrect" and "inconsistent."[15] All of this is considered to be an integral part of the

---

[15]An example of deductive reasoning (taken from equilibrium analysis and mentioned in Section 1.2) is the argument explaining the formation of observed (relative)

analysis he is undertaking.

During the course of completing his analysis, the investigator's conception of analysis, appropriate language, and appropriate rules become modified as he interacts with the real world and with his study. Meanings change as the development of discourse and knowledge proceeds, and thus it is possible that his investigation may end up by turning into a different analysis from that originally planned.

Unlike equilibrium and disequilibrium analysis, in which explanation is based on the construction of models as described in Sections 1.2 and 1.3, the mutually interactive perspective does not admit of explanations of economic reality that are reducible to formal models like (1.2-1), (1.2-3), and (1.2-5). As suggested above, the pieces of such models, indeed the models themselves, are mutually interactive with all facets of actuality (including thought processes), and the thing being explained cannot, therefore, be understood as the result of the single cause characterized (as in equilibrium analysis) by the determination of certain parameter values in an independent simultaneous equations system. Thus variables in the mutually interactive approach are defined as being constituted in and through the effects of all other variables of the analysis. They do not exist as detached, isolated, independently specified entities. The same is true of the values that variables may take on.

---

prices in terms of preferences, endowments, and technology through constrained utility maximization by consumers, profit maximization by firms, and the equilibrium of demand and supply in all markets. In this argument, the connotation of prices is given and there is a clear separation between observations of prices and the explanation (or thoughts) of how observed prices arise. Such logic may be contrasted with the following illustration of reasoning in interactive analysis about the connotation of prices themselves: prices only exist in that the effects of all economic and noneconomic parts of life – including preferences, endowments, technology, consumers, firms, and markets – come together to produce them. Also to be reckoned here are the interactions between the intellectual processes involved in thinking about the connotation of prices and the objects (some have been listed above) on which the processes act. Prices cannot be understood except in reference to all of these consequences: they are the unique points of convergence in this web of interlocking effects having the properties usually attributed to prices. (Similarly, preferences, endowments, technology, consumers, firms, and markets only exist, in part, as a result of prices. Therefore each of these elements mutually determines, again in part, the conceptual existence of each of the others.) The general notion of a variable, of which price is a particular instance, is described below.

Because variables and their values condition each other's conceptual existence, a change in the value of any variable transforms (among other things) the variable of which it is a value. The price of a good, then, represents the good's price only as it stands in relation to everything else (recall n. 15 on p. 19).

Relations among variables are also interactive with each other and are modified when brought together in the conduct of analysis. A relation between two variables is characterized by the unique way in which these variables and the relation itself are affected by all other variables and relations. It is a focal point in a myriad of interlocking effects that continually modulates in the mind of the investigator as the effects are explored. As in the case of variables, each relation can exist only in conjunction with the totality of all such relations since each is literally produced by the effects of all others on it. For example, the relation describing the way technology transforms inputs into outputs (what would be called the production function in equilibrium analysis) is understood to be the combined result of the interactions of all technological, economic, social, political, and even psychological forces that come together to determine how inputs are transformed into outputs.

Following the usual parlance, collections of relations are called systems. In parallel with variables and relations, systems can be conceived of only as they relate to other systems and all other aspects of the analysis. To illustrate, a university is a system defined by all of the relations that make it up. Reflected in this construction is the vast variety of pressures operating on and interacting with it, both inside and outside the university.

The occurrence of change in the real world is understood in mutually interactive analysis in terms of systemic variation, that is, the alteration of the multiplicity of material, economic, sociocultural, intellective, and other variables and relations of which the systems are constituted. Systems become modified in that old ones break down and new ones emerge from them in their place. Such modulation arises from the interaction of all elements of the systems with each other and with the remainder of reality, including the investigator conducting the analysis and the investigation itself. Since all of these interactions progress continually as the phenomena under investigation unfold through time and as the analysis develops, both the elements of the analysis and the analysis itself are always in flux. In this sense, mutually interactive analysis, even though it projects its own methodological and epistemological moorings and orientations, is similar to nonequilibrium analysis as described in the next section.

It is important to understand that because of their interactive properties, the variables, relations, systems, and "laws" of motion of mutually interactive analysis cannot be represented by formal mathematical symbolism in the usual manner. For example, the very act of manipulating or interpreting an equation interacts with all other aspects of the analysis and with the equation itself in such a way that the meaning of the equation is changed. But at any analytical moment, one can still "abstract" from these mutual interactions to obtain standard mathematical variables, relations, systems, and laws of motion. Such abstractions might usefully serve as heuristic devices and metaphors, illustrating certain components of the analysis. Models put together in this way would be like those employed in equilibrium and disequilibrium analysis. But it must be recognized that the process of abstraction interacts with and hence changes both analyses and models. Thus metaphors, say, may lose their relevance immediately upon construction. Moreover, metaphors are not unique. No one metaphor is intrinsically better than another.[16] Any "result" secured from a particular metaphor is pertinent only to that metaphor and is entirely dependent on it. For reasons described above, such a result can never be thought of as a "complete" explanation of the phenomena under investigation.

To illustrate the role that mathematical models play in interactive analysis, consider the general problem of explaining prices in the microeconomy. (A description of the variable "price" that might be employed in an interactive study has already been given in n. 15 on p. 19.) It clearly makes no sense to think of prices as "determined" by independently specified "forces" at work in the microeconomy. Rather, prices emerge from the interaction of all mutually constitutive variables, forces (relations), investigations, etc. One may abstract a (mathematical) Walrasian model of the microeconomy from these mutual inter-

---

[16]This follows from the rejection of traditional epistemology and the resulting consequence that there is no longer such a thing as unique truth.

actions as a metaphor for price determination, but it is subject to all of the limitations described above. Thus the metaphor is not unique; many others (*e.g.*, class conflict) can also provide equally privileged illustrations of price determination. Moreover, one must be conscious of taking a snapshot of an ongoing process of change. This changing process includes not only the phenomenon under investigation and its interface with other phenomena but what is going on in the mind of the investigator as well. For, once the particular Walrasian model is built, things may be noticed that were not seen before, and the model may, as a result, be modified by adding or subtracting variables and revising equations. Alternatively, the model may no longer seem appropriate. Thus, immediately upon construction, the metaphor may be dismantled, subsequently to be replaced with an altered version or discarded entirely.

In mutually interactive analysis, then, variables, relations, systems, and laws of motion are built up and used to explain that portion of reality for which understanding is desired. The purposes and limits of the analysis, the time interval to be covered, the language, the rules of reasoning, and the use of metaphors are all determined as part of the analysis. Since there is no dichotomy between observations and thinking, there is no gap to bridge (as there is in equilibrium and disequilibrium analysis) by identifying sightings in reality with particular elements in a model. What is seen in the real world is automatically understood in terms of the mutual interaction of the relations, systems, and laws of motion of the analysis.

An illustration of mutually interactive analysis is the Marxian explanation of the transition from feudalism to capitalism in Western Europe between 1100 and 1500 A.D. given by Resnick and Wolff [30]. Whereas others have argued that this transition was triggered by a single ultimate cause like, for example, the conflict between feudal lords and peasants over rents or the opening up of external trade to Western Europe, Resnick and Wolff do not accept the idea that one or more determinants caused the decline of feudalism and the rise of capitalism. Rather, they conceive of feudalism as a social system of relations existing in change. Contained in this system were lords, classes of people subsumed to lords, and peasants. Over time, interactions among these different groups modified the entire social and economic fabric in ways that gradually destroyed feudalism. Using the vocabulary developed above, the original system was repeatedly broken down and replaced by new systems as time went on. In the process, new relations among new groups emerged, and by the end of the period the transition to capitalism was well under way.

1.5 Nonequilibrium Analysis

The third and final alternative to be considered, *viz.*, nonequilibrium analysis, and that which is to be developed more fully in subsequent chapters, retains the essentialistic epistemologies and the essentialism in methodology of equilibrium analysis but is methodologically distinct in its focus only on, and in the nature of, its dynamics. Since all of life's events take place in historical time (rendering the notions of philosophical materialism and logical time irrelevant), the posing of static questions that give no recognition to that conceptualization of time is not meaningful. For time, in reality, can never be started over as in the machines of (1.2-3) and (1.2-5). Rather, it is irreversible and historical: time flows in a single continuous stream along which every moment is unique. Each moment, that is, has its own peculiar history, its own peculiar knowledge derived from that history, its own peculiar institutional structures and environments, and its own totality and distribution of resource endowments. Thus the recurrence of a moment of time that has already gone by cannot happen, and phenomena that arise in historical time can never repeat themselves in exactly the same way or in the same ontological and epistemic contexts. Unique histories lead into and impinge upon unique histories that are yet to be completed. It follows that explanations or understandings (which consitute analysis and may serve as the basis for behavior) of any one moment, at that moment, are necessarily different from those at all other moments. To recall the Hicksian terminology introduced earlier, such an analysis (along with mutually interactive analysis), which rests methodologically on the idea of historical time, is in time, while the equilibrium- and disequilibrium-type analyses of Sections 1.2 and 1.3 are out of time.

Throughout the passage of historical time, the present is the boundary separating the past from the future. The past, being past, is capable of historical description, and hence knowledge about the past can be secured. To the extent that the present is experienced and exposed, knowledge of the present is also obtainable. But such knowledge of the past and present is always unique to the individual possessing it and, because the world is enormously complex, so incomplete and insufficient that it cannot usually be expressed probabilistically.[17] The knowledge complex an individual has of the past and present at any moment defines what may be referred to as his epistemic status of that moment. However, knowledge, including probabilistic knowledge (assuming the structure of reality is such that probabilities exist), about the future is impossible to secure because the future cannot be known until it is past. Both future novelty and hence the totality of future possibilities is unknowable: the unexpected may happen. Not only is the investigating economist confronted by such large gaps in knowledge, but so too are the decision makers whose behavior may be part of the subject matter of his investigation. In spite of this ignorance and the (nonprobabilistic) uncertainty it imposes, these latter decision makers still imagine and guess about the future using their faulty knowledge of the past and present. They may even build models to help organize their thoughts. In any case, such imaginings, guesses, and models may also serve as the springboards for decisions or behavior in the present. Thus an individual decision maker arrives at each moment (or period) of decision with a unique background of history and with a unique epistemic status and unique thoughts derived from that history. The environment in which he decides is also unique because it, too, has its own singular history.[18] The same environment, the same background

---

[17]Only knowledge of the past and present, not, as argued below, of the future, can be probabilistic in form, and only in the following way: because observations of the past and present necessarily require abstraction and the omission of numerous details, it might appear that certain happenings reoccur in certain repeated situations. In that case, regardless of whether it exists in reality or not, a probability of occurrence over the time frame of the observations might be inferred. However, the presumption is that as soon as the present moves into the past, and a new present provides a new observation, this probability modifies. History, that is, does not, as a rule, establish probability distributions that are unchanging over time. In Davidson's terminology, our world tends to be "nonergodic" [6, p. 187].

[18]As pointed out in n. 17 immediately above, history may, in special circum-

of the individual, and hence the same decision opportunity, can never arise again.

The contrast between this vision of economic decision making and that of standard equilibrium analysis is quite stark. For the presence of historical time and human ignorance raises history to a position of paramount importance and destroys the omniscience of the typical utility- (or expected utility-) maximizing consumer and profit- (or expected profit-) maximizing firm. Indeed, Hutchison [17, pp. 1-3] has argued that such omniscience is "the most criticizable and unrealistic feature of . . . 'Economic Man'" and lies at the heart of the crisis of abstraction mentioned in the introduction to this chapter.

It should also be noted that these ideas revolving around the notions of historical time, ignorance, and uncertainty are not new. According to Hutchison [16, p. 212], historical time was present in the work of Adam Smith. More recently, Marshall, Keynes, and Popper all spoke about various aspects of historical time, or the inability to forsee the future, or the impossibility of obtaining probabilities.[19] Knight [23] dealt with all three and also deserves the credit [23, p. 233] for distinguishing between uncertainty when probability is definable, which he referred to as *risk*, and uncertainty when it is not, which is what he meant by *uncertainty* and what is meant by that term here. The pervasiveness and significance of ignorance has been described in another context by Hayek [11, pp. 519-520]: "The peculiar character of the problem of a rational economic order is determined precisely by the fact that knowledge of the circumstances of which we must make use never exists in concentrated or integrated form, but solely as the dispersed bits of incomplete and frequently contradictory knowledge which . . . separate individuals possess. . . . It is the problem of the utilization of knowl-

---

stances, give the appearance of statistically or ergodically "repeating" itself. But such repetition, if it occurs, can be perceived only after that history has unfolded, or in an *ex post* and not an *ex ante* sense. In conditions of historical time and the uniqueness of decision moments that are enshrouded in ignorance of the future, and in the context of the uncertainty that that creates, logic does not permit the assumption that the past or previously established patterns will necessarily project themselves into the future. Such an assumption is precluded by the unforseen and unforeseeable outcomes that the future hides from view.

[19]*E.g.*, Marshall [25, pp. 109, 347], Keynes [21, pp. 213-214], and Popper [28, pp. ix-x].

edge not given to anyone in its totality." Other authors who have taken up these and related issues include Bausor [3], Hicks [14], Loasby [24], Robinson [33], Shackle [37], and Vickers [39]. It is also interesting that the contrast between logical and historical time arose some time ago in physics when reconciling the laws of Newtonian mechanics, which are out of time, with the observation that, in real time, heat always flows from warmer to colder bodies.[20]

Returning to the description of nonequilibrium analysis, suppose, now, that the basic unit of time is taken to be the moment (a similar argument would apply if it were the period), and that a nonequilibrium or in-time explanation for happenings in the real world is desired for the period between time t^0 and time t'. Denote the present moment, that is, the moment at which the explanation is to be developed, by t^P. It may be supposed that $t^0 \leq t' \leq t^P$. Then t^0 is the moment at which the explanation breaks into the stream of time, and t' is the moment it breaks out. The explanation itself necessarily depends on the (historical) knowledge available at t^P. The situations in which $t^0 = t'$, $t' = t^P$, and $t^0 = t' = t^P$ may be considered as special cases. Observe that explanations of, say, individual behavior at any moment, fall under the circumstance $t^0 = t'$.

At first, in the construction of an explanation for the period between t^0 and t', nonequilibrium analysis may be conceived to proceed analogously to both dynamic equilibrium and dynamic disequilibrium analysis: a model such as (1.2-1) when $t^0 = t'$, or (1.2-3) or (1.2-5) when $t^0 < t'$, in which decision makers (if present) are subject to the ignorance and uncertainty described above, may be built up, its solutions or time-paths studied, and one solution or time-path identified (either rationalistically or empiricistically) with observed reality between t^0 and t'.[21] Then, for the case in which $t^0 < t'$, by pursuing the latter time-path beyond t', one possible description of what could happen next may be provided. It is important to understand, however, that although nonequilibrium-analytic models constructed in this way might seem similar to their equilibrium-analytic counterparts, the difference

---

[20]Porter [29, Ch. 7].

[21]This is clearly quite different from mutually interactive analysis, which, as described in Section 1.4, does not admit explanations that are reducible to models.

between them remains significant and far-reaching. For, unlike the models of equilibrium and disequilibrium analysis, a nonequilibrium-analytic model itself would be thought of as time dependent. Once t^0, t', or t^P changes, one could not expect the same model to be appropriate because historical imperatives inject a presumption that individual epistemic statuses, and, as a consequence, individual behaviors, are now different. Hence the "fixed" parameters do not remain fixed, and the structural relations themselves immediately dissolve: if, say, t' were to increase to t'', then the history of reality at t' is modified by the passage of time; and if t^P were to rise to $t^{\overline{P}}$, then the information upon which explanation is founded would be different. In the special case $t' = t^P$, understanding of occurrences between t^0 and the present undergoes such profound change as time moves on (due to the unforeseen and unpredictable novelty that enters the fabric of life) that the analytical structure of that understanding is unlikely to hold up in its wake. Clearly the methodology of nonequilibrium analysis does not allow formal prediction as permitted by the methodology of equilibrium analysis.

Still, stretches of time may unfold during which real-world newness does not appear to impinge substantively on the particular phenomena under investigation. The lack of impact could be reflected in at least two ways. First, it may be that the equations of a model seem to be roughly stable over time in the sense that for a while, as t' expands, a single time-path generated by the model continues to approximate observations of reality reasonably well.[22] Here equilibrium or disequilibrium analysis, though coming from different methodological perspectives, is capable of furnishing the same formal picture of the real world as nonequilibrium analysis. Furthermore, it is only in cases like these that the possibilities, exposed by the in-time models, of what could happen in the future actually transpire. But this, of course, does not mean that the employment of nonequilibrium models for predictive purposes is viable in general.

Second, and perhaps less likely, stability over time could also arise

---

[22]Even if all variables between t^0 and t' were constant, this time-path would still not be the stationary state defined in Section 1.2 because at each t' there is no presumption of rest, *i.e.*, that the same model and time-path will remain relevant for the next moment beyond t'.

with respect to the variables $z = (z_1, \ldots, z_K)$, even as the equations of the model modify. Regardless of whether the components z_k are quantifiable or not, criteria can be given for determining whether any pair, z' and z'', are "significantly different from" or "essentially the same as" each other.[23] With these criteria specified, it may happen that all points z observed between t^0 and t' are essentially similar. Hence reality between t^0 and t' could be viewed as in a pseudo-stationary state: novelty occurs, but either not to a sufficient extent or not in the ways that significantly affect the values of the variables in the analysis.[24] What is seen can therefore be explained in terms of an equilibrium analysis with a single model and a unique stationary state or, in the language of nonequilibrium analysis, with a "model" whose equations might modulate but whose solutions remain essentially the same over time.

During intervals of rapid transformation, the two approaches also supply quite distinct explanations of real-world phenomena. On the one hand, equilibrium analysis can only explain unforeseen change by asserting, after the fact, that "outside" forces caused alteration in the parameter values ρ. But the idea of a continually modulating equilibrium responding to repeated variations in ρ is not a very satisfying way to conceptualizing the effects of novelty. Nonequilibrium analysis, on the other hand, cannot provide much of an understanding of unforeseen change either. Yet the acknowledgment of such change is part of the internal structure of its methological tissue. Nonequilibrium analysis expects change and leaves room for it. Its emphasis is on the present state and what might happen subsequently. By comparison, equilibrium analysis, with its focus on the end result toward which time-paths, if not already there, converge, makes room for change only after it has occurred.[25]

As an illustration of nonequilibrium analysis, Bausor [3] investigates

---

[23]Suppose that the values of z exhibit, to one extent or another, a given collection of properties. Then z' may be said to be *essentially the same as* z'' provided that z' and z'' exhibit each property to the same degree. Further, z' and z'' may be referred to as *significantly different from* each other whenever they are not essentially the same. See the concept of "closeness" in Katzner [19, pp. 61-68].

[24]Bausor [3, pp. 173-177] calls this *historical equilibrium*.

[25]*Cf.* Loasby [24, p. 214].

the choice of consumption baskets by consumers in terms of a functional loop in which the existing outcome of the previous round of decision making determines (not necessarily quantifiable) perceptions for the next round. Perceptions, in turn, determine (also nonquantifiable) expectations, which, again in turn, determine strategies. Lastly, decisions are made and strategies are turned into outcomes. Further examples, discussed in much greater detail, appear throughout this book.

1.6　A Preview

It is clear, then, that unlike Edward Bear (Winnie-the-Pooh), who never did find another way to negotiate the stairs, economists do have viable substitutes for equilibrium analysis. Each of the three possibilities described above evidently constitutes a distinct conceptual foundation upon which an alternative economic analysis can be built. All three make appropriate place for formal mathematical models. Yet they differ markedly in their approach to time and uncertainty, in their interpretation of the nature and role of variables, relations, systems, and laws of motion, and in the way they deal with the complex interrelatednesses of analysis and reality. Each, together with equilibrium analysis, provides a basis from which a separate and competing explanation, and hence knowledge, of happenings in the world can be constructed.

The remainder of this volume, however, is concerned only with the last alternative, nonequilibrium analysis. It attempts to show how economic inquiry can proceed in the absence of philosophical materialism, logical time, and perfect information, that is, how explicit models of the economic behavior of individual agents, markets, and the economy as a whole can be constructed that take into account historical time and human ignorance, and how these models can be analyzed. Only one approach to such models is provided, namely, that emerging from the work of Shackle [36] as modified by Vickers [40]. Thus subsequent chapters put a very particular kind of flesh on the structure outlined in Section 1.5. In so doing, many of the arguments of that section are enhanced and expanded. For example, although it is already clear that the concept of probability has to be rejected (to be replaced in the next chapter by Shackle's notion of potential surprise), considerable effort is devoted to explaining what is involved in that rejection and how that rejection can be independently sustained. The specific contents of coming chapters are outlined in the next several paragraphs.

Part I is concerned with the basic concept of potential surprise that, in the present investigation, underlies all subsequent constructions. Of course, whether or not potential surprise differs from one-minus-probability has been the subject of some controversy. A similar issue arises in the relation, if any, of potential confirmation, a notion analogous to potential surprise, to probability without subtraction from unity. From a mathematical point of view, potential surprise and potential confirmation, like probability, may be thought of in terms of functions defined abstractly over certain σ-fields of sets. In Chapter 2, such functions are defined, and their formal properties are explored and compared with those of standard probability and one-minus-probability functions. Chapter 3 examines the ways in which the differences that arise are manifested in the associated distribution and density functions.

Part II deals with three of the cornerstones of contemporary economic theorizing, namely, decision making, aggregation, and simultaneity. A formal statement and analysis of the model of decision making in ignorance proposed by Shackle [36] and modified by Vickers [40] is presented in Chapter 4: based on a family of density functions, one function corresponding to each object of choice, objects of choice are first characterized in terms of the constrained maximization of an attractiveness function, and then a selection is made by maximizing a decision index. Two versions of the model are given, one obtained from a family of potential surprise density functions and the other from a family of potential confirmation density functions, and conditions are identified under which these constructions amount to the same thing. Chapter 5 provides five examples of the potential surprise version of this model. Two of the examples use families of "dominating" potential surprise density functions; two others employ families of "nested" potential surprise density functions. "Comparative statics" properties of the model are also derived and applied as special cases to these examples. The ways in which the model is operational in both positive and normative senses is the subject matter of Chapter 6. The latter chapter also includes, as part of a discussion illustrating positive operationality, an examination of uncertainty aversion and favor.

The case for aggregating relations in economics is often tenuous. Chapter 7 shows that under conditions of ignorance and historical time it is not possible, as a rule, to aggregate from individual demand and supply functions to either market-level demand and supply functions or macroeconomic behavioral relations. Hence, in particular, the traditional analysis of markets based on the equilibration of market demand and market supply is called into question. Three proposals for replacing that traditional market analysis are suggested that do not rely on aggregation within markets. One of these, namely, the use of market-level analogues of individual behavior, is also more generally applicable to the derivation of macroeconomic relations.

The most common method of handling simultaneous behavior in economics today is general equilibrium analysis. This method, as indicated above, relies on the assumptions that time is logical and that knowledge is perfect. But, when historical time and human ignorance are viewed as significant features of the economic landscape, and hence, in Shackle's words [37, p. 42], the world is "kaleidic" and as a result analytical structures representing it are capable of dissolving "at a touch," general equilibrium analysis is clearly inapplicable. Chapter 8 considers what it means to analyze simultaneous behavior under these circumstances, and an example is provided in a two-person, two-commodity, exchange economy.

Part III employs the building blocks of Parts I and II to construct and analyze models of the firm, the consumer, and the micro- and macroeconomies. These models may be viewed as replacements, in the framework of nonequilibrium analysis, for the corresponding well-known traditional models of equilibrium analysis. For the firm, discussed in Chapter 9, the presence of historical time and ignorance means, of course, that each decision moment has a unique, nonrepeatable place in history, and that the firm's decision maker has incomplete knowledge of the past and present and no knowledge at all of the future. In such a circumstance, the notion of probability is, as suggested earlier, irrelevant. A reformulation of the theory of the firm for this kind of environment is proposed. It employs the decision model of Chapter 4 to analyze determination of the firm's investment in durable-good input simultaneously with its estimates of present and future output demands. All production, finance, and (markup) pricing decisions follow in turn.

In Chapter 10, a model of consumer behavior under conditions of historical time and ignorance, and hence without the notion of probability, is presented that, in addition to explaining the consumer's demand for commodities and income-earning assets and his supply of initial endowments (including labor), also explains his demand for nominal money balances. A financial resources constraint together with an individual velocity of circulation of money constraint define the consumer's choice set, and the analysis of Chapter 4 is employed (once again) to derive his selection from it. One consequence is that the consumer's demand for money balances emerges as the demand for one asset, namely, money, in a portfolio of many assets.

Drawing, in part, on earlier discussions, Chapter 11 explicitly sets out a model of a monetary, kaleidic microeconomy as a complex of individuals, firms, and commercial banks that make decisions and interact simultaneously in markets under conditions of ignorance and historical time. Actually, to keep matters simple, the model is limited to one consumer, two firms, and one bank. (There is also a central bank.) But the generalization to many consumers, firms, and banks is straightforward. In either case, the resolution, in each time period, of inconsistent plans into consistent outcomes, and the consequent failure of expectations, are among the significant and unique features of the model.

Chapter 12 constructs a model of a monetary, kaleidic macroeconomy also faithful to the vision of economic activity in the context of historical time and ignorance. Since, as described in Chapter 7, macrorelations are not obtainable by invoking aggregation procedures, adherence to the tradition of methodological individualism is maintained through the use, at the macrolevel, of analogues drawn from the model of the microeconomy of Chapter 11. As in that chapter, a central bank is also present. In the macroeconomic model so developed, neither Walras' law nor Say's law obtains. Furthermore, the labor market need not clear, and money is not neutral.

Part IV considers two issues that relate theoretical analysis to the observation of reality. First, in light of the significance of history in nonequilibrium analysis as described in Section 1.5, the impact of history or, more precisely, the role of observed variables values (that is, val-

ues of variables that have occurred in the past), in determining present
variable values is examined and compared in Chapter 13 under conditions of (i) logical time and perfect knowledge and (ii) historical time
and ignorance. Included here is a discussion of two notions of hysteresis. And, finally, Chapter 14 investigates the nature and place of
empirical analysis in the context of the present volume, that is, when
historical time and ignorance preclude the use of probability and hence
the familiar distributional techniques such as hypothesis testing and estimation, along with the standard methods of probabilistic prediction,
have to be discarded. It turns out, however, that nondistributional "estimation" and nonprobabilistic "prediction" are still possible. And the
potential for empirical falsification and "corroboration" of theoretical
propositions and models remains intact.

1.7   References

1. Allen, R. D. G., *Macro-Economic Theory* (London: Macmillan,
   1967).

2. Amariglio, J. L., "Economic History and the Theory of Primi-
   tive Socio-Economic Development," Ph.D. dissertation (Amherst:
   University of Massachusetts, 1984).

3. Bausor, R., "Time and the Structure of Economic Analysis,"
   Journal of Post Keynesian Economics 5 (1982-83), pp. 163-179.

4. Bell, D., and I. Kristol, eds., *The Crisis in Economic Theory*
   (New York: Basic Books, 1981).

5. Benassy, J. P., *The Economics of Market Disequilibrium* (New
   York: Academic Press, 1982).

6. Davidson, P., "Rational Expectations: A Fallacious Foundation
   for Studying Crucial Decision-Making Processes," *Journal of Post
   Keynesian Economics* 5 (1982-83), pp. 182-198.

7. Friedman, M., "The Methodology of Positive Economics," in *Essays in Positive Economics* (Chicago: University of Chicago Press,
   1953), pp. 3-43.

8. Georgescu-Roegen, N., "Methods in Economic Science," *Journal of Economic Issues* 13 (1979), pp. 317-328.

9. Grandmont, J. M., "Introduction," in *Temporary Equilibrium*, J. M. Grandmont, ed. (San Diego: Academic Press, 1988), pp. xiii-xxiii.

10. Hahn, F. H., *On the Notion of Equilibrium in Economics*, inaugural lecture (Cambridge: Cambridge University Press, 1973).

11. Hayek, F. A., "The Use of Knowledge in Society," *American Economic Review* 35 (1945), pp. 519-530.

12. Hicks, J. R., *Capital and Time* (Oxford: Oxford University Press, 1973).

13. ———, "The Revival of Political Economy: The Old and the New," *Economic Record* 51 (1975), pp. 356-367.

14. ———, "Some Questions of Time in Economics," in *Evolution, Welfare, and Time in Economics*, A. M. Tang, F. M. Westfield, and J. S. Worley, eds. (Lexington: D. C. Heath, 1976), pp. 135-151.

15. Hutchison, T. W., *Knowledge and Ignorance in Economics* (Chicago: University of Chicago Press, 1977).

16. ———, *On Revolutions and Progress in Economic Knowledge* (Cambridge: Cambridge University Press, 1978).

17. ———, "Our Methodological Crisis," in *Economics in Disarray*, P. Wiles and G. Routh, eds. (Oxford: Basil Blackwell, 1984), pp. 1-21.

18. Katouzian, H., *Ideology and Method in Economics* (New York: New York University Press, 1980).

19. Katzner, D. W., *Analysis without Measurement* (Cambridge: Cambridge University Press, 1983).

20. ———, *Walrasian Microeconomics* (Reading: Addison-Wesley, 1988).

21. Keynes, J. M., "The General Theory of Employment," *Quarterly Journal of Economics* 51 (1937), pp. 209-223.

22. Klamer, A., and D. N. McCloskey, "The Rhetoric of Disagreement," *Rethinking Marxism* 2, no. 3 (Fall 1989), pp. 140-161.

23. Knight, F. H., *Risk, Uncertainty and Profit* (Boston: Houghton Mifflin, 1921).

24. Loasby, B., *Choice, Complexity and Ignorance* (Cambridge: Cambridge University Press, 1976).

25. Marshall, A., *Principles of Economics*, 8th ed. (New York: Macmillan, 1948).

26. McCloskey, D. N., "The Rhetoric of Economics," *Journal of Economic Literature* 21 (1983), pp. 481-517.

27. ———, "Formalism in Economics, Rhetorically Speaking," *Ricerche Economiche* 43 (1989), pp. 57-75.

28. Popper, K. R., *The Poverty of Historicism* (New York: Basic Books, 1960).

29. Porter, T. M., *The Rise of Statistical Thinking, 1820-1900* (Princeton: Princeton University Press, 1986).

30. Resnick, S., and R. Wolff, "The Theory of Transitional Conjunctures and the Transition from Feudalism to Capitalism in Western Europe," *Review of Radical Political Economics* 11, no. 3 (Fall 1979), pp. 3-22.

31. ———, "Marxist Epistemology: The Critique of Economic Determinism," *Social Text* 2, no. 3 (Fall 1982), pp. 31-72.

32. Robbins, L., *An Essay on the Nature and Significance of Economic Science*, 2nd ed. (London: Macmillan, 1952).

33. Robinson, J., *History versus Equilibrium*, Thames Papers in Political Economy (London: Thames Polytechnic, 1974).

34. Rorty, R., *Philosophy and the Mirror of Nature* (Princeton: Princeton University Press, 1979).

35. Ruccio, D. F., "Optimal Planning Theory and Theories of Socialist Planning," Ph.D. dissertation (Amherst: University of Massachusetts, 1984).

36. Shackle, G. L. S., *Decision Order and Time in Human Affairs*, 2nd ed. (Cambridge: Cambridge University Press, 1969).

37. ———, *Epistemics and Economics* (Cambridge: Cambridge University Press, 1972).

38. ———, *Keynesian Kaleidics* (Edinburgh: Edinburgh University Press, 1974).

39. Vickers, D., "On Relational Structures and Non-Equilibrium in Economic Theory," *Eastern Economic Journal* 11 (1985), pp. 384-403.

40. ———, *Money Capital in the Theory of the Firm* (Cambridge: Cambridge University Press, 1987).

41. Ward, B., *What's Wrong with Economics?* (New York: Basic Books, 1972).

42. Wiles, P., and G. Routh, eds., *Economics in Disarray* (Oxford: Basil Blackwell, 1984).

43. Winston, G. C., "Three Problems with the Treatment of Time in Economics: Perspectives, Repetitiveness, and Time Units," in *The Boundaries of Economics*, G. C. Winston and R. F. Teichgraeber III, eds. (Cambridge: Cambridge University Press, 1988), pp. 30-52.

44. Woo, H. K. H., *What's Wrong with Formalization in Economics? An Epistemological Critique* (Newark: Victoria, 1986).

PART I

Potential Surprise and Potential Confirmation as Expressions of Uncertainty

CHAPTER 2

Potential Surprise, Potential Confirmation, and Probability

One of the principal aims of economic analysis is to explain the behavior of individual economic agents (consumers and firms) as they participate in what Alfred Marshall described [19, p. 1] as the "ordinary business of life." Since an agent's behavior is the outcome of the decisions he makes, it is natural that, in this regard, considerable effort has been focused on the investigation of agent decision making. It has also been recognized that agents frequently have to make decisions in environments in which the consequences of their decisions are not known for some time after the decisions are made. To analyze agent decision making under these conditions, the main traditional approach has been to assume that time is logical and knowledge is perfect (when the consequences of decisions are not known with certainty in advance, this means that the agent is able to determine a probability function defined over possible future states that reflects his feelings of uncertainty) and that his decisions are made by maximizing a (possibly expected) objective function, often subject to constraint.[1] But as suggested in Chapter 1, when, from the perspective of nonequilibrium analysis, time is viewed as historical and knowledge as imperfect, the

---

[1]See Sections 4.1 and 4.2.

This chapter is reproduced, with considerable additions, corrections, and other modifications, from my "Potential Surprise, Potential Confirmation, and Probability," *Journal of Post Keynesian Economics* 9 (1986-87), pp. 58-78.

assumption that the agent is able to construct a probability function is no longer tenable. In such a world, uncertainty may be brought into the analysis through Shackle's notion of potential surprise.

Yet, ever since it was introduced over fifty years ago, various economists have tried to link potential surprise to (usually subjective) probability. For example, Edwards [5], Ozga [21, pp. 94-96], and Krelle [18] have attempted to show that potential surprise can always be transformed into subjective probability, and Ford [9, Ch. 5] employs a transformation of potential surprise that has clear subjective probability associations in his axiomatization of Shackle's model of decision making. Vickers [26, p. 143], however, and Shackle himself [24, Ch. 9], deny that such transformations can have significant probabilistic meaning in the historical time and ignorance context in which the concept of potential surprise is set because that context does not contain the necessary logical prerequisites for the ordinary definition of probability (subjective or otherwise). The purpose of this chapter is to explore potential surprise as an expression of uncertainty along with a second notion referred to as "potential confirmation"; to clarify the distinction between potential surprise, potential confirmation, and probability; and, in pursuing these ends, to make the Shackle-Vickers argument more precise.

The reader should be warned, however, that the notion of potential confirmation does not play any role at all in subsequent argument as that argument relates to the analysis of economic problems. Although a model of decision making in ignorance is built upon potential confirmation in Section 4.4, that model is quickly discarded as a consequence of considerations elucidated at that point. The reason why potential confirmation is introduced here and explored further in Chapter 3 is to emphasize, from an additional analytical perspective, the inapplicability and irrelevance of the probability apparatus in light of the ignorance and uncertainty presently being addressed. Moreover, the development of the idea of potential confirmation below reinforces, on the basis of its own axiomatic foundations, the fact that potential surprise, which does provide the underpinnings for later analysis, cannot be interpreted in terms of one-minus-probability.

It is, of course, true that the numbers on any finite scale can always be converted into numbers between 0 and 1 by application of a suitable mapping. Indeed, this is the method employed by Krelle to transform

Shackle's potential surprise into (subjective) probability. But such a "demonstration" of the reducibility of potential surprise to probability starts from potential surprise numbers without reference to the underlying characterization of potential surprise as a function defined on an appropriate collection of sets. By examining the latter function and its properties, and by comparing it to a standard probability function and a potential confirmation function defined over the same collection of sets, the formal differences between probability and potential surprise are exhibited more clearly and more fully.

Discussion begins, then, with the standard definition of an ordinary probability function. The potential surprise function is considered next, along with some of its attendant properties. Thereafter the potential confirmation function is introduced to sharpen the contrast, and the relationship to probability is discussed. In particular, it is argued that potential confirmation cannot be thought of as a special instance of probability; nor can potential surprise be understood as a special instance of one-minus-probability. The chapter concludes with a more philosophical exposition of the distinction between potential surprise and probability. To make it easier to keep track of the similarities and differences in the comparison of potential surprise, potential confirmation, and probability functions below, the system for numbering axioms, theorems, and relations, introduced, in part, in Chapter 1, is modified here by adding a "p" after the number if the axiom, theorem, or relation involved refers to probability, an "s" if it deals with potential surprise, and a "c" if it concerns potential confirmation. Anyone wishing to avoid mathematical technicalities and willing to accept the formal distinction between potential surprise, potential confirmation, and probability, need read only the first two paragraphs of Section 2.1 and only up through the discussions of examples of potential surprise and confirmation functions in, respectively, Sections 2.2 and 2.3. The remaining material of these sections can be omitted.

2.1 Probability Functions

Probability functions are normally defined over collections of sets called σ-fields. Let a question be asked and let Ω be a set of distinct and discrete, but not necessarily quantifiable, answers or outcomes.[2] For any subset $A \subseteq \Omega$, denote its complement by $\bar{A}$. Thus $A \cup \bar{A} = \Omega$ and $A \cap \bar{A} = \phi$, where ϕ represents the empty set. A σ-field over Ω is a nonempty collection, $\mathcal{A}^*$, of subsets of Ω such that:

(i) If A is in $\mathcal{A}^*$, then $\bar{A}$ is in $\mathcal{A}^*$.

(ii) If $\{A_i\}$ is a countable collection of sets in $\mathcal{A}^*$, then $\bigcup_i A_i$ is in $\mathcal{A}^*$.

(iii) If $\{A_i\}$ is a countable collection of sets in $\mathcal{A}^*$, then $\bigcap_i A_i$ is in $\mathcal{A}^*$.

The set Ω is often referred to as a *sample space*, and the elements of $\mathcal{A}^*$ are called *events*. Note that the empty set is an element of $\mathcal{A}^*$.

A *probability* function (*measure*) on $\mathcal{A}^*$ is a function

$$p : \mathcal{A}^* \to [0, 1]$$

such that:

(i) For all A in $\mathcal{A}^*$,

$$0 \leq p(A) \leq 1. \qquad (2.1\text{-}1\text{p})$$

(ii) For any countable collection $\{A_i\}$ of mutually disjoint sets in $\mathcal{A}^*$,

$$p\left(\bigcup_i A_i\right) = \sum_i p(A_i). \qquad (2.1\text{-}2\text{p})$$

(iii) For the empty set and the sample space,

$$p(\phi) = 0 \qquad \text{and} \qquad p(\Omega) = 1. \qquad (2.1\text{-}3\text{p})$$

Three important ideas are implicit in this definition of probability. First, the set Ω contains all possible outcomes or answers to the initial question posed. There is no such thing as an unknown possible outcome – one that cannot be identified because it has not yet been seen or cannot even be contemplated. Second, regardless of whether one interprets p as frequency probability or in some other way,[3] the notion

---

[2]Numerical representation of the elements of Ω is not required in subsequent discussion. The material of this section is quite standard and happens to be drawn from Katzner [14, Ch. 12]. See also, for example, Wilks [28, Ch. 1].

[3]The distinction between frequency and subjective probability is described in Secton 2.4.

of repeated questioning is always lurking in the background. For to say, for example, that $p(A)$ is an "objective measure of incomplete information about the truth of event A," or that $p(A)$ is the "confidence one subjectively has in the truth of A," clearly implies that if one could ask the original question over and over again, and repeatedly observe the outcome, the expected frequency of occurrence of A would be $p(A)$. Thus replication, actual or hypothetical, is intimately related to the meaning and significance of the notion of probability, no matter how probability is understood.[4] Third, the probabilistic laws governing the answers to the original question are known in their entirety. There is no uncertainty in or ambiguity of numerical magnitude in the statement that event A has probability $p(A)$. Discussion will return to these issues at various points throughout the chapter.

All well-known properties of probability functions follow from axioms (2.1-1p) through (2.1-3p). Thus, for example, it can be shown that

$$p(A) + p(\bar{A}) = 1 \qquad (2.1\text{-}4p)$$

for all A in $\mathcal{A}^*$, that

$$p(A \cup B) = p(A) + p(B) - p(A \cap B) \qquad (2.1\text{-}5p)$$

for every A and B in $\mathcal{A}^*$, and that

$$p(A) \geq p(B) \qquad (2.1\text{-}6p)$$

whenever $A \supseteq B$ and A and B are in $\mathcal{A}^*$. Furthermore, if $\{A_i\}$ is a countable sequence of events in $\mathcal{A}^*$ that is either expanding ($A_1 \subseteq A_2 \subseteq \cdots$) or contracting ($A_1 \supseteq A_2 \supseteq \cdots$), then

$$\lim_{i \to \infty} p(A_i) = p\left(\lim_{i \to \infty} A_i\right), \qquad (2.1\text{-}7p)$$

where

$$\lim_{i \to \infty} A_i = \begin{cases} \bigcup_i A_i, & \text{when } A_1 \subseteq A_2 \subseteq \cdots, \\ \bigcap_i A_i, & \text{when } A_1 \supseteq A_2 \supseteq \cdots. \end{cases}$$

---

[4] A more complete statement of this argument appears in Section 2.4.

The *conditional* probability of A given B is defined as

$$p(A|B) = \frac{p(A \cap B)}{p(B)}, \qquad (2.1\text{-}8\text{p})$$

where A and B are in $\mathcal{A}^*$ and $p(B) \neq 0$. And, finally, events A and B are said to be *independent* whenever $p(A|B) = p(A)$, or

$$p(A \cap B) = p(A)p(B). \qquad (2.1\text{-}9\text{p})$$

2.2   Potential Surprise Functions

Now let a question be asked of such a kind that the individual is in ignorance of many of the possible answers that might be given to it. In the context of economic decision making, where time is historical and knowledge is not perfect, questions like these seem to be the rule rather than the exception. For example, the question might be "What kinds of personal computers will be available for purchase two years from now?" One cannot have complete knowledge of the possible answers to this question because there is no way of knowing what the future will bring. The set of all possible outcomes (answers) cannot be known, replication of the question is not permissible even conceptually since the nature of the question is such that it can be asked only once,[5] and probabilistic laws governing the answers cannot be known with certainty.[6] But it still may be assumed that in this ignorance the individual imagines an incomplete set of outcomes and forms opinions of belief and disbelief about their possible occurrence.

Let Ω be such an incomplete set of outcomes.[7] To present ideas in their most general form, it is necessary to discard some of the "smaller"

---

[5]To ask the same question again at a later moment of time changes the question because both the questioner and the answerer have different epistemological statuses at the new moment from those which they had at the old. That is, they both have more knowledge, different perceptions, and so on.

[6]See Section 2.4. Indeed, as pointed out earlier, there might be no probabilistic laws to be known.

[7]The material of this section is a formalization of Shackle [24, Ch. 10]. A very rough correspondence between Shackle's numbered postulates and propositions on the one hand, and the following axioms and implications on the other, would be as follows: Shackle numbers 1,2,5 ↔ definition of s as a function, (2.2-1s); number 6 ↔

σ-fields, $\mathcal{A}^*$, on which probability functions are defined. Thus take $\mathcal{A}$ as a σ-field over Ω that contains, in addition to everything else, all uncountable unions of its members.[8] A *hypothesis* or set containing answers to the question (what was, in the previous section, called an event) is a subset of Ω, that is, a member of $\mathcal{A}$. The *residual* hypothesis is the collection of all unknown or unknowable outcomes that are not included in Ω. Now, of course, the residual hypothesis cannot be specified. But it is represented in the present context by the empty set ϕ.[9] Hence it is recognized that the inconceivable may occur. Note that ϕ is not an element of Ω. Rather, $\phi \subseteq \Omega$ and ϕ is a member of $\mathcal{A}$. Once again, no assumptions about the quantifiability of the elements of Ω are imposed.

Let A be in $\mathcal{A}$. The *contradictory* to A is the complement of A, namely, $\bar{A}$. A *rival* hypothesis to A is another hypothesis B in $\mathcal{A}$ such that $A \cap B = \phi$. Thus A and $\bar{A}$ are both contradictory and rival. Moreover, every rival hypothesis to A is a subset of the contradictory hypothesis $\bar{A}$, and every subset of $\bar{A}$ is rival to A. Of course, the residual hypothesis is rival to every hypothesis in $\mathcal{A}$. Let i and j denote indices, each running over the same finite, countable, or uncountably infinite indexing set containing the number 1. An *exhaustive collection* of rival hypotheses is a collection $\{A_i\}$ such that:

(i) $A_1 = \phi$.

(ii) A_i is a nonempty hypothesis, for each $i \neq 1$.

(2.2-9s); number 7 (first version on Shackle's p. 80) $\leftrightarrow$ (2.2-21s); number 7 (version on Shackle's p. 83) $\leftrightarrow$ (2.2-16s); number 8 $\leftrightarrow$ definition of the σ-field $\mathcal{A}$; number 9 $\leftrightarrow$ (2.2-3s); numbers 10, 11 $\leftrightarrow$ (2.2-11s); number 12 $\leftrightarrow$ (2.2-10s); number 13 $\leftrightarrow$ (2.2-13s); number 14 $\leftrightarrow$ (2.2-14s), (2.2-15s); number 15 $\leftrightarrow$ (2.2-19s); number 16 $\leftrightarrow$ (2.2-18s); and number 17 $\leftrightarrow$ (2.2-17s). In addition, (2.2-2s) may be interpreted to be a generalization of Shackle's postulate 4.

[8]Clearly, $\mathcal{A}$ is a topology too. In most cases, it is also the family of all subsets of Ω. Because it continues to be a σ-field, $\mathcal{A}$ may still serve as a domain of definition for probability functions.

[9]There is no obvious economic justification for identifying the residual hypothesis with the empty set. But it does provide a methodologically and mathematically convenient way of explicitly including the residual hypothesis in the analysis. This identification, moreover, is one of the principal reasons why subsequent argument falls into place so nicely and why the original ideas of Shackle come through so clearly.

(iii) A_i and A_j are rival, for all $i \neq j$.

(iv) $\bigcup_i A_i = \Omega$.

Because it contains the residual hypothesis ϕ, every exhaustive set of rival hypotheses symbolically extends "beyond" Ω.

A *potential surprise* function on $\mathcal{A}$ is a function

$$s : \mathcal{A} \to [0, 1]$$

such that:

(i) For all A in $\mathcal{A}$,
$$0 \leq s(A) \leq 1. \tag{2.2-1s}$$

(ii) For any (possibly uncountable) collection $\{A_i\}$ of nonempty subsets in $\mathcal{A}$,
$$s\left(\bigcup_i A_i\right) = \inf_i s(A_i). \tag{2.2-2s}$$

(iii) If $\{A_i\}$ is an exhaustive set of rival hypotheses, then
$$s(A_i) = 0 \tag{2.2-3s}$$

for at least one i.

The *potential surprise*, $s(A)$, of a hypothesis A is understood to be the surprise the individual imagines now that he would experience in the future if an element or outcome of A turns out to be the correct answer to the initial question.[10] It arises from the opinions of disbelief with which the individual contemplates the possible occurrence of an element in A.[11] To say $s(A) = 0$ for some A in $\mathcal{A}$ means that an element of A is "perfectly possible" or that the individual is unable to conceive

---

[10]The actual surprise the individual feels in the future if an element of A occurs bears no necessary resemblance to the presently contemplated potential surprise $s(A)$.

[11]This relation between disbelief and potential surprise is quite different from that between disbelief and one-minus-(subjective)-probability. Indeed, it will be argued in Section 2.4 that the latter is based on an assumption of knowledge whereas the former is not.

of any obstacle to the occurrence of an element in A. For the particular case in which A is the residual hypothesis, $s(\phi) = 0$ asserts the perfect possibility of something happening that the individual is not yet able to imagine. Similarly, $s(A) = 1$ identifies "perfect impossibility" in the sense that he cannot conceive of an element of A transpiring.[12] Thus the extent to which the individual believes the occurrence of a hypothesis is possible is bounded by his perception of what can happen consistent with what he knows about such things as the laws of nature and the economic structures and inheritances that he contemplates at the moment. Because Ω is not necessarily the complete collection of all possible outcomes, the potential surprise associated with the residual hypothesis need not be unity, that is,

$$s(\phi) \leq 1. \tag{2.2-4s}$$

In other words, the individual's beliefs may be such that he does not think the occurrence of an unimagined outcome (outside of Ω) is impossible. For similar reasons, and as will be clarified below, the sum of the potential surprises of a hypothesis and its contradictory may be different from, and even greater than, one.

Examples of potential surprise functions are not difficult to specify. Take Ω to be the real line and the σ-field $\mathcal{A}$ to contain all open intervals together with all complements, countable intersections, and countable and uncountable unions generated by them. Then the function defined as

$$s(A) = \begin{cases} 0, & \text{if } 0 \text{ is in } A, \\ \frac{1}{2}, & \text{if } 0 \text{ is not in } A, \end{cases}$$

for all A in $\mathcal{A}$ (including ϕ) satisfies (2.2-1s) through (2.2-3s). In this case, $s(\phi) = 1/2$. Alternatively, (2.2-1s) through (2.2-3s) also hold with

$$s(A) = \frac{1}{2}$$

for all $A \neq \phi$ in $\mathcal{A}$, and

$$s(\phi) = 0.$$

---

[12]The range of Shackle's potential surprise function is actually $[0, \alpha]$, where $\alpha > 0$ is the absolute maximum of potential surprise values, *i.e.*, that value associated with perfect impossibility [24, p. 80]. Little is lost, however, by taking $\alpha = 1$.

As a third example, let

$$s(A) = 0$$

for all A in $\mathcal{A}$.

To obtain a more complex example, consider any function $h : \Omega \to [0,1]$, which is continuous, monotone decreasing, and onto. Let Ω and $\mathcal{A}$ be specified as in the previous illustrations. For any A in $\mathcal{A}$ such that $A \neq \phi$ and $A \neq \Omega$, define

$$s(A) = h(\text{lub } A),$$

where "lub A" is the least upper bound of the set A. Write

$$s(\phi) = 1$$

and

$$s(\Omega) = 0.$$

Observe that (2.2-1s) through (2.2-3s) are met.

It is also not hard to show, by means of other examples, that axioms (2.2-1s) through (2.2-3s) are independent of each other.[13]

Axioms (2.2-2s) and (2.2-3s), and property (2.2-4s), of potential surprise functions provide immediate contrast with axioms (2.1-2p) and

---

[13]To show that axioms (2.2-1s) through (2.2-3s) are independent, choose Ω and $\mathcal{A}$ as in the previous examples. Then the function

$$r(A) = \left\{ \begin{array}{ll} 1, & \text{if } 0 \text{ is in } A, \\ \frac{1}{2}, & \text{if } 0 \text{ is not in } A, \end{array} \right.$$

for all A in $\mathcal{A}$ (including ϕ) satisfies (2.2-1s) but not (2.2-2s) and (2.2-3s). (This is actually a potential confirmation function as defined in Section 2.3). The function

$$r(A) = \left\{ \begin{array}{ll} -1, & \text{if } 0 \text{ is in } A, \\ 1, & \text{if } 0 \text{ is not in } A, \end{array} \right.$$

for all A in $\mathcal{A}$ satisfies (2.2-2s) but not (2.2-1s) and (2.2-3s). And the function

$$r(A) = \left\{ \begin{array}{ll} 1, & \text{if } 0 \text{ is in } A, \\ -1, & \text{if } 0 \text{ is not in } A, \end{array} \right.$$

for all $A \neq \phi$ in $\mathcal{A}$ and

$$r(\phi) = 0,$$

satisfies (2.2-3s) but not (2.2-1s) and (2.2-2s).

(2.1-3p) of probability functions. The additivity and the mutual disjointness of the A_i found in (2.1-2p) are replaced in (2.2-2s) by the nonadditive operation "inf" and the requirement that the A_i be nonempty. Uncountable unions of sets in $\mathcal{A}$ also are covered by the latter axiom. Clearly (2.2-2s) plays an analogous role in potential surprise constructs to that which (2.1-2p) plays for probability. Axiom (2.2-3s) discards the equalities of (2.1-3p) and introduces a restriction that has no real counterpart in terms of probability: in every exhaustive collection of rival hypotheses (each of which, recall, includes the residual hypothesis $A_1 = \phi$), there is always some hypothesis carrying zero potential surprise.[14] Thus, for example, if $s(A_i) > 0$ for all $i \neq 1$ in the exhaustive collection of rival hypotheses $\{A_i\}$, then $s(\phi) = 0$. Although not completely satisfying as a descriptive characteristic of individual thought structures, this axiom is plausible as a first-order approximation so that the characteristics of potential surprise functions can be studied. Observe that when $s(\phi) = 0$, (2.2-3s) does not place any further restrictions (beyond the requirement that $s(\phi) = 0$) on the potential surprise function whatsoever.

Several properties of potential surprise functions may be derived from axioms (2.2-1s) through (2.2-3s). Those implied by (2.2-2s) are considered first. To begin with, it follows immediately from (2.2-2s) that for all $A_1 \neq \phi$ and $A_2 \neq \phi$ in $\mathcal{A}$,

$$s(A_1 \cup A_2) = \min [s(A_1), s(A_2)]. \qquad (2.2\text{-}5s)$$

Hence, as long as there is at least one $A \neq \phi$ in $\mathcal{A}$ for which $A \neq \Omega$ and $s(A) = 0$,

$$s(\Omega) = s(A \cup \bar{A}) = 0.$$

Additional implications of (2.2-2s) are described as indicated below.

Theorem 2.2-6s. *Let A and B in $\mathcal{A}$ be such that either $A = \phi$ or*

---

[14]It is certainly true that, if a probability function p were also defined on $\mathcal{A}$, then, from (2.1-3p), any exhaustive collection of rival hypotheses would contain a set, namely, A_1, with zero probability. However, this is not the same thing as (2.2-3s) because, for any A in $\mathcal{A}$, the equation $p(A) = 0$ means that the nonoccurrence of an element in A is "certain," while $s(A) = 0$ makes the "opposite" assertion that the occurrence of an element in A is perfectly possible.

$B \neq \phi$ *(but not both). If $A \supseteq B$, then*

$$s(A) \leq s(B).$$

Proof:

If $A = \phi$, then $B = \phi$ and there is nothing to prove. Otherwise, with $B \neq \phi$, two possibilities arise. In the first case, $A = B$ and once again the conclusion is obvious. In the second case, $B \subseteq A$ and $B \neq A$. Here $A = (A - B) \cup B$, where both $A - B$ and B are nonempty. From (2.2-5s), which is implied by (2.2-2s),

$$s(A) = \min\left[s(A - B), s(B)\right].$$

Therefore $s(A) \leq s(B)$.

Q.E.D.

Theorem 2.2-6s has intuitive appeal. Just as (2.1-6p) asserts that adding outcomes to a set B cannot reduce the probability assigned to it, so Theorem 2.2-6s asserts that, with the addition of outcomes to (nonempty) B, the potential surprise of B cannot rise. This explains the use of "inf" in (2.2-2s) rather than "sup." (For an analogous reason, "sup" appears in axiom [2.3-2c] for potential confirmation functions in Section 2.3.) Note that setting $A = \Omega$ in Theorem 2.2-6s leads to the conclusion

$$s(\Omega) \leq s(B)$$

for all $B \neq \phi$ in $\mathcal{A}$.

Theorem 2.2-7s. *If $\{A_i\}$ is an expanding, countable[15] sequence $(A_1 \subseteq A_2 \subseteq \cdots)$ of nonempty hypotheses in $\mathcal{A}$, then*

$$\lim_{i \to \infty} s(A_i) = s\left(\lim_{i \to \infty} A_i\right),$$

where

$$\lim_{i \to \infty} A_i = \bigcup_i A_i.$$

---

[15]Both here and in Theorem 2.2-8s, the same result holds with the countability requirement dropped. Countability has been retained in the statements of these theorems, however, to emphasize their similarity to (2.1-7p).

Proof:

Let $\{A_i\}$ be an expanding, countable sequence of nonempty hypotheses in $\mathcal{A}$. Then, for each i,

$$A_i = A_1 \cup \cdots \cup A_i.$$

Hence, by (2.2-2s),

$$s(A_i) = \inf\,[s(A_1), \ldots, s(A_i)].$$

Taking the limit of both sides of this equality as $i \to \infty$,

$$\lim_{i \to \infty} s(A_i) = \lim_{i \to \infty} \{\inf\,[s(A_1), \ldots, s(A_i)]\},$$

$$= \inf\,[s(A_1), s(A_2), \ldots],$$

$$= \inf_i s(A_i).$$

Therefore, using (2.2-2s) once again,

$$s\left(\lim_{i \to \infty} A_i\right) = s\left(\bigcup_i A_i\right),$$

$$= \inf_i s(A_i),$$

$$= \lim_{i \to \infty} s(A_i).$$

Q.E.D.

Theorem 2.2-8s. *If $\{A_i\}$ is a contracting, countable sequence $(A_1 \supseteq A_2 \supseteq \cdots)$ of nonempty hypotheses in $\mathcal{A}$ such that $\bigcap_i A_i \neq \phi$, then*

$$\lim_{i \to \infty} s(A_i) \leq s\left(\lim_{i \to \infty} A_i\right),$$

where

$$\lim_{i \to \infty} A_i = \bigcap_i A_i.$$

Proof:

Let $\{A_i\}$ be a contracting, countable sequence of nonempty hypotheses in $\mathcal{A}$ such that $\bigcap_i A_i \neq \phi$ and set

$$A = \lim_{i \to \infty} A_i.$$

Then $A = \bigcap_i A_i \neq \phi$ and $A \subseteq A_i$ for every i. By Theorem 2.2-6s,

$$s(A_i) \leq s(A)$$

also for all i. Taking the limit of both sides of this inequality as $i \to \infty$,

$$\lim_{i \to \infty} s(A_i) \leq s(A),$$

or

$$\lim_{i \to \infty} s(A_i) \leq s\left(\lim_{i \to \infty} A_i\right).$$

Q.E.D.

The restriction that $A = \bigcap_i A_i \neq \phi$ in Theorem 2.2-8s is necessary in order to be able to apply Theorem 2.2-6s. Theorem 2.2-6s, in turn, rests ultimately – through (2.2-5s) – on axiom (2.2-2s), which, in the present case requires that A_i and A be nonempty. If (2.2-2s) were permitted to hold for possibly empty sets, then, as in (2.2-5s),

$$s(A) = s(A \cup \phi),$$

$$= \min\left[s(A), s(\phi)\right],$$

for any A in $\mathcal{A}$. Hence, whenever the potential surprise of the residual hypothesis $s(\phi) = 0$, it would necessarily follow that $s(A) = 0$ for all A in $\mathcal{A}$. Admitting the empty set in (2.2-2s), then, would reduce s to a trivial potential surprise function in certain, otherwise interesting, cases.

Axiom (2.2-2s) can also be applied to exhaustive collections of rival hypotheses. Thus, if $\{A_i\} \neq \{\phi, \Omega\}$ is a (not necessarily countable) exhaustive collection of rival hypotheses, then, since $A_1 = \phi$, for any $j \neq 1$,

$$\bar{A}_j = \bigcup_{i \neq 1, j} A_i,$$

so that (2.2-2s) implies

$$s(\bar{A}_j) = \inf_{i \neq 1,j} s(A_i). \tag{2.2-9s}$$

An obvious consequence of (2.2-9s) is stated next.

Theorem 2.2-10s. *Let $\{A_i\} \neq \{\phi, \Omega\}$ be an exhaustive set of rival hypotheses in $\mathcal{A}$ and let $j \neq 1$ be given. Then there exists a number ε such that $0 < \varepsilon < 1$ and*

$$s(A_i) > \varepsilon, \quad all \ i \neq 1, j,$$

if and only if

$$s(\bar{A}_j) > 0.$$

Attention now turns to the implications of (2.2-3s). Since A, $\bar{A}$, and ϕ always constitute an exhaustive set of rival hypotheses, a simple deduction from (2.2-3s) provides the following.

Theorem 2.2-11s. *For all A in $\mathcal{A}$, if $s(A) > 0$, then $s(\bar{A}) = 0$ or $s(\phi) = 0$ (or both).*

It follows from Theorem 2.2-11s that, if $s(A) > 0$ and $s(\phi) \neq 0$, then

$$s(A) + s(\bar{A}) \leq 1.$$

Moreover, if $s(\phi) = 0$, then it is possible to have

$$s(A) + s(\bar{A}) > 1.$$

(Recall that, for the case of probability, $p(A) + p(\bar{A}) = p(A \cup \bar{A})$, and hence the meaning of $p(A) + p(\bar{A})$ is given as $p(A \cup \bar{A})$. Here, however, in the absence of the additivity axiom (2.1-2p), $s(A) + s(\bar{A})$ can be given no such interpretation.) Applying Theorem 2.2-11s to first $A = \phi$ and then $A = \Omega$,

$$s(\phi) > 0 \quad \text{implies} \quad s(\Omega) = 0,$$

$$\tag{2.2-12s}$$

$$s(\Omega) > 0 \quad \text{implies} \quad s(\phi) = 0.$$

Of course, each of the assertions in (2.2-12s) is the contrapositive of the other. Note the converse of Theorem 2.2-11s cannot hold because $s(A) = 0$, $s(\bar{A}) = 0$, and $s(\phi) = 0$ may all be in force simultaneously for some A in $\mathcal{A}$.

The next two results give further properties of potential surprise functions.

Theorem 2.2-13s. *If $A \neq \phi$ and $B \neq \phi$ in $\mathcal{A}$ are rival hypotheses, and if $s(\bar{A}) > 0$, then $s(\bar{B}) = 0$ or $s(\phi) = 0$.*

Proof:

Suppose $s(\bar{A}) > 0$. There are two cases to consider: (i) If $\bar{A} = B$ (that is, A, B, and ϕ comprise an exhaustive set of rival hypotheses), then $s(B) > 0$, and by Theorem 2.2-11s, $s(\bar{B}) = 0$ or $s(\phi) = 0$.

(ii) If $\bar{A} \neq B$, then $\bar{A} = B \cup (\bar{A} - B)$, where $\bar{A} - B \neq \phi$. Now A, B, $\bar{A} - B$, and ϕ constitute an exhaustive collection of rival hypotheses. Applying Theorem 2.2-10s with $s(\bar{A}) > 0$ gives $s(B) > 0$. Therefore, from Theorem 2.2-11s, $s(\bar{B}) = 0$ or $s(\phi) = 0$.

Q.E.D.

Theorem 2.2-14s. *Assume $s(\phi) > 0$. Let $A \neq \phi$ and $B \neq \phi$ in $\mathcal{A}$ be rival hypotheses. Then $s(\bar{A}) = s(\bar{B})$ if and only if $s(\bar{A}) = 0$ and $s(\bar{B}) = 0$.*

Proof:

If $s(\bar{A}) = 0$ and $s(\bar{B}) = 0$, there is nothing to prove. Conversely, suppose $s(\bar{A}) = s(\bar{B})$. By Theorem 2.2-13s, $s(\bar{A}) > 0$ implies $s(\bar{B}) = 0$. Hence the only way to have $s(\bar{A}) = s(\bar{B})$ is if $s(\bar{A}) = 0$ and $s(\bar{B}) = 0$.

Q.E.D.

By setting $B = \bar{A}$ in Theorem 2.2-14s, one obtains the following proposition.

Theorem 2.2-15s. *Let $s(\phi) > 0$. For all $A \neq \phi$ in $\mathcal{A}$, where $A \neq \Omega$, $s(A) = s(\bar{A})$ if and only if $s(A) = 0$ and $s(\bar{A}) = 0$.*

Now think of the individual as facing two questions, each with the same (possibly incomplete) set of outcomes Ω and in which the answer (outcome) to one question may appear with that of the other. Let A be a hypothesis for the former question and B a hypothesis for the latter. Suppose the individual arrives at a judgment of potential surprise for A and, given that judgment, makes a judgment about the potential surprise of B. Let $s(B|_{s(A)=\alpha})$, where $0 \leq \alpha \leq 1$, be the *conditional* potential surprise of B given that a value $s(A) = \alpha$ has been assigned to A. Note that $s(B|_{s(A)=\alpha})$ is not the potential surprise associated with B after the occurrence of A. Rather, it reflects the surprise the individual, at present, expects to feel subsequently if, in the future, an element of A were to happen along with an element of B.[16] When the initial judgment $s(A) = 0$, the conditional potential surprise of B is taken to be $s(B)$, that is,

$$s(B|_{s(A)=0}) = s(B).$$

The axiom below includes this as a special case and serves to characterize values of the conditional potential surprise function in general. For all A and B in $\mathcal{A}$,

$$s(B|_{s(A)=\alpha}) = \max\,[s(A), s(B)]. \tag{2.2-16s}$$

It is clear from (2.2-16s) that if A and B are in $\mathcal{A}$, then

$$s(B) \leq s(B|_{s(A)=\alpha}). \tag{2.2-17s}$$

Two additional implications of (2.2-16s) are as follows.

Theorem 2.2-18s. *For all B in $\mathcal{A}$ and $\{A_i\}$, where A_i is in $\mathcal{A}$ and $s(A_i) = \alpha_i$ for each i,*

$$s(B) \leq \inf_i\,\{\max\,[s(A_i), s(B|_{s(A_i)=\alpha_i})]\}.$$

---

[16]Similarly, the conditional potential surprise $s(A|_{s(B)=\beta})$, for $0 \leq \beta \leq 1$, is the surprise the individual anticipates if an element of B were to transpire along with an element of A. Because order is important here, the happening of A with B or of B with A is not the same thing as the "joint occurrence" of A and B (written $A \cap B$). Moreover, the order referred to is an order by position only and not an order through time. That is, A, say, is not expected to come before B, nor is the judgment of the potential surprise assigned to A made before that assigned to B. This is why assumption (2.2-16s) below makes sense and why, as a consequence of that assumption, it turns out that $s(A \cap B) = s(B \cap A)$. For Shackle, however, the temporal order of the eventuation of A and B, and of the judgments of their potential surprise values, are important [24, pp. 83,200-203], and as a result it need not follow that $s(A \cap B) = s(B \cap A)$ in his context.

Proof:

The conclusion of the theorem is an immediate consequence of the fact that, from (2.2-16s),

$$s(B) \le \max\left[s(A_i), s(B|_{s(A_i)=\alpha_i})\right]$$

for every i.

Q.E.D.

Theorem 2.2-19s. *If* $\{A_i\}$ *is an exhaustive set of rival hypotheses in* $\mathcal{A}$, *and if*

$$s(B|_{s(A_i)=\alpha_i}) = \varepsilon, \quad \text{all} \ \ i,$$

for some hypothesis B *in* $\mathcal{A}$ *and some numbers* α_i *and* ε, *where* $0 \le \alpha_i \le 1$ *and* $0 \le \varepsilon \le 1$, *then*

$$s(B) = \varepsilon.$$

Proof:

Since $\{A_i\}$ is an exhaustive set of rival hypotheses, (2.2-3s) implies that $s(A_j) = 0$ for some j. Applying (2.2-16s) to that j and using the supposition that $s(B|_{s(A_j)=\alpha_j}) = \varepsilon$,

$$\varepsilon = \max\left[0, s(B)\right].$$

Hence

$$s(B) = \varepsilon.$$

Q.E.D.

It remains to consider the potential surprise of the joint occurrence or intersection of two hypotheses in $\mathcal{A}$. Let A and B be in $\mathcal{A}$ such that $A \cap B \neq \phi$. To maintain a partial analogy to (2.1-8p), define

$$s(A \cap B) = \max\left[s(A|_{s(B)=\beta}), s(B)\right]. \qquad (2.2\text{-}20\text{s})$$

and

$$s(B \cap A) = \max\left[s(B|_{s(A)=\alpha}), s(A)\right].$$

Of course, these definitions, by themselves, are ambiguous since, although $A \cap B = B \cap A$, they do not guarantee that $s(A \cap B) = s(B \cap A)$. Application of axiom (2.2-16s), however, eliminates the ambiguity by forcing $s(A \cap B) = s(B \cap A)$ and reduces (2.2-20s), say, to

$$s(A \cap B) = \max\left[s(A), s(B)\right]. \qquad (2.2\text{-}21s)$$

A similar expression is obtained for $s(B \cap A)$. Note that it is necessary to assume $A \cap B \neq \phi$, for otherwise

$$s(\phi) = \max\left[s(A), s(B)\right],$$

where A and B are any pair of rival hypotheses, and hence the value of $s(\phi)$ would no longer have to be unique. Moreover, although $s(A|_{s(B)=\beta})$, $s(B|_{s(A)=\alpha})$, and $s(A \cap B)$ are conceptually distinct,

$$s(A|_{s(B)=\beta}) = s(B|_{s(A)=\alpha}) = s(A \cap B).$$

Observe that, with the hypotheses of Theorem 2.2-19s in force, the conditional potential surprise of B given that $s(A_i) = \alpha_i$ is, for every i, identical to the (unconditional) potential surprise of B. Here, as is done in the case of probability, hypothesis B and the exhaustive collection of rival hypotheses $\{A_i\}$ may be said to be *independent*. However, there is no analogue in the potential surprise situation of the independence characterization (2.1-9p) in terms of intersecting sets.

2.3 Potential Confirmation Functions

Recall that $s(A) = 0$ conveys the idea that the individual is unable to imagine any obstacle to the occurrence of an element of the hypothesis A. Similarly $s(A) = 1$ refers to the notion that the happening of an element in A seems impossible. Thus, if one were contemplating the reinterpretation of potential surprise as probability, the appropriate function on which to focus would be $1 - s(A)$ rather than $s(A)$ itself. The question of the viability of $1 - s(A)$ viewed as a probability function will be taken up at the end of this section. But first it is necessary to ask about the meaning, if any, that can be attributed to the expression $1 - s(A)$ in terms of potential surprise concepts.

To deal with this issue, consider first a distinction between the nature of concepts pointed out by Georgescu-Roegen [11, pp. 43-47]. On the one hand, a concept is *arithmomorphic* when the human mind is capable of sharply delineating the boundaries of the thing to which it relates. Each arithmomorphic concept, that is to say, has the property that it can be clearly distinguished and separated from all other concepts. It is discretely distinct, and there is no overlap between the concept and its opposite. The length of a piece of chalk, the element oxygen, and the notion of a circle are all arithmomorphic concepts. On the other hand, there are concepts whose boundaries human powers seem unable to precisely and unambiguously describe. Exact specifications are either arbitrary or unattainable. Where, for example, does one quality of experience leave off and another begin? Democracy and nondemocracy are different ideas, each with a variety of shades of meaning and, more significantly, with certain shades of democracy overlapping certain shades of nondemocracy. Notions such as these are *dialectical* concepts. A dialectical concept is distinct, though not, like its arithmomorphic counterpart, discretely so. Each is surrounded by its own penumbra of meanings. Any dialectical concept is distinguishable from all others (including its opposite) because no two penumbrae are the same. Nevertheless (and this is impossible with arithmomorphic concepts) a country can be both a democracy and a nondemocracy at the same time.

In the present context of uncertainty, where ignorance is pervasive and knowledge possibly ephemeral, an individual is likely to simultaneously believe and disbelieve, with no clear and exact distinction of meaning, that a particular outcome (element) in Ω might occur. That this is the rule rather than the exception arises from the fact that there is generally no way to divide thoughts into nonoverlapping beliefs and disbeliefs about the possible transpiration of each of the elements of Ω. In other words, for any ω in Ω, "belief in its occurrence" and "disbelief in its occurrence" are opposite dialectical concepts whose distinct penumbrae of meaning, like all dialectical concepts, overlap. It follows that, since $s(A)$ is based upon opinions of disbelief alone, and since belief and disbelief are independent and distinct notions, the expression $1 - s(A)$ cannot be assigned significance in the potential surprise context. (This has already been hinted at in the discussion following

Theorem 2.2-11s, which indicates that, in general, $s(A) + s(\bar{A}) \neq 1$.)
However, a separate function may still be defined, to be named the
"potential confirmation function" and denoted by c, which captures
the essence of $1 - s(A)$, although it is not conceptually identical to
it.[17] Specifically $c(A)$, or the *potential confirmation* of hypothesis A, is
the relative absence of surprise or confirmation of opinion expressible
in degrees that the individual thinks now he would experience in the
future if an element or outcome of A turns out to be the correct answer
to the question. It emerges from the opinions of belief (the dialectical
opposite of opinions of disbelief) with which the individual ponders the
possible appearance of an element in A.[18]

Formally, a *potential confirmation* function on $\mathcal{A}$ is a function

$$c : \mathcal{A} \to [0, 1]$$

such that:

(i) For all A in $\mathcal{A}$,

$$0 \leq c(A) \leq 1. \qquad (2.3\text{-}1c)$$

(ii) For any (possibly uncountable) collection $\{A_i\}$ of nonempty subsets in $\mathcal{A}$,

$$c\left(\bigcup_i A_i\right) = \sup_i c(A_i). \qquad (2.3\text{-}2c)$$

(iii) If $\{A_i\}$ is an exhaustive set of rival hypotheses, then

$$c(A_i) = 1 \qquad (2.3\text{-}3c)$$

for at least one i.

---

[17]That the potential confirmation of A does not necessarily equal $1 - s(A)$ is
crucial to the ensuing argument. Neglect of this fact has led to a misunderstanding
by Ford [10, p. 169], who asserts a 1-1 correspondence between potential surprise
and potential confirmation values of the sets of $\mathcal{A}$.

[18]The present meaning of the term "confirmation" is similar, in certain respects,
to that employed by, say, Carnap [2, p. 19ff.], except that it is not relevant to the
context of probability. See also Ozga [21, pp. 51-53].

Observe that the differences between (2.3-2c) and (2.2-2s), and between (2.3-3c) and (2.2-3s), that is, the substitution of "sup" for "inf" in the first instance and the replacement of 0 by 1 in the second, are quite natural in view of the fact that potential confirmation is grounded in belief while potential surprise rests on disbelief. Notice also that the potential confirmation numbers 1 and 0 would appear to have "opposite" meaning to the same numbers interpreted in terms of potential surprise. More precisely, for A in $\mathcal{A}$, $c(A) = 1$ or $c(A) = 0$ would seem to be associated, respectively, with what was called perfect possibility and perfect impossibility in the previous section. But it should be emphasized once again that while perfect possibility and impossibility in the case of potential confirmation are expressed with respect to opinions of belief, when speaking of potential surprise they are based on the dialectically opposite concept of opinions of disbelief. Hence, unlike the corresponding notions defined in terms of probability functions, $c(A) = 1$ for some A in $\mathcal{A}$, say, does not imply $s(A) = 0$; nor does it follow that, for any A in $\mathcal{A}$, the sum of $s(A)$ and $c(A)$ is unity or that $c(A) = 1 - s(A)$. All that can be said is that which may be deduced from the definitions of s and c themselves, namely, that

$$0 \leq s(A) + c(A) \leq 2$$

for all A in $\mathcal{A}$. Furthermore, for the same reason given to justify the corresponding property of the potential surprise function,

$$c(\phi) \geq 0, \tag{2.3-4c}$$

that is, the potential confirmation of the residual hypothesis may be different from zero. In light of axiom (2.3-3c), if $c(A_i) < 1$ for all $i \neq 1$ in any exhaustive collection of rival hypothesis $\{A_i\}$, then $c(A_1) = 1$, where, recall, $A_1 = \phi$ is the residual hypothesis.

Note that each of the first three examples of potential surprise functions given in Section 2.2 may be converted into potential confirmation functions simply by changing the function value 0, where it arises, to 1.[19] The fourth example in that section becomes a potential confirmation function upon replacing h by a function $g : \Omega \to [0, 1]$ that is

---

[19]*E.g.*, compare the first illustration of s on p. 49 with the first illustration in n. 13 on p. 50.

continuous, monotone increasing, and onto, and upon setting[20]

$$c(\phi) = 0,$$

$$c(\Omega) = 1.$$

In addition, axioms (2.3-1c) through (2.3-3c) are independent of each other.[21]

All remaining properties of potential confirmation functions also parallel those of potential surprise functions with things such as "inf," "min," "max," 0, and certain inequalities appropriately modified. These properties are now listed with order and identifying number the same as those of the corresponding potential surprise function properties in Section 2.2 except that here, in the identifying number, 2.2 becomes 2.3 and "s" is changed to "c". Since the proofs are all analogous to those given in Section 2.2, they are omitted.

For all $A_1 \neq \phi$ and $A_2 \neq \phi$ in $\mathcal{A}$,

$$c(A_1 \cup A_2) = \max[c(A_1), c(A_2)], \qquad (2.3\text{-}5c)$$

and if there is an $A \neq \phi$ in $\mathcal{A}$ such that $A \neq \Omega$ and $c(A) = 1$, then

$$c(\Omega) = 1.$$

Theorem 2.3-6c. *Let A and B in $\mathcal{A}$ be such that either $A = \phi$ or $B \neq \phi$ (but not both). If $A \supseteq B$, then*

$$c(A) \geq c(B).$$

It follows from Theorem 2.3-6c that

$$c(\Omega) \geq c(B),$$

for all $B \neq \phi$ in $\mathcal{A}$.

---

[20]This version of the example will be employed in Section 3.3.

[21]That axioms (2.3-1c) through (2.3-3c) are independent is shown analogously to the demonstration in n. 13 on p. 50 that axioms (2.2-1s) through (2.2-3s) are independent.

Theorem 2.3-7c. *If $\{A_i\}$ is an expanding, countable[22] sequence $(A_1 \subseteq A_2 \subseteq \cdots)$ of nonempty hypotheses in $\mathcal{A}$, then*

$$\lim_{i \to \infty} c(A_i) = c\left(\lim_{i \to \infty} A_i\right),$$

where

$$\lim_{i \to \infty} A_i = \bigcup_i A_i.$$

Theorem 2.3-8c. *If $\{A_i\}$ is a contracting, countable sequence $(A_1 \supseteq A_2 \supseteq \cdots)$ of nonempty hypotheses in $\mathcal{A}$ such that $\bigcap_i A_i \neq \phi$, then*

$$\lim_{i \to \infty} c(A_i) \geq c\left(\lim_{i \to \infty} A_i\right),$$

where

$$\lim_{i \to \infty} A_i = \bigcap_i A_i.$$

If $\{A_i\} \neq \{\phi, \Omega\}$ is an exhaustive set of rival hypotheses, then, for any $j \neq 1$,

$$c(\bar{A}_j) = \sup_{i \neq 1, j} c(A_i). \qquad (2.3\text{-}9c)$$

Theorem 2.3-10c. *Let $\{A_i\} \neq \{\phi, \Omega\}$ be an exhaustive set of rival hypotheses in $\mathcal{A}$ and let $j \neq 1$ be given. Then there exists a number ε such that $0 < \varepsilon < 1$ and*

$$c(A_i) < \varepsilon, \quad all \ i \neq 1, j,$$

if and only if

$$c(\bar{A}_j) < 1.$$

Theorem 2.3-11c. *For all A in $\mathcal{A}$, if $c(A) < 1$, then $c(\bar{A}) = 1$ or $c(\phi) = 1$ (or both).*

---

[22]As with their potential surprise counterparts, the countability restriction in Theorems 2.3-7c and 2.3-8c may be omitted.

The implications of Theorem 2.3-11c are as follows. First, if $c(A) < 1$ and $c(\phi) \neq 1$, then

$$c(A) + c(\bar{A}) \geq 1.$$

Second, with $c(\phi) = 1$, the inequality

$$c(A) + c(\bar{A}) < 1$$

cannot be ruled out. And third,

$$c(\phi) < 1 \quad \text{implies} \quad c(\Omega) = 1,$$

$$c(\Omega) < 1 \quad \text{implies} \quad c(\phi) = 1. \tag{2.3-12c}$$

Theorem 2.3-13c. *If $A \neq \phi$ and $B \neq \phi$ in $\mathcal{A}$ are rival hypotheses, and if $c(\bar{A}) < 1$, then $c(\bar{B}) = 1$ or $c(\phi) = 1$.*

Theorem 2.3-14c. *Assume $c(\phi) < 1$. Let $A \neq \phi$ and $B \neq \phi$ in $\mathcal{A}$ be rival hypotheses. Then $c(\bar{A}) = c(\bar{B})$ if and only if $c(\bar{A}) = 1$ and $c(\bar{B}) = 1$.*

Theorem 2.3-15c. *Let $c(\phi) < 1$. For all $A \neq \phi$ in $\mathcal{A}$, where $A \neq \Omega$, $c(A) = c(\bar{A})$ if and only if $c(A) = 1$ and $c(\bar{A}) = 1$.*

In parallel with the circumstance of conditional potential surprise, let $c(B|_{c(A)=\alpha})$, where $0 \leq \alpha \leq 1$, be the *conditional* potential confirmation of B given that a value $c(A) = \alpha$ has been assigned to A. With

$$c(B|_{c(A)=1}) = c(B)$$

as a special case, let the following axiom be imposed: for all A and B in $\mathcal{A}$,

$$c(B|_{c(A)=\alpha}) = \min\left[c(A), c(B)\right]. \tag{2.3-16c}$$

Then, when A and B are in $\mathcal{A}$,

$$c(B) \geq c(B|_{c(A)=\alpha}). \tag{2.3-17c}$$

The remaining properties of the conditional potential confirmation function are as indicated below.

Theorem 2.3-18c. *For all B in $\mathcal{A}$ and $\{A_i\}$, where A_i is in $\mathcal{A}$ and $c(A_i) = \alpha_i$ for each i,*

$$c(B) \geq \sup_i \{\min [c(A_i), c(B|_{c(A_i)=\alpha_i})]\}.$$

Theorem 2.3-19c. *If $\{A_i\}$ is an exhaustive set of rival hypotheses in $\mathcal{A}$, and if*

$$c(B|_{c(A_i)=\alpha_i}) = \varepsilon, \quad \text{all } i,$$

for some hypothesis B in $\mathcal{A}$ and some numbers α_i and ε, where $0 \leq \alpha_i \leq 1$ and $0 \leq \varepsilon \leq 1$, then

$$c(B) = \varepsilon.$$

As with the case of potential surprise, the potential confirmation of the intersection of two hypotheses in $\mathcal{A}$ is also defined for A and B in $\mathcal{A}$ such that $A \cap B \neq \phi$. Here

$$c(A \cap B) = \min [c(A|_{c(B)=\beta}), c(B)], \qquad (2.3\text{-}20\text{c})$$

$$c(B \cap A) = \min [c(B|_{c(A)=\alpha}), c(A)],$$

and application of axiom (2.3-16c) to (2.3-20c), say, yields

$$c(A \cap B) = \min [c(A), c(B)]. \qquad (2.3\text{-}21\text{c})$$

Similarly, $c(B \cap A) = \min [c(A), c(B)]$, so that

$$c(A|_{c(B)=\beta}) = c(B|_{c(A)=\alpha}) = c(A \cap B).$$

Under the hypotheses of Theorem 2.3-19c, B and the exhaustive collection of rival hypotheses $\{A_i\}$ are independent.

Consider, now, the relationship between potential confirmation and probability. It has been implied in the previous discussion that, in general, potential confirmation applies to situations in which Ω does not necessarily represent the set of all possible outcomes, replication of the original question cannot always be accomplished, and the probabilistic laws governing the outcomes, even if they exist, usually are unknowable.

Clearly, if probability functions are not known under such conditions (an issue that is taken up in the next section), then c cannot be thought of as one. But, of course, if one were to assume as a special case (for example, when drawing red and white balls from an urn) that Ω contains all possible outcomes exactly, that replication (at least conceptually) is meaningful, and that the relevant probabilistic laws are understood completely, then for this particular circumstance c might appear to be interpretable as a probability function. In such a situation, moreover, the dialectical ambiguity between opinions of belief and disbelief would disappear and it would follow that

$$c(A) = 1 - s(A)$$

for all A in $\mathcal{A}$, and

$$c(\phi) = 0.$$

Thus axioms (2.1-1p) and (2.1-3p) for probability functions would be met.[23]

But even in this case the axiom of additivity (2.1-2p) is still not satisfied and is replaced instead by (2.3-2c) and (2.3-3c). The implications of the switch are obvious. Although probability properties (2.1-6p) and, for the case of expanding sequences, (2.1-7p) remain intact as Theorems 2.3-6c and 2.3-7c (for contracting sequences [2.1-7p] is reduced to the inequality of Theorem 2.3-8c), properties (2.1-4p) and (2.1-5p) are violated and, from the point of view of traditional probability theory, a host of dubious characteristics in the form of (2.3-4c), (2.3-5c),

---

[23]Recall that $c(\phi) = 0$ implies $c(\Omega) = 1$ according to (2.3-12c). The fact that certain σ-fields on which probability functions might be defined do not contain uncountable unions, and hence do not qualify as a domain of definition for c, is of relatively minor consequence here.

Note also that with $c(A) = 1 - s(A)$ in force, it is not hard to show that $c(A \cup B) = 1 - s(A \cup B)$ and $c(A \cap B) = 1 - s(A \cap B)$. For example, using (2.3-5c), the given equality, and then (2.2-5s),

$$
\begin{aligned}
c(A \cup B) &= \max\left[c(A), c(B)\right], \\
&= \max\left[1 - s(A), 1 - s(B)\right], \\
&= 1 - \min\left[s(A), s(B)\right], \\
&= 1 - s(A \cup B),
\end{aligned}
$$

for all nonempty A and B in $\mathcal{A}$.

and (2.3-9c) through (2.3-15c) is introduced. Furthermore, conditional probability is nothing at all like conditional potential confirmation – compare (2.1-8p) and (2.3-16c). Thus, even if one were to concede the meaning of $c(A)$ as the probability of event or hypothesis A, the difficulty of making probabilistic sense out of the formal properties of c remains. It follows, then, that potential confirmation cannot arise as a special case of probability and, in a similar way, potential surprise can never turn up as a special case of one-minus-probability. The plain fact is that, insofar as concern focuses on the formal characteristics of the functions with which they are associated, probability and potential confirmation (and hence potential surprise) are separate, distinct, and, in many respects, rather distant conceptual constructions.

2.4   Potential Surprise versus Probability

Formally, the ideas of probability and potential surprise each give rise, as has been seen, to functions defined on certain σ-fields of subsets of some set Ω. Take $\mathcal{A}$ to be such a σ-field, large enough to serve as the domain of definition of either function. Let p be a probability function and s a potential surprise function both defined on $\mathcal{A}$. Then, for any A in $\mathcal{A}$, $p(A)$ and $s(A)$ are, respectively, the probability and potential surprise associated with the occurrence of an outcome in A. And p exhibits its own unique characteristics distinct from the unique characteristics of s. So much is clear.[24] What has not yet gained general acceptance, however, is the meaning of the phrase "the probability associated with the occurrence of an outcome in A," or, for short, "the probability of A," and, in spite of the argument of Chapter 1, the circumstances in which the notion of probability in any meaning does not apply and hence could and should be replaced by that of potential surprise (or potential confirmation).

Consider the meaning of the concept of probability first. Although the practice of gambling, and hence the ideas of chance and frequency, were known to the ancients, the notion of probability as it is presently

---

[24]This approach of defining probability functions axiomatically on collections of sets, which has been imitated above in characterizing potential surprise and potential confirmation functions, dates to Kolmogorov [17].

conceived did not emerge until the decade around 1660. And when it did it seemed to spring up in the minds of many individuals, including its legendary inventor Pascal, at once. In birthing, moreover, it came into existence in two forms, neither of which had antecedents in its prehistory, and which still persist today.[25] These two forms are often connoted by using the adjectives "aleatory" and "epistemological." Thus aleatory probability is associated with the outcomes of chance mechanisms and the relative frequencies they produce upon repeated trials, while epistemological probability is concerned with measures of degrees of belief, as warranted by evidence or judgment, that outcomes will obtain.[26] The fact that philosophers have been unable in over three hundred years to bridge the gap between these two conceptualizations suggests the presence of deep and significant differences.[27]

There are alternative perspectives from which to view both forms of probability. Perhaps the dominant approach to aleatory probability is the frequentist position that $p(A)$ is the relative frequency that an outcome in A is observed in an arbitrarily large number of trials. Implicit in this definition is the requirement that the attribute defining the event A be distributed randomly over the elements of every infinite sequence of trial outcomes so that the limiting relative frequency, $p(A)$, is always the same. Observe that the frequentist notion applies only to the collective outcomes of repeated trials of a "game" of chance. One may say that the probability of a general toss of a fair coin yielding "heads" is $1/2$ in the sense that after many, many trials the relative frequency of occurrence of heads approaches $1/2$. But the notion of the probability of heads on any particular toss itself is, literally speaking, not defined.[28]

The most prevalent way of thinking about epistemological proba-

---

[25]See Hacking [13, Chs. 1,2].

[26]Recall that, although potential surprise and potential confirmation arise from opinions of, respectively, disbelief and belief, they do not express those opinions of disbelief and belief in the same way as epistemological one-minus-probability and probability. This is due, at least in part, to the fact that the opinions of disbelief and belief in the former instances are dialectical in character, whereas in the latter they either exist as, or are necessarily transformed into, arithmomorphic notions.

[27]Hacking [13, p. 15].

[28]Oaks [20, p. 102].

bility is with respect to personal or subjective probability. On this view, $p(A)$ is a measure of the belief an individual has that an outcome in A will occur. These beliefs, and hence subjective probabilities, are revised as the individual acquires more information relevant to the possible occurrence of an outcome in A. Moreover, they have to be coherent in the sense that, based upon them, "Dutch book" cannot be made against him.[29] Clearly the subjectivist approach to probability applies to a much broader class of circumstances than does the frequentist approach. In particular, although the probability of heads in many repeated tosses of a coin is definable for both, the probability of heads on any particular toss is (literally) meaningful only for the subjectivist.

Of course, most people who apply probability to statistical, decision, or other analyses in their work do not take such philosophical distinctions of meaning very seriously.[30] Indeed, individuals will often think of probability as either frequency or subjective probability to suit the circumstance at hand. When it seems reasonable to conceptualize in terms of the collective outcomes of a game, one takes cognizance of the former. Otherwise the perception is of the latter. From this perspective, since it is relevant in either case, subjective probability may be viewed as a generalization of frequency probability. In such a context, moreover, the so-called de Finetti theorem has a significant implication.[31] For the theorem applies, in part, to situations in which an individual modifies his subjective probabilities of events concerning the outcomes of a game in accordance with the observed outcomes of repeated trials of that game. And it asserts that under certain reasonable conditions, regardless of the subjective probability of an event with which the individual starts out, if his beliefs are coherent, then, as the number of repeated trials increases, the individual repeatedly revises that subjective probability to become closer and closer to the event's

---

[29]See, for example, *ibid.*, pp. 106-108. An individual can have Dutch book made against him if it is possible for someone else to devise a betting strategy such that, over a sufficiently long string of bets, the individual will always lose.

[30]Hacking [13, pp. 14,15].

[31]de Finetti [6]. An informal statement of the theorem appears on p. 142. De Finetti would not agree with this implication because he does not accept the existence of frequency probability. See pp. 99,148-154.

observed frequency.[32] But, since, as the number of trials becomes large, the observed frequency approaches the frequency probability, the subjective probability of the event must converge to its frequency probability. It follows that given the initial subjective probability of any event in general, hypothetical translation of that event into a game environment would lead, at least in theory, to a similar convergence of subjective probability, as repeatedly revised, to frequency probability. In this sense, then, subjective probability is related to both frequency probability and replication.

However, Shackle [24, Ch. 7] has questioned the use of any notion of probability in the context of human decision making that is characterized by historical time and ignorance. His argument is threefold.[33] First, the ignorance in which decisions must be made precludes the listing of all possible outcomes resulting from the selection of each decision option. Residual hypotheses are always present.[34] But with the possibility of unknown and unknowable outcomes, the determination of the probability of any subset of known outcomes is problematic because it depends on the measure of the outcome space in general and, in the finite case, on the specific number of outcomes. In other words, the existence of a residual hypothesis rules out the "permanent" assignment of probability to any other hypothesis.[35] One might think that a possible way to avoid this difficulty is to assign probabilities (they would have

---

[32]In a similar way, two persons who begin with different subjective probabilities of the same event will eventually see those subjective probabilities converge to each other.

[33]Although the following is expressed in terms of frequency and subjective probability, it clearly applies to aleatory and epistemological probability in general.

[34]Of course there is an empty set over which probability is defined. But this empty set does not function as a residual hypothesis and is always associated with zero probability.

[35]Shackle [24, p. 49]. To illustrate, suppose there are three candidates in an election and suppose an individual's subjective probabilities of each of them winning are 1/4, 1/4, and 1/2. Now, at a later date, a fourth candidate, until then unknown and with a positive (subjective) probability of winning, decides to enter the race. Then, because probabilities sum to 1, the probabilities assigned to the original three candidates must change. Note, however, that if the individual had instead assigned potential surprise or potential confirmation values to each of the original candidates winning, then these values would not necerssarily have to be changed due to the entry of the fourth candidate.

to be subjective probabilities) to some subsets of known outcomes, and then to lump all remaining outcomes, including the residual hypothesis, into one set and assign probability to it so that the probability of all outcomes combined, including those in the residual hypothesis, is unity. But such an approach still does not permit a permanent assignment of probabilities (recall the example of n. 35 on p. 71), and this lack of permanence may, according to Shackle, hide analytical features of the decision problem that turn out to be significant. The use of subjective probabilities also raises the issue, to be further considered below, of how the subjective probabilities of the subsets of known outcomes are determined.

Shackle's second objection applies mainly to frequency probability and that portion of subjective probability that relates to it. Since the decisions in which Shackle is interested take place in historical time, each moment of decision is unique and can never reappear in exactly the same way again. Decisions, that is, are "self-destructive" in that they change the nature of future state of the world or outcome configurations and the epistemic statuses of the decision makers, and thereby destroy forever the possibility of their being repeated. This being so, the replication required for frequency probability does not exist, and hence the concept itself cannot be employed in such a context.[36] Thus, for example, it would have been meaningless for Napoleon to have asked in advance about the probability of his winning the battle of Waterloo. For, were he to have won the battle, he would not have had to fight it again, and, were he to have lost, he would not have been able to fight it again.

The third difficulty with the use of probability under conditions of historical time and ignorance raised by Shackle is addressed solely to subjective probability and the source from which it comes. For to be able to assign relevant subjective probabilities in a particular decision situation, the decision maker has to employ knowledge that he has

---

[36]*Ibid.*, pp. 55-57. Knight [16, p. 226] made a similar argument some forty-five years earlier. Although observations of the past can give the false impression of replication, that replication, even if mistakenly accepted, still cannot be projected into the future (recall nn. 17, 18 on pp. 25). Thus the determination of the probability of occurrence of a future event from apparent, previous replication is not possible.

obtained appropriate to that situation from what he has learned and experienced in the past. That knowledge need not be knowledge of frequencies, but it is knowledge all the same. However, under conditions of historical time and ignorance where, as suggested above, residual hypotheses and unique decision moments are present, Shackle argues that sufficient knowledge to assign subjective probabilities is never available. Knowledge of future outcomes cannot be secured in advance, and knowledge of present and past outcomes is too replete with errors and gaps. And this is so even if the first two difficulties cited above did not happen to arise. Thus the assignment of subjective probability values to outcomes or sets of outcomes is not meaningful because there is no way to come up with suitable assignments.[37]

At any rate, to replace probability in decision making where it does not apply, Shackle [23, p. 443], in 1939, proposed potential surprise.[38] Shackle's argument, as partly outlined above, implies that this concept, together with that of potential confirmation as introduced by Katzner [15], rely for their definition on considerably less knowledge than does probability. Indeed, they are definable even when probability, due to the difficulties brought on by the presence of historical time and ignorance, is not. In previous sections, both potential surprise and potential confirmation functions have been characterized axiomatically on appropriate σ-fields of sets. It has been suggested that of these two the potential confirmation function is the more appropriate to compare to a probability function. In axiomatic structure, this function supplants, in part, the countable additivity property of the probability function (2.3-2c) by a combination operation over unions of disjoint hypotheses or events involving the supremum. Interestingly enough, partly because no satisfactory justification has ever been given for it,[39] mathematicians and statisticians have also begun to investigate properties that can be substituted for countable additivity. In particular, functions called "capacities" have been studied that satisfy, among other things, replacement axiom (2.3-2c) for countable sequences $\{A_i\}$, where the A_i

---

[37]Shackle [24, p. 60]. See also Vickers [27, pp. 9,85-87].

[38]It should be noted that there are other indices of surprise based on probability. But these bear no relationship to Shackle's construction. See Good [12].

[39]See Dubins and Savage [4, pp. 8-11] and de Finetti [7, pp. 83-98] and [8, pp. 259,348-361].

are subsets of Ω such that $A_1 \subseteq A_2 \subseteq \cdots$.[40] And probability functions (and, more generally, measures that are referred to as "charges") satisfying all standard axioms except that finite additivity is substituted for countable additivity have also been considered.[41] But, of course, all of Shackle's criticisms of probability described above apply equally well to the "probability" concepts underlying these modified probability functions because no change has been made in their preclusion of historical time and ignorance.

Another proposal somewhat closer in spirit to Shackle's ideas has been put forward by Shafer [25]. Shafer suggested the consideration of "belief" functions such that the beliefs (*i.e.*, function values) associated with ϕ and Ω are, respectively, 0 and 1, and such that countable additivity is replaced by a generalization of finite additivity having the characteristic that in the special case in which a collection of subsets of Ω are disjoint, the belief of their union is at least as large as the sum of the beliefs attached to the individual subsets separately.[42] Not only does Shafer's approach exhibit a commonality with the epistemological probability tradition, but it also overlaps with that of Sections 2.2 and 2.3 above. Thus ignorance is accounted for in the sense that zero or small belief can be assigned to all proper subsets of Ω. That is, it is not necessary for the belief assigned to a proper subset, A, of Ω together with that assigned to its complement, $\Omega - A$, to sum to unity (hence the problem described in the example of n. 35 on p. 71 is eliminated).[43] Furthermore, for a special class of belief functions called "consonant support" functions, the belief of the intersection of two subsets of Ω is the smaller of the beliefs of the two subsets by themselves.[44] The potential confirmation function has the same property. Lastly, Shafer's doubt function, which is defined in terms of his "consonant belief" function,[45] exhibits two characteristics somewhat akin to those of Shackle's potential surprise function: first, the doubt

---

[40]Dellacherie [3]. Recall that axiom (2.3-2c) applies to possibly uncountable unions of arbitrary, nonempty subsets of Ω.

[41]*E.g.*, Bhaskara Rao and Bhaskara Rao [1] and Purves and Sudderth [22].

[42]Shafer [25, p. 7].

[43]*Ibid.*, pp. 22,23.

[44]*Ibid.*, p. 224.

[45]That is, the doubt of $A \subseteq \Omega$ is the belief of its complement. See *ibid.*, p. 224.

of any subset A is the smallest of the doubts of the single-element subsets of A and, second, there always exists at least one single-element subset of Ω to which zero doubt is assigned.[46] However, it should be pointed out that Shafer's belief functions are defined over domains with only finite numbers of known elements. There is, moreover, no residual hypothesis. And even though replication is not required to conceive of them, to the extent that their construction relies on the presence of unavailable knowledge, belief functions will be as limited in use as subjective probabilities.

In the end, the choice between probability and potential surprise (or potential confirmation) as the relevant thought form for decision-theoretic analysis depends on one's vision of reality and the feelings that one has about the realism and suitability of the assumptions of the approach. The perception of real time as logical and real individuals as having enough knowledge naturally leads to the use of probability. But if one sides with Shackle in maintaining that real time is historical and real knowledge is insufficient to warrant reliance on probability, or even if one adheres to a modified version of logical time that admits to sufficient ignorance to preclude probability, then potential surprise becomes more meaningful. In the remainder of this book, the position is taken that, when dealing with human decision making, particularly, that is, in the general instances of economic decision making, probability is not acceptable for the reasons given above. It is therefore appropriate and necessary to consider, in part, how the economic analysis of decision making can proceed if potential surprise (or potential confirmation) is substituted in its place. This issue will be carefully examined in Chapters 4-6.

2.5 References

1. Bhaskara Rao, K. P. S., and M. Bhaskara Rao, *Theory of Charges* (London: Academic, 1983).

2. Carnap, R., *Logical Foundations of Probability*, 2nd ed. (Chicago: University of Chicago Press, 1962).

---

[46] *Ibid.*

3. Dellacherie, C., *Capacités et Processus Stochastique* (Berlin: Springer, 1972).

4. Dubins, L. E., and L. J. Savage, *How to Gamble If You Must* (New York: McGraw-Hill, 1965).

5. Edwards, W., "Note on Potential Surprise and Nonadditive Subjective Probabilities," *Expectations, Uncertainty and Business Behavior*, M. J. Bowman, ed. (New York: Social Science Research Council, 1958), pp. 45-48.

6. de Finetti, B., "Foresight: Its Logical Laws, Its Subjective Sources," H. E. Kyburg, Jr., trans., in *Studies in Subjective Probability*, H. E. Kyburg, Jr., and H. E. Smokler, eds. (New York: Wiley, 1964), pp. 93-158.

7. ———, *Probability, Induction and Statistics* (London: Wiley, 1972).

8. ———, *Theory of Probability*, vol. 2, A. Machí and A. Smith, trans. (London: Wiley, 1975).

9. Ford, J. L., *Choice, Expectation and Uncertainty* (Totowa: Barnes & Noble, 1983).

10. ———, *G. L. S. Shackle: The Dissenting Economist's Economist* (Aldershot: Elgar, 1994).

11. Georgescu-Roegen, N., *The Entropy Law and the Economic Process* (Cambridge, Harvard University Press, 1971).

12. Good, I. J., "Surprise Index," in *Encyclopedia of Statistical Science,* vol. 9, S. Kotz and N. L. Johnson, eds. (New York: Wiley, 1988), pp. 104-109.

13. Hacking, I., *The Emergence of Probability* (Cambridge: Cambridge University Press, 1975).

14. Katzner, D. W., *Analysis without Measurement* (Cambridge: Cambridge University Press, 1983).

15. ———, "Potential Surprise, Potential Confirmation, and Probability," *Journal of Post Keynesian Economics* 9 (1986-87), pp. 58-78.

16. Knight, F. H., *Risk, Uncertainty and Profit* (Boston: Houghton Mifflin, 1921).

17. Kolmogorov, A. N., *Foundations of the Theory of Probability*, N. Morrison, trans. (New York: Chelsea, 1950).

18. Krelle, W., "Review of Uncertainty in Economics and Other Reflections by G. L. S. Shackle," *Econometrica* 25 (1957), pp. 618-619.

19. Marshall, A., *Principles of Economics*, 8th ed. (New York: Macmillan, 1948).

20. Oaks, M., *Statistical Inference: A Commentary for the Social and Behavioural Sciences* (Chichester: Wiley, 1986).

21. Ozga, S. A., *Expectations in Economic Theory* (Chicago: Aldine, 1965).

22. Purves, R. A., and W. D. Sudderth, "Some Finitely Additive Probability," *Annals of Probability* 4 (1976), pp. 259-276.

23. Shackle, G. L. S., "Expectations and Employment," *Economic Journal* 49 (1939), pp. 442-452.

24. ———, *Decision, Order and Time in Human Affairs*, 2nd ed. (Cambridge: Cambridge University Press, 1969).

25. Shafer, G., *A Mathematical Theory of Evidence* (Princeton: Princeton University Press, 1976).

26. Vickers, D., *Financial Markets in the Capitalist Process* (Philadelphia: University of Pennsylvania Press, 1978).

27. ———, *Economics and the Antagonism of Time: Time, Uncertainty, and Choice in Economic Theory* (Ann Arbor: University of Michigan Press, 1994).

28. Wilks, S. S., *Mathematical Statistics* (New York: Wiley, 1962).

CHAPTER 3

Distribution, Frequency, and Density Functions

According to Chapter 2, the potential surprise of a hypothesis A is the surprise the individual imagines now that he would experience in the future were an element of A to occur subsequently. It emerges from the opinions of disbelief with which an individual contemplates the possible appearance of an element in A. The "opposite" idea is that of the potential confirmation of A, which is the confirmation the same person thinks now he would feel in the future were an element of A to happen subsequently and which arises from the opinions of belief he associates with the possibility that an element of A might come to pass. By contrast, the probability of A can be understood to be, say, a measure (quite different from potential confirmation) of the degree of belief the individual has that an element in A will occur (subjective probability), or the relative frequency of occurrence of an element in A (frequency probability). The three notions of potential surprise, potential confirmation, and probability were articulated formally in Chapter 2 as functions defined on appropriate σ-fields of sets, and the properties of these functions were explored and compared. Although potential confirmation and probability seem to be somewhat parallel constructs, and although economists have attempted to derive probability from potential surprise in the past, that chapter also demonstrated the logical impropriety of such derivations: potential surprise, potential confirmation, and probability are independently defined concepts, and, while

---

This chapter is reproduced with considerable rearrangement, additions, corrections, and other modifications, from my "More on the Distinction between Potential Confirmation and Probability," *Journal of Post Keynesian Economics* 10 (1987-88), pp. 65-83.

the first two are related to each other in a manner that is not true of the third, none of these concepts can be rigorously characterized by deduction from either of the others.

As suggested earlier, the problems with which the ideas of potential surprise and potential confirmation, as distinct from probability, connect arise quite naturally in the context of human decision making when viewed from a nonequilibrium vantage point. Many decisions have to be made in ignorance, without knowing much about the past, without being able to conceive of all future contingencies, and hence without being able to specify, even subjectively, an appropriate probability function in any meaningful fashion. Yet such ignorance does not prevent the decision maker from imagining some possibilities and forming opinions of disbelief or belief about their possible occurrence that are neither extensive enough nor concrete enough to serve as the basis for subjective probability. Thus the concepts of potential surprise and potential confirmation are obvious candidates for substitutes with which to replace probability as expressions of uncertainty.

To apply probability or potential surprise functions in the analysis of decision making, received theory requires their translation into an altered, more usable form. This translation propels the informational content of the function in question, defined, as it is, on a collection of sets, onto two related functions of a real scalar (or vector) variable, namely, the so-called distribution and density (or frequency) functions. Thus traditional decision models that apply to situations of risk employ the latter to calculate an expected objective function, which is then maximized under appropriate constraint to secure the decision.[1] And Shackle's [5] approach to the making of decisions in the face of uncertainty and ignorance uses, in part, a potential surprise "density" function to locate what he calls the "focus gain" and "focus loss."[2] One would also expect that the same kind of translation into the density or distribution function mode would be appropriate in models of decision making that rest on the idea of potential confirmation.

Because distribution, frequency, and density functions in the world

---

[1]See, for example, Hey [2]. The approach is outlined in relation to equations (4.1-5) and (4.1-6) of Section 4.1, and in Section 4.2 below.

[2]See Section 4.3.

to which probability relates are almost always expressed with reference to probability, as opposed to one-minus-probability, and because, as has been demonstrated above, the "natural" analogue of probability in the potential surprise context is potential confirmation, the present chapter attempts to clarify further the distinction between probability and potential surprise by examining and contrasting the distribution and frequency or density functions to which probability and potential confirmation functions give rise. It is shown that, while traditionally defined distribution and frequency or density functions may often be built up in the potential confirmation framework, their meaning and significance, as well as their properties, are not the same as in the case of probability. The main reason for the discrepancies is seen to be, not surprisingly, the replacement of the additivity of probabilities requirement in (2.1-2p) with the supremum operation of (2.3-2c). It also becomes clear in the following argument that applying the traditional (probability) definitions of frequency and density function to the potential confirmation situation is not especially useful because the frequency and density functions so obtained do not possess the same analytical content as the original potential confirmation function. That is, information is always lost in passing from the latter to the former. Starting with a frequency or density function, then, it is not possible to reconstruct the original potential confirmation function. To avoid this difficulty, different definitions of frequency and density functions are needed. Although not developed here, a similar argument leads to the same conclusion for frequency and density functions emanating from potential surprise functions. Alternative definitions of frequency and density functions for both potential confirmation and potential surprise configurations are provided at the end of the chapter to serve as the basis for subsequent development.

In parallel to Chapter 2, discussion begins with an outline of the extraction of distribution and frequency or density functions from probability functions to serve as the basis for comparison. The practice of adding a "p" in the case of probability and a "c" in the case of potential confirmation to the numbers identifying the equations and properties relating, respectively, to probability and potential confirmation circumstances will, where appropriate, be continued here. Readers not interested in pursuing mathematical details may skip immediately to

Section 3.4.

3.1 Probability Distribution, Frequency, and Density Functions

Consider the sample space Ω and the probability function p on the σ-field $\mathcal{A}^*$ as defined in Section 2.1. Let Ψ denote the real line and consider the set of open intervals[3]

$$\Gamma = \{(-\infty, \psi) : \psi \text{ is in } \Psi\},$$

where

$$(-\infty, \psi) = \{\psi' : \psi' < \psi\}.$$

The smallest σ-field over Ψ containing Γ, known as the *Borel field* over Ψ, is represented by the symbol $\mathcal{B}$. A *random variable* with respect to Ω and Ψ is a function

$$v : \Omega \to \Psi, \tag{3.1-1}$$

for which the inverse image of any set in $\mathcal{B}$, written $v^{-1}(B)$, is contained in $\mathcal{A}^*$, or for which, in other words, v is *measurable*. For A in $\mathcal{A}^*$, set

$$v(A) = \{\psi : \psi = v(\omega), \text{ for some } \omega \text{ in } A\}.$$

Given the random variable v, the *distribution* function F is defined on Ψ according to

$$F(\psi) = p\left(v^{-1}((-\infty, \psi))\right) \tag{3.1-2}$$

for all ψ in Ψ.

Axioms (2.1-1p) through (2.1-3p) ensure that F possesses the properties listed below: For all ψ in Ψ,

$$0 \leq F(\psi) \leq 1. \tag{3.1-3p}$$

For all ψ' and ψ' in Ψ,

$$\text{if } \quad \psi' > \psi'', \quad \text{then} \quad F(\psi') \geq F(\psi''). \tag{3.1-4p}$$

---

[3]As in Section 2.1, the following discussion is drawn from Katzner [3, Ch. 12]. A more detailed exposition can be found in Wilks [6, Ch. 2].

For all ψ in Ψ, if $\{\psi_i\}$ is any countable sequence in Ψ such that $\psi_{i+1} > \psi_i$, for every i, and $\lim_{i \to \infty} \psi_i = \psi$, then

$$\lim_{i \to \infty} F(\psi_i) = F(\psi). \tag{3.1-5p}$$

And lastly,

$$\lim_{\psi \to -\infty} F(\psi) = 0, \quad \text{and} \quad \lim_{\psi \to +\infty} F(\psi) = 1. \tag{3.1-6p}$$

In words, the last three properties assert, respectively, that F is monotone nondecreasing, continuous from the left, and approaches 0 and 1 as ψ declines to $-\infty$ and rises $+\infty$. Property (3.1-3p) is an immediate consequence of (2.1-1p) and equation (3.1-2); (3.1-4p) is derived from (2.1-6p) and (3.1-2); (3.1-5p) and the second part of (3.1-6p) follow from (3.1-2) and (2.1-7p) applied to expanding sequences; and the first part of (3.1-6p) comes out of (3.1-2) and (2.1-7p) applied to contracting sequences. If, in the preceding construction, the open intervals $(-\infty, \psi)$ were replaced by the half-open intervals,

$$(-\infty, \psi] = \{\psi' : \psi' \le \psi\},$$

then F could still be defined as in (3.1-2) and properties (3.1-3p) through (3.1-6p) would obtain except that F would now be continuous from the right instead of from the left.

There are two kinds of random variables of special interest. A random variable, v, is called *discrete* if its distribution function F is a step function, that is, if F is constant over Ψ except at a finite or countably infinite number of points in Ψ. At these exceptional points the distribution function jumps. Suppose $\{\psi_\alpha\}$ denotes the set of all jump points for some index α, and let $f(\psi_\alpha)$ represent the length of the jump at ψ_α. Thus

$$f(\psi_\alpha) = \lim_{\psi \downarrow \psi_\alpha} F(\psi) - \lim_{\psi \uparrow \psi_\alpha} F(\psi), \tag{3.1-7}$$

where $\psi \downarrow \psi_\alpha$ and $\psi \uparrow \psi_\alpha$ mean that ψ declines and, respectively, rises to ψ_α. For nonexceptional ψ in Ψ, that is, when $\psi \ne \psi_\alpha$ for every α, set $f(\psi) = 0$. Then f is a function defined on Ψ. It is referred to as the (*probability*) *frequency* function for the random variable v. The properties of f are stated without proof.[4] For all ψ in Ψ,

$$0 \leq f(\psi) \leq 1. \tag{3.1-8p}$$

Next,

$$\sum_\alpha f(\psi_\alpha) = 1. \tag{3.1-9p}$$

And, finally, for any A in $\mathcal{A}^*$,

$$p(A) = \sum_\alpha f(\psi_\alpha), \tag{3.1-10p}$$

where the sum is taken only over those α for which ψ_α is in $v(A)$.

The second kind of random variable obtains whenever there exists a measurable function on Ψ, also written f, such that

$$F(\psi') = \int_{-\infty}^{\psi'} f(\psi)\, d\psi \tag{3.1-11}$$

for all ψ' in Ψ. In this case, the random variable v is said to be *continuous* and f is its (*probability*) *density* function. Moreover, F is differentiable almost everywhere,[5] and at differentiable ψ

$$\frac{dF(\psi)}{d\psi} = f(\psi). \tag{3.1-12}$$

Where (3.1-12) fails to hold, $f(\psi)$ is taken to be zero. The three properties of density functions paralleling (3.1-8p) through (3.1-10p) are as follows. First, for all ψ in Ψ,

$$f(\psi) \geq 0. \tag{3.1-13p}$$

Second,

$$\int_\Psi f(\psi)\, d\psi = 1. \tag{3.1-14p}$$

And, third, for any A in $\mathcal{A}^*$ such that $v(a)$ is in $\mathcal{B}$,

$$p\left(v^{-1}\left(v\left(A\right)\right)\right) = \int_{v(A)} f(\psi)\, d\psi. \tag{3.1-15p}$$

---

[4]Wilks [6, pp. 34-35].

[5]That is, the subset of Ψ on which F is not differentiable is at most of Lebesgue measure zero.

In the special case having $v^{-1}(v(A)) = A$, property (3.1-15p) reduces to

$$p(A) = \int_{v(A)} f(\psi) \, d\psi.$$

Proofs of (3.1-13p) through (3.1-15p) are straightforward and may be found elsewhere.[6] It is a consequence of (3.1-15p) that if $\mathcal{A}^*$ contains all single-element sets $\{\omega\}$, where ω is in Ω, then for any ω

$$p\left(v^{-1}(v(\omega))\right) = \int_{\{v(\omega)\}} f(\psi) \, d\psi = 0.$$

Hence

$$p(\{\omega\}) = 0 \qquad\qquad (3.1\text{-}16\text{p})$$

for every ω in Ω. When $\mathcal{A}^*$ does not include all single-element sets, these sets may be added to $\mathcal{A}^*$ (along with the appropriate complements, countable unions, and countable intersections to maintain $\mathcal{A}^*$ as a σ-field), and the definition of p extended to the new sets in such a way that (2.1-1p) through (2.1-3p) remain in force and[7]

$$p(\{\omega\}) = 0$$

for all ω in Ω.

Properties (3.1-10p) and (3.1-15p) ensure that regardless of whether v is discrete or continuous, f conveys much the same information as p. That is, the probability of any event A in $\mathcal{A}^*$ such that $v(A)$ is in $\mathcal{B}$ and $v^{-1}(v(A)) = A$ can be calculated as either $p(A)$ or as a sum or integral of the function values $f(\psi)$ over ψ in $v(A)$. In particular, the probability of single-element sets $\{\omega\}$ are always zero unless, in the discrete situation, $v(\omega) = \psi_\alpha$ for some α. Clearly, if v is discrete, $v^{-1}(v(\omega)) = \omega$ for every ω and, with $v(\omega) = \psi$, the frequency function f is defined so that

$$f(\psi) = p(\{\omega\})$$

for all ω in Ω. But when v is continuous, even though the probability of A may often be obtained using f, it is generally true that

$$f(\psi) \neq p(\{\omega\})$$

---

[6]Wilks [6, pp. 36-37].
[7]Meyer [4, p. 22].

for all ω in Ω. In the latter case (unlike the former), $f(\psi)$ cannot be interpreted as the "probability" of ψ.

3.2   Potential Confirmation Distribution Functions

As described in Section 2.3, the potential confirmation function c is defined on the σ-field $\mathcal{A}$, which, since it also contains all uncountable unions of the elements or hypotheses of $\mathcal{A}$, may be "larger" than $\mathcal{A}^*$. A *potential* random variable (a possible counterpart to the ordinary random variable of Section 3.1 set in the potential confirmation context) with respect to Ω and Ψ is a random variable, v, as specified in (3.1-1) with the added characteristic[8] that $v^{-1}((-\infty, \psi)) \neq \phi$ for every ψ in Ψ. Given a potential random variable v, it is possible to define a "potential confirmation distribution function," F, in parallel to the probability distribution function of (3.1-2). Thus, for all ψ in Ψ,

$$F(\psi) = c\left(v^{-1}((-\infty, \psi))\right), \qquad (3.2\text{-}1)$$

where the same symbol F is employed to represent both kinds of distribution functions. Properties somewhat analogous to (3.1-3p) through (3.1-6p) are now derived for this conceptualization of potential confirmation distribution functions.

To begin with, (3.2-1) and (2.3-1c) clearly ensure that for all ψ in Ψ

$$0 \leq F(\psi) \leq 1. \qquad (3.2\text{-}2c)$$

Next, if $\psi' > \psi''$ with ψ' and ψ'' in Ψ, then $(-\infty, \psi'') \subseteq (-\infty, \psi')$. Hence $v^{-1}((-\infty, \psi'')) \subseteq v^{-1}((-\infty, \psi'))$. Since $v^{-1}((-\infty, \psi'')) \neq \phi$ from the definition of potential random variable, Theorem 2.3-6c now implies

$$c\left(v^{-1}((-\infty, \psi'))\right) \geq c\left(v^{-1}((-\infty, \psi''))\right).$$

---

[8]This added condition is very strong. It excludes all random variables whose function values are bounded away from $-\infty$. In particular, all random variables with a finite number of function values are ruled out.

Combining this with (3.2-1) provides a second property: For all ψ' and ψ'' in Ψ,

$$\text{if} \quad \psi' > \psi'', \quad \text{then} \quad F(\psi') \geq F(\psi''). \tag{3.2-3c}$$

Thus F is monotone nondecreasing.

To obtain the third property, let $\{\psi_i\}$ be a countable sequence such that $\psi_{i+1} > \psi_i$ for every i, and $\lim_{i \to \infty} \psi_i = \psi$, where ψ and the ψ_i are in Ψ. Because v is a potential random variable, $\{v^{-1}((-\infty, \psi_i))\}$ is an expanding, countable sequence of nonempty hypotheses in $\mathcal{A}$. Hence, application of (3.2-1) and then Theorem 2.3-7c yields

$$\lim_{i \to \infty} F(\psi_i) = \lim_{i \to \infty} c\left(v^{-1}((-\infty, \psi_i))\right),$$

$$= c\left(\lim_{i \to \infty} v^{-1}((-\infty, \psi_i))\right),$$

$$= c\left(\bigcup_i v^{-1}((-\infty, \psi_i))\right),$$

$$= c\left(v^{-1}\left(\bigcup_i (-\infty, \psi_i)\right)\right),$$

$$= c\left(v^{-1}((-\infty, \psi))\right),$$

$$= F(\psi),$$

where the last equality is also secured from (3.2-1). Therefore F is continuous from the left, that is, for all ψ in Ψ, if $\{\psi_i\}$ is any countable sequence in Ψ such that $\psi_{i+1} > \psi_i$, for every i, and $\lim_{i \to \infty} \psi_i = \psi$, then

$$\lim_{i \to \infty} F(\psi_i) = F(\psi). \tag{3.2-4c}$$

It should be pointed out that if, instead of (3.2-1), F were defined as

$$F(\psi) = c\left(v^{-1}((-\infty, \psi])\right)$$

for all ψ in Ψ, then, unlike the case of probability, continuity of F from the right could not, in general, be proved. This is because Theorem 2.3-8c, which replaces Theorem 2.3-7c in the previous argument, does not hold as an equality. Even so, properties (3.2-2c) and (3.2-3c), as well as (3.2-5c) below, would still obtain.

Lastly, if $\{\psi_i\}$ is a countable sequence with $\psi_{i+1} > \psi_i$ for every i and $\lim_{i \to \infty} \psi_i = \infty$, then, as in the proof of (3.2-4c),

$$\lim_{i \to \infty} F(\psi_i) = c(\Omega) \leq 1.$$

Hence

$$\lim_{\psi \to +\infty} F(\psi) = c(\Omega), \tag{3.2-5c}$$

which corresponds to the second part of (3.1-6p). It is a corollary of (3.2-5c) that if $c(\Omega) = 1$ then

$$\lim_{\psi \to +\infty} F(\psi) = 1.$$

Observe that $\lim_{i \to \infty} F(\psi_i)$, where $\psi_{i+1} < \psi_i$ and $\lim_{i \to \infty} \psi_i = -\infty$, cannot be evaluated other than to say that $F(\psi_i)$ cannot increase with i (from [3.2-3c]), and

$$0 \leq \lim_{i \to \infty} F(\psi_i) \leq 1$$

(from [3.2-2c]). In particular, recourse cannot be made to Theorem 2.3-8c (as is done with the corresponding part of [2.1-7p] when proving the first half of [3.1-6p]) since

$$\lim_{i \to \infty} v^{-1}((-\infty, \psi_i)) = \bigcap_i v^{-1}((-\infty, \psi_i)) = \phi.$$

As a rule, then, one cannot conclude that $\lim_{\psi \to -\infty} F(\psi) = 0$.

Thus the properties of the above potential confirmation distribution functions are, to a considerable extent, quite close to those of ordinary distribution functions derived from probability functions. The few differences that arise do so because the latter, defined in (3.1-2), cumulate probability as ψ rises according to the operation of addition contained in (2.1-2p), while the former, characterized by (3.2-1), "cumulate" potential confirmation as ψ rises in the sense of the operation of supremum present in (2.3-2c). This conceptual distinction concerning the means of cumulation between potential confirmation distribution functions and ordinary distribution functions, however, should not be taken lightly.

Though significant and deep, it tends to be obfuscated by the remarkable similarity of formal properties exhibited by each. On the other hand, such similarity of properties is not maintained in the respective frequency or density functions associated with these distribution functions so that here, as seen in the next section, the contrast between potential confirmation and probability stands in much sharper relief.

3.3 Potential Confirmation Frequency and Density Functions

To see how the "frequency" and "density" functions derived, in the usual way from (3.2-1), and generated by potential confirmation functions satisfying (2.3-1c) through (2.3-3c) differ from those based on probability functions, consider first the discrete case in which F is a step function. With the set of jump points taken to be $\{\psi_\alpha\}$, a potential confirmation frequency function is obtained as before by setting $f(\psi) = 0$ when ψ is not an element of $\{\psi_\alpha\}$, and, when ψ is in $\{\psi_\alpha\}$, by defining $f(\psi_\alpha)$ as in (3.1-7) for every α. Clearly the analogue of (3.1-8p) continues in force: for all ψ in Ψ,

$$0 \le f(\psi) \le 1. \tag{3.3-1c}$$

However, neither the counterpart to (3.1-9p), *viz.*, over Ψ, the frequencies sum to unity, nor the counterpart to (3.1-10p), *viz.*, over any A in $\mathcal{A}$, the frequencies identified with the points of A sum to $c(A)$, remain viable. This last assertion may be established by means of an example.

Let $\Omega = \Psi$ and suppose $\mathcal{A}$ is a σ-field over Ω that is closed under uncountable unions and is generated by all open intervals in Ψ.[9] Take the potential random variable v to be the identity function. For all A in $\mathcal{A}$, set[10]

$$c(A) = \begin{cases} 1, & \text{if } 0 \text{ is in } A, \\[2mm] \frac{1}{2}, & \text{if } 0 \text{ is not in } A. \end{cases}$$

[9]In this case, $\mathcal{A}$ is necessarily the family of all subsets of Ψ.

[10]This example has already appeared in n. 13 on p. 50, and was also referred to in the illustrations of potential confirmation functions suggested, but not explicitly defined, in Section 2.3.

Then c is a potential confirmation function satisfying (2.3-1c) through (2.3-3c). Note that $c(\phi) = 1/2$ and $c(\Omega) = 1$. According to (3.2-1), the potential confirmation distribution function is the step function

$$F(\psi) = \begin{cases} \frac{1}{2}, & \text{if } \psi \leq 0, \\ \\ 1, & \text{if } \psi > 0, \end{cases}$$

whose collection of jump points is the single-element set $\{0\}$. The potential confirmation frequency function derived from F is

$$f(\psi) = \begin{cases} 0, & \text{if } \psi \neq 0, \\ \\ \frac{1}{2}, & \text{if } \psi = 0. \end{cases}$$

In this example,

$$\sum_\alpha f(\psi_\alpha) = f(0) = \frac{1}{2}.$$

Hence $\sum_\alpha f(\psi_\alpha) \neq c(\Omega)$ and $\sum_\alpha f(\psi_\alpha) \neq 1$, violating any possible counterpart to (3.1-9p). The counterpart to (3.1-10p) fails for a similar reason. Let A in $\mathcal{A}$ contain the point 0. Then, summing over α for which ψ_α is in $v(A) = A$,

$$\sum_\alpha f(\psi_\alpha) = f(0) = \frac{1}{2}.$$

But for such A the definition of c requires that $c(A) = 1$. Therefore $c(A) \neq \sum_\alpha f(\psi_\alpha)$.

Turning to the continuous situation, when there is to exist a measurable function f satisfying the potential confirmation analogues of (3.1-11) and (3.1-12), it is necessary that the potential confirmation function be restrained by an additional condition. For in this case the distribution function F is absolutely continuous, that is,[11]

$$\int_{\psi''}^{\psi'} f(\psi)\, d\psi = F(\psi') - F(\psi'')$$

---

[11]Chung [1, pp. 10,11].

for all $\psi' > \psi''$ in Ψ. Hence, since

$$\int_{-\infty}^{\psi'} f(\psi)\, d\psi = F(\psi') - \lim_{\psi'' \to -\infty} F(\psi''),$$

an equation like (3.1-11) cannot hold unless

$$\lim_{\psi'' \to -\infty} F(\psi'') = 0, \qquad (3.3\text{-}2)$$

and, as indicated at the end of the preceding section, (3.3-2) need not be a property of potential confirmation distribution functions in general. (An illustration is provided subsequently.) It follows that, when they exist, potential confirmation density functions can be obtained from potential confirmation distribution functions only for the special cases in which (3.3-2) is satisfied.

With (3.3-2) in force, and assuming it exists, the potential confirmation density function exhibits properties parallel to (3.1-13p) and (3.1-14p). On the one hand, for all ψ in Ψ,

$$f(\psi) \geq 0. \qquad (3.3\text{-}3c)$$

On the other,

$$\int_{\Psi} f(\psi)\, d\psi = c(\Omega), \qquad (3.3\text{-}4c)$$

and, when $c(\Omega) = 1$, this becomes

$$\int_{\Psi} f(\psi)\, d\psi = 1.$$

But, as in the discrete case, there can be no counterpart to (3.1-15p). This is also seen by examining a particular example.

Choose Ω, $\mathcal{A}$, and v as in the previous example. Let g be a differentiable function mapping $\Omega = \Psi$ onto the open interval (0,1) such that the derivative

$$g'(\psi) > 0$$

for all ψ in Ψ. For all A in $\mathcal{A}$ such that $A \neq \phi$ and $A \neq \Omega$, define the potential confirmation of A by

$$c(A) = g(\text{lub } A),$$

where, recall, "lub A" is the least upper bound of A. Set

$$c(\phi) = 0,$$

$$c(\Omega) = 1.$$

Then axioms (2.3-1c) through (2.3-3c) are met.[12] Since v is the identity function, the potential confirmation distribution function is, from (3.2-1),

$$F(\psi) = c\left(v^{-1}((-\infty, \psi))\right),$$

$$= c((-\infty, \psi)),$$

$$= g(\operatorname{lub}(-\infty, \psi)),$$

$$= g(\psi)$$

for all ψ in Ψ. Hence F is differentiable and has a positive derivative everywhere. Furthermore

$$\lim_{\psi \to -\infty} F(\psi) = 0,$$

and there exists a function f such that for all ψ' in Ψ

$$F(\psi') = \int_{-\infty}^{\psi'} f(\psi)\, d\psi,$$

where

$$\frac{dF(\psi')}{d\psi} = f(\psi') = g'(\psi').$$

Observe that, since $c(\Omega) = 1$,

$$\int_{\Psi} f(\psi)\, d\psi = 1,$$

which is property (3.3-4c). As a rule, however, the potential confirmation counterpart to (3.1-15p) cannot apply. To see why, consider any

---

[12]This example was also alluded to, but not specifically defined, in Section 2.3.

finite open interval $A = (\psi', \psi'')$. Then, recalling that v is the identity function,

$$\int_{v(A)} f(\psi) \, d\psi = \int_{\psi'}^{\psi''} f(\psi) \, d\psi,$$

$$= F(\psi'') - F(\psi'),$$

$$= g(\psi'') - g(\psi').$$

On the other hand, according to the definition of $c(A)$ as $g(\text{lub } A)$,

$$c(A) = g(\psi'').$$

Therefore, since $g(\psi') \neq 0$, and since $v^{-1}(v(A)) = A$,

$$c(A) \quad \left[= c\left(v^{-1}(v(A))\right) \right] \quad \neq \int_{v(A)} f(\psi) \, d\psi.$$

It should also be pointed out that if g in this example mapped Ω onto $(1/2, 1)$ instead of $(0,1)$, then

$$\lim_{\psi \to -\infty} F(\psi) = \frac{1}{2},$$

and, for reasons indicated above, no potential confirmation density function could exist.

The failure of (3.1-10p) and (3.1-15p) to carry over into the potential confirmation context means that even when they may be derived from distribution functions defined by (3.2-1), potential confirmation frequency and density functions are unable to preserve and transmit the salient information contained in c. This is in stark contrast to the same functions when constructed on the basis of probability. The reason why analogues of (3.1-10p) and (3.1-15p) do not hold, and hence information is irretrievably lost in passing from c to f, is that both (3.1-10p) and (3.1-15p) are, like the probability distribution function, deeply rooted in the addition operation of axiom (2.1-2p). Such is obviously the case for (3.1-10p), which requires the direct summation of certain $f(\psi_\alpha)$'s. And it is equally true for (3.1-15p) since integration over a given set is merely an extension of addition that permits the "summation" of an uncountable collection of numbers. The omission of addition in axioms

(2.3-1c) through (2.3-3c), then, precludes the potential confirmation analogues of (3.1-10p) and (3.1-15p).

Note also that, for the continuous case, the absence of a counterpart to (3.1-15p) frees the potential confirmation function from always assigning zero potential confirmation to single-element sets in $\mathcal{A}$. Of course, when dealing with probabilities, (3.1-16p) asserts that there is no choice but to do so.

3.4 Alternative Definitions of Potential Confirmation Frequency and Density Functions

Given, as the previous argument demonstrates, that it is not possible to derive from traditional definitions the probabilistic kind of frequency or density function from a potential confirmation function, the question arises of whether the notions of potential confirmation frequency and density functions can be redefined so as to make them more compatible with potential confirmation functions, and possessive of the ability to convey similar information. An affirmative answer to this query is now provided.

Let Ω be a set of outcomes, and $\mathcal{A}$ a σ-field over Ω that is closed under uncountable unions and that also contains all single-element sets $\{\omega\}$, where ω is in Ω. Like the σ-field $\mathcal{A}$ in the examples of Section 3.3, this $\mathcal{A}$, too, is the family of all subsets of Ω. Take v to be any function mapping Ω into Ψ. (Although the properties characterizing random variables and potential random variables are not required of v, additional (different) conditions still have to be imposed, as shown below.) Consider a function f^c from Ψ into the closed interval $[0,1]$ such that f^c is either identically zero except for at most a countable collection $\{\psi_\alpha\}$ in Ψ where $f^c(\psi_\alpha) > 0$, in which case f^c is called a *potential confirmation frequency* function, or f^c is continuous and referred to as a *potential confirmation density* function. The former situation is illustrated in Figure 3-1(a), the latter in Figure 3-1(b). (In spite of its shape, the curve in Figure 3-1[b] is not a probability density curve.) Define the potential confirmation of single-element sets $\{\omega\}$ in

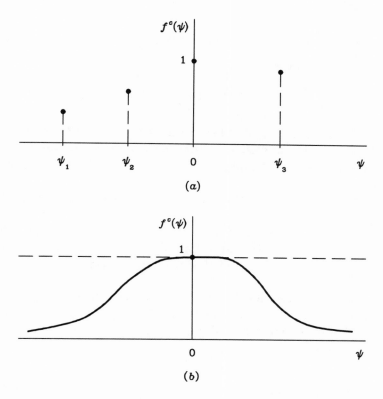

Figure 3–1. (a) Potential confirmation frequency points.
(b) Potential confirmation density curve.

$\mathcal{A}$ by

$$c(\{\omega\}) = f^c(v(\omega)), \qquad (3.4\text{-}1)$$

and for $A \neq \phi$ in $\mathcal{A}$, set

$$c(A) = \sup_{\omega \text{ in } A} c(\{\omega\}). \qquad (3.4\text{-}2)$$

When there is no $A \neq \phi$ in $\mathcal{A}$ for which, according to (3.4-2), $c(A) = 1$, fix $c(\phi) = 1$. Otherwise, $c(\phi)$ may be assigned any value in $[0,1]$. Clearly, c is a potential confirmation function on $\mathcal{A}$ satisfying (2.3-1c) through (2.3-3c).

Thus, starting with f^c, it is always possible to define a potential confirmation function c satisfying axioms (2.3-1c) through (2.3-3c). Without further conditions, however, f^c may still take on certain function values that bear no relation to c at all. The f^c value of any ψ in Ψ such that $v^{-1}(\psi) = \phi$ would exhibit this property. But if v were required to be onto, then such discrepancies between f^c and c could not arise and the two functions would contain almost exactly the same information. On the one hand, f^c would define c on $\mathcal{A}$ except for ϕ. On the other, f^c could always be recalculated from c since, for each ψ in Ψ,

$$f^c(\psi) = c(\{\omega\}), \qquad (3.4\text{-}3)$$

where ω is any element in $v^{-1}(\psi)$. (Equation (3.4-1) assigns all single-element sets $\{\omega\}$, with ω in $v^{-1}(\psi)$, the same c value.) Hence there would be an even closer relationship between f^c and c than between f and p for continuous random variables in the context of probability. Indeed, there would be no discrepancy requiring that $p(\{\omega\}) = 0$ while, in terms of the associated probability density function, $f(v(\omega)) \neq 0$ and, in the present case, $f^c(\psi)$ could properly be interpreted as the potential confirmation of ψ.

Alternatively, beginning with a given c, a potential confirmation density function f^c is well defined by (3.4-3) as long as v is one-to-one. For in this case there could not exist distinct elements ω' and ω'' in Ω such that $v(\omega') = v(\omega'') = \psi$ and $c(\{\omega'\}) \neq c(\{\omega''\})$, which would render ambiguous the correct value for $f^c(\psi)$ in (3.4-3). With both one-to-one and onto properties of v in force, f^c and c are again equivalent expressions of the same thing (except for $c(\phi)$), and $f^c(\psi)$, even when continuous, may be thought of as the potential confirmation of ψ. Of course, unlike probability frequency and density functions, there are no means and variances calculable from f^c.

Notice, in addition, that if a potential confirmation distribution function F were constructed, as in (3.2-1), for the function c characterized by (3.4-1) and (3.4-2), then the f^c in (3.4-1) or (3.4-3) could not be related to F according to (3.1-7) or (3.1-11) and (3.1-12). Likewise, if (3.1-7) or (3.1-11) and (3.1-12) were used to define F in terms of the f^c in (3.4-1) or (3.4-3), then such an F would not be the potential confirmation distribution function of Section 3.2. Nor could it generally satisfy properties (3.2-2c) through (3.2-5c). Thus, one may conclude, if frequency or density functions are to be derived from distribution functions, then either the former can be meaningfully related to a given potential confirmation function c or the latter can be meaningfully related to c, but not both. And this is quite different from the tightly interwoven structure linking frequency or density, distribution, and probability.

An argument analogous to that of this chapter applies to the relationship between potential surprise functions and their associated distribution and density or frequency functions, on the one hand, and that between one-minus-probability functions and the corresponding "distribution" and "density" or "frequency" functions on the other. With a potential surprise function defined on $\mathcal{A}$ as characterized in Section 2.2, and with v one-to-one and onto, the *potential surprise density* or *frequency* function, f^s, is defined as in (3.4-3) by

$$f^s(\psi) = s(\{\omega\}) \tag{3.4-4}$$

for all ψ in Ψ, where $\omega = v^{-1}(\psi)$. An illustration of a "typical" potential surprise density function appears in Figure 3-2. (To obtain a simple geometric example of a potential surprise frequency function, reinterpret the vertical lengths between the points in Figure 3-1[a] and the ψ axis as potential surprise instead of potential confirmation values.) Alternatively, given f^s, the potential surprise of single-element sets $\{\omega\}$ in $\mathcal{A}$ is

$$s(\{\omega\}) = f^s(v(\omega)), \tag{3.4-5}$$

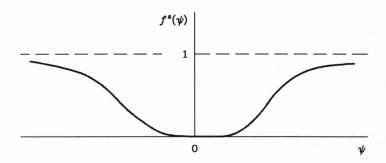

Figure 3–2.   Potential surprise density curve.

and for $A \neq \phi$ in $\mathcal{A}$

$$s(A) = \inf_{\omega \,\text{in}\, A} s(\{\omega\}). \qquad (3.4\text{-}6)$$

When there is no $A \neq \phi$ in $\mathcal{A}$ for which, according to (3.4-6), $s(A) = 0$, fix $s(\phi) = 0$. Otherwise, $s(\phi)$ may be assigned any value in $[0,1]$. Thus the potential surprise function is reconstructed from f^s. In the chapters that follow, potential confirmation and potential surprise distributions will be ignored, v will be assumed one-to-one and onto, and potential confirmation and potential surprise density (or frequency) functions will be thought of as defined, respectively, by (3.4-3) and (3.4-4).

One final point. In subsequent discussion, potential confirmation and potential surprise density functions are frequently encountered in families. Let X be a set of objects x. Then the symbolism f_x^c denotes the potential confirmation density function associated with x and the family of such density functions is

$$\mathcal{F}^c = \{f_x^c : x \,\text{is in}\, X\}. \qquad (3.4\text{-}7)$$

Similarly, the family of potential surprise density functions identified with X is

$$\mathcal{F}^s = \{f_x^s : x \,\text{is in}\, X\}, \qquad (3.4\text{-}8)$$

where f_x^s is the potential surprise density function corresponding to x.

3.5 References

1. Chung, K. L., *A Course in Probability Theory*, 2nd ed. (New York: Academic, 1974).

2. Hey, J. D., *Uncertainty in Microeconomics* (New York: New York University Press, 1979).

3. Katzner, D. W., *Analysis without Measurement* (Cambridge: Cambridge University Press, 1983).

4. Meyer, P. A., *Probability and Potentials* (Waltham: Blaisdell, 1966).

5. Shackle, G. L. S., *Decision, Order and Time in Human Affairs*, 2nd ed. (Cambridge: Cambridge University Press, 1969).

6. Wilks, S. S., *Mathematical Statistics* (New York: Wiley, 1962).

PART II

Some Basic Analytical Structures and Techniques

CHAPTER 4

Making Decisions in Ignorance

Ignorance is a fact of economic life. All decision makers face decision situations with incomplete information. On the one hand, the world is so complex that the individual is unable to collect, much less assimilate, more than a small fraction of the relevant data. On the other, human beings do not possess the ability to analyze what data they have beyond a few simplified, coarsely approximating propositions. Thus the decision context, including the set of options from which the decision maker chooses, is often imprecise and fuzzy. Moreover, even if one knew and understood everything there is to know and understand about past economic activity and present economic behavior, it would still not be possible to anticipate all future consequences of each choice option. The unexpected can, and often does, occur. For the decision maker, then, ignorance arises both from his incompetence to know and understand fully the past and the present, as well as from the impossibility of foreseeing the future.

The reality of ignorance, however, is only just beginning to have an impact on the economic analysis of decision making. Most studies, falling, as they do, in the realm of equilibrium analysis, assume it away, either by supposing that there is only one state of the world and this state is completely recognizable, or by postulating that there are many possible and describable states of the world, each subset of which having a (possibly subjective) probability of occurrence assigned

---

This chapter is reproduced, with considerable additions, corrections, and other modifications, from my "The Shackle-Vickers Approach to Decision-Making in Ignorance," *Journal of Post Keynesian Economics* 12 (1989-90), pp. 237-259.

to it. It is useful to consider some of these latter perspectives briefly before proceeding to a detailed nonequilibrium-analytic examination of decision making in ignorance.

4.1   Approaches to Decision Making

In thinking about the making of decisions by individuals in society,[1] two general facts are immediately obvious. First, all decisions are made in environments that are well defined with respect to the individual's perceptions of (a) the possible outcomes, (b) the economic structures, and (c) the endowments that are relevant to his choice. Second, the particularities of an environment necessarily influence the means by which a decision made in that environment is reached. Not surprisingly, then, the various approaches to the analysis of decision making may be classified according to the environments to which they apply. In one important classification scheme, there are three primary categories of environments, each mutually exclusive of the others. These are associated with the names "certainty," "risk," and "uncertainty." Although general definitions of the latter two concepts have been given in Section 1.5, it is worth providing more specific versions here, along with a definition of certainty, that relate, in particular, to the analysis of decision making. A decision, then, is made under conditions of *certainty* provided that the state of the world, and hence the outcome of the decision, that is to emerge as the decision is put into effect is known in advance. It is made under circumstances of *risk* if only the possible future states of the world (and hence the possible future outcomes) together with the (typically subjective) probabilities of those states (and outcomes) are known in advance. And a decision is made in an environment of *uncertainty* when not all of the many possible future states of the world (and outcomes) are known in advance, and the probabilities of those states (and outcomes) are unknown or may not exist.[2] Decision making under uncertainty is also referred to as

---

[1]The present focus on individual decision making excludes decisions made in game- and social-choice-theoretic situations.

[2]Recall that the distinction between risk and uncertainty is essentially due to Knight [17, p. 233]. Actually, the phrase "environment of uncertainty" sometimes

decision making in *ignorance*.

In addition to an environment, all analyses of decision making by individuals specify a collection of objects or options among which a choice, that is, a decision, is to be made, and either a criterion function that orders the objects of choice or a decision rule that picks out a single object of choice. The choice object selected is usually that which is "best" (assuming one exists) according to the designated criteria function or decision rule. It is the use and construction of the criteria function or decision rule that varies from environment to environment.

The numerous approaches to and applications of models of individual decision making under certainty are well known and need not be considered in detail here.[3] Suffice it to say that in many instances the objects of choice are baskets of consumption commodities, quantities of outputs, or vectors of inputs; the criteria functions associated with them frequently are, respectively, utility or profit functions; and decisions are made, again respectively, by maximizing utility subject to budget constraints or by maximizing profit. It should be pointed out, however, that the viability of such models has not been left unquestioned. Abbott [1, pp. 51-54], for example, has talked about the imperfectness of the knowledge that an individual has about his own utility function. Similarly, Simon [24, pp. 79-84; 25, pp. 272-273] has concluded that, when making decisions, ignorance arising from an inability to process sufficiently large amounts of information places bounds on the capacity of individuals to know the full extent and implications of their opportunities. Hence their ability to choose is limited and they are forced to pursue "satisficing" rather than maximizing behaviors. These criticisms would appear to suggest that actual environments are not certain environments because individuals do not really know in advance some of the outcomes, or at least their evaluations of those outcomes, produced by their decisions. But whether this kind of ignorance actually leads

---

has a slightly different meaning from that described here. Uncertain environments in this last sense are ones in which, although probabilities remain unknown, all possible future states of the world and outcomes are known in advance. Such a notion may be viewed as lying in between those of environments of risk and environments of uncertainty as originally characterized above. It is introduced as a fourth category of environments below.

[3]For example, the utility-maximizing consumer is analyzed by Katzner [13].

to certainty, risk, or uncertainty models of individual decision making depends on the particular way in which the absence of knowledge is handled. Consider, on the one hand, Radner's approach [22] to satisficing behavior, in which a manager, say, searches for improvement in the activities he supervises. Since Radner introduces a probability function as the basis for assuming that, among other things, the expected rate of improvement of each activity per unit of time depends on the search-effort devoted to it, his model is clearly located in an environment of risk. On the other hand, Winter's model [29] of satisficing behavior on the part of firms, which make pricing and production decisions by adopting rules of thumb such as the setting of output price by marking up from unit cost, is couched in a certainty-type environment.

A significant portion of the recent literature concerning individual decision making under risk can be described in the context of finite numbers of objects of choice and possible states of the world as follows. Let $X = \{x_1, \ldots, x_I\}$ represent the collection of choice options x_i, where $i = 1, \ldots, I$. The set X is called the opportunity, choice, or decision set. Denote the collection of possible states of the world, ω_j, by $\Omega = \{\omega_1, \ldots, \omega_J\}$. Write o_{ij} for the outcome of decision x_i when ω_j is the state of the world that actually comes to pass.[4] Lastly, take p_j to be the probability of occurrence of ω_j. Thus each choice option x_i can be thought of as a lottery in which the prizes are $o_i = (o_{i1}, \ldots, o_{iJ})$, and the probability of winning prize o_{ij} is p_j. The situation is summarized in Table 4-1. Probabilities are usually taken to be subjective probabilities, and it is generally assumed that

$$\sum_{j-1}^{J} p_j = 1.$$

Although objects of choice, states of the world, and outcomes, as described here, all refer to specific values, there is no reason why these elements cannot also be thought of as varying from one situation to another. In such a setting, outcome o_{ij}, now a dependent variable, may be expressed as a function, G^{ij}, of two independent variables, namely,

---

[4]In Chapter 2, states of the world were referred to as outcomes. Henceforth, however, the term "outcome" is reserved for variable values related, as indicated where appropriate, to states of the world.

TABLE 4-1. Outcomes Arising from Alternative Decisions and States of the World and the Probabilities Associated with Those States

	States of the World			
	ω_1	ω_2	. . . .	ω_J
Objects of choice				
x_1	o_{11}	o_{12}	. . . .	o_{1J}
x_2	o_{21}	o_{12}	. . . .	o_{2J}
.	.	.		.
.	.	.		.
.	.	.		.
x_I	o_{I1}	o_{I2}	. . . .	o_{IJ}
Probabilities	p_1	p_2	. . . .	p_J

the object of choice x_i and the state of the world ω_j, that is,

$$o_{ij} = G^{ij}(x_i, \omega_j), \qquad (4.1\text{-}1)$$

where $i = 1, \ldots, I$, $J = 1, \ldots, J$, and G^{ij} is defined on some suitable domain. Probabilities also depend on states of the world as in, say,

$$p_j = H^j(\omega_j), \qquad (4.1\text{-}2)$$

for $j = 1, \ldots, J$, and appropriately defined H^j.

To build a model of decision making in this framework is to construct a criterion function, F, defined over the I specified vectors of outcomes $o_i = (o_{i1}, \ldots, o_{iJ})$ and the given vector of probabilities $p = (p_1, \ldots, p_J)$ so that

$$v = F(o, p), \qquad (4.1\text{-}3)$$

where, in any particular situation, o varies over $o_1, \ldots, o_I$, p is "fixed," and v varies over the range of F. It is clear that by substituting (4.1-1) into (4.1-3) and by suppressing the state of the world variables (including those behind p as described in [4.1-2]), equation (4.1-3) can be rewritten for each i as

$$v_i = f(x_i, p), \qquad (4.1\text{-}4)$$

where (the suppressed ω_j in the G^{ij} are indicated below for the sake of clarity)

$$f(x_i, p) = F(G^{i1}(x_i, \omega_1), \ldots, G^{iJ}(x_i, \omega_J), p),$$

and v_i is the image of x_i under f, given p. An equivalent formulation of (4.1-4) is

$$v = f(x, p),$$

where x varies over $x_1, \ldots, x_I$, v varies over $v_1, \ldots, v_I$, and, of course, p remains fixed.

Perhaps the most common approach to decision making by individuals under risk is that of the expected utility model. Let u be a utility function defined over all outcome values o_{ij} and, for each i, set

$$F(o_i, p) = \sum_{j=1}^{J} u(o_{ij}) p_j. \tag{4.1-5}$$

Then f becomes the expected utility function and, from (4.1-1),

$$v_i = f(x_i, p) = \sum_{j=1}^{J} u\left(G^{ij}(x_i, \omega_j)\right) p_j, \tag{4.1-6}$$

where $i = 1, \ldots, I$ and the ω_j underlying p_j are suppressed. The decision maker is assumed to choose that x_i which maximizes this expected utility function over X.[5]

There is, however, a large (and growing) body of empirical evidence, much of it based on laboratory-type experiments, suggesting that the actual behavior of individual decision makers is not consistent with expected utility maximization.[6] As a result, scholars have investigated other formulations of the function F, often generalizations of (4.1-5), which might be better at explaining experimentally observed data. Thus, for example, Kahneman and Tversky [12], in their "theory of prospects," write

$$F(o_i, p) = \sum_{j=1}^{J} u(o_{ij}) \pi(p_j)$$

---

[5]The continuous version of this model is discussed in Section 4.2. A special case is the selection of a portfolio of risky assets to maximize the expected utility of the return on that portfolio as a whole (see Section 4.2). This, in turn, is equivalent, under certain conditions, to the selection of a portfolio by choosing a probability distribution of portfolio returns that represents the most preferred risk-return profile (*e.g.*, Katzner [13, pp. 167-173]). The latter perspective is briefly described in Section 10.1 below.

[6]See, for example, Machina [20].

for $i = 1, \ldots, I$, where u is a valuation (perhaps utility) function defined over an "edited" subset of outcomes and π is a weighting function applied to the probabilities. And Loomes and Sugden [19], in one version of their "regret theory" model, let

$$F(o_i, p) = \sum_{k=1(k \neq i)}^{I} \alpha_{ik} \left\{ \sum_{j=1}^{J} [u(o_{ij}) + r(u(o_{ij}), u(o_{kj}))] \, p_j \right\},$$

where the α_{ik} are weights, u is again a utility function, and r is a "regret/rejoicing" function reflecting the fact that, in comparing outcomes o_{ij} and o_{kj}, part of the pleasure of having o_{ij} in state ω_j depends on the psychological interplay between having o_{ij} and giving up o_{kj}. Additional examples are surveyed in Hey [9] and Machina [20]. But even these departures from the expected utility model may not go far enough. For such modified models appear to be consistent with appropriate experimentally derived observed behavior only when the individuals making decisions are given the probabilities with which to work. Otherwise there is evidence to suggest that decision makers often err in their calculations of probabilities and that these errors, rather than being random, are systematically biased. Additional evidence also hints at the possibility that decision makers' observed behavior itself may even be inconsistent with the existence of such probabilities.[7] It follows that models of this sort, although perhaps retaining some normative significance, may not be all that relevant to positive or descriptive economics.

Consider now a separate, additional class of environments, in between what have been called risk and uncertain environments, in which all possible future outcomes and states of the world are known in advance but their associated probabilities are not. Obviously, probabilities cannot be employed in analyses of individual decision making relevant to these environments. At least two approaches have been suggested that may be presented in the framework described by Table 4-1 without the probabilities. First, explicit decision rules, which do not always constitute full-blown models, can be given for use in making decisions. These rules generally require the assumption of, say, a utility

---

[7]*Ibid.*, pp. 147-148.

function u defined over the collection of all outcomes o_{ij}. To illustrate, the "maximin" rule is to select the choice option from X so as to ensure that the worst outcome is as "good" as possible or, in other words, to choose x_i such that

$$\min_j \; u(o_{ij})$$

is maximized. An alternative rule is to arbitrarily assign all states of the world equal probabilities (the "principle of insufficient reason") and apply, say, the expected utility model as if the environment were one of risk. Further examples are described by Hey [8, pp. 42-43]. In addition, Arrow and Hurwicz [2] and Maskin [21] have developed axioms that characterize and imply such decision rules. The second perspective, called the "state-preference" approach, takes the utility function to be defined over vectors of outcomes $o_i = (o_{i1}, \ldots, o_{iJ})$, conflates objects of choice x_i with vectors of their associated outcomes o_i, and requires that $x_i = o_i$ be chosen so as to maximize $u(o_i)$ subject to appropriate constraints. A discussion of such a model in which the choice set X, which has now become a collection of outcome vectors, is expanded into a Euclidean subspace of finite dimension satisfying the aforementioned constraints, is given by Diamond and Yaari [4]. Note that approaches to decision making in these "in-between" environments evidently preclude the individual from taking into account any feelings about the "likelihood" of states of the world that he may have.

It is clear that for a decision maker to employ any of the above models or rules in reaching decisions, he must necessarily be blessed with considerable information. For environments of certainty the individual must know what future states and outcomes will be; for those of risk he has to be aware of all possible future states and their associated outcomes and probabilities; and for situations in between risk and uncertainty he needs to know all possible future states and outcomes. But many economists believe, in the spirit of the complaints attributed to Abbott and Simon above,[8] that actual decision makers have no such knowledge and are really forced to operate in an environment of uncertainty. To repeat the words (previously cited in Chapter 1) of Hutchison [10, pp. 2-3] arguing that the assumption of this knowledge where it does not actually exist has led economists into a crisis

---

[8]See also Keynes [14, pp. 162-163] and [15, pp. 213-214].

of abstraction: "The most criticizable and unrealistic feature of '. . . Economic Man,' is not his materialism, or selfishness . . . [but rather] his omniscience." Or, to quote Jefferson [11, pp. 122-123], with only a minor change in focus from decision makers themselves to those who study decision making,

> Despite the pervading mist of uncertainty there is a deeply-embedded desire in human nature to impose order on disorder; to fit recalcitrant phenomena into general theories; to speak and act as if . . . [decision makers] had knowledge where it cannot exist; to seek firm answers and 'optimum' solutions as if uncertainty could be eliminated. There is thus a tendency to . . . pretend . . . [that] by developing and applying general theories, introducing . . . techniques, claiming systematic approaches and . . . [objectivity], people can come to believe that . . . [a decision maker's] capacity for sound decision making is far more robust than is the case. [This has resulted in models, some of which have been described above, that suggest that the decision maker] can conjure knowledge out of ignorance, precision out of vagueness, and certainty out of irremediable unforeknowledge.

On such a view, the earlier comment that expected utility models and their generalizations may have normative but not necessarily positive or descriptive meaning extends to all models of individual decision making in non-uncertain environments.

Of course, the Austrian School of economics reacts to the fact of human ignorance by denying the possibility of ever being able to explain how decisions are made in real environments, that is, environments of uncertainty. According to Lachmann [18, p. 168], ". . . the business of the economist consists in very little else but asking what human choices have caused a given phenomenon. . . . But behind these choices we must not go. The economic consequences . . . of . . . choice[s] once . . . [they are] made, not the psychological causes, belong to the province of Economics."[9] But the Austrians notwithstanding, Shackle

---

[9] See also Kirzner [16, pp. 142-143].

[23], as mentioned earlier, has developed a "static" maximization-type framework for analyzing the making of decisions in an environment of uncertainty that explicitly provides room for ignorance within its structure; Vickers [26, Pt. 3; 27, Ch. 12] has simplified and applied Shackle's apparatus; Ford [7] has provided, in part, a variant of it;[10] and Earl [5] has combined Shackle's ideas with elements from what he identifies as behavioral economics. In addition, a different decision model, proposed by Bausor [3], that includes ignorance as part of a dynamic process of individual decision making has already been briefly outlined at the end of Section 1.5. Thus economists have something to say about the making of decisions by individuals in a nonequilibrium environment of uncertainty. Shackle's construction as modified by Vickers is the focus of attention here.

It is possible to consider the source and meaning of ignorance in various ways. For example (and in addition to that attributed to Simon above), ignorance may be thought to arise because, at the moment of decision, the decision maker does not know, and due to the unknowability of the future he is unable to know, the state of the world that eventually will greet his decision. As a result, he cannot say what his preferences, which depend on that future state, actually are. Alternatively, ignorance may be taken to arise from the unpredictability of modifications that may occur in the decision maker's preferences as the process of making the decision unfolds. For, with the passage of time over the interval between the instant the decision maker starts the decision-making process and the instant his final decision is determined, the knowledge the decision maker has at his disposal, that is, his epistemological status, changes. New knowledge may come along that influences the decision maker's attitudes and opinions in general or he

---

[10]Ford's approach [7], which he calls "perspective theory," has two different manifestations. One uses probability and is therefore subject to the difficulties associated with the assumption of perfect knowledge and of the inconsistency with experimentally observed behavior described earlier. The other replaces probability by "degrees of credibility or belief," which is conceptually distinct from probability, potential surprise, potential confirmation, and the notion of belief behind Shafer's belief function mentioned in Section 2.4. Even so, there are striking formal similarities between the Vickers version of the Shackle model and the degrees of credibility manifestation of Ford's model.

may, say, discover new elements in or properties of his opportunity set in particular. In any case, the addition of new knowledge may result in preference modulation. Thus the decision maker is unable to specify, at each moment of the decision process, an unchanging and manipulable preference ordering.

To examine all such forms of ignorance in the present chapter would require considerations that extend well beyond analysis of the essential structure of decision criteria in the presence of the genuine uncertainty created by ignorance. A more modest goal, and the one pursued below, is to confine attention to a single kind of ignorance and assume away all others. Thus the decision maker's preference ordering is hypothesized to depend on his conception of the possible future states of the world that may arise following his decision. The opportunity set from which selections are made, together with the decision maker's epistemological status and the relationship between his preference orderings and states of the world, are presumed to be fixed and specified. This perspective permits full account to be taken of the uniqueness of the point in historical time at which the decision opportunity occurs and the choice is made. At any succeeding point in time, given the unidirectional flow of time and the implied changes emanating from variation in the decision maker's epistemological status and preference ordering, an entirely different decision situation will exist. The uniqueness of historical time points determines and colors a uniqueness in the decision maker's successive preference orderings and decision criteria as well as in the opportunity sets that he faces. It should also be borne in mind that the decision apparatus presented here is rigorously directed toward the making of the "best" decision at a particular moment in or period of time. The fact, alluded to above, that the "decision-making process" might start at one moment and terminate at a later moment is ignored. Thus, analogously to what might be conceived of as intertemporal dynamics in a strict neoclassical environment, such problems as the consistency of the decision-making process over time (in the sense, for example, of Bausor [3]) are not addressed. The question of the timing of decisions, or when to take what kind of action, is also not considered.

As indicated earlier, the vehicle subsequently employed to explore the impact of introducing ignorance into the analysis of decision making is based on the work of Shackle [23] and Vickers [27, Ch. 12]. In particular, the aim is to generalize and extend the Shackle-Vickers framework so that it may be applied to a broader range of economic problems. The approach begins with the development, by the decision maker, of a family of potential surprise density functions, each member of which is defined over possible outcomes associated with a particular choice or decision. For every option, maximization of an "attractiveness" function subject to the potential surprise density function permits the decision maker to focus his attention on a pair of outcomes that go with the selection of that option. Then, by introducing a decision function or index over the collection of all of these pairs, he is able to choose from them, and hence arrive at a decision among the options to which they correspond.

Ford [6, pp. 146-147] has argued that the final selection by the decision maker would not be affected if potential surprise in the above scheme were transformed into and replaced by subjective probability. Therefore, according to Ford, there is nothing wrong with making the switch. There are at least two reasons, however, why this is not so. First, the proposed replacement modifies both the meaning and significance of the original Shacklean construction. Shackle's model is, after all, one of decision making *in ignorance*. Since the use of even subjective probability in place of potential surprise banishes ignorance from the discussion, an important characteristic of the original is lost in substitution. Second, it has been shown in Chapter 3 that the density function generated by a potential confirmation function (the proper Shacklean expression of uncertainty to compare with probability), has different mathematical characteristics than a probability density function. Similar reasoning applied as well to the density function derived from a potential surprise function as compared to that obtained from a one-minus-probability function. Hence the replacement of a potential surprise density function (or, for that matter, a potential confirmation density function) by a probability density function may indeed alter the decision produced by the model.

Briefly, the remainder of this chapter is structured as follows. To set the stage and serve as both a source of contrast and a point of departure, Section 4.2 summarizes the continuous version of the expected utility model, the standard analysis of decision making in risky situations, as it applies in the present context. (The finite formulation, of course, is contained in equations [4.1-5] and [4.1-6].) Then, using the idea of potential surprise, Section 4.3 develops a nonequilibrium-analytic theory of decision making in ignorance as outlined above. An alternative approach that substitutes potential confirmation for potential surprise is presented in Section 4.4. For decisions based on potential surprise to be consistent with those resting on potential confirmation, it turns out that the potential surprise model and the potential confirmation model have to be related in certain, very specific ways. It should be noted that subsequent chapters will also provide examples to illustrate the potential surprise model, and examine that model's operationality. The discussions of Sections 4.3 and 4.4, however, are concerned only with the logic of the potential-surprise, potential-confirmation choice paradigm.

4.2 The Expected Utility Model

To outline the usual description of decision making under risk,[11] let Ω be the collection of all possible "outcomes of randomness" or states of the world. Each state ω in Ω is completely known to the decision maker, and there are no states that can arise which are not already contained in Ω. Let $\mathcal{A}^*$ be a σ-field of subsets (events) in Ω. Suppose the decision maker contructs a probability function p defined on $\mathcal{A}^*$ that indicates the probability of each collection of states A in $\mathcal{A}^*$. This probability function is also known in its entirety by the decision maker and satisfies the axioms and properties indicated in Section 2.1.

Take the real line to be represented by the symbol Ψ and consider a random variable, v, mapping Ω into Ψ. Let ψ range over the elements of Ψ. When v is continuous (the discrete case has already been considered in Section 4.1), the probability function p generates, as described in Section 3.1, a probability density function on Ψ, written $f(\psi)$. The axioms required of p impose certain, standard restrictions on f. In-

---

[11]See, for example, Hey [8, Ch. 5]. The following is a more detailed discussion of the expected utility model than that given in Section 4.1, and is based on the probability density function rather than, as in Section 4.1, on the probability frequency function.

deed, Ψ and f contain much the same information as Ω and p and may be used as alternative representations of, respectively, states and their "probabilities" of occurrence. From now on, values of ω will be identified only as *states of the world*, and values of ψ will be designated as *outcomes*. Recall, however, that $f(\psi)$ can not be interpreted as the probability of ψ.

Let X be the set of elements, x, from whose subsets the individual must decide or choose. Refer to X to as the *decision set* (one of the names already given to X in the discussion of finite situations in Section 4.1), and the elements of X as *objects of choice* or *choice options*. Although the objects of choice are known at the moment of decision, the effect of the randomness, that is, the state of the world or the outcome actually arising, is not discovered until later when the consequences of the decision are learned. Assume that (unlike the models of decision making in ignorance developed in the next two sections) the decision made has no effect on the state of the world or outcome actually occurring and that the utility of the decision depends on both the outcome that comes to pass as well as on the chosen x.[12] In other words, the individual possesses a utility function $u(x, \psi)$ defined over the Cartesian product $X \times \Psi$ such that for each outcome ψ, $u(x, \psi)$ defines a complete preference ordering of all elements in the decision set.[13] Suppose, moreover, that the decision is arrived at by choosing x to maximize the expected utility function

$$\bar{u}(x) = \int_{-\infty}^{\infty} u(x, \psi) f(\psi) \, d\psi, \qquad (4.2\text{-}1)$$

subject to whatever nonstochastic constraints are present. Of course, to be able to select x so as to maximize $\bar{u}$, it is necessary that $\bar{u}$ exist and exhibit properties sufficient to ensure that a (constrained) maximization can be carried out. (The expected utility function for the case in which the random variable v is discrete was given in equation [4.1-6].)

---

[12]This is analogous to the discrete-case utility function u as composed with G^{ij}, that is, $u(G^{ij}(x_i, \omega_j))$, of equation (4.1-6), except that here ω has been transformed into ψ by v.

[13]In order to ensure that subsequent argument does not depend on the particular choice of the utility representation, it is necessary to assume that either u is cardinal or variations in the choice of the representation u are offset by changes in f so that the same results obtain.

In many circumstances, the mean μ and the standard deviation σ of the density function f appear as parameters in the expected utility function $\bar{u}$ of (4.2-1). Such would be the case, for example, if f were at least a two-parameter density function with parameters μ and σ, and if $u(x, \psi)$ were a polynomial of at least the second degree in ψ for each x (with appropriate nonzero coefficients).[14] In situations like these, values of σ are thought of as measuring the risk associated with the decision maker's density function f, and the first- and second-order partial derivatives of $\bar{u}$ with respect to μ and σ describe his risk *profile* at different values of x, μ, and σ. This profile, moreover, characterizes the decision maker's attitudes toward risk in at least two different ways. First, when the sign of

$$\frac{\partial \bar{u}(x)}{\partial \sigma} \tag{4.2-2}$$

is positive, negative, or zero, the decision maker is said to, respectively, *unconditionally favor* risk, be *unconditionally averse* to risk, or be *unconditionally neutral* or *indifferent* toward risk at x, μ, and σ.[15] And the

---

[14]In this example, even if f had a third moment it could not appear as a parameter of $\bar{u}$ unless $u(x, \psi)$ were a polynomial in ψ of degree larger than two. Likewise, even if $u(x, \psi)$ were a polynomial in ψ of degree larger than two, a third moment could not appear as a parameter of $\bar{u}$ unless it existed as a parameter of f. In general, if $u(x, \psi)$ is a polynomial in ψ of degree $K > 0$, or

$$u(x, \psi) = u^0(x) + u^1(x)\psi + \cdots + u^K(x)\psi^K,$$

where $u^k(x)$ is some function of x for each $k = 0, \ldots, K$, then

$$\bar{u}(x, \psi) = u^0(x) + u^1(x)m_1 + \cdots + u^K(x)m_K,$$

where $m_k = \int_{-\infty}^{\infty} \psi^k f(\psi) \, d\psi$ is the kth moment of ψ. Thus $\bar{u}$ exists only if the first K moments of ψ exist and, in that event, those moments, and no higher moments, even if they existed, would appear as parameters of $\bar{u}$.

In this regard, it should be understood that to say, for example, that m_k exists means that the integral defining m_k exists as a finite number. Hence the equation $m_k = 0$ asserts not only that m_k exists, but also that its value is zero. An analogous interpretation applies to the statement that $\bar{u}$ exists. Note also that there are distributions, such as the Cauchy distribution, for which no moments exist. But distributions like these are not relevant or useful in, say, traditional discussions of portfolio selection (see Section 10.2) that require the existence of first and second moments to deduce their conclusions.

[15]See, for example, Hey [8, Ch. 6].

more positive or negative the value of (4.2-2), the more unconditionally favorable or, again respectively, more unconditionally averse to risk the individual is.

Whereas unconditional attitudes toward risk depend on how expected utility values change with variation in the risk parameter σ, "trade-off" risk attitudes relate to the way μ modifies in response to alterations in σ when the level of expected utility is held constant. More specifically, the decision maker is called *trade-off favorable* to risk, *trade-off averse* to risk, and *trade-off neutral* or *indifferent* toward risk at x, μ, and σ, according to whether, respectively,

$$-\frac{\partial \bar{u}(x)}{\partial \sigma} \bigg/ \frac{\partial \bar{u}(x)}{\partial \mu} \qquad (4.2\text{-}3)$$

is negative, positive, or zero. Thus trade-off risk aversion, say, means that given x, μ, and σ, a larger value of σ requires a greater value of μ to keep expected utility constant. In addition, trade-off risk aversion at x, μ, and σ increases with σ if the increment of μ necessary to maintain constant expected utility rises as σ becomes larger or, in other words, if the partial derivative of (4.2-3) with respect to σ is positive.

In the context of the theory of consumer demand, the object of choice x becomes a vector or basket of commodities and X the commodity space. Taking prices and the consumer's income to be known with certainty, x is chosen to maximize $\bar{u}$ subject to the budget constraint. One approach to the imposition of assumptions and the derivation of their implications for the consumer demand functions secured from the constrained maximization of $\bar{u}$ has been discussed in Katzner [13, Sect. 8.2]. A variant of this approach is the portfolio selection model in which

$$u(x, \psi) = x \cdot \psi - \frac{1}{2}\alpha(x \cdot \psi)^2, \qquad (4.2\text{-}4)$$

where x is a vector of quantities of assets, ψ is a vector of (random) yields per unit of asset, α is a positive constant and the dots denote inner products. As before, maximization of $\bar{u}$ from (4.2-1) subject to a budget constraint yields the demand for x as a function of current asset prices, income, and both the vector of means and the variance-covariance matrix of f. The properties of these demand functions were studied in [13, Sect. 8.3]. (Recall also n. 5 on p. 108.) Letting $\delta =$

$x \cdot \psi$ in (4.2-4), then substituting the resulting function u into (4.2-1), replacing ψ in that revised (4.2-1) with δ, and assuming μ and σ exist and $\partial \bar{u}/\partial \mu > 0$, it can be shown that, for all relevant values of μ and σ, the expected utility function $\bar{u}$ exhibits unconditional risk aversion and trade-off risk aversion, and increasing unconditional risk aversion and increasing trade-off risk aversion with expanding σ.[16]

The perfectly competitive firm may be treated similarly. Given that input and output prices and the firm's production function are known with certainty, appeal to cost minimization allows profit to be expressed, in part, as a function of the object of choice, namely, output. Profit also depends on the state of the world that arises as the firm decides on its output. Represent output by x and express this profit function as $\pi(x, \psi)$. Then in parallel with equation (4.2-1), expected profit is[17]

$$\bar{\pi}(x) = \int_{-\infty}^{\infty} \pi(x, \psi) f(\psi) \, d\psi,$$

and the firm may be thought of as choosing x so as to maximize $\bar{\pi}$.

Observe that the standard approach to decision making under risk as depicted here contains, in general, six components: (i) a collection of possible states of the world that is known completely; (ii) known probabilities of occurrence of collections of states and an appropriate random variable, or a density function defined over outcomes; (iii) a decision set containing the objects of choice from subsets of which one element (the decision) must be chosen; (iv) a utility (or profit) function expressing a complete list of preferences among all elements in the decision set for each possible outcome; (v) a method for reducing the different preference lists of (iv) into a single decision function (*i.e*, calculation of expectation) that possibly reflects risk favoring, risk aversion or risk indifference on the part of the decision maker; and (vi) selection (arriving at the decision) by maximizing the decision function obtained in (v) subject to relevant constraints. An analogous, though different, structure is present in each of the two models of decision making under ignorance developed in the remainder of this chapter.

Analogies between structures notwithstanding, it should also be

---

[16]See, for example, Vickers [27, pp. 112-116].

[17]This is a special case of the model described by Hey [8, pp. 127-129].

borne in mind that the expected utility approach and those developed subsequently all depart from the same point, namely, a nonstochastic utility, profit, or rate of return function appropriately defined over objects of choice and states of the world. But whereas the expected utility approach proceeds by redefining the state of the world variable as a stochastic variable and employs a probability function to account for its stochastic variation, the subsequent approaches move in a different direction characterized with respect to the potential surprise or confirmation functions, the attractiveness functions, and the decision indices that those approaches introduce. In the latter approaches, the state of the world variable is also redefined, this time as a nonstochastic but still uncertain variable.

4.3   Decision Making in Ignorance Using Potential Surprise

The first thing to recognize when admitting ignorance into the decision-making picture is that, since the past and present are only imperfectly perceived, and since the future is unknowable, it is no longer tenable to assume either that the decision maker can enumerate and describe all possible states of the world that may greet his decision or that he is able to assign probabilities of occurrence to subcollections of those states in a meaningful way.[18] In the midst of ignorance, unforeseen and even inconceivable states of the world may arise without warning, and there is simply not enough information available to be able to assert that a subset of states, A, has probability of occurrence $p(A)$. Hence the notions of probability and of a complete and known collection of states of the world, concepts that are fundamental to the analysis of decision making under risk, have to be discarded. They are replaced here by supposing that, based on his experience and the imperfect knowledge he has of the past and present, the decision maker imagines an incomplete collection of as many states of the world as he can think

---

[18]Indeed, Shackle [23, pp. 6-10] argues that decision makers cannot base decisions on future states that are known because once those states are known the moment of decision is past and it is too late to decide.

of that could emerge as the effects of his possible decision among the objects of choice work themselves out, and forms nonprobabilistic opinions about their possible occurrence that are expressed in the language of potential surprise or potential confirmation. At each decision moment, in other words, the decision maker contemplates the possibilities for future events, given the shape and texture of the history of which he is aware and as he perceives it. And he imagines the extent to which he might be surprised if certain states of the world rather than certain others were to occur. He can do this while, at the same time, being unable to come up with probabilities of occurrence because his sense of the structure of things is historically informed by conjured relations, not necessarily stable over time, that pertain to economic affairs.

It should be noted that the determination of a potential surprise value, say, for any subset of imagined, possible states of the world, although based on what the decision maker knows or thinks he knows, is also confronted by the same ignorance and uncertainty described above with respect to the listing of all such states. Under these conditions, then, the decision maker can only estimate and guess using his incomplete knowledge of the past and present, and hence his potential surprise function is highly personal and subjective. This is not meant to suggest, however, that the potential surprise function is a shadowy or fuzzy concept. On the contrary, it is assumed to be precisely specified and well defined. Observe further that since they depend, in part, on the individual's epistemic status, and since that status varies from moment to moment (or period to period), both the set of imagined possible states of the world and the potential surprise function are unique to each moment of historical time.

Denote the incomplete collection of states of the world by Ω. (Because it is imagined and not "known," this Ω is not the same as that employed in the previous section.) Subsets (now called hypotheses) of Ω are again written A. The residual hypothesis, or the class of all unknown or unknowable states that are not included in Ω, is represented by the empty set ϕ. Although ϕ is a subset of Ω, it is not an element of Ω. Consider only the σ-field over Ω that contains all subsets of Ω and denote it by $\mathcal{A}$, and let s and c be, respectively, the decision maker's potential surprise and potential confirmation functions defined on $\mathcal{A}$. The properties of these functions have been discussed at length in

Chapter 2. Recall that, due to the dialectical character of the opposing and underlying concepts of disbelief and belief, s and c are themselves independently defined so that, in general, one would not expect

$$s(A) + c(A) = 1 \qquad (4.3\text{-}1)$$

for any A in $\mathcal{A}$. However, the fact that (4.3-1) might hold for all A in $\mathcal{A}$ in special circumstances is of considerble importance to subsequent argument.

As demonstrated in Section 3.4, when a suitable 1-1 and onto transformation of Ω into the real line Ψ is available, the information contained in s and c can be translated into density (or frequency) functions defined on Ψ and denoted, respectively, by f^s and f^c. These functions, moreover, permit $f^s(\psi)$ and $f^c(\psi)$ to be thought of, again respectively, as the potential surprise and potential confirmation of ψ in Ψ and allow the values of ψ to be taken as proxies for the various states of the world. As with s and c, it is generally not so that

$$f^s(\psi) + f^c(\psi) = 1 \qquad (4.3\text{-}2)$$

for any ψ in Ψ. Of course, in the case of probability, when f is a (continuous) density function, $f(\psi)$ cannot meaningfully be described as the probability of ψ.

Analysis of the making of decisions in ignorance may be based on either the potential surprise or the potential confirmation function. Shackle [23] employed only the former, but a parallel argument is easily built up from the latter. Both are considered below. It should be noted that equation (4.3-2), though not holding as a rule, still turns out to have some significance in relating the two approaches to each other. Moreover, this condition and that of (4.3-1) are equivalent in the sense of the following proposition.

Theorem 4.3-3. *Let f^s, f^c, s, and c be related according to equations* (3.4-1), (3.4-2), (3.4-5), *and* (3.4-6). *Then, for all ψ in Ψ,*

$$f^s(\psi) + f^c(\psi) = 1,$$

if and only if, for all A in $\mathcal{A}$,

$$s(A) + c(A) = 1.$$

Proof:

Let f^s, f^c, s, and c and s satisfy (3.4-1), (3.4-2), (3.4-5), and (3.4-6). That is, for all ω in Ω and $A \neq \phi$ in $\mathcal{A}$,

$$s(\{\omega\}) = f^s(v(\omega)),$$

$$s(A) = \inf_{\omega \in A} s(\{\omega\}),$$

and

$$c(\{\omega\}) = f^c(v(\omega)),$$

$$c(A) = \sup_{\omega \in A} c(\{\omega\}),$$

where v is an appropriate 1-1 and onto function mapping Ω into Ψ. Clearly, if $s(A) + c(A) = 1$ for all A in $\mathcal{A}$, then, since all single-element sets $\{\omega\}$ are in $\mathcal{A}$, it follows that $f^s(\psi) + f^c(\psi) = 1$ for all ψ in Ψ.

Conversely, with the latter condition in force, for any A in $\mathcal{A}$,

$$c(A) = \sup_{\omega \in A} f^c(v(\omega)),$$

$$= \sup_{\omega \in A} [1 - f^s(v(\omega))],$$

$$= 1 - \inf_{\omega \in A} f^s(v(\omega)),$$

$$= 1 - s(A).$$

Q.E.D.

Turning to the model of decision making itself, discussion begins by taking the potential surprise approach first (that based on potential confirmation is deferred to the next section) and by following Shackle [23]. Vickers' modification of the Shacklean apparatus is introduced where it appropriately fits into subsequent development. In this case, components (i) and (ii) of the standard model of decision making under risk summarized at the end of Section 4.2, namely, the complete and known collection of all possible states of the world, and the probability function and random variable are replaced, respectively, by the incomplete, imagined collection Ω, the potential surprise function s, and a function to be specified momentarily. (Recall that, in spite of the use of the same symbol, this Ω is different from the Ω in the model of decision making under risk described in the previous section.) The second two components of the risk decision-making model carry over almost without change: let X be the decision set (the collection of choice options) and $u(x, \omega)$ a utility function defined on $X \times \Omega$. As before, the utility function orders the elements of X by the personal preferences of the decision maker,[19] and there is a distinct ordering for each state of the world ω. Note that the substitution of ω for ψ in the specification of u means that, like $u(G^{ij}(x_i, \omega_j))$ in equation (4.1-6), randomness enters the utility function directly instead of through a transformation that relates Ω to the real line Ψ. Functions that map Ω into Ψ, the aforementioned replacement for the random variable, are obtained by fixing x in $u(x, \omega)$ and taking the range of u to be Ψ. Thus utility values become the outcomes ψ in Ψ. Sometimes these are referred to as *utility outcomes*.

Naturally, in decision contexts other than those relating to a private individual, alternative functions mapping Ω into Ψ become relevant and appropriate. With respect to the firm, for example, a profit function analogous to that appearing in the definition of expected profit at the end of Section 4.2 might be used. Alternatively, a *rate of return* function

$$\psi = \mathcal{R}(x, \omega)$$

could be employed, where objects of choice x would represent various investment projects and, for each x in X, $\mathcal{R}$ would map a state of the world ω into a rate of return ψ on all money capital invested in it. (A similar function is exploited in Chapter 9.) In that case, ψ would vary over *rate of return* outcomes. The context of present discussion, however, remains the individual. Even so, it is worth noting that the construction of functions mapping Ω into Ψ for each x in X turns out to be one of the central issues in applying this model of decision making in ignorance to the firm and the consumer in, respectively, Chapters 9 and 10.

---

[19]Here, too, it must be assumed that variations in the choice of the utility representation are offset by changes in other functions (described below) so that the following argument does not depend on the selection of the representation u. Recall n. 13 on p. 116.

Of course, the facts that Ψ is taken to be the entire real line and that u (like $\mathcal{R}$ and any other function linking, for each x, Ω to Ψ) is assumed, in part, to be onto imply that utility outcomes range from $-\infty$ to ∞. This convention, adopted throughout, renders the decision-making analysis of the consumer analogous, in part, to that of the firm, where rate of return outcomes can be negative. However, it should be understood that utility values are arbitrary up to increasing transformations and that all nonpositive outcome magnitudes could, via such transformations, be converted into positive ones. In that case, the construction developed below would be limited, at least in terms of utility outcomes, to the positive half-line. The acceptance in the following discussion of the convention that, for each x, the image of Ω under u is the entire real line also leads, again in parallel with the firm, to the reference to the negative utility outcomes as "losses," but only in the sense that they reflect lower welfare resulting from the decision made.

Assuming all utility functions,

$$\psi = u(x, \omega),$$

one for every x, are 1-1 and onto, it is clear that, for each x in X, the potential surprise function $s(A)$ on $\mathcal{A}$ induces a potential surprise density function $f_x^s(\psi)$ on Ψ as described in Section 3.4. That is, given Ω and s, the set X generates a family of potential surprise density functions $\mathcal{F}^s$ through $u(x, \omega)$ as in (3.4-8). In a more general context, both Ω and s could also be thought of as dependent on choice objects x.[20] This, of course, would not imply a relation between particular values of x and particular states ω. But, in any case, such a generalization is not pursued here, and ω and x are taken to vary independently of each other. The next step is to reduce the collection of preference orderings

---

[20]It should be observed, however, that if Ω_x were the incomplete collection of possible states of the world associated with x, then the collection Ω of the present section, which is independent of x, would be obtained from

$$\Omega = \bigcup_{x \text{ in } X} \Omega_x.$$

Thus the generalization described here would not add as much to the present analysis as might, at first, have been expected.

defined by $u(x, \omega)$ to a single function of x, which is to be employed in arriving at the actual decision.

Shackle tackles the problem by introducing an attractiveness (or ascendancy) function that, like the utility function, is assumed to be constructed by the decision maker on the basis of his own intimate cognitions.[21] Let x in X be given and define the set

$$N_x^s = \{\psi : f_x^s(\psi) = 0\}.$$

Thus N_x^s is the subset of perfectly possible outcomes of Ψ or, in other words, those outcomes for which the individual is unable to conceive of any obstacle to their eventuation. Suppose that N_x^s is a nonempty,[22] bounded, and connected subset of Ψ. Identify some element in N_x^s, call it ψ_x^s, as the boundary between "more favorable" utility outcomes, often said to be gains, and "less favorable" outcomes, also referred to as losses. Write

$$\Psi_x^+ = \{\psi : \psi \geq \psi_x^s\},$$
$$\Psi_x^- = \{\psi : \psi \leq \psi_x^s\},$$

so that $\Psi_x^+ \cap \Psi_x^- = \{\psi_x^s\}$. Thus ψ_x^s is, at the same time, the minimum utility outcome that can be considered a gain and the maximum utility outcome that can be thought of as a loss. Assign the variable ξ to represent potential surprise values, that is, to vary over the range, Ξ, of the f_x^s. Symbolically,

$$\xi = f_x^s(\psi). \tag{4.3-4}$$

(Recall, $\Xi = \{\xi : 0 \leq \xi \leq 1\}$.) Assume that each pair (ψ, ξ) in $\Psi_x^+ \times \Xi$ and $\Psi_x^- \times \Xi$ has an attractiveness or "power to command the decision-maker's attention" associated with it. Thus, given x, and with attractiveness measured ordinally in terms of real numbers, an attractiveness function having two branches, each (along with the function itself) denoted by g_x^s, is defined mapping $\Psi_x^+ \times \Xi$ and $\Psi_x^- \times \Xi$ into the real line.[23]

---

[21]Shackle [23, Pt. 3]. Use of the adjective "attractiveness" in place of the Shacklean term "ascendancy," as is done here, is due to Vickers [26, p. 148].

[22]The nonemptyness of N_x^s is not guaranteed by (2.2-3s) since, in all exhaustive sets of rival hypotheses, the A_i for which $s(A_i) = 0$ may be empty.

[23]The fact that g_x^s might produce two distinct functions values, one with each branch of the function, when $\psi = \psi_x^s$ is of no consequence. This is because the two branches of g_x^s are each intended to be single-valued functions in their own right, and independent of one another.

These functions independently order the elements of $\Psi_x^+ \times \Xi$ and $\Psi_x^- \times \Xi$ according to the extent to which they stand out in the decision maker's mind in much the same way that an ordinary consumer utility function orders the relevant commodity space by the consumer's preferences. Those pairs that stand out more sharply have a higher number or attractiveness assigned to them. But the attractiveness function is not a utility function: the attractiveness of any pair reflects only its power to secure the decision maker's attention and has nothing to do with the preferences upon which his utility function is based. For example, the combinations of a large positive or negative value of ψ and a small value of ξ, given the choice option x, might have higher attractive power than more "balanced" pairs because the decision maker's experience suggests to him that such a combination, in this case, is more incongruous and warrants further investigation.

Another distinction between the attractiveness and utility functions is that the decision maker's attitudes toward uncertainty are reflected in the former but not in the latter. To see why, return, for a moment, to the analogous concepts of attitudes toward risk in the expected utility model. As indicated in Section 4.2, those attitudes (favoring, neutrality, or aversion) are characterized with respect to the parameters μ and σ in the expected utility function $\bar{u}(x)$ and, as such, account for both the individual's preferences as recorded in his utility function $u(x, \psi)$, and the riskiness associated with outcomes ψ as exhibited in the probability density function. Clearly, by itself, $u(x, \psi)$ in (4.2-1) is incapable of fully describing the individual's attitudes toward risk. The same is true of $u(x, \omega)$ in the present context with respect to his attitudes toward uncertainty because there is no representation of uncertainty, as expressed in the potential surprise density function, in it. The attractiveness function, however, is defined over pairs containing both utility outcomes and potential surprise values and is, therefore, able to encapsulate attitudes toward uncertainty within its fabric. Further discussion and an illustration of how this might happen is provided in Section 6.2.

Observe that, in general, the attractiveness function depends on the object of choice x because there can be different dividing points ψ_x^s associated with each such object. In that case, the subdomains Ψ_x^+ and Ψ_x^- would vary with x and so, as a consequence, would the attractiveness function. Only when ψ_x^s is identical for every x in X does the attractiveness function become independent of x, and the attractivenesses (*i.e.*, the function values) of all pairs (ψ, ξ) remain the same regardless of the objects of choice that generate them. Note also that, in comparison with the potential surprise density function, the attractiveness function depends on two variables whose combined domain consists of two Cartesian products of two sets, namely, $\Psi_x^- \times \Xi$ and $\Psi_x^+ \times \Xi$. By contrast, the potential surprise density function is a function of a single variable with domain $\Psi = \Psi_x^- \cup \Psi_x^+$ and range Ξ. Regardless, Shackle assumes that in making selections from subsets of the decision set X, the decision maker begins by focusing, for each x, on those pairs (ψ, ξ) that have maximum attractiveness subject to the potential surprise density function f_x^s. Due to the latter constraint, all such pairs must satisfy equation (4.3-4). The question of the existence of these constrained maximizing pairs is discussed in Section 5.2.

Suppose for now, however, that for every x there are exactly two attractiveness-maximizing pairs, (ψ_x^-, ξ_x^-) in $\Psi_x^- \times \Xi$ and (ψ_x^+, ξ_x^+) in $\Psi_x^+ \times \Xi$, such that

$$f_x^s(\psi) \leq \max \left[f_x^s(\psi_x^-), f_x^s(\psi_x^+) \right] \qquad (4.3\text{-}5)$$

for all ψ where $\psi_x^- \leq \psi \leq \psi_x^+$. As previously noted, $\xi_x^- = f_x^s(\psi_x^-)$ and $\xi_x^+ = f_x^s(\psi_x^+)$. The pair (ψ_x^-, ξ_x^-) is called the *focus loss*, while (ψ_x^+, ξ_x^+) is the *focus gain*. All utility values between ψ_x^- in the focus loss and the boundary point ψ_x^s have potential surprise at least as small as that of ψ_x^-, and the potential surprise of all utility outcomes between ψ_x^+ and ψ_x^s cannot exceed that of ψ_x^+. In effect, the decision maker's attention is drawn to two utility values for x, namely, ψ_x^- and ψ_x^+, which are the endpoints of a closed interval of utility outcomes for x having "minimal" potential surprise as characterized by (4.3-5). Another way of saying the same thing is that the decision maker ascribes to each object of choice the particularities of that object that (subject to constraint) stand out the most in his mind. That is, when assessing x in the decision process, he pays attention only to these endpoints and their potential surprise values (*i.e.*, the standout particularities) and ignores all others. Clearly such action by the decision maker is not unreasonable. Why, in contemplating losses, for example, should he worry about a low potential surprise utility outcome of -10 in the interior of the utility interval when there is also a utility outcome of $-1,000$ with low potential surprise at the endpoint? Shackle [23, p. 118] put it this way: "When many different things are all equally and perfectly possible, it is the brilliant and the black *extremes* [*sic*] which hold our thoughts." Of course, outcomes outside of the utility interval can be discarded because they are associated with relatively high potential surprise values.

As x hypothetically varies over X, repeated constrained maximization of the attractiveness function permits the definition of left- and right-endpoint functions, L and R, respectively, by setting $\psi_x^- = L(x)$ and $\psi_x^+ = R(x)$ for every x, if and only if $(\psi_x^-, f_x^s(\psi_x^-))$ and $(\psi_x^+, f_x^s(\psi_x^+))$ maximize the appropriate branch of g_x^s subject to f_x^s and also satisfy (4.3-5). The collection of closed utility intervals whose endpoints the decision maker needs to consider when making decisions is therefore

$$\mathcal{I}^s = \{[L(x), R(x)] : x \text{ is in } X\}.$$

In addition, left- and right-endpoint potential-surprise-value functions, ℓ and r, are defined at each x according to

$$\xi_x^- = \ell(x),$$

$$\xi_x^+ = r(x),$$

where, as before, $\xi_x^- = f_x^s(\psi_x^-)$ and $\xi_x^+ = f_x^s(\psi_x^+)$.

For the above construction of L, ℓ, R, and r to be viable, of course, the attractiveness function $g_x^s(\psi, \xi)$ and the potential surprise density functions $f_x^s(\psi)$, for every x, must have enough properties to guarantee that two unique, constrained maxima satisfying (4.3-5) always exist. Although not worth spelling out in mathematical detail here,[24] it is useful to illustrate these properties in a geometric example.[25] Let x be given. Figure 4-1 contains the graph of a potential surprise density function with a shape similar to those pictured by Shackle.[26] This back-to-back, elongated S-shape reflects the idea that as increasing positive

---

[24]As indicated earlier, the issue is discussed more fully in Section 5.2.

[25]Examples in which explicit algebraic form is given to each of the functions of this model are developed in Section 5.1.

[26]*E.g.*, Shackle [23, p. 155]. This is the same geometric form depicted in Figure 3-2.

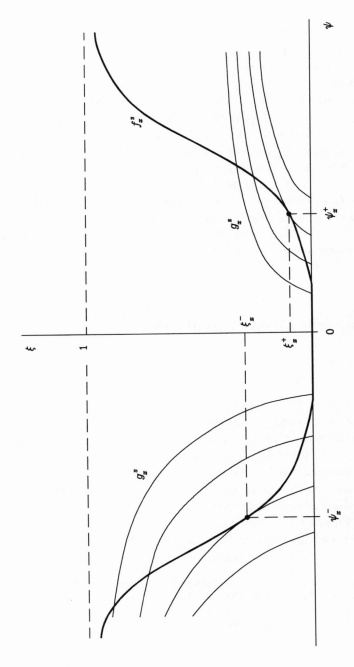

Figure 4-1. Constrained maximization of the attractiveness function in the potential surprise model.

or negative outcome magnitudes are envisaged the decision maker associates with those magnitudes potential surprise values that increase at an increasing rate. But, because no potential surprise value can rise above unity, there comes a point in both Ψ_x^+ and Ψ_x^- at which the shape of the potential surprise density curve switches from being strictly convex to strictly concave and thereafter approaches the line $\xi = 1$ assymptotically. As a rule, the two branches of the graph of the potential surprise density function defined, respectively, over Ψ_x^+ and Ψ_x^- need not be symmetrical. Iso-attractiveness contours in Figure 4-1 are drawn strictly concave and also asymptotic to the line $\xi = 1$. To the left of $\psi_x^s = 0$, they slope downward; to the right, they slope upward. Curves closer to the ψ axis have higher attractivenesses. (These curves also copy Shackle [23, p. 155]). In general, of course, the nature of the attractiveness function will depend on the subjective reactions by which the decision maker responds to the possibilities of outcome and potential surprise combinations. And the implied trade-offs between outcome and potential surprise that attract his attention may be such as to generate iso-attractiveness contours of any shape. For present purposes, however, it is convenient to employ the geometry of Figure 4-1. It will be seen in due course (and was hinted at earlier) that certain forms of the attractiveness function, and hence certain kinds of iso-attractiveness coutours, can be linked to the degree of uncertainty aversion or favor with which the decision maker contemplates possible outcomes. In any case, given the relative locations and shapes of the potential surprise density curve and iso-attractiveness contours in the example of Figure 4-1, two unique constrained maxima satisfying (4.3-5) exist and are located at (ψ_x^-, ξ_x^-) and (ψ_x^+, ξ_x^+) where iso-attractiveness contours are tangent to the potential surprise density curve. Note that, in this illustration, (4.3-5) is satisfied for all ψ such that $\psi_x^- \leq \psi \leq \psi_x^+$, and hence $[\psi_x^-, \psi_x^+]$ is the closed interval of utility outcomes having minimal potential surprise referred to above.

These tangencies between iso-attractiveness contours and the potential surprise density curve can be described mathematically assuming appropriate derivatives exist. Before doing so, however, note that to maximize $g_x^s(\psi, \xi)$ subject to $\xi = f_x^s(\psi)$ is equivalent to maximizing $h(\psi) = g_x^s(\psi, f_x^s(\psi))$ without constraint and with respect to ψ alone. Hence either applying the method of Lagrange multipliers to the former or differentiating the latter with respect to ψ and equating the derivative to zero leads to

$$\frac{df_x^s(\psi_x^0)}{d\psi} = -\frac{\partial g_x^s(\psi_x^0, \xi_x^0)}{\partial \psi} \bigg/ \frac{\partial g_x^s(\psi_x^0, \xi_x^0)}{\partial \xi}, \tag{4.3-6}$$

where the right-hand side of equation (4.3-6) is a ratio of partial derivatives of g_x^s, the left-hand side represents the (full) derivative of f_x^s with respect to ψ, and all derivatives are evaluated at the maximizing pairs $(\psi_x^0, \xi_x^0) = (\psi_x^-, \xi_x^-)$ or $(\psi_x^0, \xi_x^0) = (\psi_x^+, \xi_x^+)$. Thus, given x, at constrained attractiveness maximization the subjectively contemplated marginal trade-off between utility outcomes and potential surprise magnitudes along an iso-attractiveness contour equals the subjectively contemplated margin of potential surprise with respect to utility outcomes. Equation (4.3-6) together with $\xi_x^0 = f_x^s(\psi_x^0)$ completely characterize the tangencies in Figure 4-1 and both equations are intimately related to the comparative statics analysis of Section 5.2.

With the collection of endpoints of closed utility intervals and the potential surprise values corresponding to them (*i.e.*, the focus gains and focus losses) in hand, it is now appropriate to consider how the decision maker comes to his decisions. And it is at this point that present discussion diverges from Shackle's original presentation and takes up the contribution of Vickers [27, Ch. 12].[27] Clearly each x in the decision set X is associated with a range of possible utility values that the decision maker concludes it is necessary to consider. The least and most utility attainable in that range is, respectively, $L(x)$ and $R(x)$, but there are also in-between utility values that would not (potentially) surprise the decision maker more than the largest of $\ell(x)$ and $r(x)$ were states of the world to arise in which they emerged. In making his decision, moreover, the decision maker needs to account for the following: (*a*) an x with a higher R-value (*i.e.*, a higher utility outcome in the focus gain) is more preferable; (*b*) an x with a higher r-value (*i.e.*, a larger potential surprise magnitude in the focus gain) is less desirable because it means that the focus-gain outcome is more uncertain; (*c*)

---

[27]The specific elements of Shackle's analysis that are abandoned include the "standardization" of the focus gain and focus loss and the "gambler's preference map." See Shackle [23, pp. 161-164].

an x with a higher (less negative) L-value is more desirable; and (d) an x with a higher ℓ-value makes the focus-loss outcome more problematical and is therefore more desirable. In addition, when choosing among x's, there are trade-offs to be reckoned between pairs of function values drawn from $L(x)$, $\ell(x)$, $R(x)$ and $r(x)$, furnished for each x. One way of accommodating these ideas is to assume that, derived from his own imperfect knowledge and experience, the decision maker employs a function $Q^s(\psi_x^-, \xi_x^-, \psi_x^+, \xi_x^+)$, defined for all values of $(\psi_x^-, \xi_x^-, \psi_x^+, \xi_x^+)$ arising from constrained maximization of the attractiveness function, and having the characteristics that all partial derivatives exist continuously and

$$\frac{\partial Q^s}{\partial \psi_x^-} > 0, \qquad \frac{\partial Q^s}{\partial \psi_x^+} > 0,$$

$$\frac{\partial Q^s}{\partial \xi_x^-} > 0, \qquad \frac{\partial Q^s}{\partial \xi_x^+} < 0,$$

everywhere. When thinking about these derivatives, it should be noted that variation in ψ_x^-, ξ_x^-, ψ_x^+, and ξ_x^+ arises only from variation in x and not because of implicit relations between ψ_x^-, ξ_x^-, ψ_x^+, and ξ_x^+ for a given x. An example of a function satisfying these derivative conditions is

$$Q^s(\psi_x^-, \xi_x^-, \psi_x^+, \xi_x^+) = \psi_x^- + \xi_x^- + \psi_x^+ - \xi_x^+. \qquad (4.3\text{-}7)$$

The trade-offs described above are easily calculated for this Q^s.

Finally, the function D^s, obtained by replacing the function-value arguments of Q^s with their associated functions, that is,

$$D^s(x) = Q^s(L(x), \ell(x), R(x), r(x)),$$

defined on X, may be thought of as the *decision* function or index employed by the decision maker. This index supplants the (4.2-1) expected utility function derived from the method of component (v) in the model of decision making under risk summarized at the end of Section 4.2. Component (vi) remains unchanged: the decision is made by selecting x to maximize $D^s(x)$ over X or some subset thereof as characterized by relevant constraints. Clearly it is necessary to impose additional restrictions (beyond those required above for the existence of constrained attractiveness maxima), so that unique maximization of $D^s(x)$ over X, or an appropriate subset of X, is always possible.

It should be pointed out that the decision index is distinct from the attractiveness function because it is derived from different intellective and psychological processes. Whereas the attractiveness function emerges from the identification of what is positive or alarming about the various objects of choice, the decision index is based upon the evaluation of precisely those things that turn out to be so identified. This does not mean, however, that the independent processes determining these functions cannot overlap. In particular, it will be shown in Section 6.2 that attitudes toward uncertainty, analogous, in some cases, to those toward risk, appear in the decision index. These attitudes may influence, but not determine, the attractiveness function in that they may set limits on the forms that the attractiveness can assume.

In any event, after a family of potential surprise density functions is secured from the original potential surprise function defined over subsets of states of the world, repeated maximization of the attractiveness function subject to the potential surprise density functions produces a characterization of choice objects in terms of the properties of those objects that, subject to constraint, stand out the most in the decision maker's mind. These properties are then evaluated in the decision index in order to compare the objects of choice they characterize.

Three observations about this model of decision making in ignorance deserve mention here. First, the model contains two separate and independent subjective processes of evaluation and the functions to which each gives rise. Referring only to the functions themselves, these are (a) the utility function $u(x, \omega)$, defined on $X \times \Omega$ and employed to secure the family of potential surprise density functions $\mathcal{F}^s$; and (b) the function Q^s, whose domain is a collection of vectors of the form $(\psi_x^-, \xi_x^-, \psi_x^+, \xi_x^+)$, and which is used as the basis for the decision index and also reflects whatever attitudes toward uncertainty that exist in the mind of the decision maker. (As indicated, the model also incorporates a further nonevaluative, subjective process in the decision maker's specification of an attractiveness function.) At the initial level of analysis described above, where the utility function is defined over objects of choice and possible states of the world, no account is yet taken of the manner in which the implications of the uncertainty attached to those states of the world inform the decision maker's decision. Of course, at this point in the traditional expected utility model outlined in Section

4.2 uncertainty is distilled into risk and then introduced in the guise of a probability function defined over the subsets of Ω. But, as has been argued earlier, under conditions of historical time and ignorance, the thought forms of probability are not available. Hence a rather different method, which is encompassed in the second evaluation function Q^s, has been developed to take into account the same uncertainty without reducing it to risk. It should also be noted that the evaluation function $u(x, \omega)$ could be avoided, and often is in many applications (including the examples of Section 5.1 below), by starting the analysis with the postulation of a family of potential surprise density functions over Ψ and not considering the source of that family, that is, the underlying potential surprise function s defined on the subsets of Ω. In this manner, the complexity of the model can be reduced considerably.

Second, another way to lessen the complexity of the model is by conflating the decision index, or more precisely the function Q^s, with the attractiveness function. This means that, in addition to evaluating objects of choice, the decision index, or some transformation of it, would, on the assumption that it coincides with an independently specified attractiveness function, also serve as an identifier of attractiveness. However, it should be understood that such a conflation of the attractiveness function and the decision index can only be accomplished under highly specialized circumstances. For in general the intellective and psychological processes taking place in the mind of the decision maker need not be consistent with an attractiveness function that is coincidentally derivable from a decision index, and, in addition, the specific form of the decision index employed by the decision maker may not permit an attractiveness function capable of constrained maximization to be generated, on the basis of coincidence, from it. To indicate what is involved, an example will now be presented that preserves consistency with earlier assumptions in that the iso-attractiveness contours obtained from the decision index have the same relationship to each other and the same concave shape as in Figure 4-1.

Begin with the function $Q^s(\psi_x^-, \xi_x^-, \psi_x^+, \xi_x^+)$ and change its focus-loss arguments (ψ_x^-, ξ_x^-) to the general variables (ψ, ξ) ranging over $\Psi_x^- \times \Xi$. In like fashion, substitute (ψ, ξ) over $\Psi_x^+ \times \Xi$ for (ψ_x^+, ξ_x^+). Suppose that

$$Q^s(\psi_x^-, \xi_x^-, \psi_x^+, \xi_x^+) = Q^-(\psi, \xi) + Q^+(\psi, \xi), \qquad (4.3\text{-}8)$$

where the domain of Q^- is $\Psi_x^- \times \Xi$ and that of Q^+ is $\Psi_x^+ \times \Xi$. Suppose, further, that on their respective domains, Q^- and Q^+ are characterized by

$$Q^-(\psi, \xi) = \theta_1 \psi + \theta_2 \xi^{1/2}, \tag{4.3-9}$$

and

$$Q^+(\psi, \xi) = \theta_3 \psi - \theta_4 \xi^2, \tag{4.3-10}$$

where $\theta_i > 0$ for $i = 1, \ldots, 4$. Then define

$$\bar{Q}^s(\psi, \xi) = \begin{cases} Q^+(\psi, \xi), & \text{on } \Psi_x^+ \times \Xi, \\[2mm] Q^-(\psi, \xi), & \text{on } \Psi_x^- \times \Xi. \end{cases} \tag{4.3-11}$$

Clearly $\bar{Q}^s$ exhibits the differential properties required of decision-index functions Q^s above. Its level contours, pictured in a diagram similar to Figure 4-1, appear in Figure 4-2(a). The arrows in that latter drawing indicate directions in which varying (ψ, ξ) increases the function value $\bar{Q}^s(\psi, \xi)$.[28]

Given the special form of Q^s that results in (4.3-11), let the function that is assumed to coincide with the attractiveness function be obtained by setting $\psi_x^s = 0$ and

$$g_x^s(\psi, \xi) = \begin{cases} Q^+(\psi, \xi), & \text{on } \Psi_x^+ \times \Xi, \\[2mm] Q^-(\psi, 0) + [Q^-(0, \xi)]^4, & \text{on } \Psi_x^- \times \Xi. \end{cases} \tag{4.3-12}$$

Substituting (4.3-9) and (4.3-10) into (4.3-12) gives

$$g_x^s(\psi, \xi) = \begin{cases} \theta_3 \psi - \theta_4 \xi^2, & \text{on } \Psi_x^+ \times \Xi, \\[2mm] \theta_1 \psi + (\theta_2)^4 \xi^2, & \text{on } \Psi_x^- \times \Xi. \end{cases} \tag{4.3-13}$$

The "iso-attractiveness" contours of (4.3-13) are shown in Figure 4-2(b). Note that the contours in the $\Psi_x^+ \times \Xi$ quadrant are identical to

---

[28]A model incorporating, in part, equations similar to (4.3-8) through (4.3-11) has been used by Vickers [28, Ch. 9] to eliminate the attractiveness function altogether. Vickers, however, does not address the question of whether the decision index can be transformed into an attractiveness function.

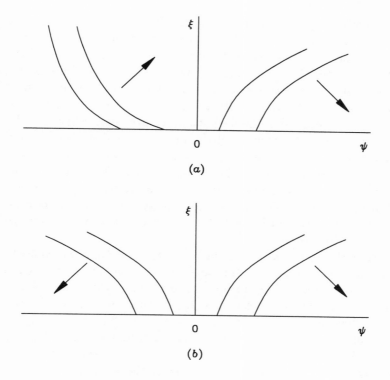

Figure 4–2. (a) Level contours of the function $\overline{Q}^s$.
(b) Iso–attractiveness contours of the attractiveness function coincident with the function derived from $\overline{Q}^s$.

those from the same quadrant in Figure 4-2(a). But in moving to Figure 4-2(b) the contours in the $\Psi_x^- \times \Xi$ quadrant switch from being strictly convex to strictly concave. This particular example will be pursued further in Section 5.1.5. Meanwhile, it should be borne in mind that in transforming the decision index into a function that coincides with the attractiveness function as indicated here, all of the attitudes toward uncertainty contained in the decision index are necessarily passed on to the attractiveness function. Indeed, in the present example the manifestation of those attitudes over $\Psi_x^+ \times \Xi$ is the same in each case since, with respect to that space, the two functions are identical. The expression in the attractiveness function of attitudes toward uncertainty contained in the decision index when the attractiveness function is not coincidentally derivable from the decision index is, as was stated earlier, taken up in Section 6.2.

Although the conflation of the attractiveness function with the decision index does serve to eliminate some of the complexity from the model of decision making in ignorance of this section, subsequent argument focuses attention on the original construction, which does not specify whether such a conflation has been introduced. For the original model, allowing, as it does, for either possibility, clearly possesses a richer structure and provides a vehicle for deeper analysis than would otherwise be the case. That is, it removes the necessity to restrict attention to specialized circumstances and, in addition, maintains a confluence with the historical development of inquiry into decision making in ignorance.

The third observation relevant at this point is that all of the elements of the present model – the choice options, the imagined states of the world, the potential surprise function, the utility and attractiveness functions, and the decision index – emerge from the past history of the individual and that of the circumstances that surround his decision (including his perception of the economic system at the time and his epistemic and economic endowments). Hence they are unique up to the moment or period of historical time at which the decision is made, and unique to the decision maker. The fact that each of these elements is unique to the decision moment does not mean that the decision maker could not think that he is repeatedly, across time, facing, with the same subjective evaluations and configurations, the same decision, in the same decision environment, over and over again. To the extent that such a perception is incorrect, the ignorance of the decision maker takes, in part, a special form, namely, ignorance of the variation that has occurred in reality. Regardless, as long as his preferences, and hence utility function, do not change, the decision maker's choice set and set of imagined future outcomes, his potential surprise and attractiveness functions, and his decision index could all remain constant through time and, should they do so, his decision making would become *routine*.[29] Evidently, that a particular decision problem might become or remain routine cannot be known in advance and can only be determined with hindsight. It has also been noted in this context that, although only the potential surprise density and attractiveness functions are formally dependent on the particularity of the choice option x in the above, the model could be generalized to require the collection of imagined states of the world Ω and the potential surprise function s to vary with x.

4.4   Decision Making in Ignorance Using Potential Confirmation

Attention now turns to the model of decision making in ignorance that employs the potential confirmation function instead of the potential surprise function. The first two components of this model, then, arguing by way of analogy to the expected utility perspective summarized at the end of Section 4.2, are (i) the incomplete collection of imagined states of the world Ω, and (ii) the potential confirmation function c and the utility function (also specified as component [iv] in the next sentence). Retain the decision set X (component [iii]) and the utility function $u(x,\omega)$ on $X \times \Omega$ (component [iv]) of the previous section. Assume, for each x in X, the function $u(x,\omega)$ is a 1-1 and onto mapping of Ω into Ψ so that a family of potential confirmation density functions $\mathcal{F}^c$, as in (3.4-7), is obtained whose individual members, $f_x^c(\psi)$, are defined on Ψ for every x. Identify the range of the f_x^c by Z and let z be the variable that assumes as values the elements of Z. (As with Ξ,

---

[29]*Cf.* nn. 17, 18 on p. 25.

remember $Z = \{z : 0 \le z \le 1\}$.) Suppose that for each x in X the set

$$N_x^c = \{\psi : f_x^c(\psi) = 1\}$$

is nonempty, bounded, and connected, and let ψ_x^c in N_x^c separate the more favorable from the less favorable utility outcomes. Define Ψ_x^+ and Ψ_x^- as in Section 4.3 using ψ_x^c in place of ψ_x^s. The two branches of the ordinal attractiveness function, symbolized, along with the function itself, by $g_x^c(\psi, z)$, are, in the present case, defined on $\Psi_x^+ \times Z$ and $\Psi_x^- \times Z$, and it is assumed that for each x the decision maker focuses on the endpoints of the closed interval $[\psi_x^-, \psi_x^+]$ and associated potential confirmation values $z_x^- = f_x^c(\psi_x^-)$ and $z_x^+ = f_x^c(\psi_x^+)$ such that $(\psi_x^-, f_x^c(\psi_x^-))$ and $(\psi_x^+, f_x^c(\psi_x^+))$ uniquely maximize $g_x^c(\psi, z)$ subject to $z = f_x^c(\psi)$ over the appropriate domains and satisfy the condition that for all ψ between ψ_x^- and ψ_x^+

$$f_x^c(\psi) \ge \min\left[f_x^c(\psi_x^-), f_x^c(\psi_x^+)\right].$$

The endpoint functions $L(x)$, $\ell(x)$, $R(x)$, and $r(x)$, and the collection of relevant intervals, $\mathcal{I}^c$, are secured as before (note that the images of x under ℓ and r become potential confirmation values instead of potential surprise values), and the same kind of decision function, now written D^c, is invoked except that here $\partial Q^c / \partial z_x^- < 0$ and $\partial Q^c / \partial z_x^+ > 0$, where Q^c is the counterpart to Q^s. Thus a single decision function of x alone emerges from the new version of component (v), and decisions are made (vi) by choosing x to maximize $D^c(x)$ over X or appropriate subsets.

One way to obtain a pictorial example of the constrained-attractiveness-maximizing pairs (ψ_x^-, z_x^-) and (ψ_x^+, z_x^+), also said to be, respectively, the focus loss and focus gain, is to look at the mirror image of Figure 4-1 with the mirror placed just above and parallel to the line $\xi = 1$. (For now, this is only intended as a method of producing a geometric example. Sufficient conditions for one model to be the "mirror image" of the other are provided below.) As shown in Figure 4-3, the line $\xi = 1$ of Figure 4-1 becomes the ψ-axis; the ξ-axis turns into the z-axis; the graph of f_x^s, which upon mirror reflection seems like (but is not) a probability density curve, becomes the potential confirmation density curve f_x^c similar to that depicted in Figure 3-1(b); and the shapes of the iso-attractiveness contours (now secured from

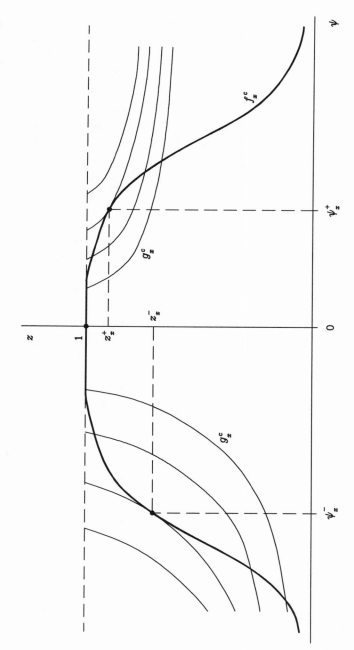

Figure 4–3. Constrained maximization of the attractiveness function in the potential confirmation model.

the g_x^c) change to strictly convex, their slopes reversing in sign. The values of ψ_x^- and ψ_x^+ are unaltered, and the values of z_x^- and z_x^+ are the lengths from the line $\xi = 1$ to, respectively, ξ_x^- and ξ_x^+ in Figure 4-1. The question of the existence of the constrained-attractiveness-maximizing pairs (ψ_x^-, z_x^-) and (ψ_x^+, z_x^+) is addressed geometrically as in Section 4.3, and the mathematical representation of the tangencies at $(\psi_x^0, z_x^0) = (\psi_x^-, z_x^-)$ and $(\psi_x^0, z_x^0) = (\psi_x^+, z_x^+)$ is derived analogously, involving, in part, an equation parallel to (4.3-6), and given by

$$\frac{df_x^c(\psi_x^0)}{d\psi} = -\frac{\partial g_x^c(\psi_x^0, z_x^0)}{\partial \psi} \bigg/ \frac{\partial g_x^c(\psi_x^0, z_x^0)}{\partial z},$$

$$z^0 = f_x^c(\psi^0).$$

The fact that, in the present case, Figure 4-3 was derived from Figure 4-1 by reflection suggests that, under very special circumstances, the two models of decision making in ignorance that these diagrams represent might lead to identical decisions. The speciality of these circumstances needs to be emphasized. For, as pointed out in Section 2.3, potential surprise and potential confirmation are, in conception, entirely distinct and independent ideas. They are defined, respectively, in conjunction with the dialectically opposite notions of disbelief and belief about possible occurrences of states of the world, and these latter notions are separated conceptually by their different, but overlapping, penumbra of meanings. All of this is contained in the assertion in Section 2.3 that, in general,

$$s(A) + c(A) \neq 1 \tag{4.4-1}$$

for all A in $\mathcal{A}$, or, equivalently, in light of Theorem 4.3-3, that

$$f_x^s(\psi) + f_x^c(\psi) \neq 1 \tag{4.4-2}$$

for all ψ in Ψ and all x in X.

Nevertheless, it is possible to demonstrate mathematically that if, perhaps by chance, the unequals symbols in equations (4.4-1) and (4.4-2) happened, in a special case, to be replaced by equals signs that held identically, and if, in addition, all pairs of attractiveness functions g_x^s and g_x^c, for every x in X, happened to coincide in a certain way, then the functions $L(x)$, $\ell(x)$, $R(x)$, and $r(x)$ of the potential surprise model would mesh with those of the potential confirmation model. If, still further, the two decision functions are appropriately linked, then identical decisions have to be made in each case. The following proposition and its corollary provide a formal statement of this result. Note that the hypotheses of Theorem 4.4-3 and the corollary constitute a rigorous statement of the conditions alluded to earlier under which the model based on potential confirmation is a mirror image of that supported by potential surprise.

Theorem 4.4-3. *If $f_x^c(\psi) = 1 - f_x^s(\psi)$ and $g_x^c(\psi, f_x^c(\psi)) = g_x^s(\psi, f_x^s(\psi))$ for all ψ in Ψ and x in X, then for any x, ψ_x^0, and z_x^0*

$$\frac{df_x^c(\psi_x^0)}{d\psi} = -\frac{\partial g_x^c(\psi_x^0, z_x^0)}{\partial \psi} \Bigg/ \frac{\partial g_x^c(\psi_x^0, z_x^0)}{\partial z}, \qquad and \qquad z^0 = f_x^c(\psi^0),$$

if and only if

$$\frac{df_x^s(\psi_x^0)}{d\psi} = -\frac{\partial g_x^s(\psi_x^0, \xi_x^0)}{\partial \psi} \Bigg/ \frac{\partial g_x^s(\psi_x^0, \xi_x^0)}{\partial \xi}, \qquad and \qquad \xi^0 = f_x^s(\psi^0),$$

where $z_x^0 = 1 - \xi_x^0$.

Proof:
Consider any x in X. Let $z = f_x^c(\psi)$ and $\xi = f_x^s(\psi)$ so that $z = 1 - \xi$. Then differentiating $f_x^c(\psi) = 1 - f_x^s(\psi)$ with respect to ψ and $g_x^c(\psi, z) = g_x^s(\psi, \xi)$ with respect to ψ and z yields

$$\frac{df_x^c(\psi)}{d\psi} = -\frac{df_x^s(\psi)}{d\psi},$$

$$\frac{\partial g_x^c(\psi, z)}{\partial \psi} = \frac{\partial g_x^s(\psi, \xi)}{\partial \psi},$$

and

$$\frac{\partial g_x^c(\psi, z)}{\partial z} = -\frac{\partial g_x^s(\psi, \xi)}{\partial \xi},$$

from which the conclusion is immediate.

Q.E.D.

Corollary 4.4-4. *Under the hypotheses of Theorem* 4.4-3, *if*

$$Q^c(\psi_x^-, z_x^-, \psi_x^+, z_x^+) = Q^s(\psi_x^-, 1 - z_x^-, \psi_x^+, 1 - z_x^+)$$

for all ψ_x^-, z_x^-, ψ_x^+, *and* z_x^+, *where* $1 - z_x^- = \xi_x^-$ *and* $1 - z_x^+ = \xi_x^+$, *then the same decisions are made under* D^c *as under* D^s.

The proof of the corollary is clear. Thus the two models of decision making in ignorance presented here overlap in a sense defined by these results. They also have similar structures and components that parallel those of the standard model of decision making under risk. And, unlike the latter, both explicitly account for the very real fact of ignorance in the making of human decisions.

However, the existence of two independent models of decision making in ignorance, each of which, in general, leads to different results, raises a serious ambiguity for the decision maker confronting decisions and the economist attempting to understand how they are made. For the decision maker, the question is which approach to take; from the economist's perspective, the question is which model is "right"? One way to resolve the issue is by arguing that the environment of ignorance in which the decision maker acts is properly described as a state of disbelief rather than belief. To structure an explanation of his behavior on the foundation of belief, then, is contrary to the meaning of ignorance. Thus it is natural for the decision maker and the economist to focus on the potential surprise model derived, as it is, from disbelief. On this view, it is only in the special circumstance that

$$s(A) + c(A) = 1$$

for all A in $\mathcal{A}$, and the remaining hypotheses of Theorem 4.4-3 and Corollary 4.4-4 are in force, that there is an equivalent way of expressing the potential surprise model in terms of potential confirmation. Alternatively, the ambiguity may be eliminated simply by imposing the hypotheses of Theorem 4.4-3 and Corollary 4.4-4 as assumptions on both models. Then the decision maker and economist cannot be misled by invoking one over the other. Of course, such assumptions restrict the undertaking and analysis of decision making in ignorance in significant and subtle ways. But they certainly do not preclude the fact of ignorance from consideration; nor do they throw the matter back into a context in which probability and the standard approach to decision making under risk become either relevant or appropriate. In particular, they do not imply that potential surprise is the same as one-minus probability. All the same, subsequent discussion, insofar as it employs an explanation of decision making in ignorance, will henceforth rely solely on the potential surprise model of Section 4.3.

4.5 References

1. Abbott, L., *Quality and Competition* (New York: Columbia University Press, 1955).

2. Arrow, K. J., and L. Hurwicz, "An Optimality Criteria for Decision-Making under Ignorance," in *Uncertainty and Expectations in Economics*, C. F. Carter and J. L. Ford, eds. (Oxford: Blackwell, 1972), pp. 1-11.

3. Bausor, R., "Time and the Structure of Economic Analysis," *Journal of Post Keynesian Economics* 5 (1982-83), pp. 163-179.

4. Diamond, P. A., and M. Yaari, "Implications of the Theory of Rationing for Consumer Choice under Uncertainty," *American Economic Review* 62 (1972), pp. 333-343.

5. Earl, P., *The Economic Imagination* (Armonk: Sharpe, 1983).

6. Ford, J. L., *Choice, Expectation and Uncertainty* (Totowa, N.J.: Barnes & Noble, 1983).

7. ———, *Economic Choice under Uncertainty: A Perspective Theory Approach* (New York: St. Martin's, 1987).

8. Hey, J. D., *Uncertainty in Microeconomics* (New York: New York University Press, 1979).

9. ———, "Towards Double Negative Economics," in *Beyond Positive Economics?* J. Wiseman, ed. (New York: St. Martin's, 1983), pp. 160-175.

10. Hutchison, T. W., "Our Methodological Crisis," in *Economics in Disarray*, P. Wiles and G. Routh, eds. (Oxford: Blackwell, 1984), pp. 1-21.

11. Jefferson, M., "Economic Uncertainty and Business Decision-Making," in *Beyond Positive Economics?* J. Wiseman, ed. (New York: St. Martin's, 1983), pp. 122-159.

12. Kahneman, D., and A. Tversky, "Prospect Theory: An Analysis of Decisions under Risk," *Econometrica* 47 (1979), pp. 263-291.

13. Katzner, D. W., *Static Demand Theory* (New York: Macmillan, 1970).

14. Keynes, J. M., *The General Theory of Employment, Interest, and Money* (New York: Harcourt Brace, 1936).

15. ———, "The General Theory of Employment," *Quarterly Journal of Economics* 51 (1937), pp. 209-223.

16. Kirzner, I. M., "Uncertainty, Discovery, and Human Action: A Study of the Entrepreneurial Profile in the Misesian System," in *Method, Process, and Austrian Economics*, I. M. Kirzner, ed. (Lexington: D. C. Heath, 1982), pp. 139-159.

17. Knight, F. H., *Risk, Uncertainty, and Profit* (Boston: Houghton Mifflin, 1921).

18. Lachmann, L. M., "Economics as a Social Science," in *Capital, Expectations, and the Market Process* (Kansas City: Sheed Andrews and McMeel, 1977), pp. 166-180.

19. Loomes, G., and R. Sugden, "Regret Theory: An Alternative Theory of Rational Choice under Uncertainty," *Economic Journal* 92 (1982), pp. 805-824.

20. Machina, M. J., "Choice under Uncertainty: Problems Solved and Unsolved," *Journal of Economic Perspectives* 1 (1987), pp. 121-154.

21. Maskin, E., "Decision-Making under Ignorance with Implications for Social Choice," *Theory and Decision* 11 (1979), pp. 319-337.

22. Radner, R., "Satisficing," *Journal of Mathematical Economics* 2 (1975), pp. 253-262.

23. Shackle, G. L. S., *Decision, Order and Time in Human Affairs*, 2nd ed. (Cambridge: Cambridge University Press, 1969).

24. Simon, H. A., *Administrative Behavior*, 2nd ed., (New York: Macmillan, 1957).

25. ———, "Theories of Decision-Making in Economics and Behavioral Science," *American Economic Review* 49 (1959), pp. 253-283.

26. Vickers, D., *Financial Markets in the Capitalist Process* (Philadelphia: University of Pennsylvania Press, 1978).

27. ———, *Money Capital in the Theory of the Firm* (Cambridge: Cambridge University Press, 1987).

28. ———, *Economics and the Antogonism of Time: Time, Uncertainty, and Choice in Economic Theory* (Ann Arbor: University of Michigan Press, 1994).

29. Winter, S. G, "Satisficing, Selection, and the Innovating Remnant," *Quarterly Journal of Economics* 85 (1971), pp. 237-261.

CHAPTER 5

Examples and Comparative Statics

The analysis of decision making under conditions of ignorance developed in Section 4.3 (*i.e.*, the potential surprise version) begins with the assumption that the decision maker is able to describe a potential surprise function defined over the subsets of an incomplete collection of possible, imagined states of the world. The potential surprise of a state of the world set A is the surprise the decision maker imagines now that he would experience in the future were an element of A to occur. Let a decision set containing the objects of choice be specified, and suppose that the decision maker has an ordinal utility function defined over the Cartesian product of the decision set and the incomplete collection of states of the world. For each state of the world, then, the utility function maps objects of choice or elements of the decision set into associated utility values. More importantly, for each object of choice the utility function also maps states of the world into utility values. Using this latter interpretation of the utility relation, the potential surprise function can be translated into potential surprise density (or frequency) functions defined over utility values that depend on the objects of choice. Thus the original potential surprise function, whose domain is a collection of state of the world sets, becomes a family of potential surprise density functions, each with a domain consisting of utility magnitudes (outcomes) or real numbers. Although, as has been seen at length, they have a different significance and meaning (due,

---

[1] This chapter is reproduced, with considerable additions, corrections, and other modifications, from my "The 'Comparative Statics' of the Shackle-Vickers Approach to Decision-Making in Ignorance," in *Studies in the Economics of Uncertainty*, T. B. Fomby and T. K. Seo, eds. (New York: Springer, 1989), pp. 21-43.

in part, to their contrasting axiomatic foundations), potential surprise density functions are often drawn to look something like inverted probability density functions.

The next step is to identify, for every object of choice, two pairs, each consisting of a utility value along with its associated potential surprise from the potential surprise density function. The utility values in these pairs represent, in every instance, one "favorable" and one "unfavorable" outcome. Each of the two pairs themselves, respectively referred to as the "focus gain" and the "focus loss," is selected so as to maximize the appropriate branch of the decision maker's attractiveness function subject to a potential surprise density function or, in other words, they are picked for their power, under constraint, to attract the attention of the decision maker. The pairs are then used in constructing a decision index defined over the decision set. In particular, the decision index is built up by assigning a value to the potential surprise numbers and the utility outcome magnitudes contained in the two pairs that correspond to each object of choice. This function is understood to be ordinal in character; it ranks the objects of choice in the decision set. In any subset of the decision set defined by relevant constraints, or in X itself, the object receiving the highest rank, that is, given the highest value by the decision function, is chosen by the decision maker.

The present chapter (and, in part, the next) attempts to elucidate the kinds of things that can be done and the manner in which investigation can proceed with this model. In the same way that conventional inquiry has identified criteria for such decisions as consumer commodity selection and producer choice among investment projects, and then developed specific examples and pursued comparative statics analysis to, respectively, illustrate and explore those criteria, the present investigation, in addition to providing the different criteria previously described for the same kinds of decisions, should also furnish specific examples and probe "comparative statics" analysis for similar reasons. With this end in mind, Section 5.1 below presents five simple examples of the model, and Section 5.2 then examines some of its comparative statics properties along with two issues that relate to them. Section 5.2 actually starts out by considering the latter issues first. These are (i) the question of what it means to do comparative statics analysis in the historical time and ignorance (nonequilibrium) context within which the model is set, and (ii) the conditions under which the constrained maxima of the two branches of the attractiveness function may be said to exist uniquely. Thereafter, discussion turns to the nature of certain comparative statics properties derived with respect to the constrained-attractiveness-maximization problem and their implications for the decision index. A final result explores a comparative statics property arising from the maximization of the decision index itself. Those desiring to skirt mathematical formalities as much as possible may leave out Examples 2, 3, and 5 and read only up to (but not including) Theorem 5.2-6 in Section 5.2.

5.1 Five Examples

Before actually presenting the examples, it is necessary to consider some general ideas, define some specific concepts, and introduce some modified and new notation.

Recall that X is the decision set, Ψ is the collection of utility outcomes over which potential surprise density functions are defined, and x and ψ are variables ranging over, respectively, X and Ψ. No constraints are imposed on X in any of the illustrations examined below. In each case, then, the problem of the decision maker is to choose an x from the full set X.

Up to this point, nothing has been said about the elements of X except that they are objects of choice. Thus, for example, x might represent scalar rates of return or vectors of quantities of commodities. Alternativly, x could vary over nonquantified objects in either scalar or vector form. For purposes of subsequent discussion, however, define a 1-1 correspondence, γ, between X and a nonempty subset, B, of the real line. Then, for all x in X,

$$b = \gamma(x),$$

where b is in B. To keep matters simple, take B to be a connected interval. (Thus B is a continuum and, through γ, so is X. Moreover, the ordering of the elements of B by $\geq$ among real numbers is induced onto the elements of X.) The function γ is an artifice introduced for analytical convenience so that the not necessarily quantifiable scalars or vectors of X can be uniquely identified with real, scalar numbers. (Were x already a real scalar variable, the transformation γ would not be needed.) Clearly such an identification, that is, γ (along with the induced ordering of X introduced through γ), is arbitrary. In a more general setting, to ensure (if appropriate) that γ did not itself interfere with the representation of the decision-making process under scrutiny, it would be necessary to suppose that γ is fixed for the duration of the analysis and, further, that all conclusions obtained with a particular γ are independent of that γ. In terms of what follows, this latter requirement would mean that changes in γ would always be accompanied by offsetting alterations in the functions introduced below so that the derived results would not vary. A similar assumption was required of the particular ordinal utility function that gave rise to the utility values ψ as indicated in n. 19 on p. 124.

Recall that, in addition to the ordering of the objects of choice in X induced by $\geq$ on B through γ, there are also orderings of those objects determined by the decision maker's utility function, $u(x,\omega)$, for each value of ω. None of the latter orderings is necessarily identical to the former. This is because each of the orderings obtained from $u(x,\omega)$ reflects the preferences of the decision maker while the ordering induced by $\geq$ on B is a consequence of the arbitrary artifice γ. Moreover, for each ω, the preference ordering defined by u can also be induced on B through the relation

$$\psi = u(\gamma^{-1}(b),\omega),$$

where γ^{-1}denotes the inverse of γ.

Ignoring its source, namely, the decision maker's potential surprise function s defined on $\mathcal{A}$, consider the family of potential surprise density functions $\mathcal{F}$ generated by s. (From now on, the superscript s, which was used in Chapter 4 to identify the potential surprise version of the model of decision making in ignorance, is dropped.) This family is characterized by the fact that, for every object of choice x in X or, equivalently, b in B, the decision maker constructs a unique potential surprise density function, $f_x(\psi)$, over the utility outcomes in Ψ. For present purposes, however, it is convenient to modify the previous symbolic representation of $\mathcal{F}$ and its members by writing, in place of

$$\xi = f_x(\psi),$$
$$\xi = f(\psi, b),$$

where f is defined on $\Psi \times B$ and ξ denotes the potential surprise associated with utility value ψ and object of choice surrogate b. Then each potential surprise density function in the family $\mathcal{F}$ is a section of f obtained for a fixed b in B. Both the section (*i.e.*, the potential surprise density function) and the family itself are often denoted by the same symbol, f. Although the decision maker is only concerned with the fact that different values of b identify his different potential surprise density functions $f(\psi, b)$, an outside investigator would also be interested in how the potential surprise density functions vary with b. The possible forms that such a potential surprise density function can take on, and the implications of these forms for decision making, will be examined in the illustrations that follow.

The relationship between the family $f(\psi, b)$ and the individual potential surprise density functions it contains is often clarified by using a symbol, say b^0, to denote a given selection of b in B. In that case, the potential surprise density function determined by that selection would be written $f(\psi, b^0)$. This would emphasize that the potential surprise density function given b^0 is a function of the single variable ψ. Such notation would also enhance derivations based on $f(\psi, b^0)$. For example, associated with $f(\psi, b^0)$, and hence with the selection b^0, is the collection of utility values N_{b^0} that are assigned zero potential surprise under $f(\psi, b^0)$. That is,

$$N_{b^0} = \{\psi : f(\psi, b^0) = 0\},$$

or, in other words, the decision maker imagines that he would not be surprised by the occurrence of any of the utility values in N_{b^0}. It is now obvious that variations in b^0 modify both $f(\psi, b^0)$ and N_{b^0}. But because notation would become too cumbersome later on, hereafter the superscript "naught" on the b is dropped. The reader may wish to keep in mind, however, that all symbols b appearing subsequently would more properly be written as b^0.

For all b in B, assume, as in Section 4.3, that N_b is a nonempty, bounded, and connected subset of Ψ. Identifying the element ψ_b of N_b as the boundary between the more favorable and less favorable utility outcomes in Ψ, the gain side of the ψ-axis is given by

$$\Psi_b^+ = \{\psi : \psi \geq \psi_b\}$$

and the loss side by

$$\Psi_b^- = \{\psi : \psi \leq \psi_b\},$$

where, of course, $\Psi_b^+ \cap \Psi_b^- = \{\psi_b\}$ and $\Psi_b^+ \cup \Psi_b^- = \Psi$. The shape of the potential surprise density function depends on the way in which the decision maker views the uncertainty of achieving the increasingly more appealing utility values in Ψ_b^+ and the increasingly less appealing utility values in Ψ_b^-.

Recall now that B is the range of the artifice γ mapping the decision set into the real line and that Ψ, the real line itself, is the collection of all utility values in the domains of the potential surprise density functions. Given, as indicated earlier, that, for each element of the decision set X, values of ψ in Ψ arise from the ordinal utility transformation of states of the world and values of b in B arise from the artifice γ, the signs and magnitudes of the partial derivatives of the function $f(\psi, b)$, when they exist, can be interpreted with respect to each of its arguments. In particular, the partial derivative with respect to utility magnitudes ψ, denoted by $f_\psi(\psi, b)$, envisages a movement along the graph of the potential surprise density function for fixed b, as shown in subsequent diagrams, and the partial derivative with respect to the object of choice surrogate b, written $f_b(\psi, b)$, represents a movement to a different potential surprise density curve at ψ (shown in only the first two diagrams).[1] It should be noted in the latter circumstance that, although the existence of $f_b(\psi', b')$ means that "small" variations of b from b' (with ψ' fixed) induce small and "smooth" changes in ξ, since γ is required to be neither differentiable nor continuous, a similar assertion about alterations in ξ with respect to x, where $b = \gamma(x)$, need not hold.

---

[1]The switch in notation here from $f_x(\psi)$ or $f_b(\psi)$ to $f_\psi(\psi, b)$ and $f_b(\psi, b)$ should be remembered. In the former notation, the subscripts x and b served to identify the members of a family of functions. With the latter, subscripts are used to denote partial derivatives. However, the designation of subscripts on f as indicators of partial derivatives appears only in Chapters 5 and 6, and the symbolizing of partial derivatives with subscripts in general is employed only in these chapters and Section 10.1.

Analogously to N_b, define the set

$$M_b = \{\psi : f(\psi, b) = 1\}$$

for all b in B. Unlike N_b, which is assumed to contain at least one ψ-value, M_b may be empty. A number of concepts relevant to the examples developed subsequently are now introduced. Each describes a special way in which variations in b transform the potential surprise density function and, in one instance, the attractiveness function. All derivatives required to define these notions are assumed to exist.

For any b' and b'' in B such that $b' > b''$, $f(\psi, b')$ is said to *dominate* $f(\psi, b'')$ if and only if

(i) $f(\psi, b') < f(\psi, b'')$, for all ψ in $\Psi_{b''}^+ - N_{b''} - M_{b'}$, and

(ii) $f(\psi, b') > f(\psi, b'')$, for all ψ in $\Psi_{b'}^- - N_{b'} - M_{b''}$.

That is, at each point ψ for which either $f(\psi, b') \neq f(\psi, b'')$ or one of $f(\psi, b')$ and $f(\psi, b'')$ is different from 0 and 1, the graph of $f(\psi, b')$ lies below that of $f(\psi, b'')$ on the gain side (condition [i]) and above it on the loss side (condition [ii]). Thus $f(\psi, b')$ dominates $f(\psi, b'')$ when the graph of the former, as illustrated by the dotted line in Figure 5-1, lies to the right of that of the latter, as exemplified by the dashed line in that diagram.[2] Although often the case, it is not necessary that the two graphs be parallel to each other, *i.e.*, that, except for translation along the ψ-axis, the graph of $f(\psi, b'')$ be identical to the graph of $f(\psi, b')$. Moreover, while not essential to do so, since b is a continuous variable, the notion of dominance with respect to a family of potential surprise density functions may conveniently be expressed in terms of signs of the partial derivative of f with respect to b. That is, the family $f(\psi, b)$ is a *family of dominating potential surprise density functions* if and only if

(i) $f_b(\psi, b) < 0$, for all ψ in $\Psi_b^+ - N_b - M_b$ and b in the interior of B, and

(ii) $f_b(\psi, b) > 0$, for all ψ in $\Psi_b^- - N_b - M_b$ and b in the interior of B.

---

[2]Of course, associating increases in b with rightward shifts of the potential surprise density curve is arbitrary. There is no reason why decreases in b could not be identified with rightward shifts instead.

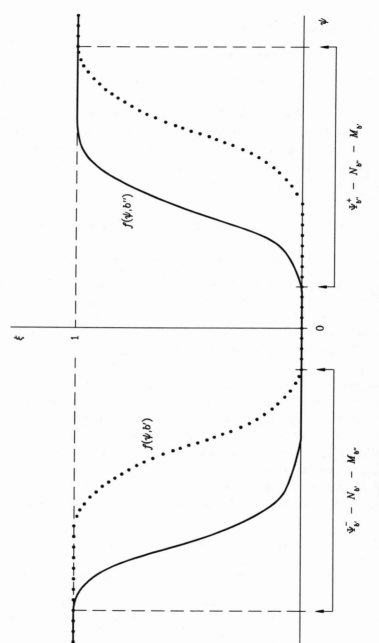

Figure 5-1. Dominating potential surprise density curves.

Examples 1 and 2 below each contain families of dominating potential surprise density functions.

For any b' and b'' in B such that $b' > b''$, $f(\psi, b'')$ is said to be *nested* in $f(\psi, b')$ if and only if

$$f(\psi, b') < f(\psi, b''), \text{ for all } \psi \text{ in } \Psi_{b''}^+ - N_{b''} - M_{b'} \text{ and } \Psi_{b''}^- - N_{b''} - M_{b'}.$$

In other words, at each ψ for which either $f(\psi, b') \neq f(\psi, b'')$ or for which one of $f(\psi, b')$ and $f(\psi, b'')$ is different from 0 and 1, the graph of $f(\psi, b'')$ always lies above that of $f(\psi, b')$. Two nested potential surprise density curves appear in Figure 5-2. In that diagram, the dashed curve (the graph of $f(\psi, b'')$) is nested in the dotted curve (the graph of $f(\psi, b')$). Neither the downward-sloping portions of the two curves nor their upward-sloping portions are required to be parallel. Note that for $f(\psi, b'')$ to be nested in $f(\psi, b')$ it is necessary that $N_{b''} \subseteq N_b$ and $M_{b'} \subseteq M_{b''}$. Again making use of the fact that b is a continuous variable, the family $f(\psi, b)$ is a *family of nested potential surprise density functions* if and only if

$$f_b(\psi, b) < 0, \text{ for all } \psi \text{ in } \Psi_b^+ - N_b - M_b \text{ and } \Psi_b^- - N_b - M_b,$$

and all b in the interior of B. Families of nested potential surprise density functions appear in Examples 3, 4, and 5.

For any b in B, $f(\psi, b)$ is said to be *symmetric* (with respect to the ξ-axis) if and only if

$$f(\psi, b) = f(-\psi, b)$$

for all ψ in Ψ. Geometrically the graph of that portion of a symmetric potential surprise density function, $f(x, b)$ given b, to the left of $\psi = 0$ is a reflection, with respect to the ξ-axis, of that to the right. The family $f(\psi, b)$ is a *symmetric family* if and only if $f(\psi, b)$ is symmetric for each b in B. Note that symmetry of a family of potential surprise density functions is neither necessary nor sufficient for it to be nested: symmetry, after all, is really a property of single potential surprise density functions, whereas nestedness has to do with the relationship between one density function and another. Even so, the potential surprise density functions in Examples 3, 4, and 5 are both nested and symmetric. Using the old notation of Chapter 4, in which the subscript

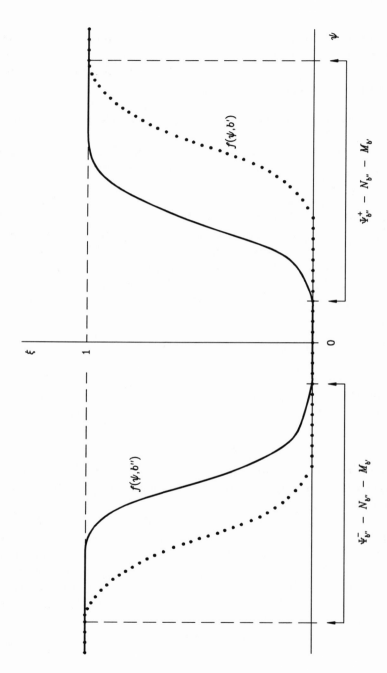

Figure 5–2. Nested potential surprise density curves.

b (the equivalent of x under γ) indicates a member of a family of functions, the attractiveness function $g_b(\psi, \xi)$ on $\Psi \times \Xi$ is *symmetric* (with respect to the ξ-axis) if and only if, for each b in B,

$$g_b(\psi, \xi) = g_b(-\psi, \xi)$$

for all $\psi \neq \psi_b$ in Ψ and ξ in Ξ. Symmetric attractiveness functions arise in Examples 1 and 3.

5.1.1 Example 1

For the first example to be considered here, let $B = \{b : 0 < b \leq 1\}$ and define for b in B, the potential surprise density function

$$f(\psi, b) = \begin{cases} 1, & \text{if } b + 1 \leq \psi, \\[2mm] (\psi - b)^2, & \text{if } b \leq \psi \leq b + 1, \\[2mm] 0, & \text{if } -b^{-1} \leq \psi \leq b, \\[2mm] (\psi + b^{-1})^2, & \text{if } -b^{-1} - 1 \leq \psi \leq -b^{-1}, \\[2mm] 1, & \text{if } \psi \leq -b^{-1} - 1. \end{cases} \qquad (5.1.1\text{-}1)$$

In (5.1.1-1), the given value of b characterizes the endpoints of the various intervals through which ψ ranges. Over each such interval the function f has its own form. It should further be recognized that, as described at the beginning of Section 5.1, the given value of b, there initially designated b^0, also fixes the boundaries of N_b and M_b. A picture of the density function (5.1.1-1) for a typical b in B appears as the curve labeled f in Figure 5-3.[3] Observe that the potential surprise density curve in that diagram is defined over the domain Ψ consisting of the points on the (horizontal) ψ-axis. The b-value in equation (5.1.1-1) and the diagram further serves the purpose, as indicated earlier, of identifying, through γ, the object of choice (in the decision set X) to

---

[3]In this and subsequent diagrams, the scales with respect to which ψ and ξ are measured on, respectively, the horizontal and vertical axes are not necessarily the same.

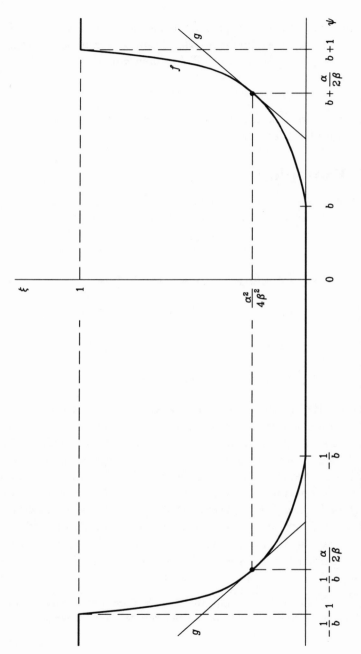

Figure 5–3. Constrained attractiveness maximization in Example 1.

which, respectively, the function and curve relate. Again, a change in the value of b would imply a move to a different object of choice and different associated potential surprise density curve. This fact is highly relevant to the interpretation of the comparative statics properties of the argument of Section 5.2. Note also that as b increases the graph of $f(\psi, b)$ moves rightward. Thus (5.1.1-1) defines a family of dominating potential surprise density functions.

Of course it is the manner in which equation (5.1.1-1) is formulated, or, more precisely, the manner in which the rule linking the domain of f to its range is broken up into subrules each defined over a particular interval or subdomain of Ψ, that causes the value of b, in addition to specifying an object of choice, to take on its further aforementioned roles. Two of the latter deserve emphasis. On the one hand, the value of b algebraically figures into the determination of the potential surprise values assigned to utility magnitudes in two subdomains according to the relevant subrule. In this regard, observe that f, where not flat, has a strictly convex, parabolic shape.[4] On the other, it delimits the subdomains of f over which each subrule is characterized. Evidently as b varies over B both of the two nonconstant subrules and all of the subdomains are modified and these modifications occur in such a way as to preserve the potential surprise function values as numbers between 0 and 1.

Clearly, in this example, $N_b = \{\psi : -b^{-1} \leq \psi \leq b\}$. For all b in B, set the boundary between the more favorable and less favorable utility values at $\psi_b = 0$. Then Ψ_b^+ and Ψ_b^- are the nonnegative reals and the nonpositive reals, respectively. The values and signs of the first-order partial derivatives of f, namely, $f_\psi(\psi, b)$ (reflecting a movement along a potential surprise density curve such as that shown in Figure 5.3) and $f_b(\psi, b)$ (reflecting a movement to a different poten-

---

[4]Although such a shape (along with that of Example 2 below) differs somewhat from the back-to-back elongated S-shape introduced earlier, it is convenient to use and easy to handle mathematically. Moreover, the absence here of the elongated S-shape's asymptotes in the upper and lower ranges of possible outcomes may not be particularly significant due to the fact that present concern only focuses on the range of outcomes within which, consistent with previous argument, the tangency of the potential surprise density curve and an iso-attractiveness contour is likely to be established.

TABLE 5-1.   Calculation of Derivatives in Example 1

Derivative	Value and Sign over the Interior of the Set			
	$[b,b+1] \times B$	$[-b^{-1}-1,-b^{-1}] \times B$	$\Psi_b^+ \times \Xi$	$\Psi_b^- \times \Xi$
$f_\psi(\psi,b)$	$2(\psi-b)>0$	$2(\psi+b^{-1})<0$		
$f_b(\psi,b)$	$-2(\psi-b)<0$	$-2b^{-2}(\psi+b^{-1})>0$		
$f_{\psi\psi}(\psi,b)$	$2>0$	$2>0$		
$f_{bb}(\psi,b)$	$2>0$	$2b^{-3}(2\psi+3b^{-1})\gtreqless 0$		
$f_{\psi b}(\psi,b)$	$-2<0$	$-2b^{-2}<0$		
$g_\psi(\psi,\xi)$			$\alpha>0$	$-\alpha<0$
$g_\xi(\psi,\xi)$			$-\beta<0$	$-\beta<0$
$g_{\psi\psi}(\psi,\xi)$			0	0
$g_{\xi\xi}(\psi,\xi)$			0	0
$g_{\psi\xi}(\psi,\xi)$			0	0

tial surprise density curve not shown in Figure 5-3), and the values and signs of the second-order partial derivatives, or $f_{\psi\psi}(\psi,b)$, $f_{bb}(\psi,b)$, and $f_{\psi b}(\psi,b) = f_{b\psi}(\psi,b)$, are indicated in Table 5-1 for the interior of the sets $[b,b+1] \times B$ and $[-b^{-1}-1, -b^{-1}] \times B$, where $[b,b+1]$ and $[-b^{-1}-1, -b^{-1}]$ are closed intervals in Ψ. In reference to Figure 5-3, where the partial derivatives of f exist, $f_\psi(\psi,b)$ describes the slope of the potential surprise density curve at each ψ in Ψ given b, while $f_b(\psi,b)$ indicates how potential surprise values change with b at every ψ. Note that potential surprise increases with ψ at an increasing rate between b and $b+1$ and increases at an increasing rate as ψ declines between $-b^{-1}$ and $-b^{-1}-1$.

Consider next the attractiveness function defined over the possible utility outcomes and the possible potential surprise magnitudes that can be associated with them. It is worth remembering that the attractiveness function is not a utility function but, rather, serves only to describe, given b in B, the ability of the various pairs (ψ,ξ) to focus the decision maker's thoughts or, that is, to describe their ability to attract his attention to the payoff and the uncertainty features that are significant in his scrutiny of the objects of choice for decision making purposes.

The attractiveness function, recall, has two independent branches, one defined on $\Psi_b^+ \times \Xi$ and the other on $\Psi_b^- \times \Xi$, where $\Xi = \{\xi : 0 \leq \xi \leq 1\}$ is the range of the family of potential surprise density functions f. The same symbolism employed earlier, $g_b(\psi, \xi)$, is used to represent both branches of the attractiveness function, where the original subscript x is replaced here by its equivalent b. (In this notation, the subscript b does not yet indicate a partial derivative. But it will be redefined to do so momentarily.) For each b in B, then, $g_b(\psi, \xi)$ on, say, $\Psi_b^+ \times \Xi$, is an ordinal function that orders the pairs of $\Psi_b^+ \times \Xi$ according to their power to attract the decision maker's attention. Given b, the decision maker is assumed to focus his attention on those pairs (ψ_b^+, ξ_b^+) and (ψ_b^-, ξ_b^-) that maximize the branch of the attractiveness function over, respectively, $\Psi_b^+ \times \Xi$ and $\Psi_b^- \times \Xi$. The comparative statics of this maximization is taken up in Section 5.2.

In the present example, let the attractiveness function be independent of b and of the form

$$g(\psi, \xi) = \begin{cases} \alpha\psi - \beta\xi, & \text{on } \Psi_b^+ \times \Xi, \\ -\alpha\psi - \beta\xi, & \text{on } \Psi_b^- \times \Xi, \end{cases}$$

where $\alpha > 0$, $\beta > 0$, $\alpha < 2\beta$, and the subscript b on g has been deleted since, in this particular case, g is not dependent on it. Because they are no longer needed to identify family members, subscripts on g, like those on f, will now denote partial derivatives.[5] Observe that this attractiveness function is symmetric and, for mathematical convenience, linear. The values and signs of the first- and second-order partial derivatives of g with respect to ψ and ξ, namely, $g_\psi(\psi, \xi)$, $g_\xi(\psi, \xi)$, $g_{\psi\psi}(\psi, \xi)$, $g_{\xi\xi}(\psi, \xi)$, and $g_{\psi\xi}(\psi, \xi) = g_{\xi\psi}(\psi, \xi)$, are given in Table 5-1. The iso-attractiveness contours of g are linear and those associated with the maximization of g subject to (5.1.1-1) are labeled g in Figure 5-3. (Increased attractiveness shifts the iso-attractiveness curves down and to the right in $\Psi_b^+ \times \Xi$ and down and to the left in $\Psi_b^+ \times \Xi$.) Using Lagrange's theorem on constrained maximization at interior points of $\Psi_b^+ \times \Xi$ and $\Psi_b^- \times \Xi$,

---

[5] As with subscripts on f, the use of subscripts on g to symbolize partial derivatives appears only in Chapters 5 and 6.

it is easily seen that for b in B, the attractiveness-maximizing pairs, that is, the focus gain and focus loss are, respectively,

$$\psi_b^+ = b + \frac{\alpha}{2\beta},$$

$$\xi_b^+ = \frac{\alpha^2}{4\beta^2},$$

and

$$\psi_b^- = -\frac{1}{b} - \frac{\alpha}{2\beta},$$

$$\xi_b^- = \frac{\alpha^2}{4\beta^2}.$$

Geometrically these values of ψ_b^+, ξ_b^+, ψ_b^-, and ξ_b^- are the coordinates of the unique points of tangency in Figure 5-3 between iso-attractiveness contours and the potential surprise density function.[6] The restrictions imposed on the parameters of g, namely, $\alpha > 0$, $\beta > 0$, and $\alpha < 2\beta$, ensure that the focus gain and focus loss occur in $\Psi \times \Xi$ where the potential surprise density function slopes, respectively, upward and downward. That is to say,

$$b < \psi_b^+ < b + 1, \qquad\qquad 0 < \xi_b^+ < 1,$$

$$-b^{-1} - 1 < \psi_b^- < -b^{-1}, \qquad 0 < \xi_b^- < 1.$$

The conclusions that

$$\frac{\partial \psi_b^+}{\partial b} > 0, \qquad \frac{\partial \xi_b^+}{\partial b} = 0,$$

$$\frac{\partial \psi_b^-}{\partial b} > 0, \qquad \frac{\partial \xi_b^-}{\partial b} = 0,$$

(5.1.1-2)

follow immediately. As already suggested in a different context, the left- and right-hand derivatives in (5.1.1-2) describe, respectively, the changes in the maximizing utility and potential surprise magnitudes as variation in b induces movement from one potential surprise density

---

[6]Note that, as required, equation (4.3-5) is also satisfied.

function to another. However, although the assertion, for example, that $\partial \psi_b^+ / \partial b > 0$ at b' in B, says something about how ψ_b^+ varies with b in a small neighborhood about b', in the absence of the assumptions that x is quantified and the artifice γ is differentiable, no parallel statement with respect to x, where $b = \gamma(x)$, is possible.

Example 1 is completed upon the introduction of a decision index. This requires, as described in Section 4.3, the specification of the decision maker's continuously differentiable function

$$Q(\psi_b^-, \xi_b^-, \psi_b^+, \xi_b^+),$$

defined over the collection of all possible vectors $(\psi_b^-, \xi_b^-, \psi_b^+, \xi_b^+)$, and such that

$$\frac{\partial Q}{\partial \psi_b^-} > 0, \qquad \frac{\partial Q}{\partial \psi_b^+} > 0,$$

$$\frac{\partial Q}{\partial \xi_b^-} > 0, \qquad \frac{\partial Q}{\partial \xi_b^+} < 0, \qquad (5.1.1\text{-}3)$$

everywhere. (Here, as before, b replaces x and the superscript s on Q is dropped.) Using the linear function of (4.3-7), that is,

$$Q(\psi_b^-, \xi_b^-, \psi_b^+, \xi_b^+) = \psi_b^- + \xi_b^- + \psi_b^+ - \xi_b^+, \qquad (5.1.1\text{-}4)$$

the decision index as a function of b, namely,

$$D(b) = Q(\psi_b^-, \xi_b^-, \psi_b^+, \xi_b^+),$$

becomes

$$D(b) = b - \frac{1}{b}$$

for all b in B. This result is obtained by substituting the constrained maximization solution values previously derived, or the focus gain and focus loss, into (5.1.1-4). Since $dD(b)/db > 0$ on the interior of B, where, recall, $B = \{b : 0 < b \leq 1\}$, the decision maker chooses that x in X corresponding, under γ, to $b = 1$. It should be remembered that to keep the above representation of decision making, and hence the results of this section (and those of the remainder of the chapter), independent of the arbitrary selections of both the ordinal utility function that produces the values of ψ, and the artifice γ that determines the values of b, it has to be assumed, in part, that alterations in either of these functions are exactly offset by corresponding and appropriate changes in f, g, and Q.

5.1.2 Example 2

In the second example, to prevent negative potential surprise values in the focus gain and focus loss, it is necessary to restrict B further to $B = \{b : 1/2 \leq b \leq 1\}$. As in Example 1, the specification of a b in B, identifying, as it does, a choice option in X, will, in Example 2, fix the location of the potential surprise density curve or, that is, will select from the given family of potential surprise density functions the precise function that is relevant. Moreover, the specification of b will further determine (also as in Example 1) the various intervals over which ψ ranges, and over which the potential surprise density function takes on special forms, and will also be employed in the calculation of certain potential surprise values. With this in mind, and for b in B, define another family of dominating potential surprise density functions according to

$$
f(\psi, b) = \begin{cases}
1, & \text{if } b + 1 \leq \psi, \\
\psi - b, & \text{if } b \leq \psi \leq b + 1, \\
0, & \text{if } -b^{-1} \leq \psi \leq b, \\
-\psi - b^{-1}, & \text{if } -b^{-1} - 1 \leq \psi \leq -b^{-1}, \\
1, & \text{if } \psi \leq -b^{-1} - 1.
\end{cases}
$$

With $\psi_b = 0$ for all b in B, the sets N_b, Ψ_b^+, and Ψ_b^- remain as in Example 1. As before, increases in b shift the potential surprise density curve to the right, but here, where its slope is not zero, the shape of each curve is linear. The graph of the potential surprise density function given b is identified as f in Figure 5-4, and the values and signs of its partial derivatives over the same sets employed in Table 5-1 are listed in Table 5-2. Due to the piecewise linearity, the rate of change of potential surprise with respect to ψ is constant, although not always the same constant, as ψ varies throughout Ψ.

Now add the attractiveness function

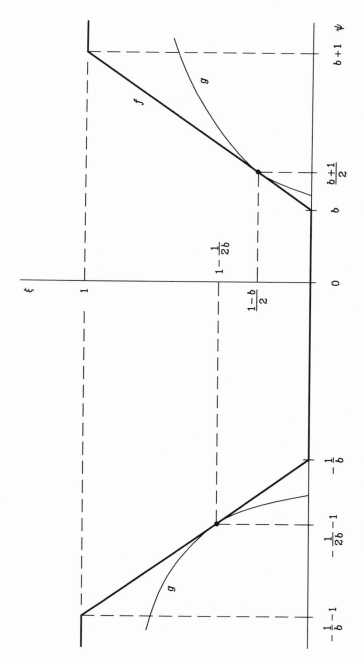

Figure 5-4. Constrained attractiveness maximization in Example 2.

TABLE 5-2.   **Calculation of Derivatives in Example 2**

Derivative	Value and Sign over the Interior of the Set			
	$[b,b+1] \times B$	$[-b^{-1}-1,-b^{-1}] \times B$	$\Psi_b^+ \times \Xi$	$\Psi_b^- \times \Xi$
$f_\psi(\psi,b)$	$1 > 0$	$-1 < 0$		
$f_b(\psi,b)$	$-1 < 0$	$b^{-2} > 0$		
$f_{\psi\psi}(\psi,b)$	0	0		
$f_{bb}(\psi,b)$	0	$-2b^{-3} < 0$		
$f_{\psi b}(\psi,b)$	0	0		
$g_\psi(\psi,\xi)$			$(1-\xi) > 0$	$(\xi-2) < 0$
$g_\xi(\psi,\xi)$			$-\psi < 0$	$\psi < 0$
$g_{\psi\psi}(\psi,\xi)$			0	0
$g_{\xi\xi}(\psi,\xi)$			0	0
$g_{\psi\xi}(\psi,\xi)$			$-1 < 0$	$1 > 0$

$$g(\psi,\xi) = \begin{cases} \psi(1-\xi), & \text{on } \Psi_b^+ \times \Xi, \\ \psi(\xi-2), & \text{on } \Psi_b^- \times \Xi, \end{cases}$$

which, like the attractiveness function of Example 1, is also independent of b. The relevant partial derivatives of g appear in Table 5-2 and the iso-attractiveness contours corresponding to its constrained maximization are labeled g in Figure 5-4. Again, from the theorem of Lagrange, at b in B, the focus gain and loss are

$$\psi_b^+ = \frac{b+1}{2},$$

$$\xi_b^+ = \frac{1-b}{2},$$

and

$$\psi_b^- = -\frac{1}{2b} - 1,$$

$$\xi_b^- = 1 - \frac{1}{2b},$$

and these values are indicated as the coordinates of appropriate tangencies in Figure 5-4. Clearly, with b in B,

$$b \le \psi_b^+ < b+1, \qquad\qquad 0 \le \xi_b^+ < 1,$$

$$-b^{-1} - 1 < \psi_b^- \le -b^{-1}, \qquad 0 \le \xi_b^- < 1,$$

and, on the interior of B,[7]

$$\frac{\partial \psi_b^+}{\partial b} > 0, \qquad \frac{\partial \xi_b^+}{\partial b} < 0,$$

$$\frac{\partial \psi_b^-}{\partial b} > 0, \qquad \frac{\partial \xi_b^-}{\partial b} > 0. \qquad (5.1.2\text{-}1)$$

Note that when $b = 1$, the attractiveness function over $\Psi_b^+ \times \Xi$ is maximized subject to the potential surprise density function at the "corner" point $(1,0)$, and when $b = 1/2$, the constrained maximum of the attractiveness function over $\Psi_b^- \times \Xi$ occurs at the corner $(-2,0)$. However, even in these situations, there is still a tangency (not shown in Figure 5-4) between an iso-attractiveness contour and the potential surprise density function at each maximizing point. Notice also that the iso-attractiveness contours in $\Psi_b^+ \times \Xi$ are asymptotic to the line $\xi = 1$, while those in $\Psi_b^- \times \Xi$ intersect $\xi = 1$. The latter contours, if extended, would be asymptotic to the line $\xi = 2$, but these extended portions are not relevant in the present context. In either case, the iso-attractiveness contours are strictly concave. Employing the same linear function Q as in $(5.1.1\text{-}4)$, once again the decision index becomes

$$D(b) = Q(\psi_b^-, \xi_b^-, \psi_b^+, \xi_b^+) = \psi_b^- + \xi_b^- + \psi_b^+ - \xi_b^+ = b - \frac{1}{b}$$

for all b in B, and the decision maker chooses that x in X whose associated value of b is $b = 1$.

5.1.3   Example 3

Adding the left-hand endpoint to the set B of Example 1, so that now $B = \{b : 0 \le b \le 1\}$, consider the family of potential surprise density

---

[7]In this case, the following partial derivatives are actually total derivatives.

functions

$$f(\psi, b) = \begin{cases} 1, & \text{if } b + 1 \leq \psi, \\[1.5em] (\psi - b)^2, & \text{if } b \leq \psi \leq b + 1, \\[1.5em] 0, & \text{if } -b \leq \psi \leq b, \\[1.5em] (\psi + b)^2, & \text{if } -b - 1 \leq \psi \leq -b, \\[1.5em] 1, & \text{if } \psi \leq -b - 1. \end{cases} \qquad (5.1.3\text{-}1)$$

Set $\psi_b = 0$, for all b in B, and define N_b, Ψ_b^+, and Ψ_b^- as in Examples 1 and 2. This family is similar to that of Example 1 except that the function values for negative ψ have been adjusted to produce a family of potential surprise density functions that are nested and symmetric instead of dominating. Thus, as b declines, the potential surprise values given by f rise over appropriate subsets of both gains Ψ_b^+ and losses Ψ_b^-. The graph of one member of (5.1.3-1) is labeled f in Figure 5-5, and the values and signs of the family's partial derivatives over the sets $[b, b+1] \times B$ and $[-b-1, -b] \times B$ are given in Table 5-3.

Employ the same symmetric attractiveness function as in Example 1, that is,

$$g(\psi, \xi) = \begin{cases} \alpha\psi - \beta\xi, & \text{on } \Psi_b^+ \times \Xi, \\[1em] -\alpha\psi - \beta\xi, & \text{on } \Psi_b^- \times \Xi, \end{cases}$$

where $\alpha > 0$, $\beta > 0$, $\alpha \leq \beta$ and g is independent of b. Note, however, that the inequality $\alpha < 2\beta$ of Example 1 has to be strengthened here to $\alpha \leq \beta$ in order to ensure that the value of b below that maximizes $D(b)$ is nonnegative, that is, remains in B. Graphs of the iso-attractiveness contours identified with the constrained maximization of g appear as the straight lines labeled g in Figure 5-5. The partial derivatives of g are calculated in Table 5-3.

Maximization of the attractiveness function subject to the potential

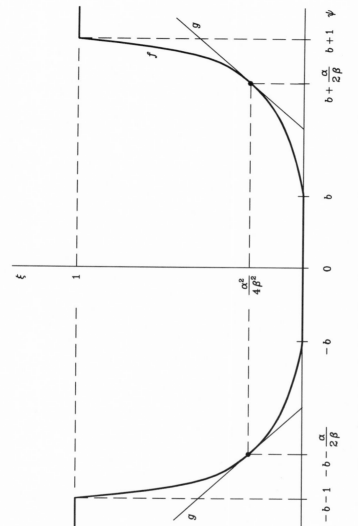

Figure 5-5. Constrained attractiveness maximization in Example 3.

TABLE 5-3.   Calculation of Derivatives in Example 3

Derivative	Value and Sign over the Interior of the Set			
	$[b,b+1] \times B$	$[-b-1,-b] \times B$	$\Psi_b^+ \times \Xi$	$\Psi_b^- \times \Psi$
$f_\psi(\psi,b)$	$2(\psi - b) > 0$	$2(\psi + b) < 0$		
$f_b(\psi,b)$	$-2(\psi - b) < 0$	$2(\psi + b) < 0$		
$f_{\psi\psi}(\psi,b)$	$2 > 0$	$2 > 0$		
$f_{bb}(\psi,b)$	$2 > 0$	$2 > 0$		
$f_{\psi b}(\psi,b)$	$-2 < 0$	$2 > 0$		
$g_\psi(\psi,\xi)$			$\alpha > 0$	$-\alpha < 0$
$g_\xi(\psi,\xi)$			$-\beta < 0$	$-\beta < 0$
$g_{\psi\psi}(\psi,\xi)$			0	0
$g_{\xi\xi}(\psi,\xi)$			0	0
$g_{\psi\xi}(\psi,\xi)$			0	0

surprise density function for each b in B yields

$$\psi_b^+ = b + \frac{\alpha}{2\beta}, \qquad \xi_b^+ = \frac{\alpha^2}{4\beta^2},$$

$$\psi_b^- = -b - \frac{\alpha}{2\beta}, \qquad \xi_b^- = \frac{\alpha^2}{4\beta^2}.$$

Observe that the values of ψ_b^+ and ξ_b^+ here are identical to those in Example 1, and the symmetry of the potential surprise density and attractiveness functions results in the equalities $\psi_b^+ = -\psi_b^+$ and $\xi_b^+ = \xi_b^-$. In addition, and based on the requirements that $\alpha > 0$, $\beta > 0$, and $\alpha \leq \beta$,

$$b < \psi_b^+ < b + 1, \qquad 0 < \xi_b^+ < 1,$$

$$-b - 1 < \psi_b^- < -b, \qquad 0 < \xi_b^- < 1,$$

and

$$\frac{\partial \psi_b^+}{\partial b} > 0, \qquad \frac{\partial \xi_b^+}{\partial b} = 0,$$

$$\frac{\partial \psi_b^-}{\partial b} > 0, \qquad \frac{\partial \xi_b^-}{\partial b} = 0. \tag{5.1.3-2}$$

Let the decision index be

$$D(b) = Q(\psi_b^-, \xi_b^-, \psi_b^+, \xi_b^+) = -\left(\psi_b^-\right)^2 + \xi_b^- + \psi_b^+ - \xi_b^+, \quad (5.1.3\text{-}3)$$

$$= \frac{\alpha}{2\beta} - \frac{\alpha^2}{4\beta^2} + \left(1 - \frac{\alpha}{\beta}\right) b - b^2.$$

Clearly Q satisfies the conditions required in (5.1.1-3). The value of b that uniquely maximizes D over B is

$$b = \frac{1}{2}\left(1 - \frac{\alpha}{\beta}\right).$$

Thus the selection of b, and the choice object x associated with b, depends on the parameters α and β. Indeed, $\partial b/\partial \alpha < 0$ and $\partial b/\partial \beta > 0$. Note that were the function Q of Examples 1 and 2 used here in place of Q in (5.1.3-3) then $D(b) \equiv 0$, and hence, based on this revised model, no unique decision could be made. It should be understood, of course, that in Examples 1 and 2, as presented earlier, the fact that the decision index value is zero at the optimal b does not mean that a unique decision does not exist.

5.1.4 Example 4

Again set $B = \{b : 0 \leq b \leq 1\}$ and use a family of nested and symmetric potential surprise density functions obtained through modification of $f(\psi, b)$ in Example 2:

$$f(\psi, b) = \begin{cases} 1, & \text{if } b + 1 \leq \psi, \\[1mm] \psi - b, & \text{if } b \leq \psi \leq b + 1, \\[1mm] 0, & \text{if } -b \leq \psi \leq b, \\[1mm] -\psi - b, & \text{if } -b - 1 \leq \psi \leq -b, \\[1mm] 1, & \text{if } \psi \leq -b - 1. \end{cases}$$

Write $\psi_b = 0$ for all b in B and define N_b, Ψ^+, and Ψ^- as before. Let the attractiveness function be

$$g(\psi,\xi) = \begin{cases} \psi(1 - a\xi), & \text{on } \Psi_b^+ \times \Xi, \\[2mm] \psi(a\xi - 2), & \text{on } \Psi_b^- \times \Xi, \end{cases}$$

where a is a parameter such that $2(b+2)^{-1} < a < 1$ and g is independent of b. This attractiveness function is identical to that of Example 2 except for the insertion of a in front of ξ. Graphs of f (labeled f) and the tangent iso-attractiveness contours of g (labeled g), and the partial derivatives of f and g appear, respectively, in Figure 5-6 and Table 5-4. The inequality restrictions $0 \le b \le 1$ and $2(b+2)^{-1} < a < 1$ guarantee that the components of the focus gain and focus loss derived below lie within the usual limits. They further imply that only the combinations of values for a and b falling in the shaded region of Figure 5-7, that is, those for which $a < 1$, $b \le 1$, and $a > 2(b+2)^{-1}$, are admissible in this example. Note that, as indicated in Figure 5-7, the inequalities also force $a > 2/3$.

For each b in B, maximizing the attractiveness function subject to the potential surprise density function gives

$$\psi_b^+ = \frac{1}{2a} + \frac{b}{2}, \qquad \xi_b^+ = \frac{1}{2a} - \frac{b}{2},$$

$$\psi_b^- = -\frac{1}{a} - \frac{b}{2}, \qquad \xi_b^- = \frac{1}{a} - \frac{b}{2}.$$

Of course, were a permitted to equal unity, the values of ψ_b^+ and ξ_b^+ would be the same as those in Example 2. It follows from the above inequality restrictions on a and b that

$$b < \psi_b^+ < b+1, \qquad 0 < \xi_b^+ < 1,$$

$$-b - 1 < \psi_b^- < -b, \qquad 0 < \xi_b^- < 1,$$

and

$$\begin{aligned} \frac{\partial \psi_b^+}{\partial b} > 0, & \qquad \frac{\partial \xi_b^+}{\partial b} < 0, \\[2mm] \frac{\partial \psi_b^-}{\partial b} < 0, & \qquad \frac{\partial \xi_b^-}{\partial b} < 0. \end{aligned} \qquad\qquad (5.1.4\text{-}1)$$

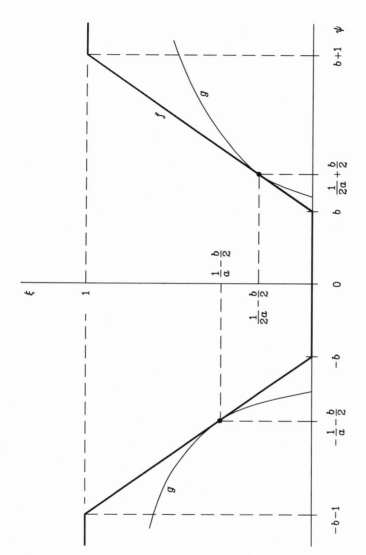

Figure 5-6. Constrained attractiveness maximization in Example 4.

TABLE 5-4.　**Calculation of Derivatives in Example 4**

Derivative	Value and Sign over the Interior of the Set			
	$[b, b+1] \times B$	$[-b-1, -b] \times B$	$\Psi_b^{+} \times \Xi$	$\Psi_b^{-} \times \Xi$
$f_\psi(\psi, b)$	$1 > 0$	$-1 < 0$		
$f_b(\psi, b)$	$-1 < 0$	$-1 < 0$		
$f_{\psi\psi}(\psi, b)$	0	0		
$f_{bb}(\psi, b)$	0	0		
$f_{\psi b}(\psi, b)$	0	0		
$g_\psi(\psi, \xi)$			$1 - a\xi > 0$	$a\xi - 2 < 0$
$g_\xi(\psi, \xi)$			$-a\psi < 0$	$a\psi < 0$
$g_{\psi\psi}(\psi, \xi)$			0	0
$g_{\xi\xi}(\psi, \xi)$			0	0
$g_{\psi\xi}(\psi, \xi)$			$-a < 0$	$a > 0$
$g_{\psi a}(\psi, \xi)$			$-\xi < 0$	$\xi > 0$
$g_{\xi a}(\psi, \xi)$			$-\psi < 0$	$\psi < 0$

With the decision index

$$D(b) = Q(\psi_b^{-}, \xi_b^{-}, \psi_b^{+}, \xi_b^{+}) = \psi_b^{-} + \xi_b^{-} \psi_b^{+} - \xi_b^{+}, \qquad (5.1.4\text{-}2)$$

$$= -\frac{3}{2a} + \frac{1}{2a^2} + \frac{b}{4a} - \frac{b^2}{4},$$

(this Q also satisfies conditions [5.1.1-3]), the value of b that uniquely maximizes D over B is

$$b = \frac{1}{2a}. \qquad (5.1.4\text{-}3)$$

As in Example 3, the selection of the choice object x associated with b depends on a parameter, in this case, a. Moreover, substitution of (5.1.4-3) into the constraints $a > 2/3$ and $a < 1$ (recall Figure 5-7) implies that the selected value of b must satisfy $1/2 < b < 3/4$. Also $db/da < 0$ or an increase in a lowers the value of b that is chosen. Here, too, use of the function Q of Examples 1 and 2 in place of Q in (5.1.4-2) would lead to $D(b) \equiv 0$, and the model would not yield a unique decision.

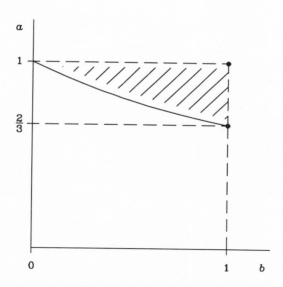

Figure 5–7. Admissible combinations (a,b) in Example 4.

Example 4 will be more fully developed in Section 6.2. In particular, it will be shown that the parameter a, which appears in both the decision index and the attractiveness function, can be interpreted in relation to the decision maker's "trade-off" aversion to or favor of uncertainty.

5.1.5 Example 5

Example 5 employs the same family of nested and symmetric potential surprise density functions f and the same definitions of $B = \{b : 0 \le b \le 1\}$, $\psi_b = 0$, and N_b, Ψ_b^+, and Ψ_b^- as Example 4. The decision index is the one given at the end of Section 4.3 from which the present attractiveness function, namely, that of (4.3-13), or

$$
g(\psi, \xi) = \begin{cases} \theta_3\psi - \theta_4\xi^2, & \text{on } \Psi_b^+ \times \Xi, \\ \\ \theta_1\psi + (\theta_2)^4\xi^2, & \text{on } \Psi_b^- \times \Xi, \end{cases} \tag{5.1.5-1}
$$

is assumed to be coincidently derivable. Observe that in keeping with the notation of this chapter, the superscript s on g in (4.3-13) has been dropped and, since g does not depend on b (or, equivalently, on x), its appearance as a subscript on g in (4.3-13) has also been eliminated. The assumptions $\theta_i > 0$, for $i = 1, \ldots, 4$, are continued, and it is further required that $\theta_1 < 2(\theta_2)^4$ and $\theta_3 < 2\theta_4$. Recall that iso-attractiveness contours associated with (5.1.5-1) have already been drawn in Figure 4-2(b). The calculation of the partial derivatives of f and g are left to the reader.

Maximization of the attractiveness function subject to the potential surprise density function for b in B yields the focus gain

$$
\psi_b^+ = \frac{\theta_3}{2\theta_4} + b, \qquad \xi_b^+ = \frac{\theta_3}{2\theta_4}, \tag{5.1.5-2}
$$

and focus loss

$$
\psi_b^- = -\frac{\theta_1}{2\,[\theta_2]^4} - b, \qquad \xi_b^- = \frac{\theta_1}{2\,[\theta_2]^4}. \tag{5.1.5-3}
$$

Enough has been assumed on the θ_i to ensure that

$$
b < \psi_b^+ < b + 1, \qquad 0 < \xi_b^+ < 1,
$$

and

$$
-b - 1 < \psi_b^- < -b, \qquad 0 < \xi_b^- < 1.
$$

Furthermore,

$$
\frac{\partial \psi_b^+}{\partial b} > 0, \qquad \frac{\partial \xi_b^+}{\partial b} = 0,
$$

$$
\frac{\partial \psi_b^-}{\partial b} < 0, \qquad \frac{\partial \xi_b^-}{\partial b} = 0. \tag{5.1.5-4}
$$

The decision index that generates the function coincident with the attractiveness function (5.1.5-1) is expressed as a function of b by combining (4.3-8) through (4.3-10) and substituting the focus loss and focus gain arguments $(\psi_b^-, \xi_b^-, \psi_b^+, \xi_b^+)$ for (ψ, ξ, ψ, ξ). This results in

$$D(b) = Q^s(\psi_b^-, \xi_b^-, \psi_b^+, \xi_b^+),$$

$$= \theta_1 \psi_b^- + \theta_2 \left(\xi_b^-\right)^{1/2} + \theta_3 \psi_b^+ - \theta_4 \left(\xi_b^+\right)^2, \qquad (5.1.5\text{-}5)$$

where, in confluence with present notation, the superscript s on Q in (4.3-8) has been discarded. From (5.1.5-2) and (5.1.5-3), $D(b)$ may be reduced to

$$D(b) = (\theta_3 - \theta_1)b + \Theta,$$

where

$$\Theta = -\frac{(\theta_1)^2}{2(\theta_2)^4} + \frac{1}{\theta_2} \left(\frac{\theta_1}{2}\right)^{1/2} + \frac{(\theta_3)^2}{4\theta_4}$$

is a constant term that does not vary with b. It follows that $b = 0$ uniquely maximizes $D(b)$ when $\theta_1 > \theta_3$, and $b = 1$ is the unique maximizer when $\theta_1 < \theta_3$. If $\theta_1 = \theta_3$, then $D(b) = \Theta$ for all b, and a unique maximum does not exist.

Example 5 also turns out to be relevant to the discussion of uncertainty aversion and favor in Section 6.2.

5.2 Comparative Statics Analysis

In conventional economic theory, that is, in what has been referred to as equilibrium analysis, comparative statics investigations involve the comparison within a given model of alternative, timeless equilibrium positions based on different parameter values. Often the equilibria are taken to be sufficiently close together to allow the analysis to proceed through the calculation of the signs of derivatives. In any case, comparative statics analysis serves two purposes. On the one hand, it leads to a more complete examination, and hence understanding, of the model under consideration. In particular, it forces the implications of assumptions and the interrelations between variables to be more fully worked out. On the other hand, it performs as an aid in the empirical corroboration of the model by providing constraints that can be used either as part of the procedure for estimating the model's functions or as a means for directly verifying the consistency of the model with observed data. For example, in the traditional theory of demand, comparative statics analysis takes, in part, the form of the derivation of the matrix of Slutsky functions and its properties. This has clearly resulted in a deeper understanding of the theory and its interrelationships, and the properties of the Slutsky functions so obtained have proved significant in many empirical studies of demand behavior.[8]

However, in the historical time environment in which the present model of decision making in ignorance is set (or, more generally, in a nonequilibrium framework), the idea of comparative statics analysis must assume a different form. First of all, timeless equilibria do not exist. Second, even if one solved the model at each moment to secure a solution for that moment alone, one could still not compare solutions of different moments because the model itself varies from moment to moment.[9] Finally, in the absence of replication and with the unavailability of probability, much of the standard empirical analysis that makes use of the comparative statics results would have to be discarded because that analysis rests on probability concepts.[10] Nevertheless, comparative statics analysis remains relevant in the model in the sense of asking what would happen if different parameter values were applied to the same moment, and therefore to the same choice-decision nexus, rather than to distinct moments in time.[11] And the two purposes that it serves, as described above, are left intact. Thus comparative statics analysis would reduce to the derivation of the implications of assumptions and the use of the results so derived in empirical work

---

[8]See, for example, Deaton and Meullbauer [1], Katzner [2], and Theil and Clements [3].

[9]This statement remains true upon substitution of the word "period" for "moment" as long as it is understood that the period now supplants the moment as the irreducible unit of time.

[10]See Section 14.2.

[11]To the extent that a single model can reasonably be employed to describe past behavior over an interval of time (see Section 6.2 below), the comparative statics analysis of that model also extends across time.

when possible. In this way, the differential equalities and inequalities of (5.1.1-2), (5.1.2-1), (5.1.3-2), (5.1.4-1), and (5.1.5-4) are legitimate comparative statics results. An illustration of the use of comparative statics analysis in exploring the implications of uncertainty aversion and favor arises in Section 6.2.

Before proceeding, in a broader setting than that provided by the examples of Section 5.1, to the actual comparative statics analysis of the maximization of the attractiveness function subject to the potential surprise density function, consider first the questions of the existence and uniqueness of such constrained maxima. For situations in which the potential surprise density function and both branches of the attractiveness function are continuous, in which the density function is identical to the line $\xi = 1$ except for a bounded, open interval in Ψ (in earlier notation this interval would be written $\Psi - M_b$), and in which the directions of increasing attractiveness in $\Psi \times \Xi$ are as they appear in Examples 1 – 4, the existence of constrained maxima poses no difficulty. Under these conditions (which are fulfilled in all of the above examples), the subset of $\Psi_b^+ \times \Xi$ consisting of the points on or above the density function, as well as that of $\Psi_b^- \times \Xi$ defined similarly, are compact. Hence, since one branch of the attractiveness function is continuous over each of these sets, appropriate constrained maxima always exist. The question of whether these maxima are unique turns on the shape of the iso-attractiveness contours in relation to the shape of the potential surprise density function. (In this connection, it should be noted that the economic realities underlying the shapes of these functions have already been alluded to in Section 4.3 and, with respect to the attractiveness function, will arise again in reference to uncertainty aversion and favor in Section 6.2.) If, as in the case of Examples 1 and 3, the iso-attractiveness contours are linear and the potential surprise density function is appropriately strictly convex, or if, as in Examples 2, 4, and 5 the iso-attractiveness contours are strictly concave and the potential surprise density function is appropriately linear, then both constrained maxima are unique. Obviously, other combinations of shapes can also produce uniqueness.

With different forms of the potential surprise density function, such as the back-to-back elongated S-shape of Figures 3-3 and 4-1, and reproduced and labeled f in Figure 5-8, and with other kinds of attractiveness functions, the questions of existence and uniqueness of constrained maxima become more complex and affirmative answers to them more problematical. In Figure 5-8, for example, a unique constrained maximum exists over $\Psi_b^+ \times \Xi$ because the curvature of the iso-attractiveness contours (labeled g) relative to the density function is sharp enough to permit it. But with the potential surprise density function crossing each iso-attractiveness contour at a single point, and with all of these curves (including the graph of the density function) asymptotic to the line $\xi = 1$, no unique constrained maximum can exist over $\Psi_b^- \times \Xi$. (Here, too, directions of increasing attractiveness are down and to the right on $\Psi_b^+ \times \Xi$ and down and to the left on $\Psi_b^- \times \Xi$.) Still other iso-attractiveness contours and potential surprise density functions can result in corner solutions (recall Example 2). When constrained maxima exist that are not unique, the present model needs to be enriched if it is to determine, and hence explain, the decision of the decision-maker. Of course, if constrained maxima do not even exist, then the model is incapable of explaining any decisions at all.[12]

As suggested earlier, the comparative statics analysis of the constrained maximization of the attractiveness function is concerned with determining, when possible, the signs of the derivatives of ψ_b^-, ξ_b^-, ψ_b^+, and ξ_b^+ with respect to b. (Recall [5.1.1-2], [5.1.2-1], [5.1.3-2], [5.1.4-1], and [5.1.5-4].) In terms of finite changes, and in reference to earlier diagrams depicting the outcome of constrained-attractiveness maximization, small variations in b shift both the potential surprise density curve and the iso-attractiveness contours tangent to it. Thus the focus of such comparative statics analysis is to discover the direction of the movement of the variable values in the focus gain and focus loss as the constrained-attractiveness-maximizing point modifies in response to alterations in b. For this purpose, inequality (4.3-5) is hereafter taken to be satisfied for all b in B and ψ, where $\psi_b^- \leq \psi \leq \psi_b^+$ (recall that b is a surrogate for x), and the derivatives of appropriate functions and the relevant unique maxima are assumed to exist. In addition, for reasons of simplicity, only attractiveness functions g that are independent of b, like those of Examples 1 through 5, are considered.

To derive general formulas for the derivatives of ψ_b^-, ξ_b^-, ψ_b^+, and ξ_b^+

---

[12]Similar assertions, of course, apply to traditional models of decision making.

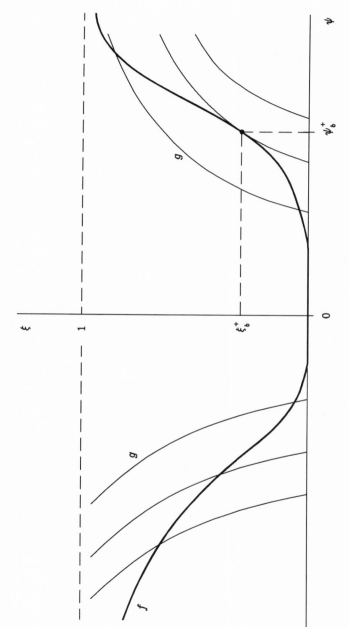

Figure 5–8. Existence and lack thereof of unique constrained maxima of the attractiveness function.

with respect to b (of which the examples in previous sections provide specific illustrations), recall the suggestion in Section 4.3 that, given b in the interior of B, the conditions defining a constrained maximum of the attractiveness function are, by Lagrange's theorem,

$$-\lambda f_\psi(\psi, b) + g_\psi(\psi, \xi) = 0,$$

$$\lambda + g_\xi(\psi, \xi) = 0, \qquad (5.2\text{-}1)$$

$$f(\psi, b) = \xi,$$

where λ is a Lagrange multiplier dependent on b. Dividing the second equation of (5.2-1) into the first (when $g_\xi(\psi, \xi) \neq 0$) yields

$$f_\psi(\psi, b) = -\frac{g_\psi(\psi, \xi)}{g_\xi(\psi, \xi)}, \qquad (5.2\text{-}2)$$

which says that, given b, at constrained maxima, iso-attractiveness contours have the same slopes as the potential surprise density curve. (This, of course, is identical to equation [4.3-6] with slightly altered notation.) When possible, solving (5.2-2) together with the last equation of (5.2-1) expresses the constrained maximizing values of ψ and ξ, the focus gain and focus loss, as functions of b. Note that for every b in the interior of B there is one system (5.2-1) defined on $\Psi_b^+ \times \Xi$ and one defined on $\Psi_b^- \times \Xi$, each reflecting the constrained maximization of a different branch of the attractiveness function.

Assuming the required derivatives and the above solutions exist, differentiate (5.2-1) with respect to b and eliminate λ and $f_\psi(\psi, b)$ by substitution from (5.2-1) and (5.2-2). This gives

$$\frac{g_\psi}{g_\xi}\lambda_b + (g_{\psi\psi} + g_\xi f_{\psi\psi})\frac{\partial \psi}{\partial b} + g_{\psi\xi}\frac{\partial \xi}{\partial b} = -g_\xi f_{\psi b},$$

$$\lambda_b \qquad\qquad + g_{\xi\psi}\frac{\partial \psi}{\partial b} + g_{\xi\xi}\frac{\partial \xi}{\partial b} = \quad 0,$$

$$-\frac{g_\psi}{g_\xi}\frac{\partial \psi}{\partial b} \quad - \frac{\partial \xi}{\partial b} = -f_b,$$

where functional arguments have been dropped to simplify notation and λ_b is the first-order partial derivative of λ with respect to b. From Cramer's rule (with $g_{\psi\xi} = g_{\xi\psi}$) and (5.2-2),

$$\frac{\partial\psi}{\partial b} = -\frac{f_b g_{\psi\xi} + g_\xi f_{\psi b} + f_\psi f_b g_{\xi\xi}}{(1/g_\xi)^2 \left([g_\xi]^2[g_{\psi\psi} + g_\xi f_{\psi\psi}] - 2g_\psi g_\xi g_{\psi\xi} + [g_\psi]^2 g_{\xi\xi}\right)}, \quad (5.2\text{-}3)$$

$$\frac{\partial\xi}{\partial b} = \frac{f_\psi f_b g_{\psi\xi} + f_b g_{\psi\psi} + g_\xi f_b f_{\psi\psi} + g_\psi f_{\psi b}}{(1/g_\xi)^2 \left([g_\xi]^2[g_{\psi\psi} + g_\xi f_{\psi\psi}] - 2g_\psi g_\xi g_{\psi\xi} + [g_\psi]^2 g_{\xi\xi}\right)}. \quad (5.2\text{-}4)$$

As indicated above, equations (5.2-3) and (5.2-4) have different expressions on $\Psi_b^+ \times \Xi$ and $\Psi_b^- \times \Xi$ for each b in the interior of B. Both are well defined as long as their denominators, as is assumed here, do not vanish.

The partial derivatives of ψ and ξ with respect to b, as determined in (5.2-3) and (5.2-4), are not possible to sign in general. Even if, around the maxima, (i) the potential surprise density function were convex with $f_{\psi\psi} \geq 0$, (ii) the attractiveness function were strictly quasi concave with $g_\xi < 0$, and (iii) the bordered Hessian determinant[13]

$$(g_\xi)^2 g_{\psi\psi} - 2g_\psi g_\xi g_{\psi\xi} + (g_\psi)^2 g_{\xi\xi} < 0,$$

thus implying that the denominators in (5.2-3) and (5.2-4) were negative, the signs in the numerator could still go either way. The same would be true if the convexity of the density function were strict with $f_{\psi\psi} > 0$. However, there are several situations of immediate interest, some based on quite modest generalizations of Examples 1 through 4, in which (5.2-3) and (5.2-4) can be signed.[14] These results, moreover, lead, occasionally under extra conditions, to conclusions concerning the outcome of the decision-index-maximization problem. This latter analysis is based on differentiation of the decision index

$$D(b) = Q(\psi_b^-, \xi_b^-, \psi_b^+, \xi_b^+),$$

---

[13]The strict quasi concavity of (ii) only ensures that this bordered Hessian determinant is nonpositive.

[14]Example 5 is not relevant to subsequent discussion because it turns out not to satisfy certain required conditions.

leading to

$$\frac{\partial D(b)}{\partial b} = \frac{\partial Q(\psi_b^-, \xi_b^-, \psi_b^+, \xi_b^+)}{\partial \psi_b^-} \frac{\partial \psi_b^-}{\partial b} + \frac{\partial Q(\psi_b^-, \xi_b^-, \psi_b^+, \xi_b^+)}{\partial \xi_b^-} \frac{\partial \xi_b^-}{\partial b}$$

$$\qquad (5.2\text{-}5)$$

$$+ \frac{\partial Q(\psi_b^-, \xi_b^-, \psi_b^+, \xi_b^+)}{\partial \psi_b^+} \frac{\partial \psi_b^+}{\partial b} + \frac{\partial Q(\psi_b^-, \xi_b^-, \psi_b^+, \xi_b^+)}{\partial \xi_b^+} \frac{\partial \xi_b^+}{\partial b}$$

for all interior b in B. (The function D is assumed to be continuous on B and continuously differentiable in its interior.) The partial derivative notation is used to the left of the equal sign in (5.2-5) because there may be parameters implicit in D with respect to which other partial derivatives can be taken (recall Examples 3 and 4). The comparative statics analyses and their implications for both the decision-index and the constrained-attractiveness-maximization problems developed here are provided in the following propositions. To maintain consistency with the examples of Section 5.1, in all cases B is taken to be an interval subset of $[0,1]$ that contains its right-hand endpoint, namely, 1.

Theorem 5.2-6. *With b in the interior of B, let $g_{\psi\psi} = g_{\psi\xi} = g_{\xi\xi} = 0$ and $g_\xi \neq 0$ in neighborhoods of the maxima (ψ_b^+, ξ_b^+) in $\Psi_b^+ \times \Xi$ and (ψ_b^-, ξ_b^-) in $\Psi_b^- \times \Xi$. If $f_{\psi\psi} > 0$ at (ψ_b^+, b) and (ψ_b^-, b), then*

$$(i) \quad \frac{\partial \psi_b^+}{\partial b} \gtrless 0 \quad and \quad \frac{\partial \psi_b^-}{\partial b} \gtrless 0, \quad according\ as \quad f_{\psi b} \lessgtr 0$$

at, respectively, (ψ_b^+, b) and (ψ_b^-, b), and

$$(ii) \quad \frac{\partial \xi_b^+}{\partial b} \gtrless 0 \quad and \quad \frac{\partial \xi_b^-}{\partial b} \gtrless 0, \quad according\ as \quad f_b f_{\psi\psi} - f_\psi f_{\psi b} \gtrless 0$$

at (ψ_b^+, b) and (ψ_b^-, b), respectively.

Proof:
Substituting $g_{\psi\psi} = g_{\psi\xi} = g_{\xi\xi} = 0$ into (5.2-3) and (5.2-4) gives, respectively,

$$\frac{\partial \psi}{\partial b} = -(g_\xi)^2 \frac{f_{\psi b}}{f_{\psi\psi}},$$

$$\frac{\partial \xi}{\partial b} = (g_\xi)^2 \frac{f_b f_{\psi\psi} - f_\psi f_{\psi b}}{f_{\psi\psi}}.$$

Hence, since $g_\xi \neq 0$ and $f_{\psi\psi} > 0$, the sign of $\partial \psi / \partial b$ in both $\Psi_b^+ \times \Xi$ and $\Psi_b^- \times \Xi$ is opposite that of $f_{\psi b}$ and the sign of $\partial \xi / \partial b$ in both $\Psi_b^+ \times \Xi$ and $\Psi_b^- \times \Xi$ is the same as that of $f_b f_{\psi\psi} - f_\psi f_{\psi b}$.

Q.E.D.

Theorem 5.2-6 is illustrated by, and is only slightly more general than, Examples 1 and 3. (That these examples satisfy the hypotheses of Theorem 5.2-6, and that Examples 2 and 4 satisfy the hypotheses of Theorem 5.2-7 as is indicated below, can readily be verified from Tables 5-1 through 5-4.) Its premise that $g_{\psi\psi} = g_{\psi\xi} = g_{\xi\xi} = 0$ locally around the focus gain and focus loss implies a linear attractiveness function in those regions, and its assumption that $f_{\psi\psi} > 0$ at (ψ_b^+, b) and (ψ_b^-, b) ensures a strictly convex potential surprise density function in neighborhoods of utility outcomes in the focus gain and focus loss. Note that Examples 1 and 3 have the property, included in Theorem 5.2-6, that $f_b f_{\psi\psi} = f_\psi f_{\psi b}$ at most points in $\Psi \times B$, thus rendering

$$\frac{\partial \xi_b^+}{\partial b} = \frac{\partial \xi_b^-}{\partial b} = 0.$$

(Recall [5.1.1-2] and [5.1.3-2].) In other words, the potential surprise values in the focus gain and focus loss are invariant with respect to transformations in the object of choice as reflected in the value of b.

Theorem 5.2-7. *With b in the interior of B, let $f_{\psi\psi} = f_{\psi b} = g_{\psi\psi} = g_{\xi\xi} = 0$, $g_{\psi\xi} \neq 0$, and $g_\xi \neq 0$ in neighborhoods of the maxima (ψ_b^+, ξ_b^+) in $\Psi_b^+ \times \Xi$ and (ψ_b^-, ξ_b^-) in $\Psi_b^- \times \Xi$. If $f_\psi > 0$ at (ψ_b^+, b), then*

$$\frac{\partial \psi_b^+}{\partial b} \underset{<}{\overset{>}{=}} 0 \quad and \quad \frac{\partial \xi_b^+}{\partial b} \underset{>}{\overset{<}{=}} 0, \quad according\ as \quad f_b \underset{>}{\overset{<}{=}} 0$$

at (ψ_b^+, b). Also, if $f_\psi < 0$ at (ψ_b^-, b), then

$$\frac{\partial \psi_b^-}{\partial b} \underset{<}{\overset{>}{=}} 0 \quad and \quad \frac{\partial \xi_b^-}{\partial b} \underset{<}{\overset{>}{=}} 0, \quad according\ as \quad f_b \underset{<}{\overset{>}{=}} 0$$

at (ψ_b^-, b).

Proof:

Substitution of $f_{\psi\psi} = f_{\psi b} = g_{\psi\psi} = g_{\xi\xi} = 0$ into (5.2-3) and (5.2-4), and noting that $g_{\psi\xi} \neq 0$ and $g_\xi \neq 0$,

$$\frac{\partial\psi}{\partial b} = -\frac{1}{2}\frac{f_b}{f_\psi},$$

$$\frac{\partial\xi}{\partial b} = \frac{1}{2}f_b.$$

Thus, with $f_\psi > 0$, the sign of $\partial\psi/\partial b$ in both $\Psi_b^+ \times \Xi$ and $\Psi_b^- \times \Xi$ is opposite that of f_b, and with $f_\psi < 0$ it is the same as that of f_b. In either case, the sign of $\partial\xi/\partial b$ in both $\Psi_b^+ \times \Xi$ and $\Psi_b^- \times \Xi$ is the same as that of f_b.

Q.E.D.

Analogously to Theorem 5.2-6, Examples 2 and 4 illustrate Theorem 5.2-7, and the situation described in that theorem is not much more general than that of the examples. The requirement that $f_{\psi\psi} = 0$ in neighborhoods of utility outcomes of the focus gain and focus loss means that, with respect to ψ, the potential surprise density function is linear there. Also, with f_ψ assumed positive at the utility outcome in the focus gain, the graph of this function is upward sloping at ψ_b^+; with $f_\psi < 0$ at the utility outcome in the focus loss, it necessarily slopes downward at ψ_b^-.

Corollary 5.2-8. *Let $f(\psi, b)$ be a family of dominating potential surprise density functions such that, for each b in B, $f_\psi(\psi, b) > 0$ on $\Psi_b^+ - N_b - M_b$ and $f_\psi(\psi, b) < 0$ on $\Psi_b^- - N_b - M_b$. Then, under the hypotheses of Theorem 5.2-7,*

$$\frac{\partial\psi_b^+}{\partial b} > 0, \qquad \frac{\partial\xi_b^+}{\partial b} < 0,$$

$$\frac{\partial\psi_b^-}{\partial b} > 0, \qquad \frac{\partial\xi_b^-}{\partial b} > 0.$$

Proof:

It follows from the definition of a family of dominating potential surprise density functions that $f_b(\psi_b^+, b) < 0$ and $f_b(\psi_b^-, b) > 0$. Now apply Theorem 5.2-7.

Q.E.D.

Corollary 5.2-9. *Let $f(\psi, b)$ be a family of nested potential surprise density functions such that, for each b in B, $f_\psi(\psi, b) > 0$ on $\Psi_b^+ - N_b - M_b$ and $f_\psi(\psi, b) < 0$ on $\Psi_b^- - N_b - M_b$. Then, under the hypotheses of Theorem 5.2-7,*

$$\frac{\partial \psi_b^+}{\partial b} > 0, \qquad \frac{\partial \xi_b^+}{\partial b} < 0,$$

$$\frac{\partial \psi_b^-}{\partial b} < 0, \qquad \frac{\partial \xi_b^-}{\partial b} < 0.$$

Proof:

From the definition of a family of nested potential surprise density functions, it follows that $f_b(\psi_b^+, b) < 0$ and $f_b(\psi_b^-, b) < 0$. Once again, apply Theorem 5.2-7.

Q.E.D.

Observe that the conditions $f_\psi(\psi, b) > 0$ on $\Psi_b^+ - N_b - M_b$ and $f_\psi(\psi, b) < 0$ on $\Psi_b^- - N_b - M_b$, for each b in B, in the hypotheses of Corollaries 5.2-8 and 5.2-9 assert that, where its slope is not zero, every potential surprise density curve obtained from the family $f(\psi, b)$ for b in B slopes, respectively, upward on the gain side and downward on the loss side. Example 2 illustrates Corollary 5.2-8, and Example 4 illustrates Corollary 5.2-9. Indeed, the conclusion of Corollary 5.2-8 is identical to (5.1.2-1), as the conclusion of Corollary 5.2-9 is identical to (5.1.4-1).

Note that, in general, even if they were weakened to allow for equality so as to accommodate, say, (5.1.1-2) of Example 1, dominance of potential surprise density functions does not, by itself, imply any of the inequalities of Corollary 5.2-8. The signs of the partial derivatives in that corollary typically depend on how the iso-attractiveness contours fit together with the potential surprise density functions as b increases.

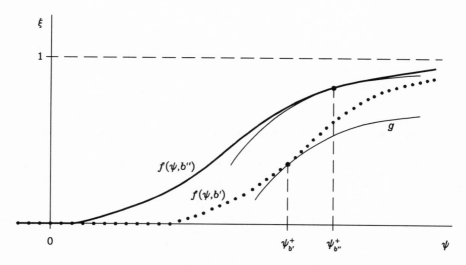

Figure 5-9.   Possible changes in constrained attractiveness
maximization with variation in b.

In this regard, recall that dominance is insufficient to ensure that the
density function moves rightward only by translation along the horizontal axis, as occurs in Examples 1 and 2. Rather, there is nothing to
prevent changes in shape from accompanying rightward shifts. Thus,
with $b' > b''$, it would be possible to have $\psi_{b'}^+ < \psi_{b''}^+$ as pictured in Figure
5-9, where $\psi_{b'}^+$ is the utility outcome in the focus gain associated with
b' and $\psi_{b''}^+$ is that associated with b''. Similarly, with different shapes
of the curves in Figure 5-9, $\xi_{b'}^+ > \xi_{b''}^+$ might occur, where $\xi_{b'}^+$ corresponds to b' and $\xi_{b''}^+$ to b''. In the same way, reversals of the inequalities
$\partial \psi_b^- / \partial b > 0$ and $\partial \xi_b^- / \partial b > 0$ could not be ruled out.

Theorem 5.2-10. *Let D be defined on B. For all b in the interior
of B, assume either the hypotheses of Theorem 5.2-6 with*

$$f_{\psi b} < 0 \ at \ all \ (\psi_b^+, b) \ and \ (\psi_b^-, b),$$
$$f_b f_{\psi \psi} - f_\psi f_{\psi b} \leq 0 \ at \ all \ (\psi_b^+, b), \ and$$
$$f_b f_{\psi \psi} - f_\psi f_{\psi b} \geq 0 \ at \ all \ (\psi_b^-, b),$$

or the hypotheses of Theorem 5.2-7 *with*

> *for each b in B, $f_\psi(\psi, b) > 0$ on $\Psi_b^+ - N_b - M_b$,*
> *for each b in B, $f_\psi(\psi, b) < 0$ on $\Psi_b^- - N_b - M_b$, and*
> *$f_b < 0$ at all (ψ_b^+, b) and $f_b > 0$ at all (ψ_b^-, b).*

Then, for all b in the interior of B, $\partial D(b)/\partial b > 0$, and $D(b)$ is uniquely maximized at $b = 1$.

Proof:

Under the first set of hypotheses, Theorem 5.2-6 implies $\partial \psi_b^- / \partial b > 0$, $\partial \xi_b^- / \partial b \geq 0$, $\partial \psi_b^+ / \partial b > 0$, and $\partial \xi_b^+ / \partial b \leq 0$. Under the second set of hypotheses, Theorem 5.2-7 yields the same inequalities except that all of them are strict. In either case, applying these inequalities and those of (5.1.1-3) to equation (5.2-5) gives $\partial D(b)/\partial b > 0$ for all b in the interior of B. Therefore $D(b)$ is uniquely maximized at the largest value of b in B or at $b = 1$.

Q.E.D.

Corollary 5.2-11. *Let $f(\psi, b)$ be a family of dominating potential surprise density functions. Then, under the hypotheses of Theorem 5.2-10, and for all b in the interior of B, $\partial D(b)/\partial b > 0$. Moreover, $D(b)$ is uniquely maximized at $b = 1$.*

Proof:

When the first collection of hypotheses of Theorem 5.2-10 are satisfied, there is nothing to prove. Otherwise, as in the proof of Corollary 5.2-8, it follows from the definition of a family of dominating potential surprise density functions that $f_b(\psi_b^+, b) < 0$ and $f_b(\psi_b^-, b) > 0$. Now apply Theorem 5.2-10 using the second collection of hypotheses.

Q.E.D.

Of course, the first group of three conditions (which go with the hypotheses of Theorem 5.2-6) listed in Theorem 5.2-10 identifies a special case of Theorem 5.2-6, while the second group points to a special case of Theorem 5.2-7. Note that Example 1 satisfies

> $f_{\psi b} < 0$ at all (ψ_b^+, b) and (ψ_b^-, b),
> $f_b f_{\psi\psi} - f_\psi f_{\psi b} = 0$ at all (ψ_b^+, b), and
> $f_b f_{\psi\psi} - f_\psi f_{\psi b} = 0$ at all (ψ_b^-, b),

and therefore illustrates Theorem 5.2-10 with the first collection of hypotheses. But Example 3 has $f_{\psi b} > 0$ at all (ψ_b^-, b) and does not illustrate the theorem. Similarly, Example 2 fulfills

$$\text{for each } b \text{ in } B, \ f_\psi(\psi, b) > 0 \text{ on } \Psi_b^+ - N_b - M_b,$$
$$\text{for each } b \text{ in } B, \ f_\psi(\psi, b) < 0 \text{ on } \Psi_b^- - N_b - M_b, \text{ and}$$
$$f_b < 0 \text{ at all } (\psi_b^+, b) \text{ and } \ f_b > 0 \text{ at all } (\psi_b^-, b),$$

and illustrates Theorem 5.2-10 with the second collection of hypotheses. Example 4 cannot illustrate the theorem since $f_b < 0$ at all (ψ_b^-, b). Both Example 1 and Example 2 illustrate Corollary 5.2-11.

Theorem 5.2-10 and Corollary 5.2-11 also suggest another notion of dominance with respect to the objects of choice. For all surrogates b' and b'' in B, refer to b' as *dominating* b'' provided that $D(b') > D(b'')$. Of course, the same notion could be expressed in terms of x' and x'' in X, where $b' = \gamma(x')$ and $b'' = \gamma(x'')$. In general, neither kind of dominance implies the other. But under the hypotheses of the corollary, $f(\psi, b')$ dominates $f(\psi, b'')$ if and only if b' dominates b''. This result arises in constructing an example of a normatively operational decision rule in Section 6.3.

Observe also that, even if dominance were maintained, as long as the remaining hypotheses of Corollary 5.2-11 were not in force it would be possible for the selected value of b to be less than the maximum b in B or unity. This could happen if it turned out that, say,

$$\frac{\partial \psi_b^+}{\partial b} < 0, \qquad \frac{\partial \xi_b^+}{\partial b} > 0,$$

$$\frac{\partial \psi_b^-}{\partial b} > 0, \qquad \frac{\partial \xi_b^-}{\partial b} > 0,$$

a circumstance alluded to above. In that event, the inequalities of (5.1.1-3) would imply that (5.2-5) contains two positive and two negative terms. Therefore, the weighting of the components of the focus gain and focus loss in Q could be such as to produce a chosen value of b for which $b < 1$.

The next proposition essentially says that if, for b in B, the iso-attractiveness contours and the portion of the potential surprise density curve on the loss side are reflections, with respect to the ξ-axis, of those contours and that part of the density curve on the gain side, then so are the components of the focus loss in that reflective relation to the components of the focus gain. It is illustrated by Example 3.

Theorem 5.2-12. *Let $f(\psi, b)$ be a symmetric family of potential surprise density functions and $g(\psi, \xi)$ be a symmetric attractiveness function for all b in B. If ψ_b^+, ξ_b^+, ψ_b^-, and ξ_b^- exist uniquely for every b in B, then*

$$\psi_b^+ = -\psi_b^- \qquad and \qquad \xi_b^+ = \xi_b^-$$

for all b in B.

Proof:
From the definitions of the symmetry of f and g,

$$f(\psi, b) = f(-\psi, b) \tag{5.2-13}$$

and

$$g(\psi, \xi) = g(-\psi, \xi)$$

over, respectively, $\Psi \times B$, and $\Psi_b^+ \times \Xi$ and $\Psi_b^- \times \Xi$. Hence on the interiors of these latter sets,

$$f_\psi(\psi, b) = -f_\psi(-\psi, b), \tag{5.2-14}$$

$$g_\psi(\psi, \xi) = -g_\psi(-\psi, \xi), \tag{5.2-15}$$

$$g_\xi(\psi, \xi) = g_\xi(-\psi, \xi). \tag{5.2-16}$$

Now, as pointed out in conjunction with (5.2-2), for all b in the interior of B, ψ_b^+ and ξ_b^+ are solutions of the system

$$f_\psi(\psi, b) = -\frac{g_\psi(\psi, \xi)}{g_\xi(\psi, \xi)},$$

$$\xi = f(\psi, b), \tag{5.2-17}$$

on $\Psi_b^+ \times \Xi$. But, in light of (5.2-13) through (5.2-16), system (5.2-17) is equivalent to the identical system on $\Psi_b^- \times \Xi$, whose solution is ψ_b^- and ξ_b^-. Therefore, $\psi_b^+ = -\psi_b^-$ and $\xi_b^+ = \xi_b^-$.

$$\text{Q.E.D.}$$

Theorem 5.2-18. *Under the hypotheses of Theorem 5.2-12, assume*

$$\frac{\partial \psi_b^+}{\partial b} \neq 0 \qquad and \qquad \frac{\partial Q}{\partial \xi_b^+} = -\frac{\partial Q}{\partial \xi_b^-}$$

everywhere. Then $D(b)$ has a critical value at b^0 in the interior of B if and only if, at the values of ψ_b^+, ξ_b^+, ψ_b^-, and ξ_b^- associated with b^0,

$$\frac{\partial Q}{\partial \psi_b^+} = \frac{\partial Q}{\partial \psi_b^-}.$$

Moreover, if all second-order, cross-partial derivatives of Q vanish identically, then a sufficient condition for the critical point b^0 to identify a unique maximum is that

$$\frac{\partial^2 Q}{\partial (\psi_b^+)^2} + \frac{\partial^2 Q}{\partial (\psi_b^-)^2} < 0$$

at the values of ψ_b^+, ξ_b^+, ψ_b^-, and ξ_b^- associated with b^0.

Proof:
Since $\partial Q/\xi_b^+ = -\partial Q/\xi_b^-$, and since, from Theorem 5.2-12, it follows that

$$\frac{\partial \psi_b^+}{\partial b} = -\frac{\partial \psi_b^-}{\partial b} \qquad and \qquad \frac{\partial \xi_b^+}{\partial b} = \frac{\partial \xi_b^-}{\partial b}, \qquad (5.2\text{-}19)$$

equation (5.2-5) reduces to

$$\frac{\partial D(b)}{\partial b} = \left(\frac{\partial Q}{\partial \psi_b^+} - \frac{\partial Q}{\partial \psi_b^-} \right) \frac{\partial \psi_b^+}{\partial b}. \qquad (5.2\text{-}20)$$

Therefore, because $\partial \psi_b^+/\partial b \neq 0$, $\partial D(b^0)/\partial b = 0$ if and only if, at those values of ψ_b^+, ξ_b^+, ψ_b^-, and ξ_b^- associated with b^0,

$$\frac{\partial Q}{\partial \psi_b^+} = \frac{\partial Q}{\partial \psi_b^-}. \qquad (5.2\text{-}21)$$

Now, with all second-order cross-partial derivatives of Q vanishing identically, further differentiation of (5.2-20) leads to

$$\frac{\partial^2 D(b)}{\partial b^2} = \left(\frac{\partial Q}{\partial \psi_b^+} - \frac{\partial Q}{\partial \psi_b^-} \right) \frac{\partial^2 \psi_b^+}{\partial b^2} + \left(\frac{\partial^2 Q}{\partial (\psi_b^+)^2} \frac{\partial \psi_b^+}{\partial b} - \frac{\partial^2 Q}{\partial (\psi_b^-)^2} \frac{\partial \psi_b^-}{\partial b} \right) \frac{\partial \psi_b^+}{\partial b}.$$

Setting $b = b^0$, and using (5.2-19) and (5.2-21), this becomes

$$\frac{\partial^2 D(b)}{\partial b^2} = \left(\frac{\partial^2 Q}{\partial (\psi_b^+)^2} + \frac{\partial^2 Q}{\partial (\psi_b^-)^2} \right) \left(\frac{\partial \psi_b^+}{\partial b} \right)^2.$$

Hence, since $\partial \psi_b^+ / \partial b \neq 0$, to have b^0 associated with a unique maximum of $D(b)$ over B, that is, to have $\partial^2 D(b^0)/\partial b^2 < 0$, it is sufficient that

$$\frac{\partial^2 Q}{\partial (\psi_b^+)^2} + \frac{\partial^2 Q}{\partial (\psi_b^-)^2} < 0.$$

Q.E.D.

Theorem 5.2-18 clearly builds on Theorem 5.2-12 and is also illustrated by Example 3. Its hypothesis requiring

$$\frac{\partial Q}{\partial \xi_b^+} = - \frac{\partial Q}{\partial \xi_b^-}$$

everywhere implies that, with respect to the function values of Q, identical changes in ξ_b^+ and ξ_b^- exactly cancel each other out. In addition, the assumption that all second-order cross-partial derivatives of Q vanish identically forces Q to be additive but not necessarily linear.

Theorem 5.2-22. *Replace ξ in g with $a\xi$, where $a > 0$ is a parameter. For each a, let b be in the interior of B, and let $f_{\psi\psi} = g_{\psi\psi} = g_{\xi\xi} = 0$ and $g_{\psi\xi} \neq 0$ in neighborhoods of the maxima (ψ_b^+, ξ_b^+) in $\Psi_b^+ \times \Xi$ and (ψ_b^-, ξ_b^-) in $\Psi_b^- \times \Xi$. Also, for each a, let $g_{\psi\xi} < 0$, $g_{\psi a} < 0$, and $g_{\xi a} < 0$ at (ψ_b^+, ξ_b^+), and $g_{\psi\xi} > 0$, $g_{\psi a} > 0$, and $g_{\xi a} < 0$ at (ψ_b^-, ξ_b^-). If $f_\psi > 0$ at (ψ_b^+, b), then*

$$\frac{\partial \psi_b^+}{\partial a} < 0 \qquad and \qquad \frac{\partial \xi_b^+}{\partial a} < 0.$$

Furthermore, if $f_\psi < 0$ at (ψ_b^-, b), then

$$\frac{\partial \psi_b^-}{\partial a} > 0 \qquad and \qquad \frac{\partial \xi_b^-}{\partial a} < 0.$$

Proof:
Differentiating (5.2-1) with respect to a, using (5.2-1) and (5.2-2) to eliminate λ and f_ψ, solving by Cramer's rule to obtain expressions for $\partial\psi/\partial a$ and $\partial\xi/\partial a$, and substituting $f_{\psi\psi} = g_{\psi\psi} = g_{\xi\xi} = 0$ into the results (with the remaining derivatives nonvanishing as required by the hypotheses of the theorem), gives

$$\frac{\partial\psi}{\partial a} = -\frac{f_\psi g_{\xi a} - g_{\psi a}}{2 f_\psi g_{\psi\xi}}, \tag{5.2-23}$$

$$\frac{\partial\xi}{\partial a} = -\frac{f_\psi g_{\xi a} - g_{\psi a}}{2 g_{\psi a}}. \tag{5.2-24}$$

The inequality hypotheses of the theorem now imply the desired results.
Q.E.D.

With its supposition that $f_{\psi\psi} = g_{\psi\psi} = g_{\xi\xi} = 0$, Theorem 5.2-22 is only slightly more general than Example 4, which illustrates it. Although the next (and last) proposition indicates, under certain conditions, how a affects the optimal value of b (and hence, through γ, the selection of x in X), and although it, too, is illustrated by Example 4, the theorem need not necessarily be regarded as a continuation of, or related to, Theorem 5.2-22. Indeed, Examples 1 and 3, neither of which satisfies the hypotheses of Theorem 5.2-22, still illustrate Theorem 5.2-25. Remember also that in a certain special situation a will be interpreted in terms of uncertainty aversion and favor by the decision maker in the next chapter.

Theorem 5.2-25. *Replace ξ in g by $a\xi$, where $a > 0$ is a parameter that also appears as a parameter of D. For each a, let a value for b exist in the interior of B that uniquely maximizes $D(b, a)$ as a function of b. Denote these maximizing values, dependent on a, by the variable b^0. Assume*

$$\frac{\partial^2 D(b, a)}{\partial b^2} < 0$$

for all b in the interior B. Then

$$\frac{\partial b^0}{\partial a} \gtrless 0 \quad \text{according as} \quad \frac{\partial^2 D(b^0, a)}{\partial b \partial a} \gtrless 0.$$

Proof:

Since, for each value of a, $D(b, a)$, as a function of b, has a unique maximum at b^0 in the interior of B,

$$\frac{\partial D(b^0, a)}{\partial b} = 0.$$

Differentiation of this result with respect to a yields

$$\frac{\partial b^0}{\partial a} = -\frac{\partial^2 D(b^0, a)}{\partial b \partial a} \bigg/ \frac{\partial^2 D(b^0, a)}{\partial b^2}.$$

Since the denominator is assumed to be negative, $\partial b^0 / \partial a$ has the same sign as $\partial^2 D(b^0, a)/\partial b \partial a$.

Q.E.D.

Additional sufficient conditions that permit the signing of (5.2-3) and (5.2-4) (as well as other derivatives of the elements of the focus gain and focus loss, such as, for example, [5.2-23] and [5.2-24]), and further theorems concerning the comparative statics of the decision-index-maximization problem, although likely to be more complex, are certainly conceivable. And the exploration of such conditions and propositions can only enrich the comparative static analysis of the model and thereby improve understanding of it. Moreover, and more generally, although the meaning, significance, and applicability of the comparative statics results developed for environments that allow for historical time, uncertainty, and ignorance are quite different from those of comparative statics explorations in more traditional models, it is clear that the possibilities for doing such analyses are every bit as rich as with any traditional model. Moving into the nonequilibrium domain of historical time, uncertainty, and ignorance, then, does not destroy the economist's ability to pursue this kind of endeavor.

Given the logical properties of the model of decision making in ignorance of Section 4.3 and the foregoing illustrative development of it, there remain the important questions of the model's operationality and the use to which it can be put in actual decision making. These issues will be addressed in the next chapter.

5.3   References

1. Deaton, A., and J. Muellbauer, *Economics and Consumer Behavior* (Cambridge: Cambridge University Press, 1980).

2. Katzner, D. W., *Static Demand Theory* (New York: Macmillan, 1970).

3. Theil, H., and K. W. Clements, *Applied Demand Analysis* (Cambridge: Ballinger, 1987).

CHAPTER 6

Operationality

To an economist, an analysis or theory is *operational* if it is demonstrably relevant to the real world or, in other words, if it relates, in some appropriate way, to real phenomena. There are at least two senses in which the operationality inherent in a theory can be understood. On the one hand, the analysis may have some competence to shed light on actually observable economic behavior. That is, it may contain assertions or propositions that, in the words of Hutchison, are conceivably capable of empirical testing or are reducible to such propositions by deduction.

> They need not . . . actually be tested or even be *practically* [*sic*] capable of testing under present or future technical conditions or conditions of statistical investigation, nor is there any sense in talking of some kind of "absolute" test which will "finally" decide whether a proposition is "absolutely" true or false. But it must be possible to indicate intersubjectively what is the case if they are true or false: their truth or falsity, that is, must make some conceivable empirically noticeable difference, or some such difference must be directly deducible therefrom. [6, pp. 9-10]

Samuelson clearly had such a notion in mind when he spoke of "operationally meaningful theorems" [13, p. 3]. This kind of operationality is henceforth referred to as *positive* operationality.

This chapter is reproduced, with considerable additions, corrections, and other modifications, from my "Operationality in the Shackle-Vickers Approach to Decision-Making in Ignorance," *Journal of Post Keynesian Economics* 15 (1992-93), pp. 229-254.

Of course, the result of an empirical test of a positively operational theory cannot establish that theory as the single correct analysis of the phenomenon in question. Such a test is only capable of concluding that, according to suitable criteria, the propositions of, or the implications drawn from those propositions in, the theory are or are not consistent with the data presented. In the latter case, the theory is falsified. In the former, the theory can be employed as an explanation of the data or, alternatively put, the data may be understood as if they were generated in accordance with the manner suggested by theory. But, even so, there may still, in this case, be other explanations as well. Thus, for example, consumer demand functions that satisfy Slutsky symmetry and negative definiteness, and other well-known conditions, can be explained by models based (a) on preference orderings having ordinary indifference curves, (b) on preference orderings with pseudo-indifference curves, (c) on ordinal or cardinal utility, or (d) on Lancaster-type characteristics.[1]

On the other hand, the analysis or theory may be operational in that it establishes propositions indicating what action ought to be taken in order to achieve the most desirable, or in some sense the best, outcome. That is, it provides optimization decision criteria for making decisions and determining (observable) behaviors in actual situations. Thus, for example, traditional theory asserts that the profit-maximizing firm ought to produce that output that equates marginal cost to marginal revenue and, in the selection of a portfolio of risky assets whose income streams are not perfectly correlated, the risk-minimizing (for a given rate of return) investor should diversify. Rules of thumb such as these tell the decision maker what ought to be done to be "rational," and operationality in this less commonly discussed, though still important, form is called *normative* operationality. Normatively operational criteria may, as in the above examples, or may not be positively operational. The only way to discover if an individual is actually using a particular normatively operational criterion to guide his behavior is to ask him. Obviously the ability to question and obtain meaningful answers is not sufficient to imply positive operationality. However, it should be noted that, although not necessarily amenable to statistical analysis, direct questioning is a perfectly valid method of ascertaining what the indi-

---

[1]*E.g.*, Katzner [8].

vidual thinks he is doing. Moreover, a "yes" answer to the question "Are you using criterion Γ?" implies not only that the individual believes he is behaving as if he were following Γ (such a conclusion, if accurate, remember, is all that is sought from models that are positively operational), but also that the criterion represents exactly what, in fact, he thinks he does. With an "I do not know" answer, clearly, or without the ability to question him and extract meaningful answers, the only recourse left to the investigator is to infer the intent of his subject by imagining, on the basis of his own (*i.e.*, the investigator's) introspection, what would most likely have been the motivating force of the subject's action. In any event, it is evident that normative operationality may imply a different relation between a theory and reality than does positive operationality.

Admittedly, the examples given above are taken from models or submodels of equilibrium analysis. That analysis, as indicated earlier, implicitly assumes that time is logical and that all decision makers have perfect knowledge (with respect to all relevant matters), at least probabilistically, of the past, present, and future. If these implicit assumptions are accepted as reasonable approximations of reality, then the positive and normative operationality of much of traditional theory, falling, as it does, within the realm of equilibrium analysis, is unquestionable. To illustrate, the utility-maximization model of consumer behavior is positively operational in that it leads to observable properties of demand, such as the symmetry and negative definiteness of matrices of Slutsky functions, which are, at least in principle, empirically testable. And it is normatively operational in its establishment of equality between marginal rates of substitution and price ratios as a criterion for achieving constrained maximum utility. But if one embraces the nonequilibrium perspective of this volume, namely, that time, in actuality, is not logical and that the knowledge possessed by individuals is not perfect, then a significant part of the assumption content of traditional theory is not in accord with, and indeed appears to directly contradict, reality. In that case, the operationality of traditional theory (*i.e.*, its "demonstrable relevance" to the real world) in both positive and normative senses is opened to doubt. Thus, referring in particular to positive operationality, an empirical test that "accepts" the presence of, say, Slutsky symmetry in observed demand behavior, either may have produced that result by accident or the test may not be fine enough to result in rejection. Alternatively, with respect to normative operationality, the criterion of equating marginal rates of substitution to price ratios may be inappropriate because it applies to an unreal world. Therefore, the answer to the question of whether a particular analysis is operational in any sense depends implicitly and critically on the acceptance or rejection of the relevance of the assumption content of that analysis as consistent with reality.

The purpose of this chapter is to explore the extent to which the present model of decision making, as developed in Section 4.3, is operational in the context of historical time and ignorance in which it is set. Shackle's original model, which, recall, is the foundation for the present one, has been criticized by Arrow [1, p. 434], Ozga [12, pp. 213-215], and others because, as applied to the problem of portfolio choice, it cannot explain, when there are more than two assets, the observed fact that people tend to select portfolios that are diversified. That is, diversification could not arise as an outcome of Shackle's model and could not, therefore, be rational. In addition, Ozga called it ". . . a conceptual framework which if generally accepted might help us to understand better each other when we speak of expectations and decisions about strategies" but then went on to assert that the requisite acceptance is unlikely to occur [12, p. 223]. Both complaints could be interpreted to have their roots in the operationality, or lack thereof, of the model. In spite of the fact that, by not summing the standardized focus gains and losses of each asset to obtain the focus gain and loss of the portfolio as a whole, and by eliminating the "gambler's indifference map," the present version of the model avoids the conclusion that diversification is not rational,[2] the question of its operationality remains.[3] In what

---

[2]This is established in Section 10.2. As explained by Ozga [12, pp. 213-215], the summing of the standardized focus gains and losses and the use of the gambler's indifference map in Shackle's original model led to the absence of diversification in it.

[3]Even though, when applied to the problem of portfolio selection, every choice option includes a nonnegative quantity of each asset as a separate component (at least in the approach of Section 10.2), and hence, since there are an immensely large number of assets in reality, the practicality of this application has yet to be established, subsequent discussion argues that the present model of decision making in ignorance is both positively and normatively operational. As suggested by the

follows, then, the positive operationality of the model is taken up first (Sections 6.1 and 6.2) and is illustrated, in part, by the application of a special case of the model to explain certain observed savings behavior of individuals in terms of one form of uncertainty aversion and favor. Section 6.3 examines the model's normative operationality.

6.1 Positive Operationality

The behavior to be explained by the model of Section 4.3 takes place in historical time and under conditions of human ignorance. Remember that to say time is historical means that each moment is unique, with its own special properties, its own special events, and its own special history. Individuals at that moment have unique and nonreplicable epistemic abilities, perceptions, and expectations, and hence decision makers necessarily face unique decision moments that can never exactly reappear in their original form. Moreover, the taking of a decision and the actions that follow from it may change the structure of the economic environment, including the decision maker's endowment and his possible scope for action, in such a way that the taking of the same decision may not be contemplatable again. Shackle, recall, referred to such decisions as self-destructive. Thus the relations of any model, as well as the model itself, depend critically on the particular moment of time at issue. Vary that moment and the presumption must be that, to understand behavior at the new moment, the existing analytical content requires modification. From the nonequilibrium perspective, then, historical time would appear to be more relevant to the analysis of actual human experience than the notion of logical time that is employed in more standard inquiry. In the latter (*i.e.*, the standard) context, the moment of real time is irrelevant to the content and outcome of the analysis.

Remember also that, in the nonequilibrium context, ignorance arises due to human limitations. That is to say, using Loasby's words [11, p. 3], the rationality of mankind is necessarily bounded rationality. Because reality is so complex, decision makers cannot have more than partial,

---

quotation attributed to Hutchison at the beginning of the chapter, operationality should not be confused with practicality.

possibly incorrect, perceptions or knowledge about relevant behavioral happenings of the past and the present. Nor can they know anything at all about the content of such matters as it will arise in the future. Indeed, due to the uniqueness of the decision moment and a genuine ignorance, and hence uncertainty, about the future, the decision maker cannot even describe the possible outcomes that the future might bequeath in terms of a probability calculus that leads to an imagined and manipulable probability distribution or density function. Therefore, rather than approximating the typically assumed situation of perfect knowledge, decision makers are actually faced with considerable ignorance and all of the uncertainty that that ignorance implies.

To be positively operational, the model of decision making in ignorance developed in Section 4.3 has to say something about the properties of observable behavior. The first question is, then, what potentially observable behavior emerges from decisions that are consistent with the model? Clearly, the potential surprise, utility, and attractiveness functions and the decision index exist only in the mind of the decision maker and are not observable. What is, of course, observable is the action taken and the seeable features of the decision environment that are (a) set by the economy independently of the decision maker and (b) those to which the action taken can be viewed as a direct response. To illustrate, suppose the decision maker is a typical consumer and the decisions to be made concern the selection of baskets of goods to consume. Ignore, for a minute, the uniqueness imposed on the moment of decision by the presence of historical time and the difficulty of knowing current prices and income, but still retain the uncertainty that arises from ignorance with respect to future states of the world. Assume that the utility provided by a given basket differs, as in the utility function of Section 4.3, depending on the future state that actually emerges at the moment of consumption. Imagine, further, for the sake of argument, that the consumer's choice set consists of vectors in a standard budget set, whose boundaries are determined by observable commodity prices and the consumer's observable income as dictated by the economy's markets. Given these prices and income, application of the present model would yield a vector of commodity demands, and hypothetically varying those prices and incomes would define demand functions analogous to those obtained from the constrained-utility-maximization procedure of the traditional theory of demand. Moreover, since a unique maximum of the decision index over the choice set would always need to exist, the decision index D would have to possess appropriate properties. One collection of properties that would do the job are the same properties customarily required of the utility function in the traditional theory mentioned above.[4] Were these latter properties forced on D by the assumed properties of the potential surprise, utility, and attractiveness functions of the model of Section 4.3, or were they independently imposed, then the observable properties of demand would be the same as those of the traditional model.[5] Therefore, under these suppositions, and subject to the previous conditions, the present model as applied to the analysis of consumer demand would appear to be positively operational with respect to the milieu of historical time and ignorance in the same manner as the traditional theory is positively operational in an environment in which logical time and perfect information are accepted as properties of reality.

There are, however, at least two difficulties with this argument that arise when full account is taken of the ignorance and historical time context, partly neglected by that argument, in which the model is set. First, because information is imperfect, the consumer cannot, in spite of the argument of the previous paragraph, be expected to have much knowledge concerning the prices he faces and the income, or total financial resources, he has, at the relevant moment, to spend.[6] Although he has, it may be supposed, perceptions of and assumptions about these prices and his income, he has no way of knowing how correct they are. Thus the prices and income actually determined in the economy may be, and in many situations are even likely to be, different from those perceived and assumed by him. Now it is clear that the consumer,

---

[4] Of course, this utility function is not the same as that employed in the model of decision making in ignorance of Section 4.3.

[5] Indeed, in terms of their demand behavior, the two models would be indistinguishable.

[6] The income the consumer actually winds up having to spend depends on the extent to which he is able to sell that portion of his endowment that he plans to sell and on the prices at which those sales take place. But, in general, none of the information on how these transactions, in fact, turn out is available to the consumer at the time he has to make his decision.

as a decision maker, has no recourse but to act on the basis of his
perceptions and his assumptions. These perceptions and assumptions,
however, are not observable. Nor can the relation between perceived
and assumed prices and income, on the one hand, and observed prices
and income, on the other, be knowable. It follows that the demand
functions described above are, when the full extent of the consumer's
ignorance is recognized, actually functions of perceived and assumed
market prices and income, and that observable demand functions (*i.e.*,
demand functions of observable prices and income) cannot be derived
from the historical time and ignorance version of the model of consumer
demand as outlined here.[7]

The second difficulty with the argument has to do with the partly
ignored presence of historical time. For, when time is fully historical,
each decision moment is unique in history and cannot be repeated.
Thus, within any specified decision moment, the decisions that produce the consumer demand functions described above must all occur
"simultaneously," and the demand functions themselves can be valid
and relevant only for that moment. It is not possible in constructing
these functions to give the consumer one set of prices and income at one
moment, ask him what he would buy, and then repeat at a later moment
the question for a different set of prices and income because the lapse of
time between the first and the second question transforms the decision
moment. At the time of the second question the consumer is (epistem-
ically and economically) a different person in a different environment,
with different potential surprise, utility, and attractiveness functions
and with a different decision index, and hence the answer to the second question is necessarily a part of a different collection of demand
functions than those to which the answer to the first relates. Therefore, even if the discrepancy between perceived and observed prices and
income were assumed away, it would still only be possible to observe
a single point on the consumer's demand functions because each moment of time permits but one observation of the consumer's behavior.
And this is certainly not enough to claim, as does the argument under
discussion, that the present model of consumer demand is positively

---

[7]In traditional analyses, by comparison, the assumption of perfect knowledge
implies that there is no difference between perceived and actual prices and incomes.

operational in the same sense as, given the usually accepted relevance of logical time and perfect knowledge, traditional demand theory.[8]

A similar conclusion emerges in reference to production, investment, and financial decisions in the firm. In general, then, application of the apparatus of Section 4.3 to any decision-making situation taking full cognizance of ignorance and historical time results in a model that, insofar as its positive operationality is concerned, is subject to these two characteristics. It is not possible to express the observable outcome of decision making in the model as a (behavioral) function of variables that are also fully observable and such that the function itself is observable through time. Inaccurate perceptions and assumptions of the decision maker distort the relation between the model and any observed behavioral function that could conceivably be generated by it and, regardless and independently of these inaccuracies, no more than one point on any such behavior function could ever be observed anyway. Although the construction of Section 4.3 was specifically created to handle environments incorporating ignorance and historical time, it is precisely the presence of that ignorance and historical time itself, and not so much the particulars of the model or any specific application of it, that causes the difficulties.

Note also that the use of the word "difficulties" here is not meant to be pejorative. Nor is it intended to suggest an impingement on the operationality (positive or normative) of the model of decision making in ignorance of Section 4.3. To the contrary, if one takes the position that the approach of Section 4.3 addresses a more realistic decision environment than does the traditional perspective, then a model based on the former would necessarily be recognized as taking certain elements of reality into account that one growing out of that latter could not. In this case, the model of Section 4.3 would, in spite of these "difficulties," be judged as having a more pervasive and significant operationality than traditional models.

But there is much more to be said in support of the assertion that the presence of the aforementioned difficulties does not vitiate the pos-

---

[8]Remember that the operationality (positive or normative) of any analysis rests, in part, on the acceptability of the assumption-content of that analysis as a "sufficiently accurate" description of reality.

itive operationality of the model developed in Section 4.3. At least two points may be made. First, as indicated at the outset, to be operational in the positive sense requires only that some assumed or implied aspects of the model be testable against observed behavior *in principle*. It is not necessary that appropriate tests be performed or even known; only the potential to falsify the theory in the light of reality must be maintained. Such tests might, under suitable conditions, be conceived of in cross-sectional terms, with one observation derived from each of an appropriate collection of cross-sectional units. Furthermore, it is very unusual in economics for anything to be actually falsified.[9] Even tests that seem to reveal "inconsistencies" with observations are often reworked to eliminate the problems or rationalized or ignored.[10] Indeed, Kuhn [10, pp. 33-37] has argued that, at least in the physical sciences, typical corroborative procedure does not involve testing at all. Rather, researchers seek "reasonable agreement" between observed data and theoretical propositions. What constitutes reasonable agreement is defined by the professional judgment of the persons doing the research and may vary from one area of investigation to another and across time. Thus, like the physical scientist, the economist too is really engaged in fitting models to data, and when, in a particular case, the fit does not seem so good, he works very hard to alter the model around the edges, locate errors in the data, and (or) adjust statistical procedures to improve it. It is only when he arrives at the judgment that all reasonable efforts have failed that he might conclude that the model has been falsified.

The requirements for positive operationality, then, are not as stringent as they might, at first, have seemed. All that is needed is to be able to compare suitable parts of the model with observed behav-

----

[9]See Caldwell [2, p. 157 and n. 47 on p. 171]. The counterfactual conclusion that, when there are more than two assets diversification in the selection of portfolios would not occur, arising, as indicated earlier, in the application of the original Shackle model to the problem of portfolio choice, is an exception. However, the use, in the portfolio selection context of Section 10.2, of the version of the model of Section 4.3 that, following Vickers [15, pp. 222-224], replaces Shackle's gambler's indifference map by a decision index, eliminates this lack of conformity with reality.

[10]See, for example, Theil's discussion of the "failure" of observed demand functions to satisfy the standard homogeneity and symmetry conditions derived in the traditionl theory of demand [14, pp. 101-115].

ior in a manner sufficient for the potential judgment of falsification to be made. And, as pointed out above, the original Shackle model of portfolio choice (not the version of Section 10.2 below) produced the empirically, clearly false result that, with two or more assets, diversification would not occur. That this result discredited the original model as an explanation of actuality does not detract from the fact that that model yielded a proposition that could be refuted by real experience. To the extent that such propositions are attainable in applications of the model of Section 4.3, which, when applied to portfolio choice in Section 10.2 avoids the absence of diversification conclusion, these applications possess a legitimate form of positive operationality. Moreover, this positive operationality is every bit as significant in the context of ignorance and historical time as the positive operationality of traditional analyses set in their environments of logical time and perfect knowledge.

The second point buttressing the positive operationality of the apparatus of Section 4.3 in the face of the difficulties discussed earlier is based on a different use of the model itself and is developed in the next section.

6.2 Uncertainty Aversion and Favor

Imagine a sequence of behaviors of an individual, observed over successive periods of time,[11] in which there is one observation per period. Because time is historical, each observation should properly be viewed as the outcome of a unique model of decision making in ignorance, of the form of Section 4.3, relevant for only the period of time in which it occurs. But it is also possible to ask if there were a single such model that could explain the entire set of observations taken together. The latter model would contain one set of defining structural relations (*i.e.*, one utility function, one family of potential surprise functions, one attractiveness function, and one decision index), and the behaviors observed would be interpreted as a consequence of specific parameter modification assumed to arise across periods. Thus the observed behaviors would be explained in terms of a hypothetical individual whose defining structural relations are stable over the given periods and who

---

[11]In this discussion, the irreducible unit of time is the period.

changes across these periods only with respect to the variation of particular parameter values.[12] Comparative statics of the model, then, would be relevant and appropriate for the entire time frame under consideration. Of course, although it may turn out, with hindsight, to the contrary, the limitations of historical time preclude any presumption that this model is relevant for explaining subsequent observations that might be added to the data set in the future. Moreover, the approach itself does a certain violence to the spirit of the model of Section 4.3 whose raison d'être is to provide a vehicle for the exploration of situations in which both decision makers and their environments modify in analytically significant ways over time. That is, this proposed use of the model ignores the possibilities of changing choice sets, changing knowledge of the decision maker (and hence his changing potential surprise, utility, attractiveness, and decision index functions), and the self-destructiveness of the decisions being made as time moves on.[13] But even so, the approach is still worthwhile because it is often capable of providing insight into the meaning and importance of past data. In addition, the unique constructions that explain the behaviors observed in each period separately might, again with hindsight, turn out, as a special case, to be actually identical to the corresponding parametric versions of the single model that explains the observed behavior over all periods. Regardless, it is worth providing an example of how the approach might work.

Before doing so, however, it should be pointed out that, in addition to the possibility of shedding light on past time series data, the model of Section 4.3 could also be applied in attempting to make sense of past cross-sectional data. Suppose, for example, a data set consisted of observations, one for each person, of the economic behaviors of a collection of individuals during the same period. Then postulating the existence of a single, hypothetical individual, analogous to the one described above, would permit the data to be interpreted as if it were made up of different observations of the same behavior function. Although the question of the stability through time of the hypothetical

---

[12]Recall the discussion of Section 1.5.

[13]It also permits the observation, through time, of multiple points of an unchanging behavioral relation, which, as argued above in terms of consumer demand functions, is not possible for behavioral relations of real persons.

person's family of potential surprise functions, his attractiveness function, and his decision index is no longer relevant, here the issue of the "aggregation" of all individuals into one, the pitfalls of which will be taken up in Chapter 7, needs to be addressed. That is, for such an approach to be employed in the present context, the assumption of stability over time has to be replaced by perhaps an equally tenuous assumption of a kind of "stability" across persons. But, again, the usefulness of the approach depends on the significance of the insights it provides.

Consider, now, the fact, suggested by the cross-sectionally observed results of Danziger *et al.* [3] that, contrary to the life-cycle hypothesis, the proportion of an individual's saving out of current income tends to increase with his age. This fact, referred to as the "Danziger fact" below, is inferred from observations of the behavior of different individuals of different ages. For present purposes, it is understood in terms of an analytical framework in which (i) there is, hypothetically, a "typical" or "average" person who in certain appropriate respects does not modify through historical time; and (ii) the observations referred to are interpreted as taken from the relevant and unchanging behavior function of that person as he ages across time. Such a framework clearly combines the time series and cross-sectional methods of elucidating observations described above. As such, it suffers from all of the weaknesses and qualifications raised previously with respect to both of those approaches. To explain the Danziger fact itself, a model of decision making by the hypothetical individual is now constructed incorporating the assumptions that his defining structural relations do not vary over time and that the specific determinations of savings and consumption at which he arrives are influenced by his attitudes toward the perceived uncertainties inherent in his decision environment. More precisely, let b denote the ratio of the hypothetical individual's current consumption to his current income or his average propensity to consume. Then, ignoring endpoints, $0 < b < 1$, and a rise in saving means a decline in the value of b. The present explanation of the Danziger fact is based on a model of the form of Section 4.3 in which the objects from which the individual chooses are the values of $x = b$ in the open interval $X = B = (0,1)$. In particular, it will show why successive selections of b as the individual grows older might be smaller and smaller. Thus the analysis that

follows is purely theoretical and is concerned only with understanding
the behavior of the hypothetical person. By itself it has no significance
for the aforementioned cross-sectional difficulties involved in interpreting observations of the behavior of several individuals as those of the
behavior of a single (hypothetical) person.

Except for the facts that B is now the open (instead of the closed)
interval (0,1), and that $x = b$, the model employed is identical to Example 4 of Section 5.1.4. For convenience, the equations of that model are
reproduced in the discussion below. Corresponding to each b in (0,1),
then, the individual has a potential surprise density function, mapping
utility outcomes ψ into potential surprise values ξ, of the form:[14]

$$\xi = f(\psi, b) = \begin{cases} 1, & \text{if } b+1 \leq \psi, \\[2mm] \psi - b, & \text{if } b \leq \psi \leq b+1, \\[2mm] 0, & \text{if } -b \leq \psi \leq b, \\[2mm] -\psi - b, & \text{if } -b-1 \leq \psi \leq -b, \\[2mm] 1, & \text{if } \psi \leq -b-1. \end{cases}$$

Recall that this is one of a nested family of piecewise linear potential
surprise density functions (one function for each object of choice $b =
x$), whose partial derivatives appear in Table 5-4 and whose graph is
illustrated in Figure 5-6. Clearly, as b declines from the value identified
with the potential surprise density curve shown in the latter diagram,
the potential surprise density function changes in such a manner that
its graph shifts "inside" and "above" that pictured in Figure 5-6. For all
b in B, remember, the utility outcome, ψ_b, separating gains from losses
is taken to be zero, so that $\Psi_b^- \times \Xi = (-\infty, 0] \times [0, 1]$ and $\Psi_b^+ \times \Xi =
[0, +\infty] \times [0, 1]$.

---

[14]As with all of the examples of Section 5.1, it is not necessary to delve behind
this family of functions and consider the underlying potential surprise function,
defined on the subsets of Ω, that generates it.

Also, for the purpose of explaining the savings phenomena described above, the
particular form of f assumed is, of course, one of many possibilities. It is chosen here
for its mathematical convenience. The same is true of the particular attractiveness
function and decision index used below.

The individual's attractiveness function is independent of b and given by

$$g(\psi, \xi) = \begin{cases} \psi(1 - a\xi), & \text{on } \Psi_b^+ \times \Xi, \\ \\ \psi(a\xi - 2), & \text{on } \Psi_b^- \times \Xi, \end{cases}$$

where a is a parameter such that $2(b + 2)^{-1} < a < 1$. Recall that, due to this latter restriction, $a > 2/3$ and the partial derivative of g with respect to ψ, or g_ψ, is positive on $\Psi_b^+ \times \Xi$ and negative on $\Psi_b^- \times \Xi$. Furthermore, the partial derivative of g with respect to ξ, calculated as

$$g_\xi(\psi, \xi) = \begin{cases} -a\psi & \text{on the interior of } \Psi_b^+ \times \Xi, \\ \\ a\psi & \text{on the interior of } \Psi_b^- \times \Xi, \end{cases}$$

is negative everywhere since $\psi < 0$ on $\Psi_b^- \times \Xi$. Thus the slopes of the iso-attractiveness contours of the attractiveness function are expressed in the formulae

$$\frac{d\xi}{d\psi} = -\frac{g_\psi(\psi, \xi)}{g_\xi(\psi, \xi)} = \begin{cases} (1 - a\xi)/a\psi > 0, & \text{on the interior of } \Psi_b^+ \times \Xi, \\ \\ -(a\xi - 2)/a\psi < 0, & \text{on the interior of } \Psi_b^- \times \Xi. \end{cases}$$

Evidently the iso-attractiveness contours are positively sloped on $\Psi_b^+ \times \Xi$ and negatively sloped on $\Psi_b^- \times \Xi$ (see Figure 5-6). In addition, the partial derivatives of these slope formulae with respect to ψ, namely,

$$\frac{\partial \left(-g_\psi(\psi, \xi)/g_\xi(\psi, \xi) \right)}{\partial \psi} =$$

$$\begin{cases} -(1 - a\xi)/a\psi^2, & \text{on the interior of } \Psi_b^+ \times \Xi, \\ \\ (a\xi - 2)/a\psi^2, & \text{on the interior of } \Psi_b^- \times \Xi, \end{cases}$$

are negative on the interior of both subdomains, given, as before, the parametric constraint $2/3 < a < 1$. It follows that the iso-attractiveness contours are everywhere strictly concave (Figure 5-6). Lastly, differentiating the slope formulae with respect to a,

$$\frac{\partial\left(-g_{\psi}(\psi,\xi)/g_{\xi}(\psi,\xi)\right)}{\partial a} =$$

$$\begin{cases} -1/a^2\psi < 0, & \text{on the interior of } \Psi_b^+ \times \Xi, \\ \\ -2/a^2\psi > 0, & \text{on the interior of } \Psi_b^- \times \Xi, \end{cases} \tag{6.2-1}$$

a result that will be used shortly in the subsequent discussion of uncertainty aversion and favor.

Recall also that, for each b in B, maximizing the attractiveness function subject to the potential surprise density function on $\Psi_b^+ \times \Xi$ leads to a focus gain consisting of

$$\psi_b^+ = \frac{1}{2a} + \frac{b}{2} \tag{6.2-2}$$

and

$$\xi_b^+ = \frac{1}{2a} - \frac{b}{2}. \tag{6.2-3}$$

A similar maximization over $\Psi_b^- \times \Xi$ gives the focus loss

$$\psi_b^- = -\frac{1}{a} - \frac{b}{2}, $$

$$\xi_b^- = \frac{1}{a} - \frac{b}{2}. \tag{6.2-4}$$

Both maximizations are pictured in Figure 5-6 at tangencies between iso-attractiveness contours and the graph of the potential surprise density function. Obviously, variation in the parameter a affects the focus gain and focus loss associated with b because, as a changes, the iso-attractiveness coutours modify against a fixed potential surprise density function. As will be described below, the value of a turns out to be a reflection of the extent of aversion to uncertainty with respect to gains and favor toward uncertainty with respect to losses present in the decision maker's decision index.

Finally, the individual has a decision index (recall that, in the present case, $b = x$) such that

$$D(b) = Q(\psi_b^-, \xi_b^-, \psi_b^+, \xi_b^+) = \psi_b^- + \xi_b^- \psi_b^+ - \xi_b^+ \tag{6.2-5}$$

defined on $B = (0,1)$. Upon substitution from (6.2-2) through (6.2-4), then, it follows that

$$D(b) = -\frac{3}{2a} + \frac{1}{2a^2} + \frac{b}{4a} - \frac{b^2}{4}.$$

The value of b that maximizes D over B is therefore

$$b = \frac{1}{2a}. \tag{6.2-6}$$

Thus the selection of the average propensity to consume b depends on the parameter a.[15] It depends, in other words (and as will be indicated below), on the uncertainty aversion and favor mirrored in the attractiveness function as that, in turn, emanates from the "trade-off" uncertainty aversion and favor of the decision index. In particular, it will be seen that enlargements in a result from a rise in that aversion and favor. Therefore the observed increased proportion of savings out of current income, that is, increases in $1 - b$ or decreases in b, as the individual ages, may be explained, in this model, as a consequence of his increased trade-off aversion to uncertainty for gains and his increased trade-off favor toward uncertainty for losses, or what will be referred to shortly as a greater conservatism in his attitude toward uncertainty, with advancing years.[16]

In the expected utility model of Section 4.2, in which uncertainty is reduced to probabilistic risk, recall that the risk facing the individual is measured by the standard deviation of possible outcomes with respect to the probability density function defined over those outcomes, and his risk profile is given by the partial derivatives of his expected utility function (4.2-1) with respect to the mean of the probability density function and that standard deviation. The individual is said to unconditionally favor risk, to be unconditionally neutral toward risk, or to be

---

[15]Recall that, in this model, a is required to satisfy the inequalities $2(b+2)^{-1} < a < 1$. Combining these restrictions with (6.2-6), it follows, as indicated in Section 5.1.4, that the value of the average propensity to consume chosen cannot be less than $1/2$ or greater than $3/4$. Moreover, the form of the relation between b and a in (6.2-6) rests on the form of the family of potential surprise density functions, the form of the attractiveness function, and the form of the decision index assumed in the model.

[16]*Cf.*, in the context of risk, Hahn [5].

unconditionally averse to risk according to whether the first-order partial derivative with respect to the standard deviation is, respectively, posititve, zero, or negative. Moreover, he is trade-off favorable to risk, trade-off neutral toward risk, or trade-off averse to risk when the negative of the ratio of the two first-order partial derivatives is, again respectively, negative, zero, or positive. Thus trade-off risk aversion, say, implies an upward sloping indifference curve in the σ-μ plane or a certain trade-off between standard deviation values and mean outcomes as the probability density function varies and expected utility is held fixed. Increasing unconditional and trade-off risk aversion requires positivity, in the first instance, of the second-order partial derivative of the expected utility function with respect to the standard deviation and, in the second, of a second-order derivative indicating the rate of change of the slope of the expected utility function's indifference curves.

The present approach to uncertainty aversion and favor, however, in addition to focusing on (nonprobabilistic) uncertainty instead of (probabilistic) risk, is considerably richer in that, including the decision index employed earlier as a special case, it allows for the possibility that the individual's unconditional and trade-off attitudes toward uncertainty when focusing on favorable outcomes or gains may be different from those relating to unfavorable outcomes or losses. Here the uncertainty the individual confronts is different for each utility outcome and is measured by the magnitude of the potential surprise value he associates with that outcome. The uncertainty *profile* of the individual is defined by the signs and magnitudes of the first- and second-order partial derivatives of his decision index $Q(\psi_b^-, \xi_b^-, \psi_b^+, \xi_b^+)$ (the analogue of the expected utility function), and unconditional attitudes toward uncertainty are expressed in terms of the signs of the first-order partial derivatives of Q with respect to the uncertainty variables ξ_b^+ and ξ_b^- as follows. The decision maker *unconditionally favors* uncertainty, is *unconditionally neutral* toward uncertainty, or is *unconditionally averse* to uncertainty *on the gain side* whenever, respectively,

$$\frac{\partial Q}{\partial \xi_b^+} \overset{>}{\underset{<}{=}} 0$$

everywhere. And he *unconditionally favors* uncertainty, is *unconditionally neutral* toward uncertainty, or is *unconditionally averse* to uncertainty *on the loss side* as

$$\frac{\partial Q}{\partial \xi_b^-} \overset{>}{<} 0$$

everywhere, respectively. For both gains and losses, then, unconditional uncertainty aversion occurs when greater uncertainty lowers the valuation assigned by the decision index, and unconditional uncertainty favor arises when enhanced uncertainty has the opposite effect. In addition, increasing unconditional uncertainty aversion means larger and larger negative increments in the decision-index value with successive rises in uncertainty, or $\partial^2 Q/\partial(\xi_b^+)^2 < 0$ for gains and $\partial^2 Q/\partial(\xi_b^-)^2 < 0$ for losses. The signs of these derivatives are reversed in the case of increasing unconditional uncertainty favor.

Like the analogous ideas for risk, trade-off uncertainty attitudes have to do with the directions of the change in possible outcomes (ψ) that leave the individual at the same decision index level for a given change in uncertainty (ξ). That is, trade-off attitudes toward uncertainty on the gain side arise in reference to the slopes of the iso-decision-index contours in the various ξ_b^+-ψ_b^+ planes in ($\psi_b^-, \xi_b^-, \psi_b^+, \xi_b^+$) space, while trade-off attitudes toward uncertainty on the loss side emerge with respect to the slopes of similar contours in the ξ_b^--ψ_b^- planes.[17] For example, the individual is *trade-off averse* to uncertainty *on the gain side* where the appropriate slopes are positive (*i.e.*, an increase in uncertainty requires compensation with a larger possible gain to maintain the same value of the decision index), and he *trade-off favors* uncertainty *on the loss side* where they are negative (*i.e.*, an increase in uncertainty, implying better perceived prospects for avoiding losses, requires toleration of, in absolute value, a larger possible loss).[18] In principle, it is possible to have any combination of trade-off attitudes

---

[17]To align properly with earlier geometry, reference here should instead be made, respectively, to ψ_b^+-ξ_b^+ and ψ_b^--ξ_b^- planes, and the ψ_b^+- and ψ_b^--axes in subsequent diagrams should be horizontal rather than vertical. But these conventions are reversed in order to perserve an analogy to the concepts and diagrams relating to risk aversion and favor in the expected utility model.

[18]On the *gain* side, the individual would *trade-off favor* uncertainty if the slopes were negative and would be *trade-off neutral* toward uncertainty if they were zero. On the *loss* side, he would be *trade-off averse* to uncertainty if the slopes were positive and *trade-off neutral* toward it if, once again, they were zero.

toward uncertainty for gains and losses. Thus a decision maker might exhibit, say, trade-off uncertainty aversion or favor for both gains and losses, or, as described in terms of the previous example, trade-off uncertainty aversion for gains and trade-off uncertainty favor for losses. A similar statement applies to unconditional uncertainty attitudes. Regardless, in deference to inequalities (5.1.1-3), which are required of all decision indices considered in this volume, including (6.2-5), only the circumstance of unconditional uncertainty aversion for gains, unconditional uncertainty favor for losses, trade-off uncertainty aversion on the gain side, and trade-off uncertainty favor on the loss side is analyzed here.

Of course, with both $\partial Q/\partial \psi_b^+$ and $\partial Q/\partial \psi_b^-$ taken to be positive everywhere, as they are, unconditional uncertainty aversion, neutrality, and favor imply, respectively, trade-off uncertainty aversion, neutrality, and favor. Under these conditons, moreover, unconditional (and hence trade-off) uncertainty favor with respect to losses is the conservative "counterpart" to unconditional (and hence trade-off) uncertainty aversion with respect to gains. For, while the latter indicates, at least insofar as the decision-index evaluation is concerned, that the less uncertainty associated with any gain the better since the possibility of securing that gain is enhanced, the former means that more uncertainty associated with any loss is better because it improves the possibility of avoiding that loss. Reflecting these ideas, a decision index exhibiting unconditional uncertainty aversion with respect to gains and unconditional uncertainty favor with respect to losses (along with $\partial Q/\partial \psi_b^+ > 0$ and $\partial Q/\partial \psi_b^- > 0$ everywhere) may be referred to as a *conservative* decision index. In addition, a rise in unconditional (and trade-off) uncertainty aversion on the gain side, or a rise in unconditional (and trade-off) uncertainty favor on the loss side, or both, signifies *increased conservatism* on the part of the decision maker in his attitude toward uncertainty. Thus the explanation, still to be completed below, of the Danziger fact in reference to the example of this section is that as the decision maker grows older and more conservative the value of the parameter a in his attractiveness function becomes larger and, as a consequence, he saves more (*i.e.*, the optimal value of b in [6.2-6] declines).

Consider, next, a situation in which unconditional uncertainty aversion on the gain side, unconditional uncertainty favor on the loss side, trade-off uncertainty aversion on the gain side, and trade-off uncertainty favor on the loss side are constant in relation to the variables of the side to which they respectively refer, and focus attention on how increases in the constant trade-off uncertainty aversion on the gain side and the constant trade-off uncertainty favor on the loss side are reflected in changes in the slopes of the relevant iso-decision-index contours. For concreteness and ease of exposition in addressing this issue, reference will be made to the example of this section. Although contours in each ξ_b^+-ψ_b^+ plane are drawn for fixed values of ψ_b^- and ξ_b^-, it is convenient for diagramatic purposes to project contours from different ξ_b^+-ψ_b^+ planes (drawn for different values of ψ_b^- and ξ_b^-) into the same ξ_b^+-ψ_b^+ plane. A similar geometry is employed for contours in the ξ_b^--ψ_b^- planes. Now, in the case of (6.2-5),

$$\frac{\partial Q}{\partial \psi_b^-} = 1, \qquad \frac{\partial Q}{\partial \psi_b^+} = \xi_b^-,$$

$$\frac{\partial Q}{\partial \xi_b^-} = \psi_b^+, \qquad \frac{\partial Q}{\partial \xi_b^+} = -1,$$

which describes part of the individual's uncertainty profile. Thus the individual is unconditionally averse to uncertainty on the gain side and unconditionally favors uncertainty on the loss side. In the latter case, the partial derivative measuring unconditional uncertainty favor at any point in $(\psi_b^-, \xi_b^-, \psi_b^+, \xi_b^+)$ space is a different constant for each object of choice b. It follows that

$$v^- = \frac{\partial \psi_b^-}{\partial \xi_b^-} = -\frac{\partial Q/\partial \xi_b^-}{\partial Q/\partial \psi_b^-} = -\psi_b^+ < 0, \qquad (6.2\text{-}7)$$

$$v^+ = \frac{\partial \psi_b^+}{\partial \xi_b^+} = -\frac{\partial Q/\partial \xi_b^+}{\partial Q/\partial \psi_b^+} = \frac{1}{\xi_b^-} > 0, \qquad (6.2\text{-}8)$$

where v^- and v^+ are abbreviations of $\partial \psi_b^-/\partial \xi_b^-$ and $\partial \psi_b^+/\partial \xi_b^+$, respectively. Taking the gain side first, two iso-decision-index contours through the same point E as projected into the ξ_b^+-ψ_b^+ plane, one identified with $v^+ = (v')^+$ and the other with $v^+ = (v'')^+$, where $(v')^+ < (v'')^+$, are drawn in Figure 6-1(a). Although, of course, it need

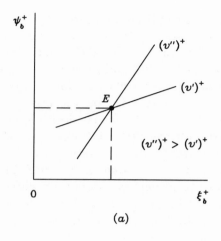

(a)

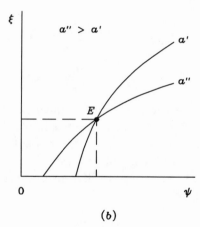

(b)

Figure 6-1. (a) Gain-side iso-decision-index contours
(b) Gain-side iso-attractiveness contours

not be so in general, the speciality of this particular example clearly yields linear contours and hence a constant value of v^+ along each. With all contours upward sloping and the individual trade-off averse to uncertainty everywhere on the gain side, the line in Figure 6-1(a) having the steeper slope with respect to the ξ_b^+-axis, $(v'')^+$, represents a larger value of v^+ and hence exhibits greater trade-off uncertainty aversion with respect to gains. Thus along each of the contours in Figure 6-1(a) the decision maker is compensated for an increase in uncertainty, ξ_b^+, with a higher ψ_b^+ outcome, that is, a larger gain value. And, in the case of the more uncertainty-averse contour, $(v'')^+$, a given increase in potential surprise ξ_b^+, from, say, point E in the diagram, necessitates compensation with a larger increase in the acceptable gain value than would be required for the less uncertainty-averse contour. Likewise, with respect to the loss side, two iso-decision-index contours through the same point F projected into the ξ_b^--ψ_b^- plane, and corresponding to $v^- = (v')^-$ and $v^- = (v'')^-$, where $(v')^- < (v'')^-$, appear in Figure 6-2(a). In this circumstance, all contours slope downward, the individual trade-off favors uncertainty everywhere on the loss side, and the contour (the one labeled $(v'')^-$) in Figure 6-2(a) having the flatter slope with respect to the ξ_b^--axis but still the greater value of v^-, reflects a larger trade-off uncertainty favor with respect to losses. In other words, along each contour, for any rise in uncertainty, ξ_b^-, the decision maker is willing to accept a lower ψ_b^- outcome or a larger absolute loss value, and along the more uncertainty-favor contour $(v'')^-$, increasing ξ_b^- from point F is associated with a smaller rise in the acceptable absolute loss value than on the less uncertainty-favor contour. That $(v'')^-$ is the more uncertainty-favor contour also reflects the fact that decreasing ψ_b^- along it from point F, or increasing the absolute loss value, the decision maker is compensated with a greater uncertainty ξ_b^- than on the less uncertainty-favor contour. Note also that the above calculation of partial derivatives implies, in this particular example, that the unconditional uncertainty favor as measured by $\partial Q / \partial \xi_b^-$ on the loss side is the negative of the trade-off uncertainty favor on that side as measured by v^-. But a parallel assertion cannot be made for the gain side.

Similar considerations apply to the analysis of attitudes toward uncertainty in the decision indices of Examples 1 and 2 of Section 5.1. More generally, when unconditional and trade-off uncertainty attitudes

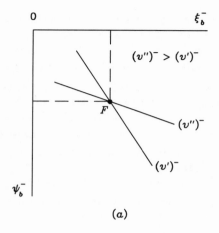

(a)

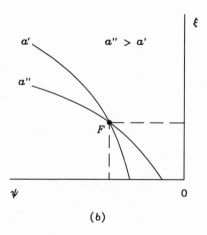

(b)

Figure 6–2. (a) Loss–side iso–decision–index contours
(b) Loss–side iso–attractiveness contours

are permitted to vary across the subdomains of the decision index to which they relate (*e.g.*, Examples 3 and 5 of Section 5.1), iso-decision-index coutours will assume nonlinear shapes. One possibility, namely, that relating to the decision index of Example 5, has already been pictured in Figure 4-2(a). The axes in that diagram are the same as in Figures 6-1(a) and 6-2(a) except that those in the latter have been reflected and rotated, and their ξ_b^+- and ξ_b^--axes have been lined up and placed on top of each other. The decision index that produced Figure 4-2(a), or (5.1.5-5), reflects unconditional and trade-off uncertainty aversion for gains, and unconditional and trade-off uncertainty favor for losses. It also exhibits increasing unconditional and trade-off uncertainty aversion on the gain side and increasing unconditional and trade-off uncertainty favor on the loss side as the uncertainty variables ξ_b^+ and ξ_b^-, respectively, rise in value.[19] However, it should be borne in mind that decision indices exist having the same unconditional and trade-off attitudes toward uncertainty as (5.1.5-5) except that the curvature of the iso-decision contours is reversed. Such is the case, for example, with

$$ Q(\psi_b^-, \xi_b^-, \psi_b^+, \xi_b^+) = \theta_1 \psi_b^- + \theta_2 \left(\xi_b^- \right)^2 + \theta_3 \psi_b^+ - \theta_4 \left(\xi_b^+ \right)^{1/2}, $$

which is obtained by switching the exponents on the terms involving ξ_b^+ and ξ_b^- in (5.1.5-5) and which, as a consequence, displays decreasing trade-off uncertainty aversion with larger values of ξ_b^+ and decreasing trade-off uncertainty favor with larger values of ξ_b^-.

To sum up, it is the partial derivatives of the decision index, or the individual's uncertainty profile, that determine if the decision index exhibits unconditional and trade-off aversion or favor to uncertainty for gains and losses. Furthermore, the unconditional and trade-off uncertainty aversion on the gain side of (5.1.5-5) are analogous to the corresponding notions of risk aversion in many expected utility situations

---

[19]In spite of its strictly concave shape, the gain side iso-decision-index contours in Figure 4-2(a) are parallel to those depicting increasing trade-off risk aversion for an expected utility function in the case of a quadratic (initially nonexpected) utility function defined over random portfolio rates of return. This is because the axis on which uncertainty is measured in Figure 4-2(a) is vertical instead of horizontal. See, for example, Vickers [15, p. 116].

in that the partial derivative of the decision index with respect to the uncertainty variable, namely, ξ_b^+, is negative, and the iso-decision-index contours in the ξ_b^+-ψ_b^+ planes all slope upward. And it is the signs of appropriate second-order partial derivatives that indicate whether either kind of uncertainty aversion or favor increases with the magnitude of the uncertainty variable.

It is also true, and has been suggested earlier, that attitudes toward uncertainty in the decision index may affect the attractiveness function. To see how this comes about in the constant trade-off uncertainty aversion situation of Example 4 discussed above,[20] consider, again, the gain side first. Substitute the second part of (6.2-4) into the expression for v^+ in (6.2-8), solve for a as a function of v^+, and partially differentiate the result with respect to v^+. Then

$$\frac{\partial a}{\partial v^+} = \frac{4}{(2 + v^+ b)^2} > 0,$$

that is, an increase in trade-off uncertainty aversion on the gain side, or a rise in v^+ (for example, from $(v')^+$ to $(v'')^+$ in Figure 6-1(a)), enlarges a (from, perhaps, a' to a''). But, according to previous calculations in (6.2-1), increasing a induces a decline in the slope of the iso-attractiveness contour on the gain side, making the curve flatter with respect to the ψ-axis, as shown in Figure 6-1(b). In the diagram, the iso-attractiveness contours corresponding to a' and a'' intersect at E, and increasing the outcome value ψ from that point along either contour necessitates an increase in potential surprise value ξ in order to maintain the same attention-attracting power for the decision maker.

---

[20]The impact on the attractiveness function of uncertainty attitudes in the decision index in general is too complex to analyze here. Suffice it to say that uncertainty attitudes in the decision index may appear in a variety of ways in the attractiveness function. For the circumstance in which the attractiveness function is coincident with a transformed decision index, as in Example 5 of Section 5.1, the manner in which uncertainty attitudes manifest themselves in the attractiveness function depends on both the specification of the decision index and the characteristics of the transformation that turns the decision into a function coincident with the attractiveness function. In this regard, it has already been remarked at the end of Section 4.3 that in the case of the gain side of Example 5 the expression of uncertainty aversion in the decision index is identical to that in the attractiveness function because the two functions are the same on $\Psi_b^+ \times \Xi$.

However, to stay on the more uncertainty-averse contour a'' when moving out from E requires a smaller increase in ξ. Thus the relationship between the two iso-attractiveness contours in Figure 6-1(b) is implied by that between the decision-index contours in Figure 6-1(a). In a similar manner, substitution of (6.2-2) into the expression for v^- in (6.2-7), solving, and differentiating leads to

$$\frac{\partial a}{\partial v^-} = \frac{2}{(2v^- + b)^2} > 0,$$

whence increasing trade-off uncertainty favor on the loss side (*i.e.*, expanding v^- by making it less negative) raises the value of a and, recalling (6.2-1), flattens the iso-attractiveness contour with respect to the ψ-axis by enlarging its slope (*i.e.*, making that slope less negative).[21] This is illustrated in Figure 6-2(b).

In the present example, however, the same value of a appears on both the gain and loss sides of the attractiveness function. Hence, to ensure consistency, it must be supposed that any change in the decision maker's attitude toward uncertainty has to impact both v^- and v^+ in such a manner that the alteration in a obtained from the gain side is identical in sign and magnitude to that derived from the loss side. In other words, again substituting (6.2-2) and the second part of (6.2-4) into (6.2-7) and (6.2-8), but now using the resulting two equations to eliminate a, v^+ and v^- have to be constrained to satisfy

$$2v^- + \frac{3b}{2} + \frac{1}{v^+} = 0, \tag{6.2-9}$$

and thus, upon differentiation, changes in v^+ and v^- that arise from modification in the decision maker's trade-off aversion to uncertainty necessarily conform to

---

[21]On the gain side, then, as trade-off uncertainty aversion falls, the slopes of the iso-attractiveness contours steepen with respect to the ψ_b^+-axis. Although it cannot happen in the present example, or with (5.1.1-3) in force, this further suggests that, under suitable modification of the example, as trade-off uncertainty aversion continues to fall, when these slopes become vertical the individual has become trade-off neutral toward uncertainty, and when their signs reverse he has begun to trade-off favor uncertainty. Thus the individual's trade-off attitude toward uncertainty would be reflected in both the slopes v^+ as well as the slopes of the iso-attractiveness contours. A similar conclusion also applies on the loss side.

$$\frac{dv^+}{dv^-} = \frac{8}{(4v^- + 3b)^2} > 0.$$

With (6.2-9) in force, it is clear that an increase in conservatism in the decision maker's attitude toward uncertainty resulting in a rise in trade-off uncertainty aversion on the gain side and a "numerically identical" increase in trade-off uncertainty favor on the loss side enlarges a and, according to (6.2-6), lowers the average propensity to consume.[22] Therefore the proportion of savings out of current income increases with the conservatism of the decision maker.

One way to explain, in part, why such a conclusion is reached in this model is based on the substitution of (6.2-6) into the focus-gain and focus-loss values of (6.2-2) through (6.2-4). Thus

$$\psi_b^+ = \frac{3}{4a}, \qquad \psi_b^- = -\frac{5}{4a},$$

$$\xi_b^+ = \frac{1}{4a}, \qquad \xi_b^- = \frac{3}{4a},$$

and it is clear that, with increased trade-off uncertainty aversion for gains and increased trade-off uncertainty favor for losses, and hence a larger value of a, the decision maker is selecting a "more conservative" choice option that attracts him with the prospect of a lower favorable outcome or gain in exchange for a less negative unfavorable outcome

---

[22]More generally, if two values of a were permitted by the attractiveness function, say, a^- on the loss side and a^+ on the gain side, so that g would appear as

$$g(\psi, \xi) = \begin{cases} \psi(1 - a^+\xi), & \text{on } \Psi_b^+ \times \Xi, \\ \psi(a^-\xi - 2), & \text{on } \Psi_b^- \times \Xi, \end{cases}$$

then it could be shown that the $D(b)$-maximizing value of b becomes

$$b = \frac{1}{a^-} - \frac{1}{2a^+}.$$

Now the question of whether or not b falls would depend on the magnitude of the increase in trade-off uncertainty favor on the loss side, and hence the magnitude of the rise in a^-, relative to the magnitude of the increase in trade-off uncertainty aversion on the gain side and the implied magnitude of the rise in a^+.

or lower (in absolute value) loss. In addition, the occurrence of both of the favorable and unfavorable outcomes that focus his attention and describe his choice option are, in his view, more plausible (*i.e.*, are associated with lower potential surprise).

It is worth recalling, at this point, the discussion in Section 4.3 relating to the fact that, depending on the specification of the image of the incomplete collection of states of the world Ω under the utility function u, the potential-surprise-attractiveness apparatus may be defined over the positive half of the real line. In the present case, in which different consumption propensities of income earners as they age are considered, the focus is on the correspondingly different utility levels that might be achieved were one consumption propensity rather than another adopted. But with such possible variation in utility outcomes in view, it might well be useful in some circumstances to employ a practice that characterizes the image of Ω under u, and hence the potential-surprise-attractiveness apparatus, over the positive half-line. In the preceeding argument, however, consistency with the conventions heretofore established has been preserved by continuing to take the image of Ω to extend from $-\infty$ to ∞.

The above analysis, of course, is based on a highly specialized representation of the model of Section 4.3. As such, two questions, both beyond the scope of the present volume, immediately arise. First, can this highly particularized representation be generalized so that the explanation of greater savings with age can arise in a larger class of theoretical circumstances? Second, is it possible to characterize the properties that data sets must exhibit in order to be explainable by some variant of the structure of Section 4.3 in general or by some subclass of these models in particular? The latter question, clearly, is answerable through further explorations of the comparative statics of the maximizations in the appropriate formulations of the model of Section 4.3. In all cases, there are two of these maximizations, namely, the constrained maximizations of the attractiveness function and decision index and, as shown in Section 5.2, under appropriate conditions both are amenable to the manipulation required to secure comparative statics results. In particular, the comparative statics analysis of the decision-index-maximization problem would permit determination of the characteristics of the behavior functions, and hence the properties of the observable data points, that

that maximization generates, while the comparative statics analysis of the attractiveness-maximization problem would, as in Section 5.2, help in setting out the implied properties of the decision index and, in that way, play a role in determining the sought-after comparative statics of the decision-index-maximization problem. But, although comparative statics analysis, in general, leads to a better understanding of the model by forcing the implications of assumptions and the interrelations between variables to be more fully explored, it only contributes to the model's positive operationality in attempts to explain historically given data. For, as indicated earlier, when the construction of Section 4.3 is applied to explain the behavior of a single person during a single period, at most only one set of values of the parameters of the decision-index-maximization problem is observable. And, disregarding the problem of perceived versus observed parameter values, since comparative statics analysis is based on at least two observations, it is not really relevant to positive operationality in the one-period context.[23]

6.3 Normative Operationality

Clearly the model of decision making in ignorance of Section 4.3 is normatively operational in its description of a decision procedure, complete with decision criteria, that could, in principle, be applied to real world decision situations. But the construction is so detailed and complex that one could not reasonably expect real decision makers to actually make use of it, if by that it is meant that the complete apparatus is to be put into operation step by step.[24] This difficulty is abbreviated somewhat when the measures described at the end of Section 4.3 to reduce the model's complexity, namely, starting with a potential surprise density function and conflating the attractiveness function with the decision index, are implemented. Still, it is both possible and significantly meaningful to derive simple, usable decision rules from the full construction that could be employed under well-defined, specific circumstances. Furthermore, it is not hard to see how actual deci-

---

[23]Clearly this problem does not arise in the application of the model of Section 4.3 to explain cross-sectional data as described earlier.

[24]Something similar could be said of some models of traditional analysis.

sion making can be interpreted as representing various elements of that framework, assuming the framework as a whole is believed to be more realistic than that of traditional analysis. Examples illustrating each of these assertions are now presented in turn. Upon completion of the presentations, it can be concluded that the normative operationality of the model extends to the practical level of everyday affairs.[25]

In developing an example of a simplified decision rule relevant to a special case of the model of Section 4.3, enough assumptions will be introduced so that it will not be necessary to use the decision index. In addition, constrained maximization of the attractiveness function will also be avoidable. And the outcome achieved by truncating, in this way, the procedure outlined in Section 4.3 to arrive at decisions in ignorance will be equivalent to that obtained with the use of the complete model of that section encompassing the full procedure.

Turn now to the example itself. As in the illustrations of Section 5.1, let b in $B = [0,1]$ (where b is generally unrelated to the average propensity to consume of the previous section) be a scalar parameter of the potential surprise density and attractiveness functions that corresponds, in a 1-1 manner, to objects of choice x in X, and suppose that constrained maximization of the attractiveness functions leads to a focus gain and focus loss with the following differential properties:[26]

$$\frac{\partial \psi_b^+}{\partial b} > 0, \qquad \frac{\partial \xi_b^+}{\partial b} \leq 0,$$

$$\frac{\partial \psi_b^-}{\partial b} > 0, \qquad \frac{\partial \xi_b^-}{\partial b} \geq 0. \qquad (6.3\text{-}1)$$

Thus, increasing the value of b raises its evaluation (*i.e.*, the utility magnitude it induces) in the focus gain but cannot enlarge its potential surprise, and increasing b also may raise both its evaluation and its potential surprise in the focus loss. Suppose the decision maker chooses from the full set B (or X). Assume further that the standard

---

[25] Parallel conclusions for more traditional analyses (when admitting logical time and perfect knowledge in explanations of reality), though possible, are not usually explored.

[26] These inequalities, though similar in some respects, are not quite the same as those relevant to the previous example and the examples and propositions of Chapter 5.

differential inequalities of (5.1.1-3) are imposed on the decision-index-determining function Q. In other words, (other things being equal) enlarging the evaluation of b in either the focus gain or the focus loss, increasing the potential surprise value in the focus loss, or lowering the potential surprise value in the focus gain, enhances the position of b in the decision index. Special cases in which all of these conditions are satisfied appear as Examples 1 and 2 of Section 5.1 and Corollary 5.2-8 of Section 5.2. It follows by applying (6.3-1) and (5.1.1-3) to (5.2-5) that

$$\frac{dD(b)}{db} > 0. \tag{6.3-2}$$

Raising the value of b, then, increases the value of $D(b)$.

One of the possible ways for the parameter b to influence the potential surprise density function is for increases in its value to shift the graph of the function to the right. This yields a family of dominating potential surprise density functions as described and illustrated in Chapter 5. Such a family is assumed here, along with the requirement that the outcome magnitude separating the more favorable utility outcomes from the less favorable ones, namely, ψ_b, vanishes for all b in B. Examples 1 and 2 (and Corollary 5.2-8) indicate that the present relationship between values of b and dominating potential surprise density functions is consistent with the inequalities of (6.3-1). Note that in the latter example, as b'' increases to b', and the graph of the potential surprise density function moves rightward, the potential surprise of utility outcomes in the focus gain falls, while that of utility outcomes in the focus loss rises. But in Example 1, variation in b produces no change in the potential surprise of utility outcomes in either the focus gain or focus loss.

Given the identification of values of b with dominating potential surprise density functions, the derivatives of (6.3-1), as indicated in a different context in Section 5.1, all reflect a shifting potential surprise density function. Those in (5.1.1-3) relate to neither shifts in nor movements along such a function. Rather, the derivatives in (5.1.1-3), as suggested in the previous section, can be associated with movements along an appropriate contour in a two-dimensional plane parallel to one of ten coordinate planes in the space formed by the Cartesian product of the range and domain of the decision-index-determining function Q.

In light of the 1-1 correspondence between values of b in $B = [0, 1]$ and x in X, let the element in X associated with the value $b = 1$ be denoted by $\bar{x}$. Then, with respect to the assumed family of dominating potential surprise density functions, the decision index D ranks the elements of B according to the values of $D(b)$.[27] Moreover, as a consequence of (6.3-2), $D(b)$ is maximized over B when b is selected so as to be as large as possible. Since the largest value of b is unity, the choice option selected must be $\bar{x}$. But the potential surprise density function identified with $b = 1$ is that member of the family of density functions whose graph is farthest to the right. Therefore, under the above conditions the choosing of b to maximize $D(b)$ over B is equivalent to selecting that choice option for which the graph of the associated potential surprise density function is as far to the right as possible.[28] Such a decision rule is applicable in the special cases of Examples 1 and 2 and Corollary 5.2-11. It also suggests a second, equivalent, decision criterion (also valid in Examples 1 and 2 and in the context of Corollary 5.2-11), which may be expressed as follows: from the collection of choice options X, each of which is associated with a unique potential surprise density function, let x, and hence the density function, be determined so that the potential surprise of the most attractive utility outcome as defined by the constrained maximization of the attractiveness function (*i.e.*, the potential surprise value in the focus gain) is as small as possible and the potential surprise of the least attractive utility outcome (or the potential surprise value in the focus loss) is as large as possible.

Evidently these last two decision rules are much simpler to apply than the full procedure of Section 4.3 involving the maximization of both the attractiveness function and the decision index, and will still

---

[27]Evidently, different families of potential surprise density functions result in different rankings of B, and hence X, by D. One possible alternative is the nested family also defined and illustrated in Section 5.1. But, as suggested by Corollary 5.2-9, not all of the inequalities of (6.3-1) need hold in this case, and hence the inequality of (6.3-2), and the ranking imposed on B by D, could depend additionally on the specific form of the attractiveness function and the decision index.

[28]This conclusion is essentially a more general restatement of the argument following Corollary 5.2-11 asserting that, under the requisite conditions, dominance among elements of B is equivalent to dominance among potential surprise density functions. Also, as intimated in n. 27 immediately above, the same conclusion is unlikely to hold for a family of nested potential surprise density functions.

lead the decision maker, under the requisite conditions, to the same decision. They also, especially the latter, have a nice intuitive appeal. Furthermore, this is only one example of a simplified decision rule that can be obtained from the model. Certainly there are others derivable and applicable in different circumstances. Thus the model of decision making in ignorance developed here is a potentially rich source of normatively operational decision rules.

Turning to the second issue raised in this section, it is not hard to find suggestions of the use of elements of the apparatus set out in Section 4.3 in real world decision making. One illustration is Jefferson's discussion of the employment and development of "scenarios" at Shell International [7]. A scenario, in this sense, is an internally consistent, sufficiently relevant and detailed story of what might happen in the future.[29] Although in Jefferson's telling, choice options were not explicitly examined in reference to scenarios in specific decision problems, the potential is clearly there to do so. Thus the scenario concept is very close to what has been referred to above as a state of the world that emerges following the making of a decision, that is, an element of Ω. Moreover, Jefferson describes how the people writing scenarios at Shell only constructed incomplete (actually, very small) sets of scenarios and "persistently refused to attach" subjective probabilities to individual scenarios,[30] and how the qualitative aspects and determinants of scenarios necessarily became more important than the numerical ones.[31] Thus, although Jefferson does not delve very far into the actual making of decisions at Shell, it is clear that some of the basic elements of the decision aparatus of Section 4.3 are present.

To give a more complete example of how certain kinds of real world decision making can be interpreted as exhibiting elements of the model of Section 4.3, consider a common decision method that dates at least to Benjamin Franklin. In responding to a request from a friend who was having trouble deciding between two alternatives, Franklin suggested [4, pp. 437-438] that his friend make a list of the likely "pros"

---

[29]Jefferson [7, p. 133].

[30]Ibid., pp. 133,134.

[31]Ibid., pp. 135-136. In this regard, techniques for analyzing nonquantifiable phenomena, though not mentioned by Jefferson, could also be useful. See Katzner [9].

and "cons" of the alternatives. Wheeler and Janis [16, Ch. 4] expand Franklin's suggestion into an entire "balance sheet" of advantages and disadvantages of possibly many choice options. Regardless, such a procedure can be thought of as determining what seem to be the most and least attractive features of each alternative or, in the lexicon of the present framework for making decisions in ignorance, the particulars of the outcomes in the focus gain and focus loss in light of the potential surprise values that correspond to them. That is, the pros and cons of any choice option are seen to be those associated with the two outcomes on which the decision maker focuses, or which stand out the most in his mind, as a result of already having maximized his attractiveness function subject to his potential surprise density constraint.[32] In deciding among options, the decision maker might very well resort to the second criterion derived above and select that option for which the attainment of the advantages would seem least surprising and the necessity of enduring the disadvantages the most surprising. To the extent that this is done, it can be said that the normative decision rule derived from the model of Section 4.3 under the above conditions is actually applied in real world situations.

It is clear, then, that the model of decision making in ignorance developed in Section 4.3 has significant depth with respect to both its positive and normative operationality. Although the presence of ignorance and historical time necessarily impairs the ability of the model to produce true behavior functions that are testable against observable data, its competence and potential to provide observably falsifiable propositions and furnish simple and usable decision rules remains intact. Therefore, there can be little doubt that this model has demonstrable relevance in explaining economic activity in the real world of ignorance and historical time.

---

[32]As pointed out in Section 4.3, it is not at all unreasonable to focus attention on only two of the possible outcomes corresponding to each choice option, where one outcome is identified with advantages and the other with disadvantages. To cite essentially the same example employed earlier, one should not, when contemplating losses, worry about an outcome of losing $10 if there is a low potential surprise associated with an outcome of losing $1,000.

6.4 References

1. Arrow, K. J., "Alternative Approaches to the Theory of Choice in Risk-Taking Situations," *Econometrica* 19 (1951), pp. 404-437.

2. Caldwell, B. J., *Beyond Positivism: Economic Methodology in the Twentieth Century* (London: George Allen & Unwin, 1982).

3. Danziger, S., J. van der Gaag, E. Smolensky, and M. K. Taussig, "The Life-Cycle Hypothesis and the Consumption Behavior of the Elderly," *Journal of Post Keynesian Economics* 5 (Winter 1982-83), pp. 208-227.

4. Franklin, B., *The Writings*, vol. 5, A. H. Smyth, ed. (New York: Haskell House, 1970).

5. Hahn, F. H., "Savings and Uncertainty," *Review of Economic Studies* 37 (1970), pp. 21-24.

6. Hutchison, T. W., *The Significance and Basic Postulates of Economic Theory* (New York: Kelley, 1965).

7. Jefferson, M., "Economic Uncertainty and Business Decision-Making," in *Beyond Positive Economics?* J. Wiseman, ed. (New York: St. Martin's, 1983), pp. 122-159.

8. Katzner, D. W., *Static Demand Theory* (New York: Macmillan, 1970).

9. ———, *Analysis without Measurement* (Cambridge: Cambridge University Press, 1983).

10. Kuhn, T. S., "The Function of Measurement in Modern Physical Science," in *Quantification,* H. Woolf, ed. (Indianapolis: Bobbs-Merrill, 1961), pp. 31-63.

11. Loasby, B. J., *Choice, Complexity and Ignorance* (Cambridge: Cambridge University Press, 1976).

12. Ozga, S. A., *Expectations in Economic Theory* (London: Weidenfeld and Nicolson, 1965).

13. Samuelson, P. A., *Foundations of Economic Analysis* (Cambridge: Harvard University Press, 1947).

14. Theil, H., "The Econometrics of Demand Systems," in *Applied Demand Analysis,* H. Theil and K. W. Clements, eds. (Cambridge: Ballinger, 1987), pp. 101-162.

15. Vickers, D., *Money Capital in the Theory of the Firm* (Cambridge: Cambridge University Press, 1987).

16. Wheeler, D. D., and I. L. Janis, *A Practical Guide for Making Decisions* (New York: Free Press, 1980).

CHAPTER 7

Aggregation

The problem of aggregation, or the combination of individual elements into a single whole, arises in different ways in, and in different areas of, equilbrium analysis. In one of its manifestations, it is expressed in terms of the notion of *consistent* aggregation: let there be K units whose character or behavior is described by the functions

$$y_k = f^k(z_{1k}, \ldots, z_{Ik}), \tag{7.0-1}$$

where y_k and the z_{ik}, for $i = 1, \ldots, I$, represent, respectively, suitably characterized dependent and independent scalar variables for unit k and $k = 1, \ldots, K$. Consistent aggregation is said to be possible if there exist scalar variables z_i and y and functions A^i and F defined on appropriate domains, such that

$$z_i = A^i(z_{i1}, \ldots, z_{iK}), \quad i = 1, \ldots, I,$$

$$y = A^{I+1}(y_1, \ldots, y_K),$$

and

$$y = F(z_1, \ldots, z_I). \tag{7.0-2}$$

Frequently one or more of the functions A^i represent simple addition formulas like, for example,

$$A^{I+1}(y_1, \ldots, y_K) = \sum_{k=1}^{K} y_k. \tag{7.0-3}$$

This chapter is reproduced, with considerable additions, corrections, and other modifications, from my "Aggregation and the Analysis of Markets," *Review of Political Economy* 3 (1991), pp. 220-231.

It is often argued that a special case in which consistent aggregation is always possible is the passage from individual (f^k) to market (F) excess demand functions. In such a circumstance, with y_k representing excess demand quantities of unit k for a particular good, and with each $z_{ik} = p_i$, where p_i, the price of good i, is assumed to be the same for every unit, A^i would be the function whose function value is always p_i, for $i = 1, \ldots, I$, and A^{I+1} would be as in (7.0-3). Then, given the individual functions f^k, the market function F would be specified as

$$F(p_1, \ldots, p_I) = \sum_{k=1}^{K} f^k(p_1, \ldots, p_I) \qquad (7.0\text{-}4)$$

on the relevant domain. The issue of the existence of consistent aggregates in general has been explored by Klein [11] and Nataf [13]. Nontrivial applications include Fisher's discussion [6] of the question of the existence of an aggregate production function. A history of the subject of consistent aggregation is provided by van Daal and Merkies [4].

A more stringent version of the consistent aggregation question seeks not merely the existence of an aggregate function (7.0-3) but, in addition, one with the same general properties exhibited by the given individual unit functions in (7.0-1). That is, it asks if there exists a consistent aggregate whose characteristics may be thought of as describing those of a fictitious unit behaving in the same general way as each of the individual units that are aggregated. When it exists, the fictitious unit is sometimes referred to as a *representative* unit, and the aggregation itself is called *representative* (consistent) aggregation. In general, consistent aggregation cannot imply representativity: it is well known, for example, that when passing from individual (f^k) to market (F) consumer demand functions the properties of the Slutsky functions of the individual consumers (assuming, in that case, that [7.0-1] is generated by maximizing a classical utility function subject to the budget constraint) do not usually carry over to the market aggregates. Thus there need not, in general, be a utility function generator of the market demand functions. Representativity, then, requires extra assumptions. Illustrations of such extra assumptions in the context of demand theory may be found in Katzner [10, pp. 243-245] and Muellbauer [12].

A second approach to the question of aggregation appears with respect to *composite* commodities and prices: given a group of commodities and their prices, is it possible to combine the goods and prices of the group into composites that can be treated as if they themselves were an ordinary good and an ordinary price? In the context of typical microeconomic models, this might mean, for example, that when maximizing utility subject to the budget constraint, the composite good and its price could be substituted for the group of goods and prices that it represents. The first-order maximization conditions would then imply that, among other things, the marginal rate of substitution between any good outside of the group and the composite commodity would equal the ratio of the price of that good to the composite price. Such composites are known to exist under the assumptions of price proportionality (within the group), quantity proportionality (within the group), or an appropriate kind of separability.[1] The problem of composite commodity-price aggregation in a general equilibrium model has been explored by Vilks [15]. And Blackorby and Schworm [3] consider the aggregation into composite commodity and price and the aggregation across individual units simultaneously.

Still other forms of aggregation include the construction of price and quantity indexes,[2] and the derivation of "social" from individual preferences.[3] In all of the above cases, however, the conditions necessary to achieve nontrivial aggregation are rather strong. So severe are they that one might reasonably ask if they do not push the thought forms that employ them too far from reality to be appropriate for use in economic analysis. Indeed, after a rigorous and thorough exploration of the issues involved in aggregating individual firm production functions, Fisher remarked that the "willing suspension of disbelief" that Solow required to take the aggregate production function seriously has become "increasingly difficult to maintain" [6, p. 576].

But the matter does not end here. In addition to the explicit assumptions that permit aggregation, there are also the implicit requirements of equilibrium analysis that all units have perfect knowledge, that

---

[1]See, for example, Katzner [9, pp. 141-145].
[2]See, for example, Diewert [5].
[3]*E.g.*, Arrow [1].

time is logical, and that the facts of historical time, uncertainty, and ignorance are ignored. For it is the assumption of perfect knowledge that allows one to write $z_{ik} = p_i$, for all i and k, in the consistent aggregation of individual into market excess demand functions described above.[4] And it is the assumption of logical time that ensures that the functions of (7.0-1) and (7.0-2), and even the A^i, can be realized in a stable enough manner over time so as to last, in any particular realization, for more than a single fleeting instant or period, and hence that permits the movement along such functions, including the aggregates, through time. But, taking the view of nonequilibrium analysis adopted in previous chapters, the world in which economic units operate is such that knowledge is not perfect and time is not logical. Human beings have only imperfect perceptions about the past and the present that are unique to each person. Nor can they know anything at all about the economic matters that are hidden by the future. Rather, the more appropriate and significant characteristic of the human condition is ignorance. And, of course, time in reality is historical not logical. Each moment (period) is unique, with its own special epistemic and ontological properties that can never be repeated again. From this perspective, then, even the most trivial aggregations are called into question. What, if anything, can it mean to aggregate individual demand or supply (or excess demand) functions into corresponding market functions when individual units do not all perceive the same prices as existing in the

---

[4]In this context, perfect knowledge generally means that every person has complete and accurate information on all present and future individual excess demand functions in the economy. Thus, at each moment or in each period of time, any person solving the system will come up with the same prices (hence $z_{ik} = p_i$ for all i and k) and will be able to say what he would buy or sell at those prices. The system has to be solved by each individual to determine his own excess demands in order for him to be sure that his income from the sale of his endowment (which includes current returns from, and possible liquidation of, past savings) will be sufficient to cover the purchases that he has chosen to demand. (Note that in the special case of perfect competition, the problem is simplifed because perfect knowledge reduces, in part, to the assumption that the individual can always buy and sell as much as he wants at prevailing market prices.) Moreover, to every vector of hypothetical prices, p^0, in the domain of the market excess demand functions, there must correspond a distinct set of such individual excess demand functions whose solution is p^0. Then, in the way outlined here, market excess demand functions can be defined throughout their domains.

economy, that is, when, for each i, $z_{ik} \neq p_i$ for most k? What can it mean to perform such an aggregation when unfulfilled expectations may imply, for example, that the consumer is unable to obtain the income from the sale of his endowment necessary to support the quantities demanded given by his excess demand functions at the vector of perceived prices? What can it mean to aggregate when individual functions may change from moment to moment or period to period according, in part, to the extent to which price perceptions and expectations turn out to be false?[5] Thus, in the present context, aggregation, in addition to everything else, has to face the further difficulties created by the realities of ignorance and historical time.

This chapter examines some of these issues. The question of aggregating to the market level under conditions of ignorance and historical time is considered first and is followed by an investigation of how markets can be analyzed when the requirements for the existence of traditional market aggregates cannot be met.

7.1 Market Aggregates

To be concrete, focus attention on the problem of aggregating individual demand behavior across consumers. Take this behavior, at some moment or period of (historical) time t, to be described by the excess demand functions

$$q_{ik} = h^{ik}(p_{1k}, \ldots, p_{Ik}), \qquad (7.1\text{-}1)$$

where $i = 1, \ldots, I$ ranges over commodities, $k = 1, \ldots, K$ indexes individuals, q_{ik} denotes excess demand quantities for good i by person k, and p_{ik} indicates the current price of i as perceived by k. Equation (7.1-1) is formally identical to (7.0-1) except that there is a separate relation for each commodity i. For every i and k, the domain of h^{ik} is

$$\mathcal{D}^k = \{(p_{1k}, \ldots, p_{Ik}) : p_{ik} > 0, \text{ for } 1 = 1, \ldots, I \text{ and } k = 1, \ldots, K\},$$

and its range is the set of all real numbers greater than or equal to the negative of k's initial endowment of good i. Although, technically, a sub- or superscript t ought to be added to each variable and function to

---

[5]These questions have been raised by Vickers [14].

place it in time, unnecessary notational complications can be avoided by not doing so. Assume that the excess demand functions of (7.1-1) reflect, for each person k, a budget constraint that allows for the receipt of income from the sale of initial endowments, and the holding and sale of assets, and hence, from the latter, that saving on the part of consumers is not, a priori, ruled out. The historical time and ignorance context in which the behavior described by (7.1-1) is set imposes at least three significant characteristics on these variables and functions that need to be brought out.[6]

First, as has been discussed at length in previous chapters, in light of the ignorance in which individuals operate, it cannot be assumed that any one person possesses complete and accurate information on the current prices of all goods. Each consumer comes to a moment (period) in time with knowledge gleaned only from his perceptions of past and present experience. The complexity of reality is so overwhelming that only a small portion of it can ever be known, and even that modicum of knowledge is usually fraught with error. In particular, it is not possible for a person to know accurately all present and future individual demand and supply (*i.e.*, excess demand) functions in the economy. The current prices of commodities, then, can only be cognized with certainty upon direct observation. But the process that determines actual current prices may not yet have worked itself out, and, in any case, there are usually too many prices to know them all simultaneously at each moment. Thus, to determine the prices he thinks he faces at any moment, the individual has to speculate and guess.[7] Moreover, as has also been indicated earlier, each consumer is a unique individual, with his own special history, his own special personality, his own special knowledge, and his own special understandings obtained from that knowledge. No two persons are alike. Therefore, the current price vector $(p_{1k}, \ldots, p_{Ik})$ perceived by person k at any moment is unique to that individual, and this is indicated symbolically by the appearance of the subscript k on each price. In general, although the domains of the functions in (7.1-1) consist of all positive price vectors, any particular

---

[6]See *ibid.*

[7]Compare this to the manner in which the individual secures price information under conditions of perfect knowledge as described in n. 4 on p. 240.

realization of perceived prices for all consumers at moment t (*i.e.*, any collection of vectors $(p_{1k}, \ldots, p_{Ik})$ for $k = 1, \ldots, K$, none of which need be actual market prices) usually has the property that $p_{i'k'} \neq p_{i''k''}$, for all $(i', k') \neq (i'', k'')$.

The second characteristic that is forced on the variables and functions of (7.1-1) by the context of historical time and ignorance has to do with the fact that, for each k, the behavior functions h^{ik}, where $i = 1, \ldots, I$, merely reflect the unrealized plans and intentions of the consumer at the moment (or period), t, under consideration. To be able to buy commodities, person k has to generate income by selling quantities of other goods inherited in his initial endowment. But in the same way that he is not sure about the prices at which these latter goods will sell, he is also uncertain about the quantities that the markets will take.[8] Hence there is no way that he can know with certainty the income he has available to spend at moment t.[9] The amounts q_{ik} in the demand functions (7.1-1), then, cannot reflect actual excess demands at t. Nor can the functions h^{ik} describe actual behavior at t. For person k simply may not wind up with enough income to follow through on the purchases intended in $(q_{1k}, \ldots, q_{Ik})$. Alternatively, he could realize unanticipated savings in the form of unsold endowment or increased holdings of assets. Clearly, the plans and intentions represented in the q_{ik} and h^{ik} are necessarily based, in part, on the individual's price and income perceptions and expectations. When, in the course of events at moment t, the latter go unfulfilled, that is, when his expectations may be said to have *failed*, person k may be unable to realize all of those plans and intentions for moment t.

The third characteristic of these variables and functions is the fact that no actualization of either variable values or functions is valid for more than the moment of time t at which they appear. The historical, psychological, and epistemic statuses of the individual are all unique to

---

[8]A similar uncertainty arises with respect to the sale of any assets that might be included in the consumer's initial endowment. For, if commodity-price perceptions turn out to be wrong, then so will asset-price preceptions since current asset prices depend on the future income streams the assets provide and these, in turn, reflect commodity-price perceptions and expectations.

[9]Remember that the presence of perfect knowledge, when it is assumed to exist, eliminates this difficulty. See n. 4 on p. 240.

moment t. The economic situation in which he behaves is also. Hence, as suggested in Section 6.1, his entire behavior rule or pattern, that is, the vector of functions $(h^{1k}, \ldots, h^{Ik})$ (assuming the individual is person k), must generally vary from moment to moment. It cannot, therefore, make any sense to "move along" any of the functions of (7.1-1) through time in the same manner that an individual is assumed to be able, under conditions of perfect knowledge and logical time, to move along an unchanging Marshallian demand curve. In spite of the fact that the individual might be inclined to say today that, if he were faced with a certain set of prices tomorrow, he would do such and such, there can still be no guarantee that he will actually be both willing and able to follow through. For even if those prices were actually to come to pass, there is no way that the individual can know today what either he or the world will be like tomorrow, and, in the final analysis, these unknowable elements are the determining factors in selecting tomorrow's choices.

Economists, of course, often explain behavior functions such as (7.1-1) as emerging from some kind of decision apparatus. Clearly one possibility that takes into account the three implied characteristics just discussed is the model of decision making in ignorance developed in Section 4.3. Translated into the present setting of the theory of demand, it may be summarized as follows: the choice options (objects of choice) facing consumer k are the collection of excess demand vectors $(q_{1k}, \ldots, q_{Ik})$ that satisfy the usual budget and initial endowment inequalities with prices $p_{1k}, \ldots, p_{Ik}$ as perceived by k and introduced above. Let k construct a potential surprise function over the subsets of an incomplete set of imagined and uncertain future states of the world. Using a utility function that depends on these states as well as on choice options, his potential surprise function is transformed into a family of potential surprise density functions over utility outcomes, where every choice option is identified with a single density function. For each choice option, maximizing an associated attractiveness function subject to the associated potential surprise density function provides a characterization of that choice option that allows its comparison to other choice options in terms of a decision index. The individual then selects the option that maximizes the decision index. Repeated hypothetical application of this apparatus for all vectors $(p_{1k}, \ldots, p_{Ik}) > 0$ at the same moment t generates the vector of functions $(h^{1k}, \ldots, h^{Ik})$ in (7.1-

1) with all of the previously described requirements of the historical time and ignorance context fulfilled.

Turn now to the question of aggregating the functions of (7.1-1) into market demand functions. To begin with, if excess demand quantities are to be added in the traditional way, it is necessary that the commodities to which the summed quantities relate be homogeneous. But under conditions of ignorance, even with physical homogeneity it is still possible for individuals to have different perceptions of a commodity's identity and, when this happens, all efforts to aggregate unrealized, planned or intended excess demand quantities have to be abandoned. Suppose, however, that, for the sake of argument, such eventualities are precluded and it is assumed that, within markets, commodities are homogeneous both in fact and across buyer perceptions of them. Then a reasonable interpretation, in the historical time and ignorance context, of the standard aggregation procedure leading to (7.0-2) would be to write

$$q_i = H^i(p_{11}, \ldots, p_{I1}, p_{12}, \ldots, p_{I2}, \ldots, p_{1K}, \ldots, p_{IK}), \qquad (7.1\text{-}2)$$

where

$$q_i = \sum_{k=1}^{K} q_{ik},$$

$$H^i(p_{11}, \ldots, p_{I1}, p_{12}, \ldots, p_{I2}, \ldots, p_{1K}, \ldots, p_{IK}) = \sum_{k=1}^{K} h^{ik}(p_{1k}, \ldots, p_{Ik}),$$

and $i = 1, \ldots, I$. In terms of the aggregation of (7.0-1) into (7.0-2) and, as suggested, in part, above, $p_{ik} = z_{ik}$, $q_{ik} = y_k$, $q_i = y$, $h^{ik} = f^k$, the variable z_i and the functions $A^1, \ldots, A^I$ have been dropped, and A^{I+1} and $F = H^i$ are defined as in, respectively, (7.0-3) and (7.0-4). For each i, the domain of H^i is the Cartesian product, $\mathcal{D}^1 \times \cdots \times \mathcal{D}^K$, of the domains of the h^{ik}, and the range of H^i is the collection of real numbers at least as large as the negative of the combined initial endowments of good i. The problems that these aggregate demand functions create for the analysis of markets are considered in the next section. For the moment, however, focus attention on the properties they possess.

Like the individual excess demand functions from which it is derived, the aggregate function H^i contains all relevant perceptions of prices as arguments, reflects only plans and intentions, and is applicable only at moment t. However, there is a property of the aggregate function H^i that is not present in the individual functions h^{ik}. To describe it, consider any prespecified collection of price perceptions and initial endowment quantity sale expectations for all persons and assume that if transactions actually occur at more than one price within, say, market i at time t, there are still not as many prices in that market as there are buyers. Clearly, at the level of the individual, the possibility exists that the given price perceptions and the given initial endowment quantity sale expectations of any one person, say, person k, will both turn out to be correct at moment t. In that event, one point on that individual's demand function, h^{ik}, will actually be realized at t. But, be that as it may, except in the unlikely circumstance that the remaining realized individual excess demand quantities happen to offset each other in an appropriate way, the given price realization cannot satisfy (7.1-2) because the individual price perceptions across persons, unless they are coincidentally identical, contradict each other. That is, with $(p_{11}, \ldots, p_{I1}, p_{12}, \ldots, p_{I2}, \ldots, p_{1K}, \ldots, p_{IK})$ specified subject to these conditions, the corresponding q_i identified by (7.1-2) cannot be realized because at least one person's expectations other than k's fail and, as a result, that person is unable or unwilling to purchase the portion of q_i he intended to buy. Thus, excluding the exceptions in which the effects of failed expectations cancel each other out, in the context of historical time and ignorance where the actual price perceptions of each individual are likely to be distinct, as long as at least one market permits fewer price values than the number of buyers participating in it, in any prespecified realization at least one person's intentions, and hence the aggregate of intentions as represented in (7.1-2), cannot be met.

Several additional features of this aggregation should also be noted. First the aggregation that produces (7.1-2) cannot be said to be consistent aggregation because individual perceptions of the same price are not combined into one (*i.e.*, there are no functions $A^1, \ldots, A^I$ and no variable z_i). Nor can the aggregation be called representative since the H^i do not have the same realization properties as the h^{ik}. Second, the only candidates for such aggregation are, generally, the behaviors that occur simultaneously at each moment or period of time. Aggregation in period t, say, of demand functions relevant to periods t and $t+1$, is not possible because the demand function for period $t+1$ cannot be known at t. Aggregation at period t of demand functions relevant to periods t and $t-1$ is appropriate only in the unlikely event that each demand function itself turns out, with hindsight, to be relevant to both periods in the sense that nothing about the consumer or his environment changed enough between periods to cause a change in that function. Such might be the case when decisions become routine, as described at the end of Section 4.3. Similar conditions permitting aggregation of the same h^{ik} to (7.1-2) across several (past) periods are also satisfied if all consumers are of the hypothetical variety introduced at the start of Section 6.2. Individuals in those circumstances, recall, have unchanging potential surprise, utility, attractiveness, and decision-index functions over the entire interval of time under consideration. Finally, it is clear that if one were to impose the requirements of perfect knowledge and logical time on H^i in (7.1-2) then the traditional aggregate-type excess demand function would emerge as a special case.

Thus the aggregation of individual consumer excess demand functions under conditions of historical time and ignorance produces aggregate excess demand functions with considerably different properties from those when knowledge is perfect and time is logical. Analogous arguments apply to the aggregation of firm excess demand functions and to the aggregation of microrelations into macrorelations in general. Accepting the facts of historical time and ignorance, then, means that, in particular, the usual market demand and supply functions, mainstays of Marshallian and Walrasian inquiry, are no longer available. The question remains as to how markets can be analyzed under such circumstances.

7.2 The Analysis of Markets

To analyze markets, it is necessary to describe the buying behavior of buyers, the selling behavior of sellers, the ways in which these behaviors resolve themselves to determine the quantities that are bought and sold in the markets, and the one or more prices that exist in each. In the traditional analysis of perfectly competitive markets (which supposes physical homogeneity of goods within those markets), planned buying and selling behavior on the part of consumers is summarized in the standard market demand and supply functions described in excess demand form earlier and often grounded in individual utility maximization subject to budget constraints. Additional planned buying and selling behavior is similarly encapsulated in market demand and supply functions that emerge, say, from profit maximization on the part of firms. And actual market quantities and (normalized) prices are determined as the simultaneous solution (assuming it exists) of this system of demand and supply relations that includes a price-normalizing equation and explicitly equates market demand to supply, or equivalently sets market excess demand at zero, in each market. Thus all markets clear in that planned quantity demanded equals planned quantity supplied everywhere. The result is a unique equilibrium price and quantity determined for each commodity such that all of the plans and intentions of everyone are fully realized.

Now attempting to do something similar under conditions of ignorance and historical time (with the added supposition of homogeneous perceptions of commodities within every market) leads to a simultaneous system built up by combining (7.1-2), say, with correspondingly obtained aggregate excess demand functions derived from individual firms. However, equating all market excess demands to zero in this case yields only I equations to determine IK consumer price perception variables plus whatever additional price perception variables are introduced by the inclusion of firms. The system, in other words, is vastly underdetermined. Thus little is explained by such a construction and it becomes necessary to reformulate the analysis of markets along different lines.

There are several possibilities, each of which, in the absence of any formal aggregation per se, nevertheless remains based on its own version of "individualistic" decision making. The first is to reason at the market level by employing analogues from the individual level. This would involve something like the following: assume the existence of a fictitious consumer named C whose decision-making apparatus generates market demand and supply functions of consumers in the excess demand form

$$q_i = G^i(p_1, \ldots, p_I), \quad i = 1, \ldots, I, \tag{7.2-1}$$

in the same manner that individual decision-making structures generate (7.1-1). These functions include the excess demand functions that reflect consumer supplies of factors and other goods and are defined for all positive price vectors. Any realization of $(p_1, \ldots, p_I)$ at moment or period t reflects the price perceptions of $\mathcal{C}$ at t. Moreover, the functions of (7.2-1) have the same properties as (7.1-1) and do not suffer from the general impossibility of realization difficulty peculiar to (7.1-2). When there are buying and selling units in the economy that are independent of $\mathcal{C}$, that is, when there are firms, let there be an additional fictitious being, namely, a producer, $\mathcal{P}$, whose decision apparatus begets the market excess demand functions derived from firms. Include in these latter functions those excess demand functions depicting firms' demand for inputs. The price variables, that is, the arguments of the excess demand functions generated by $\mathcal{P}$, represent $\mathcal{P}$'s price perceptions and not $\mathcal{C}$'s. Now, in such a case, where the same two "persons" are the only participants in every market, it is reasonable to assume that, taken together, the markets operate to eliminate differences in perceptions and avoid failed expectations.[10] Thus equating planned market demand to supply, or reducing market excess demand to zero in every market, yields a system of I equations in I unknown, commonly perceived, and hence actual, prices. Usually it will be necessary to add a normalization (since, if there are no leakages in the flow of goods and expenditures, $\mathcal{C}$'s budget constraint, together with whatever constraint or profit equation that restricts $\mathcal{P}$, imply that only $I - 1$ equations can be independent), and to impose enough restrictions so that a unique solution exists. Clearly the market quantities and (normalized) prices that emerge are valid only for moment t. Thus the economy is understood to behave as if it were driven solely by the decisions of $\mathcal{P}$ and $\mathcal{C}$.

Note that the aggregate excess demand functions employed here are

---

[10]With three or more persons, the complexity of market dealings is likely to leave differences in perceptions in place until it is too late and, therefore, result in expectations that are unfulfilled.

not representative in the sense defined at the beginning of the chapter. This is because they are not obtained by combining individual functions in any particular way. They are, rather, assumed to exist merely as aggregative analogues of corresponding individual functions. Furthermore, there is historical precedent in the economics literature for the method of analysis that employs aggregative analogues. Such precedent is traceable at least to Jevons, who said, "The general forms of the laws of Economics are the same in the case of individuals and nations . . ." [8, p. 15]. And, although Hicks incorrectly thought he had demonstrated the proposition that ". . . the behavior of a group of individuals . . . obeys the same laws as the behavior of a single unit" [7, p. 245], a good portion of macroeconomic analysis has operated, and continues to operate, as if it were true.[11] A further application of aggregative analogues, in a less traditional approach to macroeconomic analysis that recognizes the presence of historical time and ignorance, is developed in Chapter 12 below.

A second way of reformulating market analysis does away with aggregate excess demand or market demand and supply functions entirely. The idea is to let each seller, say, determine, at period (moment) t, the price at which he sells his commodities, perhaps according to some specified rule, and let buyers purchase what they wish.[12] For example, if the seller is a firm, he might develop an estimate of the demand for his output and, based on that estimate and the wage of labor, set the price he charges by marking up a fixed amount from his unit labor cost.[13] The assumptions that (i) commodities supplied by different sellers in the same market are homogeneous and (ii) perceptions of the nature of the same commodity by different buyers are homogeneous need not be maintained. In any case, this usually determines a multiplicity of prices in the market for the firm's output in period t. Assuming sellers are able to obtain the resources to supply the quantities demanded by buyers, assuming buyers are able to secure enough income from the sale of their initial endowments (at prices that they, as suppliers, set), and assuming all markets clear at prices set by suppliers that cover depreci-

---

[11]See Weintraub [16, p. 11].

[12]In labor markets it might be more appropriate to assume that buyers are the price setters and sellers dispense as much as they like.

[13]See Chapter 9.

ation costs and provide the expected rates of return on money capital invested in firms, then all plans and intentions are realized in the consummation of transactions in period t. Otherwise, and more generally, the so-called *short-side trading rule* applies and the actual quantities transacted are the smaller of the amounts that buyers want to buy and sellers want to sell.[14] Under these latter circumstances, moreover, additional mechanisms, usually referred to as *rationing* schemes, have to be specified that indicate how commodities are to be allocated to buyers when, at the fixed prices, they are in short supply, and how sales are to be allocated among sellers when, also at the same fixed prices, there is too much supplied.[15] Clearly, when the short-side trading rule comes into play, expectations fail, markets do not clear, and plans and intentions are likely to be modified in period $t + 1$ beyond what might ordinarily be called for (given preferences and technology at $t + 1$) to make up for the surprises and disappointments that arose in period t. However, even if all plans and expectations are fulfilled at t, there could still be changes at $t + 1$ because preferences, technology, perceptions, or expectations might be different then or because the distributional effects of the goings on at t may have affected the initial endowments in place at $t+1$. Note that, although there may be multiple price values actually appearing in a market in period t, when the products within that market are homogeneous, there is only one actual market quantity – namely, the sum of all quantities actually transacted in the market at t. An application of this approach to the analysis of commodity and labor markets appears in Chapter 11.

The third way of thinking about the operation of markets considered here also avoids the aggregation issue and will be used as the basis for examining IOU markets in Chapter 11. Let buyers and sellers meet, say, randomly in a market and suppose that each has his own independent decision-making procedure and perception of the price at which the good of the market is transacted. Assume that when a buyer and seller meet for which the buyer's perceived price of the good is at least as large as the seller's perceived price, and the buyer's planned

---

[14]See, for example, Benassy [2, pp. 10,11].

[15]Examples of rationing schemes have been suggested and analyzed by Benassy [*ibid.*, Ch. 2]. See also Section 11.5 below.

purchase quantity of it is no greater than the seller's planned sale quantity, a transaction is effected in which the price is the seller's (lower) perceived price and the quantity is the buyer's (lower) planned purchase quantity. When the above conditions are not met, this particular buyer and seller do not do business, and each may move on to attempt to make a deal with another partner. Generally, with a market operating in this way, at least some expectations fail, and the market does not clear. A possibility for analyzing barter markets, with yet a different mechanism for making offers and resolving them into trades, is suggested, though not fully developed, in Chapter 8.

The usefulness of these proposed substitutes for traditional market analysis depends on the purpose of the inquiry that has been undertaken. The latter two, highly microeconomic approaches would be appropriate if, for example, the aim were to explain how the economic interaction among individual units in the economy might lead to "coherence" instead of chaos. The resulting vision of coherence would not be one of an economy passing, over time, through a sequence of temporary equilibria or through a sequence of positions that converges, or is in some other relation, to an equilibrium (recall Section 1.2) but, rather, of a world that lurches from one nonequilibrium posture to another (see Chapters 8 and 11). Alternatively, if the aim were to investigate more overarching market or even macroeconomic phonomena, say, to explain the level of unemployment or inflation, then the first approach based on the postulation of analogues would be more suitable. For investigations such as these, the microeconomic structures detailing individual interactions are too fine and lean, and their aggregation into coarser and fleshier market-level and macroeconomic models is not possible. Moreover, the issue of the microfoundations of market-level and macroconstructs is, in the compelling sense that microeconomic structures and principles underlie their postulation, fully resolved through the use of analogues as described above. (In this regard the reader is again referred to Chapter 12.)

At any level, then, it is possible to analyze markets without resort to aggregating individual demand and supply (or excess demand) functions into market demand and supply (or excess demand) functions. When doing so, however, market clearing is often lost. But by avoiding aggregation the additional restrictions that aggregation requires are eliminated. This is desirable in general because it brings any analysis in closer touch with the actuality that it is intended to explore. And in the case of explaining markets, in particular, it allows the investigation to account for the facts of historical time and ignorance.

7.3   References

1. Arrow, K. J., *Social Choice and Individual Values*, 2nd ed. (New York: Wiley, 1963).

2. Benassy, J. P., *The Economics of Market Disequilibrium* (New York: Academic Press, 1982).

3. Blackorby, C., and W. Schworm, "Consistent Commodity Aggregates in Market Demand Equations," in *Measurement in Economics*, W. Eichhorn, ed. (Heidelberg: Physica-Verlag, 1988), pp. 577-606.

4. van Daal, J., and A. H. Q. M. Merkies, "The Problem of Aggregation of Individual Economic Relations; Consistency and Representativity in a Historical Perspective," in *Measurement in Economics*, W. Eichhorn, ed. (Heidelberg: Physica-Verlag, 1988), pp. 607-637.

5. Diewert, W. E., "Index Numbers," in *The New Palgrave,* vol. 2, J. Eatwell *et al.*, eds. (London: Macmillan, 1987), pp. 767-779.

6. Fisher, F. M., "The Existence of Aggregate Production Functions," *Econometrica* 37 (1969), pp. 553-577.

7. Hicks, J. R., *Value and Capital*, 2nd ed. (London: Oxford University Press, 1946).

8. Jevons, W. S., *The Theory of Political Economy*, 5th ed. (New York: Kelley, 1965).

9. Katzner, D. W., *Static Demand Theory* (New York: Macmillan, 1970).

10. ——, *Walrasian Microeconomics: An Introduction to the Economic Theory of Market Behavior* (Reading: Addison-Wesley, 1988).

11. Klein, L. R., "Macroeconomics and the Theory of Rational Behavior," *Econometrica* 15 (1946), pp. 93-108.

12. Muellbauer, J., "Community Preferences and the Representative Consumer," *Econometrica* 44 (1976), pp. 979-999.

13. Nataf, A., "Sur la Possibilité de Construction de Certains Macromodèles," *Econometrica* 17 (1948), pp. 232-244.

14. Vickers, D., "The Illusion of the Economic Margin," *Journal of Post Keynesian Economics* 12 (1989), pp. 88-97.

15. Vilks, A., "Consistent Aggregation of a General Equilibrium Model," in *Measurement in Economics*, W. Eichhorn, ed. (Heidelberg: Physica-Verlag, 1988), pp. 691-703.

16. Weintraub, E. R., *Microfoundations: The Compatibility of Microeconomics and Macroeconomics* (Cambridge: Cambridge University Press, 1979).

CHAPTER 8

Simultaneity and Kaleidics

Economists recognized long ago, indeed, at least as far back as Cournot [3, p. 127], that simultaneity is a fundamental fact of economic life. At present, their most sophisticated expression of this idea is represented, possibly, by so-called general equilibrium or Walrasian analysis. In its microeconomic form, a fully developed general equilibrium analysis involves, as suggested in Section 1.2, the construction of a dynamic mathematical model whose equations characterize, at each moment or in each period, the behavior of consumers, the behavior of firms, and the operation of markets. (A government may also be included.) Consumer and firm behaviors emerge from distinct decision-making mechanisms, the former maximizing utility subject to a budget constraint, the latter maximizing profit subject to technological production possibilities. For each vector of equilibrium and other price values, announced, perhaps, by an auctioneer, the unique solution of the relevant equations of the model for a period on the model's time clock (assuming such a solution exists) represents the result of the simultaneous interaction of the consumers, firms, and markets in that period in light of the endowments and the history of the interactions of previous periods already determined by the model. Each sequence of these solutions starting with a fixed initial endowment and generated by changing prices determines a unique time-path. A time-path along which there is neither change in economic behavior by any consumer or firm nor change in economic value in any market is an equilibrium path. It is frequently supposed in general equilibrium analysis not only that an equilibrium

---

[1]This chapter is reproduced, with considerable additions, corrections, and other modifications, from my "Simultaneous Economic Behavior under Conditions of Ignorance and Historical Time," in *Measurement, Quantification and Economic Analysis*, I. H. Rima, ed. (London: Routledge, 1995), pp. 379-395.

exists and is (globally) stable but also that, at this equilibrium, all markets clear and trade takes place only after market-clearing equilibrium is achieved.[1] As parameters and other "fixed" elements modify, the equilibrium changes. The presence of fixed-element variation across a succession of given dates thus generates a sequence of equilibria and resulting trades at those dates. Such a model is often referred to as a *sequence* economy.[2]

As described earlier, however, the general equilibrium approach to simultaneity carries with it certain methodological assumptions that, from the vantage point of nonequilibrium analysis, severely limit its applicability to real world phenomena. First, time is logical – it can be restarted over and over again by repeatedly placing the same, fixed, dynamic equations at their initial values. Moreover, the equilibrium itself, when it exists, is timeless, that is, the relations that determine the equilibrium values do not depend on time. Second, all decision makers in the general equilibrium framework have perfect knowledge in that they know all of the relevant possible outcomes that can result from their actions or decisions, they know the probabilities of future occurrences of those outcomes when the actual outcomes are uncertain, and they know their evaluations of each of their actions (in light of the probabilities if appropriate) in a manner that is invariant over time. Third, learning, novelty, and the unimagined are precluded. Only things that are consistent with the working out over time of the fixed equations of the model can happen, and, of course, upon reaching equilibrium, as long as parameters do not modify, all change must cease. It is clear, then, that these assumptions remove general equilibrium analysis, along with the simultaneity it depicts, from the realities of historical time and ignorance.

To face up to the presence of historical time and ignorance requires, in part, the recognition that functions describing individual behavior (such as, for example, a consumer's excess demand functions), to the

---

[1]For a discussion of equilibrium without market clearing, see, for example, Benassy [2].

[2]*E.g.*, Hahn [4, p. 230]. The word "economy" is used here to mean a particular kind of model. However, as is often the case in the economics literature, "economy" will sometimes refer in this volume to the thing being modeled. The context in which the word appears determines its meaning.

extent that they can be given economic meaning, have to be defined separately and hypothetically in each period of time (recall Section 7.1). Such functions, often called *behavioral* or *notional* functions, can be ascertained, in principle, by repeatedly asking the individual how he would behave under various circumstances in which everything that does not explicitly vary is held rigidly fixed. But, since people behave only in historical time, and, since they always acquire new knowledge and react to new and unique situations as time passes, decisions to act are made independently in each period. In practice, then, and except in the case of the hypothetical individual of Section 6.2, who does not change over past periods, repeated questioning, which also takes place only in historical time, necessarily yields responses on successively different behavioral functions. Thus behavioral functions can have only hypothetical meaning and, as concluded in Section 7.1 with respect to consumer excess demand functions, the individual cannot be thought of as moving along a behavior function through historical time.

Another aspect of notional or behavioral functions worth remembering is that they only reflect the planned activity of individuals under the assumption that they are able to carry out these plans (Section 7.1). That is, if, under a particular price regime, say, an individual's behavioral functions indicate that he wants to sell some of his initial endowment and use the funds obtained to buy a certain basket of commodities, these plans make sense only if the individual believes that, at the given prices, he will be able to sell the intended endowment, thereby permitting him to buy the intended basket of goods. But just because plans are made does not mean they can be carried out. In the swirl of simultaneous economic activity of the period, as the individual interacts with other individuals and with firms, if markets do not clear, then the assumption that he can buy and sell what he wants at prevailing prices may turn out to be incorrect and he may be frustrated in achieving the intentions expressed in his behavioral functions.

A second element that has to be accounted for, if historical time and ignorance are to be fully recognized, is that in making decisions individuals look not only to the past and present for knowledge and experience but also contemplate and evaluate the future possible consequences of various present choices. Unlike general equilibrium analysis, in this process the individual has only imperfect and usually nonprobabilistic knowledge of the past and present, and no knowledge at all of the future. Thus contemplations and evaluations of future outcomes necessarily fall in the realm of informed, albeit nonprobabilistic, conjecture and guesswork.

In the absence of logical time and perfect knowledge, that is, outside the domain of general equilibrium analysis and the sequence economy, individuals still make decisions, simultaneous activity still occurs, and sequences of events can still be discerned. Individual behavior across time, either from the perspective of the person making decisions or the analyst trying to understand them, can still be analyzed in the tradition of Marshall. And the interaction of the behaviors of two or more individuals taking place simultaneously through time can still be examined in the tradition of Walras. Of course, the analytical visions of Marshall and Walras need careful reconstruction in this nonequilibrium context, and consequently the results of such analyses are decidedly quite different from those of traditional partial equilibrium and general equilibrium analyses and the sequence economy. Models of sequences of simultaneous and interacting behaviors that emerge may be called, to use Shackle's term [6], *kaleidic* economies. As Shackle put it [6, p. 42], a kaleidic economy is an expression of

> the view that the expectations, which together with the drive of needs or ambitions make up the 'springs of action,' are at all times so unsubstantially founded upon data and so mutably suggested by the stream of 'news,' that is, of counter-expected or totally unthought-of events, that they can undergo complete transformation in an hour or even a moment, as the patterns in the kaleidoscope dissolve at a touch. . . .

Even the structures of kaleidic models themselves, that is, the numbers and natures of the relations of these models, as well as the way they fit together, need not remain stable over time. In any event, it is the character of expectations arising from the uncertainty created by the presence of historical time and ignorance that ultimately colors the sequences of simultaneous actions and their outcomes. Uncertainty, then, is the primary "kaleidic factor."

Clearly, to deal with economic simultaneity under conditions of historical time and ignorance requires specification of the particular behaviors that are to be viewed as occurring simultaneously. These behaviors, as indicated above, necessarily emerge from decision making that takes place in the face of uncertainty and require some sort of resolution in each period of (historical) time. In particular, the hypothetical relations describing the simultaneous behavior in, say, period t, have to be solved uniquely if the outcome of the simultaneous interaction of that behavior in period t is to be defined. There are many options. At one extreme, all relevant actions happen together in every period (as occurs along the equilibrium path in general equilibrium analysis); at the other, each act has its own opportunity at the center of the stage while all others watch and wait. Of course, the precise specification of simultaneity employed will depend on the intent of the investigation.

The aim of the present chapter is to show how simultaneity can be represented and analyzed in a kaleidic economy under the nonequilibrium conditions of historical time and ignorance. This is accomplished by providing an example in which a model of simultaneous economic activity is constructed without the limiting methodological assumptions of logical time and perfect knowledge, and hence in which the equilibrium of general equilibrium analysis, even without the extra requirement that all markets clear, cannot be expected to be achieved. Of course, models of present-day economic reality that account for historical time and ignorance are exceedingly complex. Not only do such models have to describe simultaneous behavior, but they also must include a realistic concept of money and be applicable to an arbitrary number of persons, goods, and firms. Although models of this sort are the ultimate aim of the line of inquiry proposed here, the analysis that follows, being an initial step, is necessarily more modest. Indeed, the present strategy is to invoke enough simplifying assumptions to be able to focus exclusively, under conditions of historical time and ignorance, on the most elementary version of the phenomenon of simultaneity alone. Since these assumptions, in part, exclude both production and money, and reduce the number of persons and goods to a minimum, the model obtained cannot be said to represent true economic reality. Nevertheless, the role of simultaneity in understanding situations of historical time and ignorance, and the problems that arise when attempting to model simultaneity in such a context, can still be meaningfully explored. A more interesting model that contains production and money is developed in Chapter 11.

The next section, then, details the example: a simple exchange economy in which two individuals trade from real initial endowments. Time, that is, historical time, is measured in discrete periods.[3] The chapter concludes with some comments and generalizations.

8.1   Two-Person, Two-Commodity Exchange

Imagine an economy, with neither production nor money, in which individuals come together, each with an initial endowment, seeking to improve themselves through trade. But trade requires negotiation (*i.e.*, offers and counteroffers), and negotiation takes time. It is assumed that each person involved in negotiations can make only one offer in any given period. While negotiating, individuals and situations change. Uncertainty is present in at least three forms. First, in any negotiating period, since individuals are unable to peer into the minds of others, they cannot know in advance the offers that will be presented to them, and hence the trading possibilities, at that period. Second, because historical time precludes any knowledge of what individuals will be like in the future, subsequent offers and trading possibilities to be faced are shrouded in mystery. Therefore the final outcome of the negotiating process is also uncertain. And, third, as a special case of the above, no individual can know what he himself will know or will be like in the future. Thus individuals are even uncertain of what their own preferences will be when trade, if it occurs, takes place. Suppose that decisions of offers to propose are made so as to account for these forms of uncertainty in the manner described in Section 4.3. Then, in constructing a potential surprise function over possible, imagined states of the world, the individual takes cognizance of the first two of these forms of uncertainty by looking to his past and present experience, in-

---

[3]It will be convenient to measure time in this way throughout much of the remainder of this volume.

cluding his accumulated knowledge up to the period of decision, as well as to his conjectures of possible future effects at, and perhaps even beyond, the cessation of negotiation and trade. And he recognizes and accounts for the third form of uncertainty in his translation of this potential surprise function over imagined states of the world into a family of potential surprise density functions over utility outcomes.

Next suppose that there are only two goods and two persons. In this simplified circumstance, offers made are not contingent on potential trades involving a third commodity or a third person. Quantities of one of the goods can only be swapped for quantities of the other, and possible trading prices are irrelevant to the making of offers. Since actual trading prices are defined by trades if and when they occur, and since the individual has no knowledge of which trades might eventuate, actual trading prices and their associated budget constraints cannot be known to him. It follows that there is no reason to subject maximization to budget constraints. Maximization is constrained instead by the limited quantities in the individual's initial endowment. Assume further that both individuals propose offers simultaneously in each period and that each person's offer proposal is a set that contains many acceptable trades from his initial endowment. With proposals stated in period t, a specific mechanism (two illustrations are given below) determines which trade, if any, takes place at t. To the extent that trade occurs, a relative trading price is determined for period t, and the traders' real initial endowments are modified accordingly. Actual trading thus affects subsequent offers. The process continues until the individuals involved in negotiating decide to stop.

More precisely, let x_{ik} denote quantities of good i for person k, where $i, k = 1, 2$, and write $x_k = (x_{1k}, x_{2k})$ for each k. (In this and in subsequent notation, except for the individuals' "base points," offer-proposals, and trades, the time indicator t, which should properly appear as a superscript on all symbols, is dropped for purposes of simplification.) Suppose these individuals have initial endowments $\hat{x}_1 = (\hat{x}_{11}, \hat{x}_{21})$ and $\hat{x}_2 = (\hat{x}_{12}, \hat{x}_{22})$, respectively, from which they may be willing to trade. Each person is assumed to have his own perception or expectation of the other's initial endowment. Symbolically, $\hat{x}_1^{e^2} = (\hat{x}_{11}^{e^2}, \hat{x}_{21}^{e^2})$ is person 2's perception of person 1's endowment, and $\hat{x}_2^{e^1} = (\hat{x}_{12}^{e^1}, \hat{x}_{22}^{e^1})$ is person 1's perception of person 2's. Note that, for each $i = 1, 2$, the values $\hat{x}_{i1}$ and $\hat{x}_{i2}$ can be larger than, smaller than, or the same as $\hat{x}_{i1}^{e^2}$ and $\hat{x}_{i2}^{e^1}$, respectively. Negotiation for trade is initiated when one individual, say person k, offers to move from his initial endowment $\hat{x}_k$ to other baskets of commodities x_k, thus suggesting exchanges such as $|x_{1k} - \hat{x}_{1k}|$ for $|x_{2k} - \hat{x}_{2k}|$. As indicated above, the present approach is to take offers to be independent of the exchange values of the initial endowments as defined by the implied rates of exchange and to be proposed in sets, that is, person k offers to move to any one of a collection of baskets B_k. All trades are constrained by the facts that what is given up by one person is received by the other and there are no more than $\hat{x}_{i1} + \hat{x}_{i2}$ units of good i available, where $i = 1, 2$. Since each person has a perception of the other's initial endowment, this may be interpreted to mean, in part, that in any single offer one person cannot ask for more in exchange than he thinks the other possesses.

Focus next on a period in time, t, at which person k determines a collection of offers B_k^t to propose. Take person k to be the type of decision maker described in Section 4.3. His decision set or collection of choice options (objects of choice) is

$$X_1 = \left\{ x_1 : x_1 = (x_{11}, x_{21}) \leq (\hat{x}_{11} + \hat{x}_{12}^{e^1}, \hat{x}_{21} + \hat{x}_{22}^{e^1}) \right\}$$

if $k = 1$ and

$$X_2 = \left\{ x_2 : x_2 = (x_{12}, x_{22}) \leq (\hat{x}_{11}^{e^2} + \hat{x}_{12}, \hat{x}_{21}^{e^2} + \hat{x}_{22}) \right\}$$

when $k = 2$. Observe that, in each case, X_k contains person k's initial endowment. In addition, because X_k depends on the perceptions or expectations of person k, it can vary from period to period, even though initial endowments remain fixed. For each option x_k, and in light of the uncertainty about his preferences, about the current offer proposal he may face, and about the end result of trade, let person k contemplate the (incomplete) collection of possible, imagined states of the world, along with the preference ordering he might have at the end of trade, and determine his corresponding collection of utility outcomes, his family of potential surprise density functions defined over those outcomes, and his attractiveness function. These elements are all time dependent, and the specification of them is grounded in the forms of uncertainty discussed above. Recall that, as envisaged in Section

4.3, to conjure them up the decision maker has to ponder what he has learned in the past and present as well as the possibilities that may arise in the future as the effects of the various decision choices play themselves out. Also, in the manner outlined in Section 4.3, let person k build his time-dependent decision index, $D^k(x_k)$, over X_k. Finally suppose that person k independently selects, at each t, a *base* point $\tilde{x}_k^t$, such that $D^k(\tilde{x}_k^t) \geq D^k(\hat{x}_k)$, from which he determines his offers, and define his proposal of offers at time t as

$$B_k^t = \left\{ x_k : x_k \text{ is in } X_k, \text{ and } D^k(x_k) \geq D^k(\tilde{x}_k^t) \right\}. \qquad (8.1\text{-}1)$$

Thus, with time starting at $t = 0$, say, person k produces a "kaleidic" sequence of offer proposals $B_k^0, B_k^1, B_k^2, \ldots$. Note that, as mentioned earlier, trading prices do not figure into the individual's decisions. Furthermore, because initial endowments change when trade occurs, and because other elements of the construction determining the B_k^t vary with time, no relation between any pair $B_k^{t'}$ and $B_k^{t''}$ can be known before both t' and t'' have passed.

The selection of a base point by an individual may be thought of as setting his "negotiating strategy" for the relevant period of time. Although not done here, it is also possible to characterize behavior B_k^t as a function of strategies $\tilde{x}_k^t$, for each k at every t. Such a behavioral function would indicate the set of proposed offers that are associated with each strategy $\tilde{x}_k^t$. But, as suggested at the outset, these behavioral functions would generally be valid only for the period t at which they are defined, nor would it be possible to move along them through time in any way.

Suppose both individuals propose offers simultaneously in each period $t = 0, 1, 2, \ldots$. Write the proposals of person 1 in terms of his own coordinate system as described in (8.1-1), that is,

$$B_1^t = \left\{ x_1 : x_1 \text{ is in } X_1, \text{ and } D^1(x_1) \geq D^1(\tilde{x}_1^t) \right\}.$$

It is instructive to look at the trading possibilities and potential outcomes from a perspective akin to that of the traditional Edgeworth box analysis. For this purpose, one might assume that each person knows the initial endowment of the other with complete accuracy and certainty, that is, $\hat{x}_1 = \hat{x}_1^{e^2}$ and $\hat{x}_2 = \hat{x}_2^{e^1}$. Under such conditions, all trade offers would satisfy the vector equation

$$x_2 = \hat{x}_1 + \hat{x}_2 - x_1,$$

and the proposals of person 2 could be expressed in the coordinate system of person 1. Denote person 2's proposals in this form by B_2^{*t}, for all t, so that

$$B_2^{*t} = \left\{ x_1 : \hat{x}_1 + \hat{x}_2 - x_1 \geq 0, \text{ and } D^2(\hat{x}_1 + \hat{x}_2 - x_1) \geq D^2(\tilde{x}_2^t) \right\}.$$

Then the feasible trades that the two individuals could make at time t would be given by the intersection $B_1^t \cap B_2^{*t}$. Were $B_1^t \cap B_2^{*t} = \phi$, no trade would be possible at t. In these circumstances, however, due to the continued presence of historical time and the other manifestations of ignorance set out above, the analytical aparatus that emerges (as will be described subsequently) is quite different from that which generally corresponds to the standard Edgeworthian construction.

Return now to the more general situation in which neither person is sure of the other's endowment. To complete the model, it remains to specify what it means to say that agreement is reached in any period t. If agreement is reached at t, then the individuals trade at t and, should they negotiate further at $t + 1$, they necessarily bargain from a new initial endowment. If agreement is not reached at t, then trade does not take place at t. In this case, too, the individuals have the option of continuing to negotiate at $t + 1$. Thus the kaleidic sequences of the offer proposals of the two persons may exhibit the reaching of agreement in more than one period of time.

Consider, first, a highly restricted and simplified characterization of reaching agreement. An alternative approach is discussed later. Suppose that agreement is said to be *reached* in a period t provided there exists unique vectors $\bar{x}_1^t = (\bar{x}_{11}^t, \bar{x}_{21}^t)$ in B_1^t and $\bar{x}_2^t = (\bar{x}_{12}^t, \bar{x}_{22}^t)$ in B_2^t such that

$$|\bar{x}_{11}^t - \hat{x}_{11}| = |\bar{x}_{12}^t - \hat{x}_{12}|$$

and

$$|\bar{x}_{21}^t - \hat{x}_{21}| = |\bar{x}_{22}^t - \hat{x}_{22}|.$$

In the special Edgeworthian-type case introduced above, in which both initial endowments are known to the two individuals, this is equivalent to the statement that $B_1^t \cap B_2^{*t} = \{\bar{x}_1^t\}$. At any rate, upon reaching agreement, $|\bar{x}_{11}^t - \hat{x}_{11}|$ is exchanged for $|\bar{x}_{21}^t - \hat{x}_{21}|$, and the individuals move from their initial endowment positions to $\bar{x}_1^t$ and $\bar{x}_2^t = \hat{x}_1 + \hat{x}_2 - \bar{x}_1^t$, respectively. Moreover, the trading price or rate of exchange, that is, the relative price of good 1, for example, is established as

$$\frac{|\bar{x}_{11}^t - \hat{x}_{11}|}{|\bar{x}_{21}^t - \hat{x}_{21}|}.$$

If agreement cannot be reached in finite time, then no agreement is possible: it makes no sense in historical time to let t approach infinity.

It also does not make any sense to ask, when $t = 0$ is the present, say, whether the parameters and functions of the model are such that agreement can eventually be reached. One cannot know in advance if agreement can be secured because one cannot know in advance how the parameters and functions of the model, indeed how the model itself, will evolve as historical time moves on. And, anyway, with hindsight it will always be possible in the future to tell through observation if agreement is ultimately obtained. Of course, one could always ask, if functions and parameters were stable over time, under what conditions would agreement always be reached? But in practically all situations such a question would not be interesting because it would not have any relevance for what is happening in historical time.

Thus the kaleidic model developed here is, in a very real sense, both open and closed. On the one hand, it is open in that there is not enough information available to the individual traders or the investigator for the model to determine a unique time path along which, in the absence of parameter shifts, future negotiation (i.e., subsequent values of the B_k^t) will proceed. One cannot tell in advance if and when trade will take place. On the other hand, the model is closed in that the simultaneous behavior in each period t is uniquely resolved at t to determine the outcome of the simultaneity and if trade actually occurs at t. Such a resolution depends on the offer proposals of the two persons and on the compatibility of those offers, and results in the occurrence of trade should agreement be reached. Clearly, when agreement is not reached at t, the outcome of the simultaneous behavior at t consists of the pair (B_1^t, B_2^t); when it is, the outcome reduces to $(\bar{x}_1^t, \bar{x}_2^t)$. The simultaneity described by the model, then, is only a "partial" simultaneity. Because the individuals' preferences might turn out to be different from what they initially expected, even if agreement were reached, it could still, unlike the traditional general equilibrium tâtonnement, leave both individuals desirous of further trade. This, then, underscores the fundamental methodological property of models of simultaneous economic behavior under conditions of historical time and ignorance just stated: that behavior that is seen as occurring simultaneously in each period must be uniquely resolved in some way in a closed submodel valid only at that moment while, at the same time, the overall model itself necessarily remains open to allow for the unforeseen novelty that the future hides. And, as the kaleidics of uncertainty unfold, the evolving model, with its changing internal structure, the changing functions of that structure, and its changing parameter values, generates an unpredictable sequence of outcomes across time.[4]

For the particular Edgeworthian-type case in which both individuals know both endowments, that is, in which a significant part of the uncertainty facing them is assumed away, the geometry of the offer proposals and possible trades that emerge in any period of time can be illustrated in the familiar Edgeworth box diagram of Figure 8-1. Person 1's origin is in the lower left corner and person 2's origin is in the upper right. The initial endowment appears at the point labeled ε and determines the dimensions of the box. Assume, for the purposes of the diagram only, that each $D^k(x_k)$ is (like individual utility functions in the traditional theory of demand) differentiable, increasing, and strictly quasi concave. Then level contours through ε of the decision indices exist and may be identified as d_1 and d_2, respectively. (Evidently, these coutours are valid only for the particular period of time t under consideration. In any other period of negotiation, the decision index, and hence the level coutours, are different.) Furthermore, with $\tilde{x}_k^t = \hat{x}_k$ at

---

[4]As indicated earlier, trades are contemplated and may take place at successive time dates. In this sense, the sequential decision making that occurs captures an alternative meaning of what is, in effect, a "sequence" economy. Clearly the notion of sequence economy as it is here understood, because of its considerations of historical time and uncertainty, and because of the decision processes it involves, is quite different from the traditional vision described at the beginning of this chapter. Indeed, its kaleidic character has been discussed at length above.

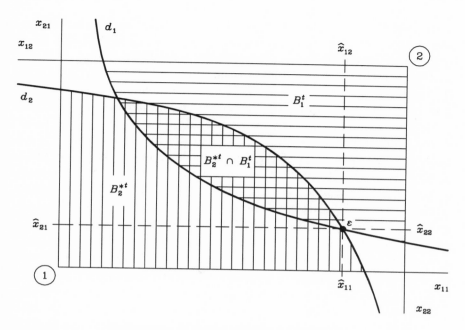

Figure 8–1.   Offers proposed in a two–person, two–good exchange
situation with known initial endowments.

moment t for each k, B_1^t is the horizontal shaded region; B_2^t, or, in the
coordinate system of person 1, B_2^{*t}, is the vertically shaded region; and
$B_1^t \cap B_2^{*t}$ is the crosshatched area between the two contours.[5] Clearly,
for these $\tilde{x}_1^t$ and $\tilde{x}_2^t$, agreement is not reached since $B_1^t \cap B_2^{*t}$ contains
more than one point. For other values of $\tilde{x}_1^t$ and $\tilde{x}_2^t$, agreement might
be reached at t and, if so, then the vector to which the individuals
would trade, namely, $(\bar{x}_1^t, \bar{x}_2^t)$, would necessarily (due to the extreme
speciality of the assumptions made in this case) appear in the diagram
at a tangency between a level contour for person 1 and a level contour

[5]Note that there is still uncertainty in this diagram in that neither person knows
the basket of commodities with which he will wind up and the decision index that
he will have at the conclusion of the negotiations.

for person 2. (One or the other of these latter level contours can be the same as, respectively, d_1 or d_2, but not both.) Observe that under the specialized conditions imposed in Figure 8-1 this $(\bar{x}_1^t, \bar{x}_2^t)$ would be pairwise Pareto optimal in the sense that, given the decision indices in the period of agreement and exchange, it is impossible through further trading *in that period* to push higher up on one person's decision index without sliding lower on the other's. However, although the slope of the straight line connecting $(\bar{x}_1^t, \bar{x}_2^t)$ to the initial endowment in a suitably redrawn version of Figure 8-1 is the trading price as defined above, the line itself need not be tangent to the tangent level contours at the point of tangency $(\bar{x}_1^t, \bar{x}_2^t)$. That is, $(\bar{x}_1^t, \bar{x}_2^t)$ together with the established trading price is not necessarily a momentary "equilibrium" and, if not, trading out of equilibrium or "false trading" has occurred.[6]

It is important to recognize that the analogy of trading to the tangency between level contours of the two decision indices arises in this special case only because of the particular characterization of reaching agreement employed above. Moreover, there are at least three reasons why a person might be willing to participate in trading that involves a different characterization of reaching agreement and hence be willing to accept a trade to a nontangency point where two level contours only intersect. First, the individual might have, or think that he has, relevant information that the other person does not possess. Second, he might hold expectations of the future that would render such a move appropriate. And, third, he may misperceive the other person's intentions or decision index. In any event, an alternative way to characterize the reaching of agreement is in terms of some random mechanism whose outcome at time t reflects these possibilities and determines, when $B_1^t \cap B_2^{*t} \neq \phi$, whether trade takes place and, if it does, which $\bar{x}_1^t$ in $B_1^t \cap B_2^{*t}$ is secured. (As before, when $B_1^t \cap B_2^{*t} = \phi$ no trading occurs.) A similar characterization could be expressed in the context in which each person is only able to guess at the other's initial endowment. With such a characterization in either situation, although individuals are still trying to improve their positions, the resulting vector to which they trade if agreement is reached at t, namely, $(\bar{x}_1^t, \bar{x}_2^t)$,

---

[6]In more general models, of course, neither trading nor false trading necessarily takes place at the equivalent of tangency points.

will not, in general, even be pairwise Pareto optimal. That is, pairwise Pareto optimality can arise only by accident.

8.2 Some Generalizations

In the presence of more than two goods and two persons, a more complex model, involving more than just the obvious addition of goods and persons, is needed. One of the added requirements is that each person conjures up in his own mind estimated or perceived trading prices with which to value his initial endowment.[7] For one person's willingness to propose an offer to another may now depend on, say, the relative values or prices he perceives of two of the goods that could possibly be exchanged for a third, or on the terms of trade, and hence relative values or prices, he expects to secure in a different trade with a third party. Each choice set X_k is thus defined by a budget constraint, and maximization effectively takes place subject to that constraint. Another added requirement is to determine who trades with whom. A simple, if not entirely realistic, possibility here is to assume that, at every t, some specified rule such as a random drawing assigns a trading partner to each individual desiring one. (If there were an odd number of persons looking to trade, then one of them would not be able to do so at time t.) Note, however, that under the conditions of Figure 8-1, although pairwise Pareto optimality may be achievable among all pairs of traders in some period t, such a situation, when it obtains, still might not be Pareto optimal with respect to all traders simultaneously. Moreover, the introduction of a generally acceptable medium of exchange (money) that allows purchasing power command over commodities to be transported and temporarily stored, would facilitate the possible movement toward an overall Pareto optimum.[8] In that case, an individual might, for example, accept more of the medium of exchange now, hoping to trade it away to someone else (or even the same person) at a later date. In any event, if trade takes place between two partners in period t, their

---

[7] Due to the kaleidic uncertainty in which individuals operate, such estimates are likely to vary across persons and bear little relation to actual trading prices.

[8] *Cf.* Starr [7] and the papers following it in the same volume. See also Section 10.1.

initial endowments change for the next period, $t + 1$. Then, at period $t+1$, those individuals wishing to find new trading partners participate in the drawing at that moment, and the process continues.[9]

Observe that when trade takes place between two persons with more than two goods, the established rates of exchange are necessarily consistent in that the rate at which good i exchanges for good j is the same as the product of the rate at which good i exchanges for good n, say, and the rate at which good n exchanges for good j. But in the presence of more than two individuals, since each pair of persons establishes, if they trade, their own rates of exchange, such consistency usually does not extend to the market level. Indeed, in a kaleidic world where exchanges take place in historical time, it is not generally possible to define the market rates of exchange to which such consistency might relate. Even if all possible cross-rates of exchange were mutually consistent, individuals might still want to engage in additional trading because their expectations concerning their own preferences upon completion of their original exchanges might not have been fulfilled. A similar statement applies to the comparison of rates of exchange across time regardless of the number of persons involved in trade.

Expressed in its generalized form, however, the model outlined above still describes a highly specialized situation. Clearly markets that do not function in terms of pairwise negotiation and trade, that provide for the sale of newly produced commodities, or that possess true monetary intermediation, in other words most markets in the real economic world, cannot be modeled in this way. (A more realistic model is constructed in Chapter 11.) But in any system of markets that is viewed from the perspective of historical time and ignorance, to the extent that simultaneity in individual (and firm) decision making or behavior is present, such simultaneity has to be handled in a manner analogous to that depicted here.

To glimpse how simultaneous microeconomic behavior can be modeled more universally, and to anticipate, in part, the analysis of Chapter 11, consider very briefly a world with production and many consumers,

---

[9]Such a model provides a fourth approach, in addition to the three of Section 7.2, to analyzing markets in the absence of the ability to aggregate and obtain market demand and supply functions.

firms, and goods. As in the above example it is first necessary to determine the forms of uncertainty that are introduced by the presence of ignorance, the simultaneous decisions (and hence behaviors) that arise in their milieu, and the mechanism that resolves this (partial) simultaneity in each period of time. One possibility is as follows: let markets operate on the basis of short-side trading rules and associated rationing schemes.[10] Let each consumer decide on quantities of comodities to buy, amounts to save in the form of the purchase of IOUs issued by firms, and quantities of factors to sell. Let each firm estimate the demand for its output and plan its investment in real capital and financial assets. Then, based partly on these estimates and decisions, let it determine the quantities of inputs it demands and hence the output it wants to produce, the price at which it sells that output, and the quantity of IOUs it will try to sell (positive or negative) to finance these operations. All market allocations and consumer and firm decisions are made simultaneously in each period, and each decision requires the relevant decision maker to face appropriate forms of uncertainty. Such uncertainty may arise, in part, from ignorance about preferences, and ignorance of the extent to which plans and intentions will turn out to be realized. And, as before, this uncertainty imparts a kaleidic quality to the model. In consequence, the resolution of the simultaneous behavior produced by these decisions necessitates consideration of the possibility that, in any period, not all markets clear and hence that consumers might not have enough income to purchase what they originally intended, that firms might not be able to secure sufficient quantities of inputs so as to meet the demand for their output, that firms' revenues might not be enough to cover their costs, and so on. The ability, or lack thereof, to realize plans and intentions in one period is one of many elements that influences the decisions made at the next. Thus, as in the example of the previous section, the model is closed in its unique resolution of the simultaneity of each period and open in its awareness of kaleidic change across time.

In general, it is clear that models of simultaneous economic activ-

---

[10]Recall Section 7.2. Actually, the model of Chapter 11 treats only the markets for goods and labor in this way and, as suggested in Section 7.2, deals with the IOU markets somewhat differently.

ity accounting for ignorance and historical time have a different conceptual basis than their perfect knowledge, logical time counterparts. Their main focus necessarily is on the possibility of a unique and independent coherence among appropriately specified activities in each period that is unrelated to the possibility of coherence in any other period. (A formal and more complete definition of coherence is given in the introduction to Chapter 11.) Such coherence, assuming it exists, is a nonequilibrium solution notion. That is, it can be described as the unique solution of a system of equations valid only in that period. Furthermore, the solution itself is not an equilibrium (*i.e.*, a position from which no change over time takes place without parameter modification), nor can it be a part of a time-path that converges to one.[11] By contrast, the standard perfect knowledge, logical time, Walrasian microeconomic model is a system whose equations are fixed over time and whose unique solutions lie either on an equilibrium path along which, in the absence of parameter variation, no change occurs or on a time-path that stands in some relation (*e.g.*, converging) to the equilibrium path.

Any of these models can be used to explain what is seen. As indicated in Section 1.2, this is accomplished in the Walrasian case by interpreting observations taken over time either as separate equilibria that arise from variations in functions and parameter values (in which case dynamic movement such as convergence toward an equilibrium path is hidden from view), or as points along a time-path that is converging, say, toward the equilibrium path (in which case the equilibrium itself cannot be seen). In the latter situation, of course, functions and parameters could modify in time, and subsequent observations would then lie on a different time-path converging to a different equilibrium path. However, there is no such choice of interpretation when using kaleidic models that recognize historical time and ignorance. Nor can there be any interpretation of observations in reference to equilibrium. The only possibility in these circumstances is to identify what is seen with the unique coherence of the period in the model, as the model itself evolves kaleidically through historical time. In terms of the example

---

[11]In particular instances, it could, of course, be constant across periods if, with hindsight, the equations of the model turn out to be stable over those periods (recall Section 1.5). Alternatively, the solution could be part of what was referred to as "historical equilibrium" in n. 24 on p. 29.

presented earlier, the model of Section 8.1 explains an observed process of negotiation that may or may not end in agreement. Thus, rather than trying to clarify particular static postures, these kinds of models attempt to illuminate an ongoing and changing process.[12]

8.3 References

1. Arthur, W. B., *Increasing Returns and Path Dependence in the Economy* (Ann Arbor: University of Michigan Press, 1994).

2. Benassy, J. P., *The Economics of Market Disequilibrium* (New York: Academic Press, 1982).

3. Cournot, A., *Researches into the Mathematical Principles of the Theory of Wealth*, N. T. Bacon, trans. (New York: Kelley, 1960).

4. Hahn, F. H., "On the Foundations of Monetary Theory," in *Essays in Modern Economics*, M. Parkin and A. R. Nobay, eds. (London: Longman, 1973), pp. 230-242.

5. Loasby, B. J., *Choice, Complexity and Ignorance* (Cambridge: Cambridge University Press, 1976).

6. Shackle, G. L. S., *Keynesian Kaleidics* (Edinburgh: Edinburgh University Press, 1974).

7. Starr, R. M., Introduction to a paper by A. M. Feldman, in *General Equilibrium Models of Monetary Economics*, R. M. Starr, ed. (San Diego: Academic Press, 1989), pp. 83-84.

---

[12]*cf.*, Loasby [5, pp. 214,220]. In this respect they also have much in common with those investigated by Arthur [1].

PART III

Modeling the Economy and Its Constituent Parts

CHAPTER 9

The Firm

The theories of simultaneous economic behavior that arise in both microeconomic and macroeconomic contexts lie at the heart of twentieth century economic thought. But, as has been and will continue to be emphasized here, these theories, with their emphasis on equilibrium and their requirements that individuals possess knowledge of the future, are unable to accommodate an analysis in which things are always in kaleidic flux and ignorance is a fact of economic life. Based on the discussion of simultaneity in Chapter 8, building on the model of decision making developed in Section 4-3, and avoiding the aggregation shown to be inappropriate in Chapter 7, Part III constructs a historical time and ignorance framework within which simultaneous economic behavior can be handled at the micro- and macrolevels. It thus provides a vision and analysis of simultaneity that is alternative to, and may serve as a replacement for, the traditional approach. This is not to say, however, that the entire body of conventional economic analysis is to be discarded. To the contrary, abundant use is made of traditional elements such as, for example, production and utility functions. But, of course, these elements are necessarily employed in different ways and in different contexts. The present chapter begins with the firm; subsequent chapters engage the consumer, the microeconomy, and the macroeconomy, in that order.

It is a generally accepted fact that the primary role of the firm in modern economies is production or the employment of inputs to produce outputs. Concomitant with this, as a necessary support for the

This chapter is reproduced, with considerable additions, corrections, and other modifications, from my "The Firm under Conditions of Ignorance and Historical Time," *Journal of Post Keynesian Economics* 13 (1990-91), pp. 125-145.

carrying out of production, are the firm's investment in durable inputs and work in progress, and the financing, by the sale of debt securities and the issuance of equity capital shares, of its production and investment operations. Production, investment, financing, the distribution of net revenues to the providers of debt and equity capital, and the provision for expansion structure the firm's interdependent activities. Traditionally the analysis of such a firm has been set in the equilibrium-analytic context of logical time and perfect knowledge. In terms of the assumption content of the analyses themselves, this has meant, respectively, that the period of time for which an analysis or model is constructed and applied to a given firm is irrelevant to the nature of that model and its constituent relations, and that enough information is available so that decision making in the firm either does not have to contend with uncertainty or, if it does, the uncertainty is reducible to an expression of probability.[1] Thus, under these conditions, the firm only has to concern itself with maximizing such things as profit,[2] expected profit,[3] the rate of return on the money capital invested in it,[4] or the economic value of the owners' investment in the firm.[5]

However, from the nonequilibrium perspective adopted in this volume, and as alluded to immediately above, it is clear that economic realities render the assumptions of logical time and perfect knowledge unusable. On the one hand, because each period of time has its own unique properties, events, and history associated with it, and because individuals in each period have their own unique epistemic statuses, perceptions, and expectations, the decisions contemplated by firms or their decision makers in each period are also necessarily unique. On

---

[1] It is well known that, when information is costly, firms will usually not have "complete" information at their disposal. Indeed, they will only seek information up to the point at which the marginal value of additional information equals the marginal cost of securing it. Under such circumstances, and, perhaps, not surprisingly, analysis has frequently taken refuge in probability (*e.g.*, Hey [2, Ch. 7]). However, as described earlier, an assumption of probability is taken here to be a manifestation of perfect knowledge.

[2] Katzner [3, Ch. 5].

[3] This is a special case of the maximization of the expected utility of profit described by Hey [2, pp. 127-129].

[4] Katzner [3, Ch. 12].

[5] Vickers [5, Ch. 10].

the other hand, with the complexity of reality rendering knowledge about economic matters of the past and present largely incomplete, if not inaccurate, and with knowledge of the future unobtainable, the construction by decision makers of a manipulable probability density function for use in making decisions, even if such a density function could be assumed to exist in reality, is out of the question. Hence, logical time and perfect knowledge have to be replaced by historical time and ignorance, and the issue immediately arises of how to reformulate the analysis of the firm, and decision making within it, to reflect that replacement.

One possibility for decision making proposed by Carter [1] involves the successive elimination of alternative actions according to a sequence of very specific criteria, with the final decision "falling out" in a relatively simple way from a greatly reduced choice set. Vickers [6, Pt. 3; 7, Ch. 12] has suggested an alternative in which the firm decides among investment projects using the model of Section 4.3. But Carter's proposal is only sketched without any in-depth analysis, and Vickers' analysis is applied only to the investment decisions of the firm. Thus a complete theory of the firm in the context of ignorance and historical time is not yet available. It is the purpose of the present chapter to begin the attempt to fill this gap by showing how Vickers' analysis of the determination of firm investment decisions can be extended into the areas of production and finance.

The chapter starts with a brief, general description of the approach to be employed. It then develops a model of the firm in historical time and ignorance that identifies the estimates and decisions that the firm has to make. Lastly, employing the apparatus of Section 4.3, the determination of these estimates and decisions is examined amid the uncertainty that is created by the presence of historical time and ignorance. In this latter regard, one of the basic elements that needs clarification is the construction of 1-1 and onto functions mapping imagined states of the world in Ω into outcomes in Ψ so that the decision maker's potential surprise function on the subsets of Ω can be translated into a family of potential surprise functions defined on Ψ. To keep matters simple, consideration of the firm's selection of a portfolio of marketable, income-earning assets and money is deferred to Chapter 11.

It should also be borne in mind that, as already mentioned, the main focus of this chapter and the next two is the construction of a model of the "full" microeconomy. Thus Chapter 10 analyzes the consumer's demand for goods and supply of factors, including his selection of a portfolio and his demand for money balances. And Chapter 11 takes this analysis and combines it with an analysis of banks and an expansion of the present analysis of the firm (which adds in the firm's choice of a portfolio and money balances) to secure the total picture.

9.1   An Overview

It is assumed for present purposes, and with a certain violence to realism, that the firm is financed by, or, in other words, obtains its money capital only through, the sale of debt securities that are referred to as IOUs. Equity capital is ignored. Time is discrete. The firm is thought of as a "steady-state" entity that is analytically "reconstructed" in each period. It is run by a single, human decision maker who can be the principal owner of the firm's debt (*i.e.*, the principal supplier of its money capital), an employee (manager), or both. As an owner, the decision maker receives a rate of return on the money capital he has provided; as an employee, he is paid a salary or wage.

An obvious way to proceed from here is to conceive of the decision maker as constructing independent potential surprise functions over σ-fields of sets with respect to such variables as current sales or output, labor available to employ, durable inputs available for purchase, the price at which its outstanding IOUs can be bought back, and so on. Next, all but the first of these potential surprise functions would be combined into a potential surprise function over sets of costs and this, together with that over sets of sales, would be reduced to a potential surprise function over sets of rates of return on the money capital invested in the firm. Of course, some of these potential surprise functions would be conditioned on the potential surprise values assigned to sets of values of the other variables. For example, the potential surprise of a collection of cost values would depend, in part, on the potential surprise value assigned to the outputs that are produced at those levels of cost. In any case, based on this structure of potential surprise functions, a model would then be built that uses the procedure of Section

4.3 (appropriately modified to fit this context) to derive the decisions made by the decision maker.

However, the method of analysis just described is exceedingly complex, involving, as it does, consideration of rather intricate interrelations between a sizable number of potential surprise functions characterized with respect to very specific economic variables. The present perspective avoids these difficulties by having the decision maker think in terms of only one potential surprise function that is defined in a more general context, namely, over collections of imagined states of the world. In this way, the model of Section 4.3 can be applied directly.

It is supposed, then, that in each period of time t, the decision maker formally estimates certain "fundamental" things such as, for example, the current demand function for the firm's output (the estimates so obtained are referred to as primary estimates), and makes an investment decision that sets the stage for future production and earnings.[6] In addition, based on his primary estimates and investment decision, he also comes up with a price determination and further projections (called secondary estimates) that fix the firm's output price and reflect its implied production and financial needs. Thus the decision maker maps out an operating program for the firm at each t. Estimates and decisions are relevant only for the period of time at which they are made. Each vector consisting of one collection of primary estimates and one investment decision possibility is viewed as an object of choice or choice option. Although situations and estimates may be imagined for many subsequent periods in advance, analytical constructions involving decisions for more than one period at a time are not considered.

---

[6]If only a marginal investment involving a project with a well defined economic life were under consideration, then the worthiness of that investment would depend on the relation between the present value of the future income stream it is expected to produce, discounted at the current required rate of return on money capital, and its current cost. But in the context of the steady-state firm, understood to be reconstructed in each successive period t, attention may focus instead, as it does here, on the steady-state rate of return earned on the firm's investment as a whole, assuming that its real capital stock is maintained intact through appropriate depreciation provisions. Specifically, in determining its investment decision, the firm's decision maker need only consider, as described in Section 9.3, the demand curve for the firm's output that he expects the firm to face in the next period, that is, in the next steady state.

Upon selecting a choice option, the decision maker can also estimate the resulting rate of return he expects the firm to earn on the money capital invested in it in period t. This rate of return is the steady-state rate of return that would be realized supposing that net investment in all subsequent periods is zero, that appropriate functions and parameter values do not change, and that all other relevant variables remain fixed through time at suitable values. Because time is historical, the estimate of the steady-state rate of return has to be recalculated at each t (since at every moment the firm faces a unique situation)[7] and, based on the new estimate, the question of whether the firm should liquidate its durable-good assets or continue production must be re-evaluated before implementation of the decision maker's operating program.[8] It is assumed that this re-evaluation always results in the continued operation of the firm or, in other words, that the recalculated estimate of the steady-state rate of return is always greater than what could be obtained elsewhere upon liquidation of the firm and reinvestment of its realized capital value. Thus, even if the decision maker thought the firm could earn more in some future period $t + k$, say, than in period t (where t is the present and $k > 0$), there would still be no need to cease operations in the present and shift the firm's resources through time to the period with the larger rate of return.

As indicated above, the main thrust of the analysis of decision making to be employed follows Section 4.3. The first step, then, is to identify the particular decision and primary estimates (which are actually viewed here as additional decisions) that the firm has to make and the ignorance and consequent uncertainty that it has to face in making them. The outcome of the decision, as well as the accuracy of the estimates, depends on the imagined present and future states of the world that arise as the impacts of the decision work themselves out. Possible

---

[7]The duration of calendar time between any t and $t + 1$ is not specified and may vary depending on business conditions.

[8]This, of course, assumes the existence of a viable spot market for second-hand durable goods. The prices established in this market presumably would take into account the depreciated value of the durable goods and their possible economic value when put to work in some alternative line of economic activity. In actual fact, the realizable value of any used durable good may be minimal due to its high economic specificity.

states of the world are combined into vectors, with each vector containing a possible present state (the present not yet having been revealed) and a collection of possible future states, one for each of an appropriate finite number of subsequent periods.[9] It is over sets of these possible vectors, as imagined by him, that the decision maker is assumed to construct his potential surprise function.[10]

The next step is to translate the potential surprise function defined over such vectors into a family of potential surprise density functions defined over possible (scalar) implicit rate of return outcomes for the firm as a whole across the finite sequence of periods under consideration. That is, the realization of a hypothetical state of the world in period t would give rise to a collection of outcomes relating to the specific primary estimates and decision made in that period and this, in turn, would determine the actual steady-state rate of return that the firm would earn in period t on the money capital invested in it. Similarly, the realization of a present state and a finite sequence of future states beginning with $t + 1$ would generate, assuming no change in the relevant functions and parameters, an actual future steady-state rate of return for each subsequent future state. This finite sequence of rates of return starting in period t would define an implicit rate of return over the entire time interval of all periods taken together. To perform the required translation to a potential surprise density function necessitates, for each vector of possible estimates and decision, that is, for each vector of choice options, the construction of a 1-1 correspondence between the imagined vectors of present and future states of the world, on the one hand, and (scalar) implicit rate of return outcomes on the other.

Finally, given the decision maker's family of potential surprise density functions, application of the remainder of the apparatus of Section

---

[9]Only the special case in which the dimensionality of such state of the world vectors is two, that is, in which there is a present period and a single future period, is actually analyzed below.

[10]In addition to this potential surprise function, a potential surprise function over sets of scalar states of the world emerging in any subsequent single period $t + k$, where t is the present and $k > 0$, could be introduced that is conditional on potential surprise values for sets of vectors whose components consist of a present state at t and future states for $t + 1, t + 2, \ldots, t + k - 1$. But the analysis and use of such functions in the present context is not pursued here.

4.3 leads to the selection of a particular choice option. This, recall, is achieved by first characterizing the properties of each possible alternative in terms of the maximization of the decision maker's attractiveness function for that alternative, subject to that alternative's potential surprise density function, and then choosing the option with the best characterization as defined by his decision index.[11]

Having made his estimates and decision for period t, the decision maker awaits period $t + 1$ to see how things turned out in period t. The likelihood is that not all of his estimates will have been correct, nor will all of his intentions have been realized. Thus it may be appropriate to make allowances in estimates and the decision in period $t + 1$ in an attempt to compensate for the unexpected occurrences in period t. Furthermore, the decision maker may even find himself severely constrained in $t + 1$ by the implications of his previous decision. And, of course, since both the decision maker and the economy are different at $t + 1$ from what they were at t, that is, since time is historical, the decision maker's choice options, the future states he imagines, his potential surprise and attractiveness functions, and his decision index, are all new.

9.2   A Model of the Firm

In order to identify the specific primary estimates and the decision that have to be made by the decision maker, it is convenient to have a model of how the firm operates. The following will suffice for present purposes.

Suppose the firm produces a single output, employing both durable inputs and labor. The durable inputs used by the firm that have been acquired in the past and have not yet worn out constitute the firm's real or physical capital stock. The money capital with which to finance the purchase of durable inputs and work in progress is obtained by selling IOUs in one-dollar denominations. New issues of IOUs always sell at their par value of one dollar. Every IOU comes with a contractual

---

[11]It should be noted that the decision maker may not attempt to maximize his decision index if by going to a nonmaximum position he can build flexibility into the firm's operations and thereby make future adjustments easier. (See, for example, Vickers [5, p. 197].) However, this possibility is not explored here.

commitment of a specific rate of return its holder is to receive at each moment of time and is assumed to be issued in perpetuity.[12] To the extent that the firm is able to save by accumulating funds to replace worn-out durables (depreciation) and by earning a return beyond what is required to service its debt, the need to issue new IOUs in order to meet its current money capital requirement is diminished.

Two rates of return on the money capital invested in the firm are of interest. The *required* rate of return is the rate of return described above that the buyer contractually requires the firm to pay when it issues and sells an IOU. The prices of outstanding IOUs always adjust in the IOU market so as to reflect their required rates of return. Clearly outstanding IOUs with different required or contractual rates of return will sell at different prices. (Recall that the price of new issues of IOUs has been fixed at one dollar.) It is assumed for convenience that in making its decisions in period t the firm takes the rate of return it will be required to pay on any new IOUs it issues, along with the prices of any outstanding IOUs it intends to buy back, as those determined in the IOU market in period $t-1$. To the extent that this supposition turns out to be incorrect, the planned operating program of the firm, as set out momentarily, will not be realized.[13] The *actual* rate of return is the rate of return that the firm actually earns on the money capital obtained from the sale of the IOUs. If all plans and intentions of the firm were actually and fully realized, then the required and actual rates of return would be brought into equality with each other. But, from the perspective of the firm, no assumptions of realization of plans and intentions are legitimate. Indeed, there is no guarantee that the firm will be profitable enough to even meet the required obligations on its debt.

Since the firm is likely to have issued IOUs at different times in the past, and since the required rate of return can differ in different periods, the firm typically has to pay different required rates of return

---

[12]In the absence of the latter assumption, the contractual return and hence the resale price of each outstanding IOU would depend, in part, on its maturity date.

[13]The firm's planned net supply of new issues of IOUs, or its planned net demand for outstanding IOUs to buy back, which contribute in period t to the subsequent setting of the required rate of return and the prices of outstanding IOUs in the IOU market, are determined according to equation (9.2-15) below.

for batches of IOUs issued on different dates. Let $\hat{\rho}^t$ be the (weighted) average required rate of return over all outstanding IOUs of the firm at time t. Clearly $\hat{\rho}^t$ is a fixed, known parameter at every t.

As suggested above, depreciation funds accumulate as savings in the firm and may be used to finance investment. Current depreciation charges depend on the past price histories and on the current prices or replacement costs of the durable inputs.[14] If the price of replacing a durable good is rising over time, without appropriate modification in the depreciation charge on each occasion that such an increase occurs, accumulated depreciation charges will be insufficient to replace the input when it wears out. Assuming the absence of technological advances, current depreciation charges must, therefore, include adjustments over and above what would normally be required to replace this durable input at its current price. Only in this way can the firm maintain intact both its real capital stock and its revenue-generating ability.

In any event, in each period of historical time, past purchases of durable goods have left the firm with a given, accumulated, but depreciating, stock of durable inputs awaiting present use, and previous sales of IOUs have resulted in a given accumulated stock of debt on which required rates of return (required, that is, at the time of issue) must be paid. It also has an accumulated stock of work in progress left over from past operations. The firm uses the revenue from the sale of its output to cover its current labor expenses, the depreciation on its stock of durable-good inputs, and the required rate of return payments on its debt. It sells IOUs whenever the remaining revenue plus accumulated depreciation funds are insufficient to permit the necessary replacement of worn-out durables and, if it is expanding, the purchase of new ones and additional work in progress. It buys back outstanding IOUs if it has more revenue than it needs to cover its labor expenses, the accumulated depreciation funds for future replacement of worn-out durables, the required payments on its debt, and the necessary current replacement of worn-out durables. In this second case, sources of the means for repurchasing IOUs when the firm is contracting will include

---

[14]It is assumed for present purposes that the economic lives of real capital assets are given independently of both the intensity of their use and of efforts to maintain them. Indeed, maintenance expenditures are taken to be zero.

depreciation funds that are no longer used up in replacing worn-out durable-good inputs and the savings secured by maintaining a lower level of work in progress.[15]

Turn, now, to the specifics. Designate a period of time t as the "present" and denote the firm's current inventory of output by the scalar $\hat{x}^t$ (not to be confused with the use of x or $\hat{x}$ in the previous chapter), its current stock of durable inputs by the vector $\hat{y}^t$, and its current debt, that is, the par value of its currently outstanding IOUs, by the scalar $\hat{a}^t$. Assume, for convenience, that the firm's desired level of output inventory at time t is zero.[16] Assume also that production at time t employs only the current stock of the durable inputs in the firm according to the time-dependent production function[17]

$$x = F^t(\hat{y}^t, \ell), \tag{9.2-1}$$

where x varies over nonnegative output quantities, ℓ is a scalar representing nonnegative quantities of labor hired by the firm, and F^t is twice, continuously differentiable with respect to ℓ. (In this notation, the superscript t does not appear on x and ℓ because specific values of these variables for period t have not yet been designated.) Thus the acquisition of real capital in period t does not affect output in that period. Furthermore, the stock of work in progress inherited from period $t-1$ and available for period t is implicit in F^t. Assume that labor is not required and is not employed to carry inventory from one period to the next.

Denote the price of the firm's output by p and the wage of labor by w. Suppose $w = \hat{w}$ so that labor's wage becomes an exogenous

---

[15]Were a market for second-hand, real capital to exist, then, to the extent that contraction implies the firm sells its real assets, still additional funds for repurchasing IOUs are obtained.

[16]This does not imply, nor is it intended to imply, a situation in which desired inventory is constant over time. Rather, desired inventory at time t is some number that, for convenience when considering this particular period, is taken to vanish.

[17]This is not necessarily the actual production function that governs the firm's combining of inputs into outputs. Rather, it is the production function the firm *thinks* it faces, given the technology of which it is aware. In practice, the firm might not know with certainty everything it needs to know about its actual production function or the technology behind it. A similar interpretation applies to the money capital requirement function introduced momentarily.

variable that is, say, contractually fixed.[18] The output price at time
t is set by the firm as described momentarily. Letting c vary over its
possible money capital requirements for current operations, take the
firm's money capital requirement function[19] to be

$$c = \Lambda^t(p, \hat{w}, x + \hat{x}^t, \hat{y}^t, \ell), \qquad (9.2\text{-}2)$$

where $\Lambda^t(p, \hat{w}, x + \hat{x}^t, \hat{y}^t, \ell) > 0$ everywhere except that $\Lambda^t(p, \hat{w}, 0, 0, 0) =$
0. Note that money capital is needed to support the holding of inven-
tory. In the present approach as described subsequently, the firm determines the current price it charges for its output, and estimates targets
for its current production of output, its current labor input needs, and
the associated part of its IOU sales or buy-back requirements by appeal
to established and automatic rule of thumb procedures. It has only one
real operating decision to analyze and contemplate, namely, how much
of the durable inputs it should buy for future production (*i.e.*, in what
durable inputs and in what quantities should it invest, if at all), and
this decision sets the remainder of its IOU sales or buy-backs. These
estimates, the price determination, and the operating decision (that is,
the firm's plan of operation), together with the present state of the
world that concurrently emerges, set the firm's actual profitability, the
actual money capital it requires, and the actual rate of return it earns
in period t. They also fix the actual quantities of durable inputs in the
firm for period $t + 1$.

Represent the vector of gross quantities of durable-good inputs that
the firm decides it wants to purchase in period t by y_e^t. Then the
planned change in the firm's (physical) capital stock at t, namely, the
vector Δy^t, is the difference between y_e^t and the amounts of durable
inputs wearing out at t. To have $\Delta y^t > 0$, each component of y_e^t must
be larger than the quantity of that respective input in the firm that
wears out. If no component of y_e^t has this property or, alternatively, if

---

[18]Of course, $\hat{w}$ may still vary over time.

[19]See, for example, Katzner [3, p. 395]. Although Katzner's money capital requirement function was developed for a world of perfect knowledge and certainty,
a similar construction is introduced here as a simplifying device. Note also that
this notion of required money capital includes both the cost of the work in progress
inherited from period $t - 1$ (working capital) and the cost still to be recovered of
the durable good inputs in use in period t (fixed capital).

$y_e^t < 0$, then $\Delta y^t < 0$.[20] Consideration of the investment decision, that is, the selection of a value for y_e^t, is postponed until the next section. For the present, it is assumed that an investment made and actually realized at time t becomes a part of the firm's productive capital stock at time $t + 1$. Each of the remaining estimates and the output-price determination is now discussed in turn.

Since current demand is unknowable until the firm's output price has been announced and buyers have completed their purchases, the price the firm charges for its output is assumed to depend on the (primary) estimate it makes of the demand function for that output and on the cost of its operation. The calculation of this estimate emerges along with the firm's investment decision and is considered in Section 9.3. In the meantime, let the estimated function for period t be written as $\mathcal{D}_e^t(p)$, where[21]

$$x = \mathcal{D}_e^t(p) - \hat{x}^t, \qquad (9.2\text{-}3)$$

$\mathcal{D}_e^t$ is continuously differentiable, and $\mathcal{D}_e^t(p) > 0$ for all $p > 0$, and solve the production function (9.2-1) to obtain the inverse

$$\ell = G^t(\hat{y}^t, x), \qquad (9.2\text{-}4)$$

which is assumed to exist in a continuously differentiable manner with respect to x on a suitably defined domain.

Suppose, as is typical in a non-perfectly-competitive environment,[22] that the firm determines the price it charges in period t by marking up from its current unit labor cost in order to cover, per unit, at least that labor cost plus its current depreciation charge and the required payments on its outstanding debt. Were it to mark up so as to cover these costs exactly, and assuming that it starts out with its desired inventory level $\hat{x}^t = 0$ and that it sells everything it produces, its revenues, px,

---

[20]Clearly $\Delta y^t > 0$ generally implies an increase in the firm's money capital requirement at $t + 1$, while $\Delta y^t < 0$ implies a decrease. When some of the components of Δy^t are positive and others negative, the money capital requirement will still rise if the cost of the net increase in the durable inputs associated with the positive components is larger than the savings due to the net decline in the durable inputs associated with the negative components.

[21]In the present notation and, except in Section 10.1, hereafter, subscripts on functions no longer indicate partial derivatives as they did in Chapters 5 and 6.

[22]*E.g.*, Pearce [4, pp. 114-116].

would be identical to $\hat{w}\ell + \hat{\rho}^t\hat{a}^t + \delta^t(\hat{p}^t_y)$, where, $\hat{p}^t_y$, the vector of durable-good prices in period t, is also exogenously set, $\delta^t(\hat{p}^t_y) > 0$ is the firm's current depreciation charge function described earlier and, recall, $\hat{\rho}^t$ is the average required rate of return over its outstanding IOUs. (The value of $\delta^t(\hat{p}^t_y)$ is implicitly assumed to be independent of the rate of usage of the durable inputs y.) Thus the firm's markup factor, k, would be defined by the equation

$$p = k\frac{\hat{w}\ell}{x} \tag{9.2-5}$$

or

$$\hat{w}\ell + \hat{\rho}^t\hat{a}^t + \delta^t(\hat{p}^t_y) = k\hat{w}\ell. \tag{9.2-6}$$

Upon solving (9.2-6) for k,

$$k = 1 + \frac{\hat{\rho}^t\hat{a}^t + \delta^t(\hat{p}^t_y)}{\hat{w}\ell}. \tag{9.2-7}$$

Clearly, with revenue varying at "break-even" levels to maintain (9.2-5) and (9.2-6) in force, $k > 1$ and

$$\frac{\partial k}{\partial \hat{w}} < 0. \tag{9.2-8}$$

Under the same revenue constraint, it also follows, using (9.2-5) and (9.2-6), that

$$\frac{\partial k}{\partial \ell} = -\frac{k-1}{\ell} < 0 \tag{9.2-9}$$

and

$$\frac{\partial^2 k}{\partial \ell^2} = \frac{2(k-1)}{\ell^2} > 0.$$

Inequalities (9.2-8) and (9.2-9) reflect the fact from (9.2-7) that hypothetical increases in ℓ or $\hat{w}$ spread depreciation and debt costs over a larger labor cost so that k declines. It should be emphasized, however, that general relations among $\hat{w}$, ℓ, k, x, and p, reflecting the maintenance of break-even revenue levels are implicit in equations (9.2-7) through (9.2-9). For example, it follows from (9.2-1) that an alteration of ℓ, in addition to causing a change in k as described in (9.2-9), would also imply a transformation in x. This, in turn, could have further impact on p. (Such possibilities are explored further in Section 12.2.1 below.) Moreover, in practice, since it cannot know in advance the labor input it will actually be able to hire and the output it will actually be able to produce and sell, the firm's markup is not likely to wind up being exact as assumed in (9.2-6). Indeed, due to the uncertainty created by its ignorance of the input supply and output demand conditions it faces, the firm is assumed to set its markup factor at the beginning of the period[23] and hope that subsequent events as the period unfolds allow it to at least cover all of its costs. With this in mind, the markup factor is henceforth taken to be exogenous and denoted by $\hat{k}$. It is supposed that $\hat{k} > 1$. Notice that the assumption of exogeneity of $\hat{k}$ does not mean that $\hat{k}$ cannot modify over time. Furthermore, to the extent that variation across periods occurs, $\hat{k}$ need not respond to modulations in ℓ and $\hat{w}$ as described by the inequalities of (9.2-8) and (9.2-9). Regardless, given $\hat{k}$, assuming the firm plans on selling all of its current output inventory plus what it produces (remember the desired level of output inventory is zero), and using (9.2-3), (9.2-4), and (9.2-5), the firm's output price at time t, or p^t, is determined as the solution of the markup equation

$$p = \hat{k} \frac{\hat{w} \left[G^t(\hat{y}^t, \mathcal{D}_e^t(p) - \hat{x}^t) \right]}{\mathcal{D}_e^t(p) - \hat{x}^t}. \tag{9.2-10}$$

Thus the firm applies an established and automatic rule of thumb markup factor, $\hat{k} > 1$, over its per unit labor cost to set its output price.

Intuitively, it would seem from the markup rule that, other things being equal, increases in $\hat{k}$ and $\hat{w}$ would be passed on by the firm to its customers in a higher output price. Also a lowering of $\hat{y}^t$ (which reduces output from the same labor input), or a fall in $\hat{x}^t$ (raising the need for production) might have a similar effect. Sufficient conditions for obtaining such conclusions are given by the proposition below. The

---

[23]One way the firm's decision maker might do this is to use its most recently employed markup amended, as described in the context of the macroeconomic analogue of the firm in Section 12.4, in light of any revised estimates of market conditions and profit opportunities.

theorem itself may be thought of as providing comparative statics results, in the sense of Section 5.2, that emanate from the solving of
(9.2-10).

Theorem 9.2-11. *Let* $p^t = \nu(\hat{k}, \hat{w}, \hat{y}^t, \hat{x}^t)$ *describe the solutions of*
(9.2-10) for all appropriate vectors $(\hat{k}, \hat{w}, \hat{y}^t, \hat{x}^t)$, *where* ν *is continuously*
differentiable on its domain. Assume that the firm's estimated demand
curve and isoquants slope downward, that is, $\partial x / \partial p < 0$, *and* $\partial \ell / \partial \hat{y}^t < 0$
everywhere. Then for

$$\frac{\partial p^t}{\partial \hat{k}} > 0, \ \frac{\partial p^t}{\partial \hat{w}} > 0, \ \frac{\partial p^t}{\partial \hat{y}^t} < 0, \quad and \quad \frac{\partial p^t}{\partial \hat{x}^t} < 0$$

to hold for those $(\hat{k}, \hat{w}, \hat{y}^t, \hat{x}^t)$, *it is sufficient that, from the production*
function,

$$\frac{\ell}{x} \frac{\partial x}{\partial \ell} < 1 \tag{9.2-12}$$

everywhere.

Proof:
Differentiating (9.2-10) with respect to, say, $\hat{w}$, leads, upon simplification, to

$$\frac{\partial p^t}{\partial \hat{w}} = \frac{\hat{k}\ell}{x + \hat{k}\hat{w}\left[(\ell/x) - \partial \ell/\partial x\right] \partial x/\partial p}.$$

Since $\partial x/\partial p < 0$, it follows that if (9.2-12) is in force then $\partial p^t/\partial \hat{w} > 0$.
A similar argument establishes the remaining inequalities. (The re-
quirement that $\partial \ell / \partial \hat{y}^t < 0$ everywhere is only needed in the demonstration that $\partial p^t / \partial \hat{y}^t < 0$.)

Q.E.D.

Observe that condition (9.2-12) says the elasticity of output with
respect to labor input is less than unity. That this does not imply
diminishing marginal productivity of labor can be seen from the production function

$$F^t(\hat{y}^t, \ell) = \hat{y}^t \sqrt{\ell^2 + 1},$$

which fulfills (9.2-12) everywhere but, as a function of ℓ, is strictly
convex. (The fact that $F^t(\hat{y}^t, 0) \neq 0$ for $\hat{y}^t \neq 0$ in the example does

not diminish its significance.) A production function satisfying (9.2-12) throughout its domain and exhibiting diminishing marginal productivity of labor for all $\ell > 0$ is

$$F^t(\hat{y}^t, \ell) = \hat{y}^t \sqrt{\ell}.$$

Evidently, for both of these production functions, $\partial \ell / \partial \hat{y}^t < 0$ everywhere.

More generally, it is worth digressing for a moment to show that diminishing marginal productivity of labor together with the property $F^t(\hat{y}^t, 0) = 0$ are sufficient for inequality (9.2-12). This is the focus of the next theorem, where, for notational simplicity, the argument $\hat{y}^t$ and the superscript t on F^t are dropped and the first- and second-order derivatives of F^t (now just F) as a function of ℓ are written, respectively, as $F'(\ell)$ and $F''(\ell)$.

Theorem 9.2-13. *If $F(0) = 0$ and $F''(\ell) < 0$, for all $\ell > 0$, then*

$$\frac{\ell}{F(\ell)} F'(\ell) < 1$$

for all $\ell > 0$.

Proof:
By the Mean Value Theorem, for any $\ell' > 0$ and $\ell'' \geq 0$ with $\ell' > \ell''$, there is an ℓ^0 such that

$$F(\ell') - F(\ell'') - (\ell' - \ell'')F'(\ell') = [F'(\ell^0) - F'(\ell')](\ell' - \ell''),$$

where $\ell' > \ell^0 > \ell''$. A second application of the Mean Value Theorem gives an $\bar{\ell}$ such that

$$F(\ell') - F(\ell'') - (\ell' - \ell'')F'(\ell') = F''(\bar{\ell})(\ell^0 - \ell')(\ell' - \ell''),$$

where $\ell' > \bar{\ell} > \ell^0 > \ell''$. Setting $\ell'' = 0$ and noting $F(0) = 0$ now implies

$$F(\ell') - \ell' F'(\ell') = F''(\bar{\ell})(\ell^0 - \ell')\ell'.$$

Therefore, because $F''(\bar{\ell}) < 0$ and $\ell' > \ell^0$,

$$F(\ell') - \ell' F'(\ell') > 0,$$

whence, since ℓ' is arbitrary, the conclusion of the theorem follows.

$$\text{Q.E.D.}$$

Note that if the hypothesis $F''(\ell) < 0$ were replaced by the condition that F is a strictly concave function of ℓ, and if $F(0) \geq 0$ were substituted for $F(0) = 0$, then Theorem 9.2-13, although still correct,[24] could not be proved in the above manner. This is because there could be "isolated" values of ℓ at which $F''(\ell) = 0$ even though F is strictly concave.[25]

Return now to the original production function notation of (9.2-1) and the determination of the firm's output price p^t as the solution of (9.2-10). Based on that solution, the firm calculates that it will sell $\mathcal{D}_e^t(p^t)$ units of output at time t. Hence, using (9.2-3), it should produce an estimated output in period t of

$$x_e^t = \mathcal{D}_e^t(p^t) - \hat{x}^t$$

by hiring (from [9.2-4]) an estimated labor input of

$$\ell_e^t = G^t(\hat{y}^t, x_e^t),$$

where the added subscript e denotes estimated quantities. (These estimates, together with those remaining in this section, are what have earlier been referred to as the decision maker's secondary estimates.) Assume that the firm attempts to produce x_e^t with labor input ℓ_e^t at

---

[24]See Katzner [3, p. 116].

[25]For example, the function defined for all $\ell \geq 0$ by

$$F(\ell) = \int_0^\ell g(z)\, dz,$$

where

$$g(\ell) = 2 - \int_0^\ell (1 + \cos\, 2\pi\theta)e^{-\theta^2}\, d\theta$$

for all $\ell \geq 0$, has the properties that $F'(\ell) = g(\ell)$ and

$$F''(\ell) = -(1 + \cos 2\pi\ell)e^{-\ell^2}.$$

It can also be shown that $F(0) = 0$, $F(\ell) > 0$ for all $\ell > 0$, $F'(\ell) > 0$ for all $\ell \geq 0$, $F''(\ell) = 0$ where $\ell = 1/2, 3/2, 5/2, \ldots$, and $F''(\ell) < 0$ otherwise for $\ell \geq 0$.

time t.[26] The firm's projected current earnings in excess of current operating cost, written π_e^t, are[27]

$$\pi_e^t = p^t \left[x_e^t + \hat{x}^t \right] - \left[\hat{w} \ell_e^t + \hat{\rho}^t \hat{a}^t + \delta^t(\hat{p}_y^t) \right]. \tag{9.2-14}$$

These earnings may be reserved for financing, insofar as possible, any additional increments in output and work in progress that are not covered by the current stock of money capital, along with the current purchases of the durable inputs to be discussed below. (Note, however, that the value of π_e^t notwithstanding, were positive earnings actually realized at t, whether they are returned to the firm's owners or not, a larger than contractually required rate of return is thereby generated for those owners, and the firm is in a position to offer a higher rate of return on subsequent new issues of IOUs in order to attract new capital.) The money capital required to support operation at these levels is found from (9.2-2) to be

$$c_e^t = \Lambda^t(p^t, \hat{w}, x_e^t + \hat{x}^t, \hat{y}^t, \ell_e^t),$$

and the firm's estimated actual rate of return in period t on the money capital invested in it is

$$\rho_e^t = \frac{\pi_e^t + \hat{\rho}^t \hat{a}^t}{c_e^t}. \tag{9.2-15}$$

Therefore, given $\hat{p}_y^t$, the firm has to "sell" (net of buy-backs)[28]

$$\Delta a_e^t = \frac{c_e^t + \hat{p}_y^t \cdot y_e^t - \delta^t(\hat{p}_y^t) - (\hat{a}^t + \pi_e^t)}{q_e^t} \tag{9.2-16}$$

---

[26]Because the firm does not determine its planned output supplies in response to given output-price values, it is not possible to define an output supply function in the traditional sense. However, a different kind of firm supply function is introduced in Section 12.2.

[27]It should be understood in (9.2-14) that the required payments on the firm's debt, $\hat{\rho}^t \hat{a}^t$, may vary depending on the extent to which the firm incurs additional obligations by issuing new IOUs or, alternatively, reduces obligations by repurchasing outstanding IUOs. But to keep matters simple these complications are ignored in calculating the firm's planned cost.

[28]Since y_e^t represents gross investment demand, it includes that portion of investment demand that is designated to replace worn-out real capital. But the funds for such replacement are already available to the firm in the form of the depreciation charge $\delta^t(\hat{p}_y^t)$. Thus, $\delta^t(\hat{p}_y^t)$ has to be subtracted from $\hat{p}_y^t \cdot y_e^t$ in determining necessary IOU sales Δa^t.

IOUs at time t, where the dot denotes "inner product," Δa_e^t is the estimated target sale of IOUs, and q_e^t (assumed to be positive) is the "estimated price" of IOUs, which will be clarified momentarily.

Observe that if the numerator of the fraction in (9.2-16) is positive, then $\Delta a_e^t > 0$ and the firm intends to participate in the IOU market as a net supplier of new issues of IOUs. In this case, since new issues are assumed to sell at their par values, $q_e^t = 1$. But if the numerator in (9.2-16) is negative, $\Delta a_e^t < 0$ and the firm would, on balance, be planning to buy back outstanding IOUs. Because the current prices of its outstanding IOUs are fixed in the IOU market, the firm pays par value for an outstanding IOU only when the currently set required rate of return for new issues turns out to equal the required rate of return on the outstanding IOU as of its date of issue. As pointed out earlier, outstanding IOUs issued on different dates, since they contractually require different rates of return, will have different current market prices. Thus the size of Δa_e^t in equation (9.2-16) depends on which of the firm's outstanding IOUs are purchased. The formula in (9.2-16) applies as written only under the assumption that all IOUs bought by the firm in period t have the same contractually required rate of return, and hence the same price q_e^t. On the basis of earlier assumptions, the firm takes as its value of q_e^t the appropriate price determined in the IOU market in period $t - 1$. The situation in which the firm simultaneously buys back IOUs with different required rates of return is not considered.

It is clear from previous discussion that quantities of the durable inputs (real capital) relative to the amounts of labor employed in production need not remain constant over time. Variation can result from either technological change or modification in relative input prices. However, higher capital intensities or durable-input-labor ratios (assuming the appropriate functions and parameters remain fixed) imply a greater potential variablity in the firm's future net income stream by virtue of the resulting increase in the firm's ratio of fixed to variable cost at all levels of output. Hence the risk of investing in the firm is larger and the IOU market is likely to set a higher required rate of return on the sale of new issues of the firm's IOUs. The firm's decision maker must take this into account when coming up with the vector of durable input demands y_e^t.

Notice also that if the presence of historical time and ignorance were eliminated by introducing, as is done in more traditional equilibrium analyses, the assumptions of logical time and perfect knowledge, and if the firm described here were positioned at "long-run equilibrium," then the conclusions of those traditional analyses would apply. For in that instance all desires and plans would be realized, and $\hat{x}^t$, and π_e^t in equation (9.2-14) would vanish.[29] In addition, since investment would only be made to replace worn-out durable inputs, it would follow that $\hat{p}_y^t \cdot y_e^t = \delta^t(\hat{p}_y^t)$ and $c_e^t = \hat{a}^t$. Thus $\rho_e^t = \hat{\rho}^t$ from equation (9.2-15), and $\Delta a_e^t = 0$ from equation (9.2-16).

In the present context, however, the values p^t, x_e^t, ℓ_e^t, π_e^t, c_e^t, ρ_e^t, Δa_e^t, and q_e^t reflect only the plans and expectations of the firm, given parameters $\hat{\rho}^t$, $\hat{x}^t$, $\hat{y}^t$, $\hat{a}^t$, $\hat{w}$, $\hat{p}_y^t$, and $\hat{k}$, and given the investment decision y_e^t and the underlying primary estimate $\mathcal{D}_e^t$ that have yet to be discussed. To the extent that the firm's plans and expectations are not realized, decisions and estimates at subsequent moments may be affected.

9.3 Decision Making in the Firm

Although the derivation of investments and the calculation of primary estimates of demand functions are usually thought of as distinct and separate procedures, it is useful and convenient here to characterize them both in terms of the same decision-making format. Within such a framework, it immediately becomes clear that the choosing of decision values for the vector y_e^t and the function $\mathcal{D}_e^t$ are interrelated processes. For the making of an estimate of the current demand for output may influence the willingness of the firm, that is, the firm's decision maker, to further invest in durable good inputs. And, conversely, the decision maker's development of a vision of the need for future investment may have an impact on what he thinks current demand will turn out to be. Thus it is appropriate to conceive of the decision maker as selecting both together.

However, due to the assumption that investment in period t does not add to the productive capital stock until period $t + 1$, the actual choice by the decision maker of a value for y_e^t is necessarily related to a second primary estimate, namely, an estimate of the demand function

---

[29]Recall that desired inventory has been assumed to be zero.

that the firm faces at $t + 1$. In particular, the decision maker will not
attempt to increase, say, the firm's capital stock unless he believes that
such an increase is warranted by his expectation of future demand.
This estimated function is written similarly to that of equation (9.2-3),
except that the symbol $\mathcal{D}_e^t$ is replaced by $\mathcal{D}_e^{t+1}$, and the decision maker's
calculation of it is assumed to be made simultaneously as part of the
same process that produces decision values for y_e^t and $\mathcal{D}_e^t$. In addition
to the just-described relation between y_e^t and $\mathcal{D}_e^{t+1}$, the decision maker
may also perceive a relation between $\mathcal{D}_e^{t+1}$ and $\mathcal{D}_e^t$. For buyers often
develop habits and loyalties that induce them to repeat their buying
patterns over and over again, and therefore general economic conditions
may suggest a stable relation between buyer expenditures over time.[30]
Out of a single decision process, then, the problem for the decision
maker is to choose a value for the vector $(y_e^t, \mathcal{D}_e^t, \mathcal{D}_e^{t+1})$, where various
relations among the components of this vector constrain his selection.

Focus, again, on period t. Abbreviate $(y_e^t, \mathcal{D}_e^t, \mathcal{D}_e^{t+1})$ by the symbol
z and think of each possible value for z (after all of the above relational
constraints among the components of z are taken into account) as a
choice option. Note that the components of z consist of both functions
and variable values. In deciding among choice options, the decision
maker has to deal with two broad categories of uncertainty. On the
one hand, to come up with a value for $\mathcal{D}_e^t$ requires him to face the
uncertainty attendant with period t. Because he is unable to read
the minds of others, and because the world is overwhelmingly complex
and the future unknowable, the decision maker is unable to discern in
advance the current demand for his firm's output and the currently
available supply of labor and durable good input. Thus, in period
t, he is uncertain about the quantity of output he can and should
produce, the quantity of durable input he can buy, the amount of money
capital he needs, and the actual rate of return he can realize on the
money capital invested in the firm. On the other hand, because current
investment influences only future rates of return, to select a value for
y_e^t (and $\mathcal{D}_e^{t+1}$) necessitates the taking cognizance of the uncertainty
associated with periods $t + 1$ and beyond. This category of uncertainty

---

[30]As indicated earlier, although current conditions may point toward such a relation, they can neither logically imply nor guarantee it. Recall n. 18 on p. 25.

comes about from the historical nature of time. Not only is the decision maker unable to know what will be going on outside of his firm in subsequent periods, but he is also unable to know what he himself and his firm will be like in those periods. He cannot even say what his production function, his money capital requirement function, and his output-price markup factor will be in period $t + 1$. (Indeed, although the possibility is not considered here, he might also employ a procedure entirely different from that based on equation [9.2-10] to arrive at the firm's output price and other determinations described in Section 9.2.) All of these forms of uncertainty are accounted for in the analysis of decision making undertaken below. As indicated earlier, the approach constitutes an application, to the firm outlined in Section 9.2, of the model of decision making in ignorance of Section 4.3.

Thus suppose, in period t, that the decision maker is aware of a collection Z of choice options $z = (y_e^t, \mathcal{D}_e^t, \mathcal{D}_e^{t+1})$ that takes into account all of the constraining relations among the components of z as described earlier. Although not indicated by this notation, both the vector z and the choice set Z are time dependent. To keep matters simple, assume that only two periods, namely, t and $t + 1$, are taken into account.[31] Let the decision maker imagine various present and future states of the world, denoted, respectively, by ω^t and ω^{t+1}, and contingent on the occurrence of unknown and unknowable events in periods t and $t + 1$. Write $\omega = (\omega^t, \omega^{t+1})$ and note that, in general, ω^t and ω^{t+1} are not independent of each other. Moreover, due to the ignorance he faces, the decision maker is incapable of specifying all possibilities for ω^t and ω^{t+1}. As in Section 4.3, let Ω be the incomplete collection of all values of ω that he imagines in period t as resulting from the selection of options z, and suppose that the decision maker constructs his potential surprise function over the collection of all subsets of Ω.

For each $z = (y_e^t, \mathcal{D}_e^t, \mathcal{D}_e^{t+1})$ in Z and every ω in Ω, think of the decision maker as calculating, based on equations like those of Section 9.2, the possible steady-state rates of return on the money capital invested in the firm for periods t and $t + 1$ according to some pair of functions

$$\rho^t = \mathcal{R}^1(z, \omega) \tag{9.3-1}$$

---

[31]The generalization of the argument to cover any finite number of periods is straightforward.

and

$$\rho^{t+1} = \mathcal{R}^2(z,\omega). \tag{9.3-2}$$

The function $\mathcal{R}^1$ reflects, in part, the combination of equations (9.2-14) and (9.2-15), together with the secondary estimates of various variable values based on the particular $\mathcal{D}_e^t$ in z. (Observe that, of course, y_e^t and $\mathcal{D}_e^{t+1}$ in z are irrelevant for $\mathcal{R}^1$.) And $\mathcal{R}^2$ mirrors a similar calculation that rests on the y_e^t and $\mathcal{D}_e^{t+1}$ (but not, directly, on the $\mathcal{D}_e^t$) in the same z, and the assumption that all of the firm's plans in period t are fully realized.[32] Both $\mathcal{R}^1$ and $\mathcal{R}^2$ depend on the period of time t on which the analysis focuses and at which the decision is made.[33] The rates of return ρ^t and ρ^{t+1} characterize an implicit (scalar) rate of return ψ over the combined time interval from the start of period t to the end of period $t + 1$ according to the equation[34]

$$\psi = \sqrt{(1 + \rho^t)(1 + \rho^{t+1})} - 1. \tag{9.3-3}$$

[32]In determining $\mathcal{R}^2$, equations (9.2-14) and (9.2-15) are used with t replaced by $t + 1$, and with appropriate revisions in variable and parameter values. To illustrate the latter revisions, since the realization of an investment of y_e^t leads to a change in capital stock of Δy^t, the capital stock employed in production at time $t + 1$, namely, $\hat{y}^{t+1}$, is $\hat{y}^t + \Delta y^t$. This figures into the setting of the firm's output price, p^{t+1}, and estimated variables like x_e^{t+1} and c_e^{t+1} as described in Section 9.2. Moreover, to calculate the parameter $\hat{\rho}^{t+1}$ (the average required rate of return over all outstanding IOUs at time $t + 1$), it is necessary to know Δa_e^t and, if $\Delta a_e^t > 0$, the required rate of return on new issues of IOUs in period t. But, as indicated earlier, the values of these variables are available to the firm because the required rate of return is taken as determined in the IOU market in period $t - 1$, and all of the firm's plans at t are assumed to be realized. Observe also that the required rate of return in period t is not needed in computing $\mathcal{R}^1$.

[33]Recall that it does not matter if $\rho^{t+1} > \rho^t$ since an earlier assumption precludes the possibility of substituting inputs through time.

[34]In a three periods of time model (with a present period and two future periods), the formula of equation (9.3-3) becomes

$$\psi = \left[(1 + \rho^t)(1 + \rho^{t+1})^2\right]^{\frac{1}{3}} - 1,$$

where ρ^t is the steady-state rate of return starting with period t, and ρ^{t+1} is the steady-state rate of return starting with period $t + 1$ and continuing to period $t + 2$. In general, $\psi + 1$ is the geometric mean of the steady-state rate of return starting with period t and the (equal) steady-state rates of return that start with period $t + 1$ and are maintained in each subsequent period included in the model.

This implicit return also depends on z and ω:

$$\psi = \mathcal{R}(z, \omega),$$

where $\mathcal{R}$ is defined by the substitution of (9.3-1) and (9.3-2) into (9.3-3). Now suppose, for each z in Z, that $\mathcal{R}$ defines a 1-1 correspondence between the image, Ψ, of Ω under $\mathcal{R}(z, \cdot)$, and Ω.[35] Then, as indicated earlier, the decision maker's potential surprise function is translatable into a family of potential surprise density functions $f_z(\psi)$ defined over the collection Ψ of future outcomes expressed in terms of implicit rate of return scalars ψ. Using this density function, it is legitimate to speak of the potential surprise ξ $[= f_z(\psi)]$ of a single rate of return outcome ψ. Note that R takes the place of the utility function of Section 4.3.

The remainder of the model of Section 4.3 carries over without change. Thus the decision maker constructs, for each z in Z, an attractiveness function, $g_z(\psi, \xi)$, over the collection of all pairs consisting of a rate of return outcome ψ and the potential surprise value ξ identified with that outcome. Corresponding, again, to each z in Z, the domain of g_z is split into two parts, and the function itself is maximized subject to the potential-surprise-density constraint $\xi = f_z(\psi)$ to obtain the focus gain and focus loss (ψ_z^+, ξ_z^+) and (ψ_z^-, ξ_z^-). Finally, to make decisions among the various choice options, the decision maker chooses z so as to maximize his decision index,

$$D(z) = Q(\psi_z^-, \xi_z^-, \psi_z^+, \xi_z^+),$$

over Z.

Thus the firm's decision maker selects a value for $z = (y_e^t, \mathcal{D}_e^t, \mathcal{D}_e^{t+1})$ in period t. At the same time, the IOU market sets q^t, and the decision maker fixes both the firm's output price p^t according to equation (9.2-10) and its planned demand or supply of IOUs from equation (9.2-15). Also in period t the decision maker attempts to put the remainder of his plan of operation, namely, that portion relating to production, into effect. He then watches the economy generate values for the variables

---

[35]This assumption, although quite strong, does not seem overly restrictive for the purpose of translating and condensing a potential surprise function of the two variables ω^t and ω^{t+1} into a family of potential surprise density functions of the single variable ψ.

x^t, ℓ^t, π^t, c^t, and ρ^t that he could only estimate in advance (Section 9.2). Also determined by the economy is the actual value of Δy^t. Given the values of these variables that come to pass, the parameters $\hat{\rho}^{t+1}$, $\hat{x}^{t+1}$, $\hat{y}^{t+1}$, and $\hat{a}^{t+1}$ for period $t+1$ are set as described earlier. And, with $\hat{w}$ and $\hat{k}$ known and $\hat{p}_y^{t+1}$ specified, the firm and its decision maker are ready to move on to period $t+1$.

9.4 References

1. Carter, C. F., "On Degrees Shackle: or, the Making of Business Decisions," in *Uncertainty and Expectations in Economics*, C. F. Carter and J. L. Ford, eds. (Oxford: Basil Blackwell, 1972), pp. 30-42.

2. Hey, J. D., *Uncertainty in Microeconomics* (New York: New York University Press, 1979).

3. Katzner, D. W., *Walrasian Microeconomics: An Introduction to the Economic Theory of Market Behavior* (Reading: Addison-Wesley, 1988).

4. Pearce, I. F., "A Study in Price Policy," *Economica*, n. s., 23 (1956), pp. 114-127.

5. Vickers, D., *The Theory of the Firm: Production, Capital, and Finance* (New York: McGraw-Hill, 1968).

6. ———, *Financial Markets in the Capitalist Process* (Philadelphia: University of Pennsylvania Press, 1978).

7. ———, *Money Capital in the Theory of the Firm* (Cambridge: Cambridge University Press, 1987).

CHAPTER 10

The Consumer and the Demand for Money

Set within the confines of nonequilibrium analysis, two major concerns direct the thrust of argument in this chapter. The first is the application of the analysis of decision making in ignorance of Section 4.3 to the development of a model of the consumer as a buyer of goods, a supplier of factors, a buyer and seller of marketable, income-earning assets, and a holder of money balances. The construction so generated will appear later as an integral part of the model of the full microeconomy built up in the next chapter. The second matter is the investigation and derivation of the demand for money.

As remarked earlier, the traditional perspective in economics from which to explain simultaneous economic behavior is built upon an equilibrium foundation and goes under the rubric of general equilibrium or Walrasian analysis. Such an approach is characterized, in part, by the complete elimination of the nonprobabilistic uncertainty produced by the realities of historical time and human ignorance. When introducing a demand for money and monetary equilibrium[1] into a model of this sort, economists often take the position that it is first necessary to set out the particular "indispensible" function, or functions, that money is

---

[1] A *monetary* equilibrium is an equilibrium in which money has a positive purchasing power value arising from its capacity to function in some significant manner, usually as a medium of exchange and store of value, even though money itself may have no intrinsic value as a commodity.

The original version of this chapter will be published as "The Demand for Money in an Uncertain World," in *Economics as the Art of Thought*, S. Boehm, ed. (London: Routledge, forthcoming).

to perform in that model.[2] Thus one must begin by asking about the purpose to be served by holding money and about the role that money is to play in furthering economic activity. Thereafter a derivation of the demand for money emanating from the answers to these questions can be given. From such perspectives, a number of specifications of a role for money and a consequent demand for money, some of which are described below, have been proposed. But if one believes, along with Keynes [6, p. 216], Shackle [13, pp. 4,61,62], and others, that money is primarily a (nonprobabilistic) "uncertainty phenomenon,"[3] then none of these proposals is satisfactory since they are all embedded in an environment in which uncertainty is not present.

In Chapter 8, however, simultaneous economic behavior was explored outside of the traditional realm of equilibrium analysis and, in particular, was considered in a nonequilibrium framework that allowed for the uncertainty arising under conditions of historical time and ignorance. That analysis focused on the kaleidic sequence of decisions and market events occurring across historical time without reference to a general equilibrium. Indeed, a general equilibrium could not have existed within that configuration; nor, in the context of the analysis, would it even have made sense to raise the question of its existence. This setting, then, provides an environment in which money, as an uncertainty phenomenon amid simultaneous economic behavior, can be studied. The present chapter shows, in part, how money might be introduced into a nonequilibrium-type model of consumer behavior and a consumer demand for money derived within it. Although postponed until Section 11.3, the demand for money by firms is obtained similarly.

The next section attempts to provide some insight into the problems involved by examining several examples of the ways in which a role for money has been justified and a demand for money derived within the traditional general equilibrium boundaries. Section 10.2 offers a role for money and analyzes the demand for money in a manner that accounts for the uncertainty created by the presence of historical time and ignorance. As was the case when investigating the firm in Chapter 9, it is necessary here, too, to come up with 1-1 and onto functions

---

[2]See Hoover [4, p. 121].
[3]Vickers [17, p. 388].

mapping imagined states of the world in Ω into outcomes in Ψ.

10.1 Perspectives on Money Demand

Economists generally agree that there are three main roles for money to play in an economy: money functions as a standard of value or unit of account, as a medium of exchange, and as a store of value. To introduce money into a general equilibrium model, then, requires that a place for each of these functions be located within that construction.

Now all general equilibrium models contain within their structures a good, called the numéraire, that can be singled out to function as a standard of value. Any good, in fact, can serve that purpose; it is only necessary to employ the normalization that fixes its price at unity. Thus the role of money as a standard of value is always present, at least implicitly, in general equilibrium analysis and need not be considered further. However, with all trades taking place only at equilibrium (as they often do in such models), there is usually no need for a money commodity whose purposes are to facilitate exchange and carry purchasing power through time. The notion of monetary equilibrium is irrelevant. To be able to speak meaningfully about money as a medium of exchange and store of value therefore requires the presence of trading out of the traditional general equilibrium or at least some conceptualization of the actual effectuation of the trades envisaged in the general equilibrium. In these latter contexts, money has a role to play and the efficiency with which it plays that role can be analyzed.[4] To the extent that the use of money as a medium of exchange and a store of value economizes by reducing transactions and opportunity costs in the process of, say, out of equilibrium exchange, the purchasing power value of money (*i.e.*, its value as a medium of exchange and store of value) will be positive even if it has no intrinsic value as a commodity.

With money successfully functioning as a medium of exchange, its use in transactions permits the consumer or firm to achieve a higher

---

[4]For example, the presence of, say, bank charges for handling checks generally causes a decline in the efficiency with which money performs its medium of exchange function. If, in addition, its purchasing power is declining, money will also function less efficiently as a store of value.

level of, respectively, utility or profit than would otherwise be the case. Hence there is a demand for money balances for such transaction purposes. Similarly, money performing a successful store of value function gives rise to an *asset* demand for money balances. In this case, money balances are stored to cover a possible lack of coincidence between income receipts and expenditures that cannot be overcome efficiently through the use of futures markets, to cover unforseen expenditures that might arise in the future, and because of (in light of potential interest rate movements) the possibility of a capital loss on nonmonetary assets that might be avoided by holding money balances. (These last three reasons for storing money balances are sometimes referred to as, respectively, the *transactions, precautionary*, and *speculative* motives.) The combined demand for money balances of, say, a consumer is the sum of that person's transactions and asset demands and would appear, as suggested implicitly above, to depend on at least his wealth, his total anticipated expenditure, the rate of interest, commodity and nonmonetary asset prices, and expectations of future possible changes in those prices and changes in the rate of interest. (The nonmonetary asset prices themselves, of course, depend on the interest rate.) With these ideas in mind, attention now turns to some examples of the way in which the role of money and the demand for money balances have been handled in the literature.

One reason put forward to warrant the holding of money in general equilibrium analysis is simply that people have a preference for doing so.[5] (The rationale for this preference will be considered later.) That is, money balances enter as an argument in each person's utility function, and individual demands for money arise as the outcome of constrained utility maximization. To illustrate, let $x = (x_1, \ldots, x_I)$ vary over nonnegative baskets of commodities in a person's commodity space, and let $p = (p_1, \ldots, p_I)$ represent vectors of respective and positive prices of goods. Take m to denote his nonnegative (nominal) money balances and set the price of money at unity. Then this individual's utility function is often written as

$$\kappa = u(m, x, p), \qquad (10.1\text{-}1)$$

where u is homogeneous of degree zero in m and p for each value of x,

---

[5]See, for example, Patinkin [8] and Samuelson [9].

and κ varies over the range of u. In this approach, money balances are the only asset held by the individual, and the homogeneity property of u suggests the absence of money illusion in his relation to money functioning as a medium of exchange. With $r > 0$ indicating (scalar) rates of interest and $y > 0$ values of the individual's income, his budget constraint is

$$rm + p \cdot x = y,$$

where the dot symbolizes inner product.[6] Sufficient additional assumptions concerning the differentiability, increasingness, concavity, etc., of u are imposed to make the subsequent derivation of demand functions valid.[7]

From the homogeneity of u, the partial derivative of u with respect to the ith good, namely, $u_i(m, x, p)$, is also homogeneous of degree zero in m and p for each x, while that with respect to m, written $u_0(m, x, p)$, is homogeneous of degree minus one in m and p for each x. Hence[8]

$$u_i(m, x, p) = u_i\left(\frac{m}{y}, x, \frac{p}{y}\right), \qquad i = 1, \dots, I,$$

$$u_0(m, x, p) = \frac{1}{y} u_0\left(\frac{m}{y}, x, \frac{p}{y}\right),$$

where $p/y = (p_1/y, \dots, p_I/y)$. The first-order Lagrangean maximization conditions, together with the budget constraint, are therefore

$$\frac{u_i(m/y, x, p/y)}{u_0(m/y, x, p/y)} = \frac{p_i/y}{r}, \qquad i = 1, \dots, I,$$

$$r\frac{m}{y} + \frac{p}{y} \cdot x = 1.$$

---

[6]If money balances must be borrowed in order to be held, then rm reflects the interest cost of holding m. If borrowing is not necessary, either because the individual has a sufficient endowment of money balances to begin with or because he is paid in money balances upon selling his endowment, then rm represents forgone interest and y must include the income that would have been earned had the interest not been forgone.

[7]The following development follows Samuelson and Sato [11].

[8]Apart from Chapters 5 and 6, this is the only place in the present volume where subscripts on functions denote partial derivatives.

This is a system of $I + 1$ equations in $I + 1$ unknowns m/y, $x_1, \ldots, x_I$. Solving yields the demand functions

$$x_i = \hat{h}^i\left(r, \frac{p}{y}\right), \qquad i = 1, \ldots, I,$$

$$\frac{m}{y} = \hat{h}^0\left(r, \frac{p}{y}\right),$$

or

$$x_i = h^i(r, p, y), \qquad i = 1, \ldots, I,$$

$$m = y h^0(r, p, y). \tag{10.1-2}$$

Observe that, as in the traditional theory of demand for commodities only, the demand functions for goods, that is, the h^i for $i = 1, \ldots, I$, are homogeneous of degree zero in all prices and income for each r. However, the demand function for money balances, namely, $y h^0(r, p, y)$ in (10.1-2), is homogeneous of degree one in all prices and income, again for each value of r. This, as, in part, suggested earlier, is consistent with the old notions of the absence of money illusion and the neutrality of money.

The justification usually provided for including money balances in the utility function, or the reason given to explain why individuals have preferences for them, is that money balances have utility in their functioning as a store of value. Holding an average money balance, says Samuelson [9, p.118],

> yields convenience in permitting the consumer to take advantage of offers of sale, in facilitating exchanges, in bridging the gap between receipt of income and expenditure, etc. The average balance is both used and at the same time not used; it revolves but is not depleted; its just being there to meet contingencies is valuable even if the contingencies do not materialize, *ex post*. Possession of this balance then yields a real service, which can be compared with the direct utilities from the consumption of [ordinary goods]. . . .

According to Patinkin [8, p. 63],

> Were it not for . . . [money balances], the lack of synchro-
> nization between the inflow and outflow of money in the
> course of the week would almost certainly force the individ-
> ual to default on some of the hourly payments he is called
> upon to make [randomly during the week]. The security
> that money . . . [balances] provide against financial em-
> barrassment of this type is what invests them with utility.

Samuelson, however, does qualify his position: "Given physical amounts of . . . [goods] have significance in terms of the want pattern of the consumer, but it is not possible to attach similar significance to a given number of physical units of money . . ." [9, p. 118]. Thus ". . . as an ultimate desideratum, money is no more in the utility function than is . . . any . . . intermediate good. We must, therefore, regard . . . [equation (10.1-1)] as already the result of some behind-the-scenes opti-mizing and time-averaging" [11, p. 601]. But the real problems with this approach are twofold: first, money balances are not the only means for storing value. Nonmonetary assets, to the extent that reliance can be placed on their marketability and liquidity, perform a similar function, and these, it may be argued, should be in the utility function too so that the consumer can choose an appropriate portfolio for storing value from among competing assets. Second, and more serious, since the ir-regular timing of expenditures and receipts is, like everything else in a general equilibrium framework, known in advance (at least probabilis-tically), and can therefore be overcome (assuming complete markets) through the use of futures markets as described below, a vindication for the existence of a store of value role for money balances has not really been supplied, and hence the previously stated justification for placing money balances in the utility function collapses. Thus the approach, as it stands, is not much help in resolving the issues raised in this chapter.

Consider now a typical general equilibrium model that accounts for the allocation of resources in the present period and at each of a finite number of successive future periods. Every quantity of every commod-ity is associated with the date of the period in which it is delivered. There is a single date, that is, the date of the present period, at which all trades occur. On that date, goods to be delivered in the present period (*i.e.*, present goods) are exchanged in present spot markets, and contracts for the purchase and delivery of goods in future periods (*i.e.*, future goods) are traded in futures markets. For the moment, transactions costs and uncertainties are assumed away. Consumers and firms optimize by choosing "lifetime" purchase and sales plans. There are lifetime budget constraints and lifetime profit equations in which future prices are discounted to the present.[9] Once trade takes place, all markets are closed forever. If a market were reopened at some future date, nothing would be exchanged in it because there would have been no changes in preferences and technology. In such a world, there is no role for money (except, possibly, as a standard of value) and no reason for anyone to hold it. As suggested above, since all trades (in both present spot markets and futures markets) are equilibrium trades occurring at the same time, and since everything about the present and future is known with at least probabilistic certainty, the use of money either as a medium of exchange or as a store of value cannot lower costs or raise utilities. However, the next approach to introducing money and a demand for money balances explored here is based on Hicks' [3, p. 6] idea that a role for money arises in this model, or a condensed version of it, as soon as certain kinds of frictions or impediments to trade are inserted and, in that case, the introduction of money balances enhances economic efficiency.[10] The general equilibrium that obtains therefore becomes a monetary equilibrium. The frictions and impediments inserted direct attention to the process of trading itself by forcing exchanges to take place out of, or by focusing on the effectuation of the exchanges that occur at, general equilibrium.

For example, Feldman [1] considers a barter situation, without either futures markets or production, in which he inserts the impediment that all trades occur only on a pairwise basis. Feldman is interested in sequences of pairwise trades (starting at initial endowments), between traders taken two at a time, in which each trade increases the utility of both traders. He shows that, under certain conditions, such sequences converge to "optimal" situations that cannot be improved upon through further trading. But these situations are optimal with respect to the

---

[9]This model also presumes unlimited borrowing and lending opportunities at the market rate of interest.

[10]See, for example, Starr [14].

two-person trading requirement only and need not be Pareto optimal in general. Feldman also demonstrates that if there were a universally held good, which he calls money, then general Pareto optimality would be assured. Therefore, by allowing individuals to trade for money as an intermediate step in achieving their final consumption goals, that is, by introducing money as a medium of exchange to be carried from one trade to another, efficiency can generally be increased. Feldman, however, does not derive a demand for money balances in his model.

As a second example of this genre, return to the general equilibrium model described above, with a full complement of futures markets, but still without production. Suppose, however, that resources have to be employed both to deliver goods and write contracts for future delivery. Suppose also that, although delivery costs are still incurred, contracts are not written for delivery (and hence the cost of writing those contracts is eliminated) whenever the agreement to purchase (*i.e.*, trade) and the delivery of the goods involved occurs on the same date. Thus trading in futures markets would result in higher transactions costs (contract plus delivery costs) than trading in present and future spot markets (only delivery costs). In the face of these transaction cost frictions, it is clear that, to avoid the higher costs, the use of futures markets in the present would be diminished and, to that extent, markets would reopen and trades would occur at future dates.[11] Furthermore, the single lifetime budget constraint in the original model would be replaced by a sequence of temporary budget constraints ensuring that expenditure equals income in each period, and utility maximization against those constraints would be repeated correspondingly across time.

Under these conditions, futures markets would be used instead of the cheaper future spot markets when the timing of future receipts and expenditures does not coincide and when the storage costs of holding the appropriate goods through time until they can be exchanged for the desired commodities is high. However, Starrett [15] shows that use of the futures markets in this case would result in allocative in-

---

[11]This would be true regardless of whether the future is known with certainty or only probabilistically. However, the presence of risk in the latter case means that the costs of using futures markets could be even higher.

efficiency due to the extra resources they require and that efficiency
(*i.e.*, Pareto optimality) could be restored by introducing a good, again
called money, that has zero transactions and storage costs, that does
not enter as an argument in the individual's utility function, and whose
purchasing power value remains constant over time. Rather than go to
expensive futures markets, money, functioning as a store of value, would
overcome gaps in timing between expenditure and income receipts by
carrying purchasing power forward costlessly through time. In this kind
of model, money would be used by individuals to balance their bud-
gets, that is, to ensure that expenditures equal receipts, at each date.
Those who spend more than they earn would use the money balances
they posses or borrow to make up the difference; those who spend less
would retain the difference in the form of money balances or lend it out.
Thus there is an implicit excess demand for nominal money balances
implied in each person's constrained utility-maximizing excess demand
for commodities.

One can imagine that this model is generalizable to include production and certain forms of probabilistic uncertainty or risk. But none of
these generalizations addresses the fact that money is one among many
assets that the individual might hold for storage of value purposes. In
particular, they provide no answer to the question of why the individual
should hold money balances when there are marketable, nonmonetary,
income-earning assets available of varying degrees of liquidity. To deal
with such issues requires a conceptualization of money in terms of a
portfolio of assets.

There are several standard ways to treat the demand for money as
a demand for an asset in a portfolio. The one described here is founded
on the riskiness of holding assets and is due to Tobin [16].[12] Suppose
there are J assets, with the Jth, say, representing (nominal) money
balances.[13] Let j index these assets and write β_j for the fraction of the
total value of the portfolio held as asset j, where $\beta_j \geq 0$, $j = 1, \ldots, J$,

---

[12]The presentation here follows that of Katzner [5, pp. 169-173].

[13]Except for money, assets issued on different dates, *i.e.*, in different periods, are
different assets.

and

$$\sum_{j=1}^{J} \beta_j = 1. \tag{10.1-3}$$

Denote the nominal rate of return on asset j by r_j, and its per dollar nominal capital gain or loss due to changes in its price by γ_j. Clearly $r_j \geq 0$, and γ_j is positive, zero, or negative, according to whether γ_j reflects, respectively, a gain, neither gain nor loss, or a loss. Moreover, $r_J = 0$ so that $\gamma_J = 0$. Thus the overall return to each dollar of the portfolio is

$$\sum_{j=1}^{J-1} \varepsilon_j,$$

where

$$\varepsilon_j = \beta_j(r_j + \gamma_j), \qquad j = 1, \ldots, J-1. \tag{10.1-4}$$

Assume that $(\gamma_1, \ldots, \gamma_{J-1})$ is a vector of random variables with zero means and variance-covariance matrix $\|\sigma_{jk}^{\gamma}\|$. Then $(\varepsilon_1, \ldots, \varepsilon_{J-1})$ is also a vector of random variables. Let its means and variance-covariance matrix be written, respectively, as $\mu = (\mu_1, \ldots, \mu_{J-1})$ and $\|\sigma_{jk}\|$. Then, from (10.1-4),

$$\mu_j = \beta_j r_j, \tag{10.1-5}$$

$$\sigma_{jk} = \beta_j \beta_k \sigma_{jk}^{\gamma},$$

where $j, k = 1, \ldots, J-1$. It follows that $0 \leq \mu_j$ and

$$0 \leq \sigma_{jk} \leq \sigma_{jk}^{\gamma}, \tag{10.1-6}$$

$$r_j r_k \sigma_{jk} = \mu_j \mu_k \sigma_{jk}^{\gamma}, \tag{10.1-7}$$

for all j and k distinct from J. In addition, the overall expected rate of return on the portfolio as a whole is given by

$$\sum_{j=1}^{J-1} \mu_j = \sum_{j=1}^{J-1} \beta_j r_j,$$

and the *risk* associated with the portfolio is defined as[14]

---

[14]For two interpretations of the risk associated with each individual asset, see Vickers [18, p. 138]. Of course, all of these notions of risk are distinct from that defined with respect to the analytical environment in Section 1.5.

$$\left(\sum_{j=1}^{J-1}\sum_{k=1}^{J-1}\sigma_{jk}\right)^{\frac{1}{2}} = \left(\sum_{j=1}^{J-1}\sum_{k=1}^{J-1}\beta_j\beta_k\sigma_{jk}^{\gamma}\right)^{\frac{1}{2}}.$$

Suppose that each specification of μ and $\|\sigma_{jk}\|$ corresponds to a unique, joint probability distribution over vectors $(\varepsilon_1,\ldots,\varepsilon_{J-1})$ in some admissible collection of distributions. Consider an individual with a utility function, $u(\mu,\|\sigma_{jk}\|)$, representing his preferences among these distributions. Given values for $r_1,\ldots,r_{J-1}$ and $\|\sigma_{jk}^{\gamma}\|$, let this person choose μ and $\|\sigma_{jk}\|$, and hence a probability distribution, so as to maximize his utility subject to constraints (10.1-6) and (10.1-7).[15] But selection of μ implies, from (10.1-3) and (10.1-5), the determination of $\beta_1,\ldots,\beta_J$. In particular, as $r_1,\ldots,r_{J-1}$, and $\|\sigma_{jk}^{\gamma}\|$ hypothetically vary, the demand for money balances per portfolio dollar, β_J, is obtained as the function g^J, where

$$\beta_J = g^J(r_1,\ldots,r_{J-1},\|\sigma_{jk}^{\gamma}\|).$$

Observe that to have a positive demand for money balances (*i.e.*, to have $\beta_J > 0$) associated with any particular collection of parameter values $r_1,\ldots,r_{J-1}$ and $\|\sigma_{jk}^{\gamma}\|$ requires that the β_j, for $j \neq J$, determined with respect to these parameter values have the property that

$$\sum_{j=1}^{J-1}\beta_j \neq 1.$$

In any case, the demand for money balances in toto thus depends on the total value of the portfolio, and on current rates of return and the variance-covariance matrix associated with capital gains. Clearly, this demand for money balances emerges from speculative motives in conjunction with the store of value function of money. But of course it is not, as outlined above, integrated with the nonportfolio decisions of individuals to demand and supply commodities.

There is one further general-equilibrium-type approach to the introduction of money that speaks to the store of value function and that

---

[15]It is assumed that u has sufficient properties so that this maximization can always be carried out.

is worthy of description here. That approach is based on the overlapping generations model of Samuelson [10]. The presentation below is indebted to Hoover [4, Ch. 6].

Imagine a world in which individuals live for two periods. In the first period, they are "young" and are able to work a fixed number of hours; in the second, they are "old" and cannot. The collection of all persons born in period t is known as generation t, and there is a new generation born every period. There is a single, perishable good that is produced each period and must be completely used up during that period. This good (like, say, sunflower seeds) can either be consumed (eaten) or invested (planted) to increase consumption for the next period. (The per unit return on that investment is the quantity of sunflower seeds produced for next period per unit of sunflower seeds planted this period minus one.) Clearly, since they do not work, if the old are to survive they have to be able either to invest or carry income earned when they were young through time to their old age for consumption. But with the produced good perishable the only way to accomplish the latter is to introduce a good, money, that is capable of storing value so that purchasing power can be moved across time. Of course, since investment is possible, there is, at this point, no necessity for individuals to store value by holding money balances.

Suppose further, however, that the young are paid for their work only at the end of the period. Then they are not able to spend their income while they are young and are now forced to carry it over to spend when they are old. To permit this to happen, there is no alternative but to pay them with money that can be stored for consumption in the next period. It is also necessary to give each person an initial endowment of money when young so that he is able consume and not starve in his youth, and to tax him a fixed amount of money when he is old in order to be able to maintain, if desirable, a constant money supply over time. Under these conditions, the overlapping generations model is able to provide a specification of intertemporal monetary equilibrium.[16]

---

[16]In such a model, problems can arise because changing price expectations may generate nonstationary equilibria. This, in turn, may lead to a deteriorioration in the purchasing power value of money over time, which, if it eventually approaches zero, would destroy the possibility of speaking of a monetary equilibrium in the sense in which that concept has been defined.

Mathematically, the overlapping generations model described above can be expressed in terms of each person of generation t maximizing a utility function of the form[17]

$$\kappa = u^t(x_1^t, x_2^t),$$

subject to the constraints

$$\hat{m}^t + w^t \hat{\ell}^t = p_1^t x_1^t + p_1^t k^t + m^t, \qquad (10.1\text{-}8)$$

$$\hat{m}^t \geq p_1^t x_1^t + p_1^t k^t, \qquad (10.1\text{-}9)$$

$$m^t + \left(1 + r^t\right) p_1^t k^t = p_2^t x_2^t + \hat{\zeta}^t, \qquad (10.1\text{-}10)$$

where, for this person, x_1^t, x_2^t, p_1^t, and p_2^t represent, respectively, quantities and prices of the perishable good consumed in periods 1 and 2; k^t is the quanity of the perishable good invested in period 1 at rate of return r^t; the parameter $\hat{\ell}^t$ indicates the fixed amount of labor time supplied in period 1 at money wage w^t; the parameters $\hat{m}^t$ and $\hat{\zeta}^t$ are, respectively, the initial endowment and tax of nominal money balances; and m^t denotes nominal money balances carried over from period 1 to period 2. Adding (10.1-8) to (10.1-10) yields the usual budget constraint asserting that, for both periods combined, the individual's income equals his expenditures. Assuming $\hat{m}^t = \hat{\zeta}^t$, this budget constraint is

$$w^t \hat{\ell}^t + r^t p_1^t k^t = p_1^t x_1^t + p_1^t x_2^t.$$

Inequality (10.1-9), known as the *finance* constraint, says that no matter what their incomes, the young cannot spend more in their youth than the money balance they inherit in their initial endowment. Its purpose is to avoid the indeterminacy that would otherwise arise if the rate of return on capital were so high that the individual does not want to hold sufficient money to cover his period 1 expenditures. Evidently out of the above maximization the demand for money by an individual of generation t in his youth emerges residually as a function of p_1^t, p_2^t, w^t, r^t, $\hat{\ell}^t$, $\hat{m}^t$, and $\hat{\zeta}^t$. The demand for money so obtained is a demand for money as a store of value. Individuals do not demand money in their

---

[17]Again, the utility function is assumed to possess sufficient properties so as to be able to perform the maximization.

old age. Rather, they use all of the money balances they have carried over from their youth to purchase quantities of the consumption good and to pay taxes.

From the models surveyed above, it is clear that, in general, money functions as a medium of exchange to increase efficiency in trading. It functions as a store of value to permit the shifting of consumption forward through time and to eliminate the inefficiency that arises from known (or probabilistically known) irregularities in the timing of income receipts and expenditures. In performing its store of value function it is one among many assets in a portfolio of assets that stores value over time. Nevertheless, an important aspect of money has been omitted from these analyses because all of them rely on the implicit general equilibrium assumptions that individuals have perfect knowledge and that time is logical. To briefly recall earlier discussion once again, saying that a person has perfect knowledge means that he knows everything there is to know about the past and the present and that, in addition, he also knows with certainty either the actual states of the world that will arise in appropriate future periods or at least the collection of possibilities together with their probabilities of occurrence in those periods. To take time to be logical is to ignore the factual uniqueness of each period in history and to permit, merely by restarting an analytical clock, the replication of those historical periods. The end result is to prevent the realities of the uncertainty that arises out of the ignorance in which real decisions are made, and out of the historical uniqueness of actual decision periods, from permeating the analytical structures of the inquiry undertaken.

This exclusion is especially striking in view of Keynes' argument that it is mostly because of the uncertainty created by the presence of historical time and ignorance that money has any role as a store of value to play at all. According to Keynes [6, p. 216],

> our desire to hold Money as a store of wealth is a barometer of the degree of our distrust of our own calculations and conventions concerning the future. . . . [This] feeling about Money . . . takes charge at the moments when the higher, more precarious conventions have weakened. The possession of actual money lulls our disquietude. . . .

The role of money as a store of value, then, is to provide "a refuge from uncertainty."[18] In particular, the demand for money as a store of value emerges, in part, from ignorance concerning the timing of expenditures and income receipts, since the purposes for which money will be needed in the future, as well as the time at which it will be needed, is often unknown or unknowable and hence uncertain.[19] And money may also be demanded for storage purposes as a consequence of ignorance of future asset prices and the accompanying "disquietude" associated with the possibility of capital losses on nonmonetary assets. The demand for money as a store of value, then, is, in Shackle's words, "a substitute for knowledge" [12, p. 216].

The next section adds to the analysis of the roles of money set out above by developing a new model that explains the demand for money in the context of the uncertainty begat from historical time and ignorance. In so doing, it accounts for both medium of exchange and store of value functions. Without commitment to perfect knowledge and logical time, the model focuses, in part, on the Tobin perspective that money is one asset in a portfolio of many assets. Although money balances appear as an argument of the individual's utility function, this inclusion, unlike the previously described Samuelson-Patinkin inclusion, is given a justification that, hopefully, stands up. And, in contrast with the analysis of Starrett and the overlapping generations model discussed above, since money balances provide utility to the individual, the demand for money is explained as the direct outcome of an authentic optimization procedure. The model also incorporates the decision to buy and sell goods simultaneously with the selection of a portfolio that includes money balances.[20]

---

[18]Vickers [17, p. 389].

[19]See Shackle [13, pp. 4,61,62]. In the context of historical time and ignorance, futures markets are of no use in circumventing this demand for money because neither the future goods that will be needed nor the timing of their purchase relative to income receipts is known. However, futures markets may still be employed for other purposes.

[20]In this sense, the present analysis is actually more in the tradition of Friedman [2], who employs a "portfolio" containing multiple assets (including money), physical goods, and human capital. Recall that the Tobin portfolio, as introduced above, has only multiple assets.

10.2 A Model of the Consumer

The analytical approach is based on Section 4.3. Let there be, as before, J financial assets indexed by $j = 1, \ldots, J$ and identify the Jth as (nominal) money balances. (Recall that nonmonetary assets issued on different dates are different assets.) Although each nonmonetary asset j provides a yield in perpetuity, the decision maker, here taken to be the individual or consumer, plans on holding j for only a predetermined finite number of periods.[21] Suppose the anticipated future rate of return on the entire portfolio is determined by the individual along with the composition of the portfolio itself. Rather than focusing on the fractions of the total value of the portfolio held in each asset, take portfolios to be defined as vectors $a = (a_1, \ldots, a_J)$, where a_j indicates a number of units of asset j. In addition to assets, let the individual also select quantities of goods (including leisure) to consume and represent vectors of excess demand quantities based on such selections by the symbol x. Thus, since leisure time is included among goods consumed, one of the components of x represents quantities of labor time supplied. In any case, the individual's decision set, X, consists of all nonnegative vectors, (x, a), that satisfy budget and any other constraints under which he operates. Note that the selection of a new portfolio necessarily carries savings or dissavings implications. Moreover, if the individual currently holds portfolio $a^0 = (a_1^0, \ldots, a_J^0)$, and if he chooses to hold portfolio a instead, then his vector of asset excess demands is given by $a - a^0$. In particular, his excess demand for money balances is $a_J - a_J^0$.

As in the traditional theory of demand, the parameters of the constraints that define the individual's decision set X, when these constraints are effective, are the variables upon which demand or excess demand quantities are said to depend.[22] Such constraints always include the following: first, assuming for the sake of simplicity that borrowing is not permitted, the dollar amount of the individual's expenditure on commodities and assets cannot exceed his income plus the revenue he would expect to obtain upon the sale of all initial endowments and

---

[21]The question of the optimal number of periods to keep j is ignored.

[22]The parameters of the remainder of the decision structure (such as, for example, the parameters of the utility function introduced below) are, as is typical, suppressed and implicit.

currently held assets (including money); that is, for all (x, a) in X,

$$p \cdot x + q \cdot (a - a^0) \leq (q \cdot a)v, \qquad (10.2\text{-}1)$$

where $p > 0$ is a vector of perceived, current, (nonasset) commodity prices; $q = (q_1, \ldots, q_J) > 0$ is a vector of perceived, current, asset prices such that $q_J = 1$; and v is the anticipated, per period rate of return on the portfolio, which will be discussed shortly. Inequality (10.2-1) includes both income and wealth and may be thought of as a *financial resources* constraint. Second, for choice options (x, a) such that $a_J > 0$, the ratio of (i) expenditure on goods and income-earning assets, ε, in (x, a), to (ii) the money balances held in the individual's portfolio in (x, a), is no larger than some anticipated number, ν, determined, in part, by his perception of the limit (imposed by his environment) on the "velocity" with which he is able to spend receipts from the sale of his initial endowment of factors and nonmonetary assets and, in part, by his perception of the current rate of interest.[23] This second constraint, referred to as the *velocity* constraint, is written

$$\varepsilon \leq \nu a_J \qquad (10.2\text{-}2)$$

and incorporates the idea that a stock of money of a certain size is held by the individual for the purpose of facilitating a flow of payments or transactions. Although ε clearly depends on appropriate components of p, x, q, and $a - a^0$, and although ν depends partly on the interest rate, to the extent that (10.2-1) and (10.2-2) are effective in the selection of (x, a) from X, the excess demands $(x, a - a^0)$ so obtained may still be thought of as dependent on, at least, p, q, ε, and ν. Further dependence on the initial endowment a^0, and hence wealth, is implicit. The rate of interest, in the guise of v, comes in indirectly through q and ν. These same variables (except for possible future price changes – which enter the present model in the specification of asset rates of return below) were the ones initially suggested as relevant in determing the consumer's demand for money balances at the start of Section 10.1.

For each (x, a) in X, let ω vary over an incomplete collection Ω of possible states of the world, as imagined by the individual, that

---

[23]A higher rate of interest, say, may induce the individual to hold a larger proportion of liquid assets in nonmonetary from, thereby forcing an increase in ν.

might greet his selection of (x, a). Suppose the individual defines a potential surprise function on the subsets of Ω. Although, in general, both the imagined set Ω and the potential surprise function defined over its subsets depend on the choice option (x, a), it is convenient to continue the simplifying assumption of Section 4.3 that they are independent of (x, a).[24]

Consider any asset $j \neq J$. Let $t = 0$ denote the present period, let y_j^t be the income anticipated from holding one unit of this asset for one period, t periods hence (call the period, "period t"), and take q_j^t to be the asset's anticipated price during that period. The perceived current price of the asset, $q_j = q_j^0$, is assumed to be known and fixed. Define the total anticipated rate of return on asset j in period t as v_j^t, where

$$v_j^t = \frac{y_j^t + q_j^{t+1} - q_j^t}{q_j^t},$$

and let t run over all periods, $t = 0, \ldots, T_j$, that the individual plans to hold asset j. To keep matters simple, assume that $T_j = T$, for $j = 1, \ldots, J - 1$ and some positive integer T. Clearly the y_j^t and the q_j^t depend on the state of the world in period t. Hence so do the v_j^t. Since the v_j^t, in turn, determine the per period average anticipated rate of return, v_j, on asset j, according to the formula

$$v_j = \left[\prod_{t=0}^{T} (1 + v_j^t) \right]^{\frac{1}{T}} - 1,$$

it follows that v_j, too, depends on these states of the world.[25] It is not necessary, however, to suppose that the individual imagines relations between future states of the world and both the y_j^t and the q_j^t clearly enough to explicitly derive v_j as a function of ω. Rather, it is assumed instead that, without any specification of how, he is able to hypothesize a working condensation or summary of these relations in the form

$$v_j = \rho^j(\omega), \qquad j = 1, \ldots, J - 1, \tag{10.2-3}$$

---

[24]Of course, as indicated in Section 4.3, to say that Ω depends on the choice option (x, a) is not to say that an element of Ω depends on that choice option. Recall, also n. 20 on p. 125.

[25]Possible serial correlation in the sequences of values $v_j^0, \ldots, v_j^T$ is of no consequence for the logic of the present argument.

linking the average anticipated rate of return on each asset j to future states of the world.

Three things about (10.2-3) should be noted. First, v_j accounts, in its own way, for both the rates of return r_j and the capital gains γ_j of the Tobin model as described in Section 10.1. Second, the approach abstracts from the manner in which future changes in the general level of commodity and asset prices might affect the purchasing power value of money. Third, since v_j, as indicated above, depends on a future collection of states of the world, one for each period $t = 1, \ldots, T+1$, the state of the world variable ω should really be thought of as a vector $\omega = (\omega^1, \ldots, \omega^{T+1})$, where ω^t is the state of the world in period t. However, as subsequent analysis remains substantively the same regardless of whether ω is taken to be a scalar or a vector, little harm will be done if, to keep exposition simple, ω continues to be referred to as a scalar.

Now the value, at currently perceived prices, of any portfolio a of (x, a) in X is $q \cdot a$ or

$$\Gamma(a) = a_J + \sum_{j=1}^{J-1} q_j a_j. \tag{10.2-4}$$

Hence the anticipated per period rate of return on the entire portfolio over all relevant periods can be characterized as

$$v = \sum_{j=1}^{J-1} \frac{q_j a_j}{\Gamma(a)} v_j, \tag{10.2-5}$$

where each v_j is weighted by the current fraction of the portfolio invested in asset j. Note that under this weighting scheme the weight assigned to money balances in the portfolio is, from (10.2-4),

$$\frac{a_J}{\Gamma(a)} = 1 - \sum_{j=1}^{J-1} \frac{q_j a_j}{\Gamma(a)}.$$

In light of (10.2-3), equation (10.2-5) defines an anticipated portfolio rate of return function

$$v = \mathcal{S}(a, \omega), \tag{10.2-6}$$

where

$$\mathcal{S}(a, \omega) = \sum_{j=1}^{J-1} \frac{q_j a_j}{\Gamma(a)} \rho^j(\omega). \tag{10.2-7}$$

Let Υ be the collection of all anticipated portfolio rates of return under $\mathcal{S}$.

Since the individual is uncertain as to the state of the world that will emerge after his selection of (x, a), he is also uncertain about what his preferences will be as the effects of his decision work themselves out. Thus suppose that the individual's utility function is of the form

$$\psi = u(x, v, \omega), \tag{10.2-8}$$

where u is defined over the Cartesian product $X \times \Upsilon \times \Omega$ and ψ ranges over the collection Ψ of all anticipated utility values or outcomes. Evidently utility is derived from the consumption of a vector x, the anticipated rate of return, v, of the entire portfolio, and the state of the world that comes to pass with the realization of x and v. Substitution of (10.2-7) into (10.2-6) and then the result into (10.2-8) yields

$$\psi = U(x, a, \omega), \tag{10.2-9}$$

where

$$U(x, a, \omega) = u\left(x, \sum_{j=1}^{J-1} \frac{q_j a_j}{\Gamma(a)} \rho^j(\omega), \omega \right). \tag{10.2-10}$$

Clearly nonmonetary assets have utility because they provide a (nonprobabilistically) uncertain income stream. Moreover, money balances a_J now appear as an argument in the utility function. The latter is justified in that money may be said to have utility as a refuge from uncertainty, that is, as a means of calming the fears about the future alluded to by Keynes in the quotation cited in Section 10.1. (It is understood here that money is not dominated in rate of return by a nonmonetary financial asset also providing perfect liquidity.) In particular, stored money balances avoid the possibility of capital loss on nonmonetary assets that might otherwise be held in place of money and are available for covering unknown and unknowable future expenditures.[26] Money also has utility as a medium of exchange since, as shown by Feldman

---

[26]Recall, again, that futures markets cannot necessarily be used to avoid such future expenditures since neither their timing nor the nature of the purchases involved may be known in advance.

and described in the previous section, it increases utility by permitting
purchasing power to be carried from one transaction to another.

Note also that equation (10.2-9) suggests substitutability between
assets, between goods, and between assets (including money) and goods
(including leisure). In general, there will be a distinct marginal rate of
substitution defined for each pair involving two assets, two goods, or
one of each.

Assume that u and the ρ^j have sufficient properties that for every
(x, a) in X, the utility function U, thought of as a function of ω alone,
given (x, a), defines a 1-1 and onto relation between Ω and Ψ. Then it
follows that, for each (x, a) in X, the potential surprise function over
subsets of Ω can be translated into a family of potential surprise density
functions, $f_{(x,a)}$, over Ψ such that $f_{(x,a)}(\psi)$ is the potential surprise of
utility outcome ψ.

Utility outcomes are not, of course, the only things over which the
individual can construct potential surprise density functions. Any function that he thinks relevant and that maps Ω into values of an economic
variable such as, for example, a future price, a future capital gain, or
future income will automatically confer the potential surprise of each
single-element set $\{\omega\}$, for ω in Ω, on the variable value onto which
ω is mapped. However, should such a function not be 1-1, that is, if
two values of ω, say, were mapped into the same economic value, then
confusion would exist as to the appropriate potential surprise value to
assign to that economic value. At any rate, it is certainly possible for
the individual to conjure up in his mind an entire system of implicit
relations among any subset of variables, taken from the collection of
the state of the world variable combined with the economic variables,
whose simultaneous solution eliminates the state of the world variable
and yields some of the economic variables as functions of the remaining economic variables. To the extent that this is done, the individual
would then be able to determine his expectation for the effect of, say,
a change in a commodity price on the rate of interest. Conversely, the
prior presence of such a system in his mind might, instead, lead to his
determination of the initial potential surprise function over collections
of state of the world values postulated for him above.

Returning to the utility function situation, a hypothetical example
in which $\rho^1, \ldots, \rho^{J-1}$ and u are such that U is appropriately 1-1 and

onto is obtained by setting

$$u(x, v, \omega) = \lambda(x, v), \qquad (10.2\text{-}11)$$

for some function λ that is 1-1 and onto for each x, and

$$\rho^j(\omega) = \theta_j \rho^{J-1}(\omega), \qquad j = 1, \ldots, J-1, \qquad (10.2\text{-}12)$$

where $\theta_1, \ldots, \theta_{J-2}$ are positive constants, $\theta_{J-1} = 1$, and $\rho^{J-1}(\omega)$ is also 1-1 and onto. That is, uncertainty, as it impinges on the state of the world variable, influences utility only as it affects the anticipated rate of return on the portfolio, and the anticipated rate of return on each nonmonetary asset moves in its own proportion to the anticipated rate of return on asset $J-1$. In this case, equations (10.2-6) through (10.2-12) together imply

$$U(x, a, \omega) = \lambda \left\{ x, \rho^{J-1}(\omega) \left[\sum_{j=1}^{J-1} \frac{q_j a_j \theta_j}{\Gamma(a)} \right] \right\}.$$

Since (x, a) and the q_j are fixed, since the θ_j are independent of ω, and since $\lambda(x, v)$ and $\rho^{J-1}(\omega)$ are suitably 1-1 and onto, it follows that U is 1-1 and onto for each (x, a) in X.

Given the potential surprise density function $f_{(x,a)}(\psi)$ on Ψ, introduce the decision-making individual's attractiveness function for (x, a) and his decision index as described earlier. Then the apparatus of Section 4.3 permits the decision index to be expressed as a function of the objects of choice, that is, as a function $D(x, a)$ defined on X, and the individual chooses (x, a) so as to maximize $D(x, a)$ over X. The portfolio selected, of course, contains a unique, nonnegative quantity of each asset,[27] and the excess demands for those assets, including money balances, are determined as (behavioral) functions of price, expenditure, and velocity variables as described earlier. Insufficient restrictions have been imposed above on the decision index and the potential surprise, utility, and attractiveness functions to ensure that the demand function for money balances exhibits an absence of money illusion, but there is

---

[27]In the general case, money will always exist in the portfolio, that is, $a_J > 0$, by virtue of its use as a medium of exchange.

little harm in adding such restrictions should that be desirable. Further-more, if the financial resources constraint (10.2-1) holds as an equality, then the choice of x as part of (x, a) fixes (as does the choice of a) the new perceived current dollar value of the entire asset portfolio, a, as $\Gamma(a)$. The question of whether the selected portfolio is diversified, that is, whether it does not lie on one of the coordinate axes of the object of choice space, depends on the characteristics of D as built up from the potential surprise function, the function U, and the attractiveness function.

Observe that the traditional approach to portfolio selection, which, under certain conditions, is equivalent to the analysis attributed to To-bin in Section 10.1, is primarily concerned with the spreading of invest-ment over assets whose income streams are not perfectly correlated.[28] It solves the problem by selecting the weights in the individual's port-folio, earlier symbolized as the β_j, so as to minimize the risk (standard deviation) associated with the entire portfolio for a given expected rate of return over the portfolio as a whole.[29] The argument of Section 10.1 showed, in part, that in this traditional context the structure of the variance-covariance matrix of the returns on the individual nonmone-tary assets plays a significant role in determining the choice of these weights. In any case, the utility-maximizing portfolio obtained by pick-ing weights to minimize risk for a specified expected rate of return is referred to as *optimal*. One of the conclusions drawn from the analysis is that, in general, risk is reduced by diversification.

It should be pointed out, however, that these notions of risk and its reduction have no place in the framework of Section 4.3 in the sense in which those concepts are relevant to probabilistic portfolio analy-sis. Because the decision event and the decision outcome are seen in the context of Section 4.3 as unique in historical time, because such uniqueness implies that neither the event nor the outcome are replica-ble, and because knowledge, in general, is so meager, there is not enough information available to speak meaningfully of means, variances, and other moments of probability distributions from which outcomes might

---

[28]See, for example, Vickers [18, pp. 136-147].

[29]Of course, for such an analysis to hold up, it is necessary that all first- and second-order moments of the asset rate of return random variables exist. In this regard, the discussion of n. 14 on p. 117 should be kept in mind.

be drawn. In addition, potential surprise density functions do not possess meaningful parameters like means and variances that are amenable to manipulation and interpretation. Hence it is not even possible to define risk with respect to such parameters, let alone to speak of reducing it. Instead, the model proposed here chooses one portfolio and one consumption vector from a set of consumption-portfolio options in much the same spirit (though in a vastly different environment) as the traditional consumer chooses commodities from a budget set.[30] All of the uncertainties and the hazards involved, together with whatever other factors that also influence decisions, are accounted for within the confines of the model. In this way, a full treatment of uncertainty is provided.

Note that, in particular, an assumption such as (10.2-12) from the traditional perspective implies that the returns on all assets are perfectly correlated and hence that the risk of the portfolio does not vary with a change in weights. Thus all portfolios are associated with the same risk and there is no advantage to diversification. But this conclusion does not apply in the present context because the decision-making individual is not choosing a portfolio to minimize risk. Rather, he selects his portfolio-consumption vector so as to maximize $D(x, a)$ over X.

Regardless, it is clear that, in addition to the selection of portfolios, the model proposed here opens the way for understanding the changes that might occur in portfolios on successive dates. These changes generally arise because, as indicated earlier, all of the elements of the construction of Section 4.3 (*e.g.*, the potential surprise function and the decision index) are unique to each period of historical time. Hence there is no presumption that the demand for any asset, including money (or, for that matter, the demand for any good), will remain constant through time. This provides, in particular, an explanation of the instability of the demand for money over time observed by Keynes [6, p. 219] – something that the more standard approaches to the demand

---

[30]Recall from p. 202 (including n. 2 at the bottom) that because it does not employ the gambler's indifference map and does not sum the focus gains and focus losses of individual assets to obtain the focus gain and focus loss of the portfolio as a whole, the present model avoids the conclusion implied by Shackle's original analysis and described by Ozga [7, pp. 213-216] that diversification is not rational.

for money outlined in Section 10.1 do not adequately address.

10.3   References

1. Feldman, A. M., "Bilateral Trading Processes, Pairwise Optimality, and Pareto Optimality," *Review of Economic Studies* 40 (1973), pp. 463-473. Reprinted as Ch. 8 in R. M. Starr, ed. *General Equilibrium Models of Monetary Economies: Studies in the Static Foundations of Monetary Theory* (San Diego: Academic Press, 1989).

2. Friedman, M., "The Quantity Theory of Money – A Restatement," in *Studies in the Quantity Theory of Money*, M. Friedman, ed. (Chicago: University of Chicago Press, 1956), pp. 3-21.

3. Hicks, J. R., "A Suggestion for Simplifying the Theory of Money," *Economica*, n. s., 2 (1935), pp. 1-19. Reprinted as Ch. 2 in R. M. Starr, ed. *General Equilibrium Models of Monetary Economies: Studies in the Static Foundations of Monetary Theory* (San Diego: Academic Press, 1989).

4. Hoover, K. D., *The New Classical Macroeconomics* (Oxford: Blackwell, 1988).

5. Katzner, D. W., *Static Demand Theory* (New York: Macmillan, 1970).

6. Keynes, J. M., "The General Theory of Employment," *Quarterly Journal of Economics* 51 (1937), pp. 209-223.

7. Ozga, S. A., *Expectations in Economic Theory* (London: Weidenfeld and Nicolson, 1965).

8. Patinkin, D., *Money Interest and Prices* (Evanston: Row Peterson, 1956).

9. Samuelson, P. A., *Foundations of Economic Analysis* (Cambridge: Harvard University Press, 1947).

10. ———, "An Exact Consumption-Loan Model of Interest with or without the Social Contrivance of Money," *Journal of Political Economy* 66 (1958), pp. 467-482.

11. Samuelson, P. A., and R. Sato, "Unattainability of Integrability and Definiteness Conditions in the General Case of Demand for Money and Goods," *American Economic Review* 74 (1984), pp. 588-604.

12. Shackle, G. L. S., *Epistemics and Economics* (Cambridge: Cambridge University Press, 1972).

13. ———, *Keynesian Kaleidics* (Edinburgh: Edinburgh University Press, 1974).

14. Starr, R. M., ed. *General Equilibrium Models of Monetary Economies: Studies in the Static Foundations of Monetary Theory* (San Diego: Academic Press, 1989).

15. Starrett, D., "Inefficiency and the Demand for 'Money' in a Sequence Economy," *Review of Economic Studies* 40 (1973), pp. 437-448. Reprinted as Ch. 17 in R. M. Starr, ed. *General Equilibrium Models of Monetary Economies: Studies in the Static Foundations of Monetary Theory* (San Diego: Academic Press, 1989).

16. Tobin, J., "Liquidity Preference as Behavior Towards Risk," *Review of Economic Studies* 25 (1957-1958), pp. 65-86.

17. Vickers, D., "On Relational Structures and Non-Equilibrium in Economic Theory," *Eastern Economic Journal* 11 (1985), pp. 384-403.

18. ———, *Money Capital in the Theory of the Firm* (Cambridge: Cambridge University Press, 1987).

CHAPTER 11

A Model of the Microeconomy

As with simultaneous behavior, the traditional perspective for analyzing the microeconomy as a whole focuses on the equilibrium-analytic notion of Walrasian or general equilibrium. From this vantage point, consumer decision making, firm decision making, and market interaction based on the decisions taken occur simultaneously in each period. All decision making produces behavioral, that is, demand and supply, functions that are stable over time and can be combined into market aggregates. When specific individual decisions are such that markets are unable to clear, a dynamic mechanism is set in motion that, as (logical) time passes, guides the system toward a market-clearing equilibrium. But as has been pointed out, under conditions of ignorance and historical time, behavioral functions cannot be presumed stable over time, aggregation of them to the market level may not be useful, and markets might not clear. Furthermore, to the extent that market clearing is prevented, plans cannot be realized and equilibrium cannot be achieved. Thus it becomes necessary to look for an alternative approach.

The purpose of this chapter is to set out, in the context of nonequilibrium analysis, a microeconomic model of a monetary, kaleidic economy[1] as a complex of individuals, firms, and banks that make decisions

---

[1] An economy is kaleidic if, recalling p. 258, its structure and outcomes are highly

and interact simultaneously through markets under conditions of historical time and ignorance. In doing so, the models of the consumer (Section 10.2), the firm (Chapter 9),[2] and the market (Section 7.2) developed earlier will be employed and integrated into a unified whole. The present discussion, then, will also serve to tie together several of the loose threads that remain from previous inquiry. To avoid the distraction of unnecessary detail, a highly uncluttered world is considered in which many simplifying assumptions are made. The effects of relaxing some of these assumptions are taken up very briefly at the end.

Before proceding, it is worth pointing out that the focus of attention of subsequent argument is on the construction of a model that coheres. A model is *coherent* if it is internally consistent in the sense that, at every t, its relations representing simultaneously occurring behavior have unique solutions (*i.e.*, solution vectors) and, where those solutions represent inconsistent planned economic activity, they are resolved into unique realized variable values according to appropriate allocative and other rules of market operation.[3] The realized values themselves are sometimes called *outcomes*,[4] and a (necessarily kaleidic) sequence of such outcomes, one for each period t, is a realized kaleidic time-path generated by the model. Thus a model is coherent whenever it produces unique outcomes at each t, and coherence is an attribute of the structure of a model rather than of its outcomes. Clearly, in light of the essentialistic epistemology and methodology of nonequilibrium analysis, only models that are coherent are capable of explaining what is observed in reality. Recall that, as suggested there, the model of simultaneous barter behavior in Chapter 8 is coherent.

---

sensitive to the vagaries of exogenous changes in the environment and individual expectation modification. It is *monetary* if, within its structure, and as described in Section 10.2, money performs an intermediating function in exchange and provides a means for storing value.

[2] Actually the model of Chapter 9 will be expanded to include the selection by the firm of a portfolio of marketable, income-earning assets and money balances.

[3] When solution values reflect consistent activity, then all plans are automatically realized and solution values become, in effect, realized values.

[4] This is a different usage of the term "outcomes" from that heretofore employed. (Previous discussion, recall, referred to the elements of Ψ as outcomes.) Context will determine the appropriate meaning hereafter.

11.1   A Description of the Microeconomy

The specific economy to be examined here consists of a single consumer, two firms, a (commercial) bank, and a central bank.[5] One firm manufactures a nondurable consumer good by hiring labor time and employing a previously produced durable good. The other fashions the durable good (it can be used only in production) out of similar inputs. The bank employs the durable good and labor in the creation of money. Its reserves consist of deposits held at the central bank. As the repository of the commercial bank's reserves, the central bank is able to influence the amount of monetary creation, or the money supply, through the setting of certain parameters.[6] Each firm finances its productive operations (that is, carrying inventory and purchasing both the durable input and the labor necessary to produce work in progress and final output) by issuing and selling debt, in the form of IOUs, to raise money capital. (IOUs are issued in perpetuity and in one-dollar denominations.) The bank also obtains money capital to finance its operation by issuing and selling its own IOUs, but the consumer is not allowed to borrow. To keep matters simple, central bank activity is assumed to be sustainable without recourse to either the selling of IOUs issued by itself for the purpose of raising money capital or the employment of labor or durable-good inputs.

Each of the two firms, the consumer, and the bank is permitted to hold the debt, that is, buy the IOUs, of any of the others that issue it. An IOU held in this manner is an income-earning asset. There are three such assets – the IOUs issued by the two firms and the bank. Moreover, since the two firms and the bank evaluate the past, present, and future independently and make their own output and investment decisions, their present and future profitabilities, as well as their present and future abilities to make the contractually required payments on

---

[5]The following account necessarily includes characteristics of the firm and consumer already set forth in, respectively, Chapter 9 and Section 10.2.

[6]This is the only element of government and the only aspect of government economic policy to be considered here. Although it would not be hard to introduce government taxation and expenditure in terms of the usual exogenous parameters, no new substantive issues apart from those relating to government policy itself would arise.

their debts, are likely to be unique to each. In general, then, holding the IOUs of either firm or the bank is associated with a distinct risk.[7] These risks vary though historical time and are perceived differently by different holders and potential buyers of IOUs. In other words, perceived or expected risk is heterogeneous over time and across the consumer, the firms, and the bank.

Another income-earning asset, held only by the two firms and the bank, is real capital consisting of previously purchased units of the durable good that have not yet been completely used up in production. It is assumed that once bought, durable goods cannot be resold.[8] The one method by which a firm or the bank can reduce its real capital is by not replacing it when it wears out. Thus, among income-earning assets, only the debt issued by the firms and the bank is marketable. Real capital assets are not.

Money is a fifth asset that does not earn income. It can be held as a store of value by anyone and, though not required, can be used as a medium of exchange in all purchases. However, as in the context established in the discussion of the demand for money in Section 10.2, reasons exist why consumers, firms, and the bank will always avoid barter in exchange and make use of money instead. Thus the economy is a monetary economy. Money balances that are held between purchases, or not used for purchases, must be kept as bank deposits. Furthermore, all money balances are backed up fractionally by a monetary base consisting of the reserves on deposit at the central bank. The (commercial) bank creates money (within certain limits) by buying the IOUs of the firms, that is, by using its excess reserves to increase its loans. (In addition, money is created or destroyed according as, respectively, the bank's operating expenditures are greater or less than its revenues.) The funds that the bank has to lend out (and to buy inputs and pay the contractual obligations on its debt) come from the excess

---

[7]The term "risk," as it is used here, is intended to have a more general meaning than in its earlier appearances and is not connected in any way to the notion of probability.

[8]Although the model of Chapter 9 permitted the firm to liquidate its real capital assets by selling them in a second-hand, real capital asset market, no significant modification in that model is required to transpose it into the present context in which the possibility of such sales is eliminated.

reserves created by the interest it receives on outstanding loans and the money capital it raises, and from its previously existing holdings of excess reserves, which depend on the reserve requirement set by the central bank. The decision problem of the bank is to select a quantity (positive, negative, or zero) of durable input to buy (*i.e.*, respectively, investment or disinvestment in, or maintenance of, its own real capital stock), an amount of excess reserves to hold, and a portfolio consisting of the debt of the two firms.

Now the firms have an initial endowment of assets inherited from the past that includes, possibly, an unplanned and undesired inventory of previously produced but as yet unsold output. They acquire revenue from the sale of output (taken out of inventory or newly produced) and additional money capital from the sale of IOUs. The firms use some of these funds to purchase inputs and pay the required return on their debt. That which remains accumulates to replace worn-out durable-good input and for possible future investment in additional durable input and work in progress. Thus, along with the standard operating decisions, the two firms have further to determine the forms in which to hold their accumulated funds, or, in other words, they, too, have to select a portfolio of marketable, income-earning assets and money.

Lastly, the consumer purchases the nondurable manufactured good, supplies homogeneous labor time to the two firms and the bank by giving up leisure time, and acquires his own portfolio containing marketable, income-earning assets and money. In addition to money balances, the consumer's initial endowment consists of given quantities of firm and bank debt obtained from previous investments and a quantity of time for allocation between leisure and labor. The initial endowment imposes specific constraints on his economic activity.

This economy, then, contains four decision-making units or agents, two outputs, two factors, three marketable assets, and money. The durable factor, when new, and the durable good produced are the same, as are labor time supplied and leisure time retained by the consumer. There is a market for the sale of each output, a market for labor time, and a separate market for each marketable asset and money. Both new and old issues of IOUs may be traded in the income-earning asset or IOU markets. (Recall that the market for used but not completely worn out durable input has been eliminated.)

Clearly consumer, firm, and bank activities occur and interact in markets simultaneously at each moment of historical time. However, because of the ignorance in which decisions are made, agent activity is likely to be inconsistent in the sense that few, if any, of the plans that emerge from agent decision making are capable of being realized. Therefore, to obtain coherence in a model representing such an economy, that is, to obtain realized quantities utilizing the model's simultaneous equations, this inconsistent activity has to be resolved into unique outcomes by trading rules and rationing schemes in the economy's markets. But resolution necessarily means that while the inconsistent activity is turned into outcomes that are consistent with each other, certain plans are still not realized. In general, then, markets do not clear and subsequent activity partly reflects adjustments that are made to correct for unrealized plans. Even so, preferences, technologies, perceptions, expectations, and, hence, behavior functions still vary from period to period, and nothing resembling a general equilibrium is likely to be achieved. Rather, as the process of interacting decision making in light of trading rules and rationing schemes churns through historical time, unpredictably reacting to unpredictable environmental and expectational variation, the kaleidic economy works itself out. Hence analytical attention can only center on the process whereby the economy arrives at its present state[9] (or how the economy achieved its previous states) as opposed to the general equilibrium focus on the future state in whose direction the economy (which, in that case, is assumed to be dynamically stable) is proceeding.[10]

More precisely, the model set out below assumes that all agents make the relevant decisions to determine their economic behaviors, that the two firms set the prices of their own outputs, that market yields and the prices of previously issued IOUs are determined in IOU markets, that all markets allocate quantities according to certain trading rules and rationing schemes, and that all of this occurs simultaneously in each period of historical time. As in general equilibrium analysis, to obtain consistent outcomes from potentially inconsistent simultaneous

---

[9]This includes consideration of, among other things, how current consumption, production, and asset investment decisions are made.

[10]The parallels to the model of two-person, two-commodity exchange analyzed in Section 8.1 should be noted. Recall, also, the general discussion of Section 8.2.

activity requires that internal consistency among all of the relations of the model be present. In the absence of such internal consistency, for example, since the two firms as modeled below must purchase inputs without knowing what quantity of output they can sell, they may wind up with insufficient funds to cover the costs that the equations say they have incurred. They also may be unable to secure all of the labor required to manufacture the "output" that the equations depict them as having produced.[11] Likewise the consumer may not have enough income to cover the quantities of goods and IOUs that the equations indicate he purchased. In any case, inequalities that ensure internal consistency are introduced later. The net effect of resolving the system, then, is to determine "realized" magnitudes for all market prices (except the wage which is taken to be exogenously set) and all agent demand and supply commodity, labor-time, IOU, and money-balance quantities in each period of time. However, it is not necessarily true that at these realized magnitudes all expectations have been met and all plans have been fulfilled. For, even when the activities that occur simultaneously are internally consistent, and even with the consumer switching the labor he supplies from one firm to the other, firms may still not produce enough at the existing prices and wages to meet output market demands or to employ all of the labor available to them. They also may not realize sufficient income to be able to meet the obligations on their previously issued IOUs.[12] And decision makers, in general, may not earn enough income elsewhere to be able to follow through on planned IOU expenditures. Evidently, the extent to which plans are actually realized depends, in part, on the extent to which price perceptions and income expectations turn out to be accurate. In any case, what actually transpires is not often the same as what is intended, and desired behavior has to be modified subsequently to fit the circumstances. This cannot usually happen in the standard general equilibrium models because the trading rules and rationing schemes are

---

[11]See Benassy [1, p. 12].

[12]Even so, the present model assumes that such firms continue to exist. If earnings were insufficient to permit the full service of their IOUs, the continued existence of these firms may depend on favorable future earnings expectations and the firms' ability to issue new IOUs as a means of borrowing funds to finance their temporary cash flow deficits.

replaced by market-clearing relations.

Since IOUs are issued in perpetuity, the current market yield on an outstanding IOU is the current dollar return on it expressed as a percentage of its current market price. The current dollar return on the IOU is determined by the contractually required rate of return specified at its date of issue. In the case of a current new issue, the price of the IOU is one dollar. Price determination in the market for the IOUs of a given firm, say, ensures that prices of old issues adjust until the current market yields on all outstanding IOUs of that firm and on the firm's new issues are the same.[13] The market yield then becomes the required rate of return on new issues. In this way, the firm's required rate of return on new issues is fixed in its IOU market. The latter return depends, among other things, on the perceived risk of investing in the firm. Although equalization of the market yields across all of the firm's outstanding IOUs establishes a market price of risk for the IOUs of that firm, perceived risk is still heterogeneous across the buyers of the firm's IOUs. Perceived risk is also heterogeneous across the two firms and the bank. Hence the required rates of return on their new issues in any period would tend to be different.[14]

Note that the presence of different required rates of return on new

---

[13]To illustrate, suppose a new issue of IOUs were sold in one-dollar denominations for one dollar each. Then the market yield is the percent required dollar return per IOU. In a model with more than one person, if some of these IOUs were resold to another consumer at a later date when, say, the then-current rate of return is higher, their selling price would be less than a dollar. Hence the market yield on the now old IOUs would rise since the originally contracted required dollar return would be divided by a smaller price.

[14]As indicated above, the required rate of return on new issues for either firm or the bank depends on the perceived riskiness of its future income stream. And while the future incomes of the firms tend to rest on the extent to which they are able to sell their output, that for the bank turns on the productivity of its loans, that is, its holdings of the IOUs of those firms. Thus the perceived risk associated with the bank depends on the perceived risk associated with the two firms. But, since its portfolio is diversified, the perceived risk associated with the bank could be judged to be lower than the risk associated with either of the firms, depending on the extent to which the historical correlation coefficient between the firms' rates of return is less that unity. In that case, the required rate of return that the bank would have to pay on the new IOUs it issues would be lower than that demanded on the new issues of both firms.

IOUs issued by the firms and the bank means that these agents have the option of diverting funds from investment in their own productive capacity (*i.e.*, in the purchase of new durable-good input) to investment in marketable, income-earning assets (*i.e.*, in the buying of the IOUs of the other firm or the bank), or to the buying back of their own previously issued IOUs. Generally a firm or the bank will divert investment in this way if the available rate of return outside is greater than the anticipated real rate of return that can be earned internally from investing in real capital formation. However, due to the lags involved in the time structure of its cash flows, an agent may still use temporarily available excess funds to purchase outside IOUs even if investment in its own productive capacity or replacement of worn-out durable input is expected to take place eventually. Such a possibility is consistent, of course, with the earlier assumption that all firms remain in existence.

11.2   The Consumer

Denote the consumer by γ, the nondurable good and the nondurable-good-producing firm by x, the durable good and the durable-good-producing firm by y, and the bank by β. Let x and y also represent quantities of the nondurable and durable good, respectively. Quantities of labor time supplied to, and numbers of IOUs issued by x, y, and β are, respectively, ℓ_x, ℓ_y, ℓ_β and a_x, a_y, a_β. (Recall that all labor time supplied is supposed homogeneous.) The symbol a_m indicates sizes of nominal money balances. Although historical time, designated by t, is referred to here as a succession of discrete periods, the same model could be conceived without alteration if, instead, time were thought of as passing in continuous moments.

Taking up the consumer first, consider the following version of the model of his economic behavior developed in Section 10.2: Write the consumer's initial endowment of total available time in period t as $\hat{\ell}_\gamma^t$. (It is assumed that $\hat{\ell}_\gamma^t$ is large enough to accommodate current production and bank needs, including those that arise from the additions to the real capital stock that occurred due to purchases of new durable goods during the last period.)[15] Let $a^t_{x\gamma\tau}$ represent the (net) number of IOUs issued by firm x in period τ that is held by γ in period t. With $\tau = t$ denoting the present period and $\tau = 1$ the first period under consideration (*i.e.*, the past period farthest removed from the present), the consumer's currently planned holding of firm x's debt is the vector $a^t_{x\gamma} = (a^t_{x\gamma1}, \ldots, a^t_{x\gamma t})$, and his initial holding at the start of period t is $\hat{a}^t_{x\gamma} = (\hat{a}^t_{x\gamma1}, \ldots, \hat{a}^t_{x\gamma t-1}, 0)$. (In terms of symbolism to be employed later on, $\hat{a}^t_{x\gamma\tau} = \bar{a}^{t-1}_{x\gamma\tau}$ for $\tau = 1, \ldots, t-1$, where $\bar{a}^{t-1}_{x\gamma\tau}$ is the quantity of $a^{t-1}_{x\gamma\tau}$ actually realized in period $t-1$.) Similarly, his currently planned and initial holdings of firm y's and the bank's debt are described as, respectively, $a^t_{y\gamma} = (a^t_{y\gamma1}, \ldots, a^t_{y\gamma t})$, $\hat{a}^t_{y\gamma} = (\hat{a}^t_{y\gamma1}, \ldots, \hat{a}^t_{y\gamma t-1}, 0)$, $a^t_{\beta\gamma} = (a^t_{\beta\gamma1}, \ldots, a^t_{\beta\gamma t})$, and $\hat{a}^t_{\beta\gamma} = (\hat{a}^t_{\beta\gamma1}, \ldots, \hat{a}^t_{\beta\gamma t-1}, 0)$. The notation $s^t_\gamma = (a^t_{x\gamma}, a^t_{y\gamma}, a^t_{\beta\gamma}, a^t_{m\gamma})$, where $a^t_{m\gamma}$ is a scalar indicating the (average) desired nominal quantity of money held by γ during period t, denotes his currently planned (asset) portfolio, and $\hat{s}^t_\gamma = (\hat{a}^t_{x\gamma}, \hat{a}^t_{y\gamma}, \hat{a}^t_{\beta\gamma}, \hat{a}^t_{m\gamma})$, where $\hat{a}^t_{m\gamma} = \bar{a}^{t-1}_{m\gamma}$, his initial endowment portfolio passed on from the previous period. The currently perceived or expected price of an IOU issued by firm x in period τ is written $q^t_{x\tau}$. Since $q^t_{xt} = \bar{q}^t_{xt} = 1$, where the bar indicates the price actually realized, the vector of currently perceived or expected prices of all issues of firm x's IOUs is $q^t_x = (q^t_{x1}, \ldots, q^t_{xt-1}, 1)$. The corresponding vectors of currently perceived or expected prices of the IOUs of firm y and the bank are $q^t_y = (q^t_{y1}, \ldots, q^t_{yt-1}, 1)$ and $q^t_\beta = (q^t_{\beta1}, \ldots, q^t_{\beta t-1}, 1)$, respectively. The "price" of money, that is, its unit asset value, is always unity, or $q^t_m = \bar{q}^t_m = 1$. Thus the currently perceived or expected value of γ's planned portfolio is $q^t \cdot s^t_\gamma$, where the price vector $q^t = (q^t_x, q^t_y, q^t_\beta, 1)$ and the dot denotes inner product.

Now, at time t, the consumer's decision set consists of vectors $(x^t_\gamma, \ell^t_{x\gamma}, \ell^t_{y\gamma}, \ell^t_{\beta\gamma}, s^t_\gamma)$, such that

$$\ell^t_{x\gamma} + \ell^t_{y\gamma} + \ell^t_{\beta\gamma} \leq \hat{\ell}^t_\gamma,$$

where x^t_γ is a quantity of the nondurable good consumed by person γ, and $\ell^t_{x\gamma}$, $\ell^t_{y\gamma}$, and $\ell^t_{\beta\gamma}$ are, respectively, quantities of labor(-time) supplied to x, y, and β by γ. Two further restrictions also impose limitations on the consumer's decision set. The first is the financial

---

[15]However, depending on the decisions of the supplier of labor, namely, γ, not all of $\hat{\ell}^t_\gamma$ need be forthcoming to meet these needs.

resources constraint

$$\bar{p}_x^t x_\gamma^t + q^t \cdot \left(s_\gamma^t - \hat{s}_\gamma^t\right) \leq \hat{w}^t \left(\ell_{x\gamma}^t + \ell_{y\gamma}^t + \ell_{\beta\gamma}^t\right) + \left(q^t \cdot s_\gamma^t\right) v_\gamma^t, \quad (11.2\text{-}1)$$

where, at time t, $\bar{p}_x^t$ is the realized price of the nondurable good set by firm x, v_γ^t is the anticipated, per period rate of return on his planned portfolio as a whole (which depends on q^t), and $\hat{w}^t$ is the wage, assumed to be given exogenously. It is supposed that $\bar{p}_x^t$ is known to the consumer by virtue of its announcement by firm x, and $\hat{w}^t$ is known from its exogeneity. (Of course, the consumer also knows his initial endowments of labor time, IOUs, and money balances.) The IOU price vector, q^t, represents only the perceptions or expectations of γ and is subject to error. The second restriction is the velocity constraint, or

$$\varepsilon_\gamma^t \leq \hat{\nu}_\gamma^t a_{m\gamma}^t,$$

where $\hat{\nu}_\gamma^t$ is γ's velocity of circulation of money at time t, assumed, for present purposes, to be exogenously set by γ and his environment; and ε_γ^t is expenditure on goods and income-earning assets.[16] It should be noted that if γ's plans are not all realized then the actual value of the velocity parameter may turn out to be different from $\hat{\nu}_\gamma^t$.

The consumer is hypothesized to have a utility function dependent on quantities of the nondurable good x_γ^t, vectors of labor supplies $(\ell_{x\gamma}^t, \ell_{y\gamma}^t, \ell_{\beta\gamma}^t)$, anticipated portfolio rates of return v_γ^t, and possible imagined states of the world ω_γ^t that, he conjectures (during period t), may emerge with his decision.[17] As shown in Section 10.2, this function reduces to

$$\psi_t = U^t(x_\gamma^t, \ell_{x\gamma}^t, \ell_{y\gamma}^t, \ell_{\beta\gamma}^t, s_\gamma^t, \omega_\gamma^t),$$

defined over an appropriate domain. Under the requisite conditions, including the existence of suitably defined potential surprise and attractiveness functions and a decision index (all with the necessary prop-

---

[16]It is legitimate to treat $\hat{\nu}_\gamma^t$ as a parameter here since IOU prices, and hence marketable asset yields, are perceived as fixed in the IOU markets. But in general, with market yields changing, $a_{m\gamma}^t$, and therefore $\hat{\nu}_\gamma^t$, will vary with those yields.

[17]With the vector, $(\ell_{x\gamma}^t, \ell_{y\gamma}^t, \ell_{\beta\gamma}^t)$, of labor supplies in the utility function, and with the consumer having no initial endowment of the nondurable good x, insofar as the nondurable good and leisure is concerned, utility is actually a function of excess demands.

erties), application of the analysis of the consumer developed previously yields quantity demands and supplies as functions of the specified parameters.[18] But, since there is no reason to believe that the behavior functions so obtained are stable over time, only the actual selections of quantities based on the parameter values existing at time t are of interest here. These are designated as follows: the quantity of the nondurable good desired is $x_{\gamma e}^t$; the planned quantities of labor time supplied are $\ell_{x\gamma e}^t$, $\ell_{y\gamma e}^t$, and $\ell_{\beta\gamma e}^t$; and the portfolio the consumer wants to hold is $s_{\gamma e}^t = (a_{x\gamma e}^t, a_{y\gamma e}^t, a_{\beta\gamma e}^t, a_{m\gamma e}^t)$. The latter translates, respectively, into asset excess demands by the consumer, at time t, of planned vectors $a_{x\gamma e}^t - \hat{a}_{x\gamma}^t$, $a_{y\gamma e}^t - \hat{a}_{y\gamma}^t$, and $a_{\beta\gamma e}^t - \hat{a}_{\beta\gamma}^t$ and the planned scalar $a_{m\gamma e}^t - \hat{a}_{m\gamma}^t$. In this and subsequent notation, the subscript e, meaning a specific planned, desired, or estimated magnitude (or function) that has been selected or determined, is affixed only to those values (or functions) that emerge from agent decision making in the model and hence might not turn out to be realized. Thus, for example, $a_{m\gamma}^t$ represents a variable ranging over possible planned values, whereas $a_{m\gamma e}^t$ designates the particular planned value that has been chosen. In addition, the appearance of a bar over a planned variable (as in, say, $\bar{q}_{xt}^t$ and $\bar{a}_{x\gamma\tau}^{t-1}$) denotes, as described above, the value of that variable actually realized at time t. It should be noted, however, that as is customary in economic theorizing, under suitable analytical circumstances barred variable values can also be thought of as variables themselves. Where appropriate, this switch in meaning will be made below without comment.

11.3   The Two Firms

Consider next the nondurable-good-producing firm x. To construct an appropriate model of this firm, it is necessary to supplement the model of the "steady-state" firm originally developed in Chapter 9 to allow for the further choice of a portfolio that includes marketable assets and nominal money balances. However, determination of the firm's output

---

[18]In the present case, the functional arguments of these behavior functions would be $\hat{\ell}_\gamma^t$, $\hat{s}_\gamma^t$, $\hat{w}^t$, $\bar{p}_x^t$, q_x^t, and $\hat{\nu}_\gamma^t$. In addition, as pointed out in Section 10.2, sufficient restrictions could be added to the model to ensure the absence of money illusion.

price and its planned output and desired labor input remain as before.

Let the firm's current inventory of finished output be designated by $\hat{x}^t$ and its current stock of durable input by $\hat{y}_x^t$. The desired level of finished output inventory is always zero. Moreover, the acquisition of additional durable input in period t does not affect output until period $t+1$. The firm's production and money capital requirement functions at time t are, respectively,

$$x = F^{xt}(\hat{y}_x^t, \ell_x)$$

and

$$c_x = \Lambda^{xt}(p_x, \hat{w}^t, x + \hat{x}^t, \hat{y}_x^t, \ell_x). \tag{11.3-1}$$

To set the price it charges for its output, firm x estimates the output demand function it faces and marks up from unit costs as described earlier. Its estimated demand function for period t (the actual selection of this estimate is outlined subsequently) is symbolized as $\mathcal{D}_{xe}^t(p_x)$ in

$$x = \mathcal{D}_{xe}^t(p_x) - \hat{x}^t. \tag{11.3-2}$$

There are no superscripts t on x, ℓ_x, and p_x in the above relations because these variables do not yet reflect plans or desires on the part of the firm. However, the price the firm charges is set by solving the markup equation (9.2-10) for p, and, since this price is actually realized, it is written (recall the previous section) as $\bar{p}_x^t$. Now, by substituting $\bar{p}_x^t$ into the estimated demand function and subtracting off current output inventory $\hat{x}^t$ as in (11.3-2), the firm's planned output production is obtained as x_e^t (its planned output supply is $x_e^t + \hat{x}^t$), and its desired labor input derives from x_e^t and the inverse of the production function as ℓ_{xe}^t. The money capital required to support operation at these levels, c_{xe}^t, is found upon substitution of the just-determined values for production and labor input into the money capital requirement function (11.3-1).

The current debt of the firm, that is, the par value of its currently outstanding IOUs, is given by

$$\hat{a}_x^t = \sum_{\tau=1}^{t-1} \left(\hat{a}_{x\gamma\tau}^t + \hat{a}_{xy\tau}^t + \hat{a}_{x\beta\tau}^t \right),$$

where $\hat{a}_{x\gamma\tau}^t$, $\hat{a}_{xy\tau}^t$, and $\hat{a}_{x\beta\tau}^t$ are, respectively, the (net) number of the firm's IOUs issued in period τ held by γ, y, and β at the start of period

t. Write $a^t_{yx\tau}$ and $a^t_{\beta x\tau}$ for the (net) number of IOUs issued by firm y and the bank in period τ that firm x plans to hold during period t,[19] and let a^t_{mx} be the firm's currently planned holdings of (nominal) money balances. Take $\hat{\rho}^t_x$ to be the (weighted) average required rate of return at time of issue over all IOUs of firm x outstanding at the start of period t and let $\delta^{xt}(\bar{p}^t_y)$ indicate its current depreciation charge function dependent on the current (realized) price asked by firm y on newly produced units of the durable good.[20] Then, using this notation and the estimated variable values determined above, the firm's estimated earnings in excess of current operating cost, written π^t_{xe}, are

$$\pi^t_{xe} = \bar{p}^t_x\left[x^t_e + \hat{x}^t\right] - \left[\hat{w}^t\ell^t_{xe} + \hat{\rho}^t_x\hat{a}^t_x + \delta^{xt}(\bar{p}^t_y)\right]$$
$$+ \left[\left(q^t_y, q^t_\beta, 1\right) \cdot s^t_{xe}\right] v_x, \tag{11.3-3}$$

where $s^t_{xe} = (a^t_{yxe}, a^t_{\beta xe}, a^t_{mxe}) = (a^t_{yx1e}, \ldots, a^t_{yxte}, a^t_{\beta x1e}, \ldots, a^t_{\beta xte}, a^t_{mxe})$ is the desired portfolio, to be considered momentarily, that the firm plans to hold in period t and v_x is (in analogue to the model of the consumer) the per period rate of return anticipated by the firm on its planned portfolio as a whole.[21] (The firm is not permitted to hold its own debt in its portfolio.) Note that q^t_y and q^t_β in equation (11.3-3), that is, the firm's perceptions or expectations of IOU prices, although symbolically identical to, are generally different from the components q^t_y and q^t_β of q^t in inequality (11.2-1) relating to the consumer. Firm x's

---

[19]As suggested earlier, to the extent that firm x is holding the IOUs of firm y and the bank, and depending on the level of its realized earnings, it may refrain from replacing worn-out durable inputs and investing accumulated revenue in the expansion of its own activities. This may, of course, be a short-run phenomenon while the firm is awaiting more permanent investment opportunities.

[20]Remember that, in the context of the model as a whole, where all agents interact with each other, $\bar{p}^t_x$ and $\bar{p}^t_y$ are determined simultaneously along with other variables.

[21]At this point a special property of (11.3-3) should be noted. It was indicated in n. 27 on p. 295 that the firm's payment on its outstanding IOUs did not take account of the possible complications arising from additional required outlays on any new IOUs issued or from savings from any outstanding IOUs repurchased. In (11.3-3), however, the firm's revenue projections include the anticipated earnings on its planned portfolio holdings of the IOUs of the other firm and the bank. This slight difference in treatment of the revenue and cost sides of the firm's profit function is maintained here in the interest of simplicity.

estimated, actual rate of return at time t on the money capital invested in it is

$$\rho^t_{xe} = \frac{\pi^t_{xe} + \hat{\rho}^t_x \hat{a}^t_x}{c^t_{xe}},$$

and its current net demand to buy back outstanding IOUs or net supply of new issues, namely, Δa^t_{xe}, is deduced as indicated in the original model of Section 9.2. Of course, depending on what happens in the commodity, labor, asset, and money markets, ρ^t_{xe} is larger than, equal to, or smaller than $\bar{\rho}^t_x$, where $\bar{\rho}^t_x$ is the realized market yield on, or the current return that firm x is required to pay on, the new IOUs it issues. Moreover, $\bar{\rho}^t_x$ is also generally different from the rate of return actually earned during period t on the money capital invested in firm x.

Observe that as long as

$$\pi^t_{xe} \geq \left[\left(q^t_y, q^t_\beta, 1\right) \cdot s^t_{xe}\right] v_x,$$

$$\rho^t_{xe} \geq \rho^t_{yxe},$$

and

$$\rho^t_{xe} \geq \rho^t_{\beta xe},$$

where ρ^t_{yxe} and $\rho^t_{\beta xe}$ are, respectively, firm x's estimate of the actual rates of return in y and β during period t, the firm will maintain its real capital intact. If the first inequality did not hold, then, from (11.3-3), the firm's estimated earnings would be negative; failure of the second or third would imply that the firm anticipates it could earn more, at least in period t, by purchasing the IOUs of firm y or the bank than by investing in itself. Provided it believed that such a situation was going to persist in the long run, the firm would divert funds earmarked for expansion of its own real capital or the replacement of its own worn-out capital to the IOU markets. However, the assumption of the firm's continued existence precludes the latter and, in any case, the firm could still not liquidate its existing real capital stock since there is no second-hand market for the durable good.

As has been argued in prior investigation, the present discussion is incomplete because the firm still has to choose (i) the current gross quantity of planned durable input, y^t_{xe}, which provides for both replacement of worn out durable input and investment for the future; and (ii) estimates, $\mathcal{D}_{xe}^t$ and $\mathcal{D}_{xe}^{t+1}$, of current and next period's output demand functions. These decisions were originally modeled in Section 9.2 using the apparatus for decision making in ignorance developed in Section 4.3. But in the present context, a fourth decision has to be made, namely, the selection of a portfolio of marketable assets and money balances in which to hold the funds from the revenues that already have accumulated and continue to accumulate in the firm. Because one of the assets it contains is money, the choice of such a portfolio implies a firm demand for money balances. Supposing that the firm only returns what is contractually required to the holders of its debt, through period t the anticipated accumulated revenues, κ_{xe}^t, consist of those built up in the past plus those expected to be currently added:

$$\kappa_{xe}^t = (q_y^t, q_\beta^t, 1) \cdot \hat{s}_x^t + \pi_{xe}^t - \bar{p}_y^t y_{xe}^t,$$

where $\hat{s}_x^t = (\hat{a}_{yx}^t, \hat{a}_{\beta x}^t, \hat{a}_{mx}^t)$ is the portfolio held initially at the start of the period. (The last component of each of $\hat{a}_{yx}^t$ and $\hat{a}_{\beta x}^t$ is zero because $\hat{s}_x^t$ only contains firm x's portfolio holdings of IOUs issued prior to the present period.) Thus the selection of the firm's desired portfolio is constrained by

$$(q_y^t, q_\beta^t, 1) \cdot s_x^t \le \kappa_x^t, \qquad (11.3\text{-}4)$$

where the subscripts e on s_x^t and κ_{xe}^t have been dropped since s_x^t and κ_x^t now vary with the particular choice option selected. A further constraint is

$$\varepsilon_x^t \le \hat{\nu}_x^t a_{mx}^t, \qquad (11.3\text{-}5)$$

where, as with the consumer, ε_x^t is expenditure on goods and income-earning assets, and $\hat{\nu}_x^t$ is an exogenous velocity parameter for the firm.[22] The firm's decision set, then, consists of vectors $(y_x^t, \mathcal{D}_x^t, \mathcal{D}_x^{t+1}, s_x^t)$, which satisfy (11.3-4) and (11.3-5),[23] and the other relations introduced in the original model.[24] (Again the subscript e is eliminated because $\mathcal{D}_x^t$ and

---

[22]As in the case of the consumer, $\hat{\nu}_x^t$ may be regarded as a parameter. See n. 16 on p. 341.

[23]The fact that κ_x^t is determined by the choice option $(y_x^t, \mathcal{D}_x^t, \mathcal{D}_x^{t+1}, s_x^t)$ in conjunction with other equations of the model is of no consequence in ensuring that (11.3-4) is satisfied.

[24]These other relations take into account such things as the effect of $\mathcal{D}_x^{t+1}$ on y_x^t. Recall Section 9.3.

$\mathcal{D}_x^{t+1}$ represent possible, and not particular, components of the choice vector.)

Remember that, as in many decision models, the parameters that define the decision set are also the parameters on which the actual choice is said, at least in part, to depend. Moreover, variations in such things as the firm's revenue flows and the amount of work it has in progress have an impact too, since they influence κ_x^t in (11.3-4) through π_x^t in the appropriate analogue of (11.3-3) with the subscripts e dropped so that specific estimated or planned values are replaced by general variables. In particular, these elements play a role in setting the firm's demand for money balances.

Now employ the same application of Section 4.3 used in the model of Section 9.3 to determine the actual selection $(y_{xe}^t, \mathcal{D}_{xe}^t, \mathcal{D}_{xe}^{t+1}, s_{xe}^t)$. Thus, for each vector of possible, imagined, present and future states of the world ω_x conceived by it, the firm is able to calculate, as in (9.3-3), possible, per period, overall rates of return on the money capital invested in it, ψ_x^*, from equations that either are unchanged from the original or that, like (11.3-3), have been slightly modified so as to fit present circumstances.[25] Using its own potential surprise function, attractiveness functions, and decision index, its choice is made as before. In addition to the quantities demanded and supplied already mentioned, the firm's demand for new durable input, y_{xe}^t, and its excess demands for assets, namely, $a_{yxe}^t - \hat{a}_{yx}^t$, $a_{\beta xe}^t - \hat{a}_{\beta x}^t$, and $a_{mxe}^t - \hat{a}_{mx}^t$, are determined.

The firm producing the durable good y is handled similarly except that it uses the output that it produces as its durable-good input and it acquires this input at the input's cost of production instead of at its market price. In parallel to the nondurable-good-producing firm, firm y has a current finished output inventory $\hat{y}^t$, a current stock of durable input $\hat{y}_y^t$, outstanding debt

$$\hat{a}_y^t = \sum_{\tau=1}^{t-1} \left(\hat{a}_{y\gamma\tau}^t + \hat{a}_{yx\tau}^t + \hat{a}_{y\beta\tau}^t \right),$$

an initial portfolio $\hat{s}_y^t = (\hat{a}_{xy}^t, \hat{a}_{\beta y}^t, \hat{a}_{my}^t)$, and production, money cap-

---

[25]Recall that ψ_x^* is the geometric mean of the ρ_x^t (that is, the ρ_{xe}^t without the subscript e) over an appropriate span of periods.

ital requirement, and depreciation charge functions similar to those described for firm x. Thus, in this case, the production function, for example, would be written

$$y = F^{yt}(\hat{y}_y^t, \ell_y)$$

and the depreciation charges depend on $\hat{w}^t$, reflecting the firm's cost of producing its own output. Additional parameters include the average required rate of return over all outstanding debt, $\hat{\rho}_y^t$, and the firm's money circulation velocity $\hat{v}_y^t$. As with firm x, it selects a choice option $(y_{ye}^t, \mathcal{D}_{ye}^t, \mathcal{D}_{ye}^{t+1}, s_{ye}^t)$ consisting of, respectively, additions of part of its own output to its capital stock (i.e., real capital investment), estimates of this period's and next period's demand functions (that include its own possible demand), and its desired portfolio $s_{ye}^t = (a_{xye}^t, a_{\beta ye}^t, a_{mye}^t)$. (The fact that the estimates $\mathcal{D}_y^t$ and $\mathcal{D}_y^{t+1}$ are related to y_y^t adds an additional constraint to the characterization of this firm's decision set but does not substantively alter the analysis.) It also determines (analogously to firm x) its price, demand, excess demand, and supply values $\bar{p}_y^t$, $y_e^t + \hat{y}^t$, ℓ_{ye}^t, $a_{xye}^t - \hat{a}_{xy}^t$, $a_{\beta ye}^t - \hat{a}_{\beta y}^t$, $a_{mye}^t - \hat{a}_{my}^t$, and Δa_{ye}^t, along with its projected earnings π_{ye}^t and actual rate of return ρ_{ye}^t.

There is, however, at least one further issue, irrelevant for firm x, that firm y may have to face. Suppose, in period t, that at the price $\bar{p}_y^t$ set by firm y, it were to turn out that the quantity demanded on the market (including firm y's own demand) is greater than $y_e^t + \hat{y}^t$. Then the firm would have to decide whether it will sell the output designated for its own use to other firms. To the extent that it were to do so, firm y's expansion plans would be curtailed.

11.4   The Bank

The bank β, as pointed out above, creates money or (demand) deposits by using its excess reserves to buy the IOUs of the two firms. Money may also be created or destroyed depending on the effect of the operations in which it engages. Designate the value of β's reserve "endowment" in period t by $\hat{g}^t$. If $\hat{r}^t$ is the fraction of total deposits, as specified by the central bank, that β is required to keep in its possession during period t, where $0 \leq \hat{r}^t \leq 1$, then the maximum quantity of money that the bank is able to create by expanding loans and suffering losses on its operations is

$$\frac{\hat{g}^t}{\hat{r}^t}.$$

Therefore raising the value of $\hat{g}^t$ or lowering the value of $\hat{r}^t$ increases the potential for monetary creation.[26] The actual supply of money itself, that is, the sum of all demand deposits held in β, depends on the past and present decisions made by individual agents, including the bank. In particular, the bank decides on the durable and nondurable inputs it plans to buy, the portfolio it will realize, and the IOUs it will actually issue. At any t, then, β's purchases and sales of IOUs, together with the extent to which it is able to secure the inputs it seeks and the revenues from its loans it expects, determine the money supply in that period. In this manner, the actual money supply can expand or contract from period to period.

In general, β's balance sheet lists its reserves (on deposit in the central bank), the loans it has made to firms x and y (that is, the IOUs of x and y that it currently holds, valued at the prices at which β purchased them), and its real capital, $\hat{y}^t_\beta$, as assets. Its liabilities consist of the (demand) deposits held in β by consumers and firms and the par value of its own outstanding IOUs (representing the money capital it has raised). At the start of period t, total deposits in the bank, $\hat{m}^t$, constitute the money supply. It follows that the bank's required reserves are $\hat{r}^t\hat{m}^t$, and its excess reserves, $\hat{R}^t$, are given by $\hat{R}^t = \hat{g}^t - \hat{r}^t\hat{m}^t$. Rearranging the terms of this last equation and dividing by $\hat{r}^t$,

$$\frac{\hat{g}^t}{\hat{r}^t} = \hat{m}^t + \frac{\hat{R}^t}{\hat{r}^t}. \tag{11.4-1}$$

Therefore, in any period t, the money supply can be expanded by, at most, $\hat{R}^t/\hat{r}^t$.

When the bank buys an IOU issued by firm x or firm y, it pays par value for a new issue and the market price for an outstanding issue. In

---

[26]It has already been noted that $\hat{r}^t$ is set by the central bank. One way that $\hat{g}^t$ can be increased is by β borrowing funds from the central bank. Thus the central bank can influence $\hat{g}^t$ by changing the price at which it lends reserves to β. Alternatively, the central bank can engage in open-market operations, $i.e.$, buying or selling the IOUs of x, y, and β. But these possibilities are not explored further here.

either case, it uses up excess reserves and the money supply rises by the amount of the transaction. When the bank sells one of these IOUs, it receives the market price for that issue, its excess reserves increase, and the money supply falls.[27] Note also that when the bank sells an IOU that it has issued itself to obtain money capital, the transaction appears on its balance sheet as an enlargement of its outstanding debt offset by an equal decline in its deposits. That is, because the purchaser of the IOU draws down his (or its) deposits to pay for the IOU, the money supply falls by the amount of the purchase. Similarly, the money supply rises when the bank buys back any of its own outstanding debt. In addition to all of this (and as indicated earlier), if during any period the bank receives more income from its loans than it pays out for its durable input and labor, and for returns to the holders of its own outstanding IOUs, then the money supply decreases. Likewise, if it receives less than it pays out, the money supply increases. Only when receipts exactly offset payments (*i.e.*, when β earns zero economic or abnormal profit) does the operation of the bank itself have no impact on the money supply. Therefore another, equivalent, way to describe the money supply in period t is as the accumulated result of all of β's transactions.

To describe this symbolically, let $\breve{a}^{\eta}_{x\beta\tau}$ and $\breve{a}^{\eta}_{y\beta\tau}$ be the number of IOUs issued, respectively, by firms x and y in period τ and purchased by the bank in period η, and let $\tilde{a}^{\eta}_{x\beta\tau}$ and $\tilde{a}^{\eta}_{y\beta\tau}$ be those respective issues sold by the bank in period η. In addition, let $\breve{a}_{\beta\tau}$ be the total number of new issues of the bank's IOUs sold to γ, x, and y in period τ and let $\tilde{a}^{\eta}_{\beta\tau}$ be the total number of the bank's IOUs issued in period τ and bought back in period η. With $\eta = t$, these are all planned rather that realized variables. Clearly $\tilde{a}^{\tau}_{x\beta\tau} = \tilde{a}^{\tau}_{y\beta\tau} = \tilde{a}^{\tau}_{\beta\tau} = 0$ for all τ. Use $\zeta_{\beta\tau}$ to denote the expected excess of the bank's revenue receipts over operating expenditures (including purchases of durable input but excluding unrealized capital gains and losses) in period τ.

---

[27]The bank may want to sell an IOU if it thinks it can replace it with one yielding a higher return. Such an exchange would imply that the bank is trading an IOU with lower risk for one with higher risk. But this, in turn, would mean that the bank would be selling the first IOU at a higher price than that at which it is buying the second and hence that the money supply would still decline.

Then, mathematically, when $\tau = t$,

$$\zeta_{\beta t} = \left(q_x^t \cdot a_{x\beta e}^t + q_y^t \cdot a_{y\beta e}^t \right) v_\beta - \left(\hat{w}^t \ell_{\beta e}^t + \hat{\rho}_\beta^t \hat{a}_\beta^t + \bar{p}_y^t y_{\beta e}^t \right), \quad (11.4\text{-}2)$$

where v_β is the per period rate of return anticipated on the marketable portfolio, $s_{\beta e}^t = (a_{x\beta e}^t, a_{y\beta e}^t)$, that β plans to hold, and, as before, $\ell_{\beta e}^t$ represents its employment plans, $\hat{\rho}_\beta^t \hat{a}_\beta^t$ the required payments on β's outstanding debt, and $y_{\beta e}^t$ its planned purchase of durable input for the future. (The bank's determination of $s_{\beta e}^t$, $\ell_{\beta e}^t$, and $y_{\beta e}^t$ is considered subsequently.) In this notation, $a_{x\beta e}^t = (a_{x\beta 1e}^t, \ldots, a_{x\beta te}^t)$ and $a_{y\beta e}^t = (a_{y\beta 1e}^t, \ldots, a_{y\beta te}^t)$, where $a_{x\beta\tau e}^t$ and $a_{y\beta\tau e}^t$ denote, respectively, the planned holdings of the IOUs issued in period τ by firm x and firm y, and q_x^t and q_y^t are the bank's perceptions and expectations of the prices of the IOUs issued by x and y. Reserves and real capital, although assets, are not in the portfolio because they are not marketable. Money is not included because it is a liability, not an asset, for β. Note $\zeta_{\beta\tau}$ can be positive, negative, or zero for $\tau = 1, \ldots, t$. Now the anticipated money supply during period t is calculated as

$$m^t = \left[\sum_{\eta,\tau=1}^{t} \left(q_{x\tau}^\eta \check{a}_{x\beta\tau}^\eta - q_{x\tau}^\eta \tilde{a}_{x\beta\tau}^\eta + q_{y\tau}^\eta \check{a}_{y\beta\tau}^\eta - q_{y\tau}^\eta \tilde{a}_{y\beta\tau}^\eta \right. \right.$$

$$\left. \left. + q_{\beta\tau}^\eta \tilde{a}_{\beta\tau}^\eta \right) \right] - \sum_{\tau=1}^{t} \left(\check{a}_{\beta\tau} + \zeta_{\beta\tau} \right), \quad (11.4\text{-}3)$$

where the $q_{x\tau}^\eta$, $q_{y\tau}^\eta$, and $q_{\beta\tau}^\eta$ for $\eta = 1, \ldots, t-1$ are previously realized IOU prices and, for $\eta = t$, represent current IOU prices as perceived or expected by the bank.[28] (Recall that $q_{x\tau}^\tau = q_{y\tau}^\tau = q_{\beta\tau}^\tau = 1$ for every τ.) The bank's outstanding debt at the start of period t is

$$\hat{a}_\beta^t = \sum_{\tau=1}^{t-1} \left(\check{a}_{\beta\tau} - \sum_{\eta=1}^{\tau} \tilde{a}_{\beta\tau}^\eta \right).$$

---

[28]Observe that variation in the bank's payments on its outstanding IOUs arising from possible repurchases of those IOUs or the sale of new issues is ignored in (11.4-2) as it was in the case of firms x and y. (Recall n. 21 on p. 344.) It is recognized, however, that a fuller accounting of such variation may impact on the money supply by virtue of the presence of $\zeta_{\beta\tau}$ in (11.4-3). But again, for the purpose of preserving simplicity, this complication is not considered.

To support a supply of money, m, in period t, think of the bank as needing labor ℓ_β and durable input $\hat{y}^t_\beta$ according to a money supply "production" function[29]

$$m = F^{\beta t}(\rho^t_x, \rho^t_y, \hat{y}^t_\beta, \ell_\beta) \qquad (11.4\text{-}4)$$

and a money capital requirement function

$$c_\beta = \Lambda^{\beta t}(\hat{w}^t, \hat{y}^t_\beta, \ell_\beta), \qquad (11.4\text{-}5)$$

where ρ^t_x and ρ^t_y are the bank's perceived or expected market yields on (or current required rates of return on the new issues of) the IOUs of firms x and y, and the domain of $F^{\beta t}$ is constrained so that

$$F^{\beta t}(\rho^t_x, \rho^t_y, \hat{y}^t_\beta, \ell_\beta) \leq \frac{\hat{g}^t}{\hat{r}^t},$$

everywhere. Assume for convenience and simplicity that when β's decisions (to be spelled out shortly) require a net expansion of its money capital (*i.e.*, the issuing and sale of new IOUs), $\tilde{a}^t_{\beta\tau} = 0$ for $\tau = 1, \ldots, t-1$, or, in other words, that the bank does not plan to buy back any of its outstanding IOUs. Thus the planned values of the $\tilde{a}^t_{\beta\tau}$ and $\breve{a}_{\beta t}$ depend on β's anticipated change in its money capital requirement

$$\Delta c^t_\beta = c^t_\beta - \hat{c}^t_\beta, \qquad (11.4\text{-}6)$$

where the superscript t has been added and $\hat{c}^t_\beta$ is the money capital with which β began the period, and, possibly, on the perceived or expected market prices, q^t_β, of its outstanding IOUs.

The portfolio with which the bank begins period t is $\hat{s}^t_\beta = (\hat{a}^t_{x\beta}, \hat{a}^t_{y\beta})$, where $\hat{a}^t_{x\beta} = (\hat{a}^t_{x\beta 1}, \ldots, \hat{a}^t_{x\beta t})$, $\hat{a}^t_{y\beta} = (\hat{a}^t_{y\beta 1}, \ldots, \hat{a}^t_{y\beta t})$,

$$\hat{a}^t_{x\beta\tau} = \sum_{\eta=1}^{t-1} \left(\breve{a}^\eta_{x\beta\tau} - \tilde{a}^\eta_{x\beta\tau} \right), \qquad \text{and} \qquad \hat{a}^t_{y\beta\tau} = \sum_{\eta=1}^{t-1} \left(\breve{a}^\eta_{y\beta\tau} - \tilde{a}^\eta_{y\beta\tau} \right)$$

---

[29]This production function has a different logical significance from that of the standard production function of the typical firm because "output produced" represents the total money supply in circulation and not merely that added in the current period.

for $\tau = 1, \ldots, t$. As indicated in (11.4-2), the holding of the IOUs of the two firms is what produces the bank's revenue. If, in period t, the bank were to attempt to hold portfolio $s_{\beta e}^t = (a_{x\beta e}^t, a_{y\beta e}^t)$ then, given $\hat{s}_\beta^t = (\hat{a}_{x\beta}^t, \hat{a}_{y\beta}^t)$, certain values of the $\breve{a}_{x\beta\tau}^t$, $\tilde{a}_{x\beta\tau}^t$, $\breve{a}_{y\beta\tau}^t$, and $\tilde{a}_{y\beta\tau}^t$ would be implied. With $y_{\beta e}^t$ determined independently as described below, with the subscript e on $\ell_{\beta e}^t$ in (11.4-2) eliminated, and with perceived or expected IOU prices given, substituting these period-t IOU quantities into (11.4-2) and (11.4-3), using (11.4-2) to eliminate $\zeta_{\beta\tau}$ in (11.4-3), and applying previous discussion, m^t is seen[30] to be a function of ℓ_β^t and Δc_β^t. Write this latter function as

$$m^t = M^t(\ell_\beta^t, \Delta c_\beta^t). \qquad (11.4\text{-}7)$$

Now, given the current perceived or expected market yields ρ_x^t and ρ_y^t (which are also the current perceived or expected required rates of return on newly issued IOUs), and with ℓ_β^t and c_β^t replacing ℓ_β and c_β where the latter arise, equations (11.4-4) through (11.4-7) consitute a system of four equations in the four unknowns m^t, ℓ_β^t, c_β^t, and Δc_β^t. Solving (assuming unique solutions exist) determines the planned values m_e^t, $\ell_{\beta e}^t$, $c_{\beta e}^t$, and $\Delta c_{\beta e}^t$ based on perceived or expected IOU market prices q^t, the desired portfolio $s_{\beta e}^t$, and the desired purchase of durable input $y_{\beta e}^t$. Hence β's current earnings would be estimated as

$$\pi_{\beta e}^t = \left(q_x^t \cdot a_{x\beta e}^t + q_y^t \cdot a_{y\beta e}^t \right) v_\beta - \left(\hat{w}^t \ell_{\beta e}^t + \hat{\rho}_\beta^t \hat{a}_\beta^t + \delta^{\beta t}(\bar{p}_y^t) \right),$$

where $\delta^{\beta t}(\bar{p}_y^t)$ is its depreciation function. In parallel with firm x of Section 11.3, the bank's expected, actual rate of return on the money capital invested in it would be given by

$$\rho_{\beta e}^t = \frac{\pi_{\beta e}^t + \hat{\rho}_\beta^t \hat{a}_\beta^t}{c_{\beta e}^t},$$

and the current expected net change in its outstanding debt, $\Delta a_{\beta e}^t$, would be calculated from Δc_β^t, and possibly q_β^t, as indicated in Section 9.2.

---

[30]It is understood in this calculation that the perceived or expected market yields, ρ_x^t and ρ_y^t, on loans made by the bank, that is, on IOUs purchased by it, are already implicit in the perceived or expected IOU prices included in (11.4-3).

Suppose the bank estimates the excess reserves it expects to have available to lend, that is, with which to buy IOUs, during period t. In so doing, of course, the bank may plan on maintaining a positive excess reserve position. Denote this estimate variable by R^t; its selection will be considered momentarily along with the choices of the desired portfolio and the future investment in durable input. Then, according to (11.4-1), β's decision set, A_β, is a subset of

$$\left\{ (a^t_{x\beta}, a^t_{y\beta}, R^t, y^t_\beta) : m^t \leq \frac{\hat{R}^t}{\hat{r}^t} + \hat{m}^t \right\},$$

where $s^t_\beta = (a^t_{x\beta}, a^t_{y\beta})$ determines m^t as described above and y^t_β, recall, represents the bank's current investment in real capital for the future (the subscripts e are dropped since here s^t_β, m^t, and y^t_β are variable). The exact form of the subset A_β depends on the effects on R^t of selling assets already existing in the portfolio, and on the relations between y^t_β and the remaining choice variables. No velocity parameter is required since the bank does not hold money as an asset. Consider any choice option $(a^t_{x\beta}, a^t_{y\beta}, R^t, y^t_\beta)$ in A_β. Following Section 9.3, for each vector of possible, present and future states of the world ω_β imagined by it, the bank calculates possible, per period, overall rates of return, ψ^*_β, on the money capital invested in it. Then the bank characterizes the choice option in terms of the maximization of that option's attractiveness function subject to its potential surprise density function defined over the values of ψ^*_β, and chooses between choice options (all of which are characterized similarly) according to a decision index. In this way, the estimate R^t_e, the bank's planned investment $y^t_{\beta e}$, and its planned marketable portfolio $s^t_{\beta e} = (a^t_{x\beta e}, a^t_{y\beta e})$ are determined for period t. The bank's respective vectors of excess demands for IOUs are therefore $a^t_{x\beta e} - \hat{a}^t_{x\beta}$, and $a^t_{y\beta e} - \hat{a}^t_{y\beta}$, and, using these planned and realized variable values, β can project the expected money supply m^t_e, as shown above, from (11.4-3).

It should be pointed out that in this model, although output quantities produced and sold by firms x and y are eventually used up, money created by β generally remains in existence and circulates. Thus, if the money supply were actually to increase as a result of the activities of individual agents, there would be a reduction in the overall (actual) velocity of circulation of money[31] unless (realized) aggregate expenditure in the economy (including nonbank expenditure on assets and bank purchases of durable input and labor) rose proportionately with the money supply.[32] This would be reflected in the fact that the individual agent velocity parameters, $\hat{\nu}_\gamma^t$, $\hat{\nu}_x^t$, and $\hat{\nu}_y^t$, would likely end up being different from what those agents initially took them to be. Because firms issue new IOUs to finance expansion of their real capital, enlargement of the money supply would often coincide with an increase in aggregate expenditure. But such increases could be mitigated by declines in the prices of both goods and assets.

11.5 The Markets and Coherence

There are seven markets in this model, one for each of the two goods, three marketable assets, labor time, and money. Agent demands, excess demands, or supplies in these markets are listed in Table 11-1, and the important parameters identified above in agent decision making, which include, in part, the parameters exogenous to the model as a whole, are summarized in Table 11-2. The markets for durable and nondurable goods function by having the two suppliers set their prices

---

[31]The *overall* velocity of circulation is defined as the ratio of aggregate expenditure to the money supply. In terms of realized variable values it is related to the individual agent velocity parameters introduced earlier: disregarding the time superscript and indexing nonbank agents by $i = 1, \ldots, 3$, let ε_i, ν_i, and m_i be, respectively, the realized expenditure of, the realized velocity for, and the actual (average) quantity of money held by agent i, where $\varepsilon_i = \nu_i m_i$ for every i. In the case of the bank, ε_4 is realized expenditure on β's durable and labor input. But the bank does not hold money balances (*i.e.*, there is no m_4) and has no velocity parameter. Let ε be realized aggregate expenditure, m the actual money supply, and ν the realized overall velocity of circulation of money such that $\varepsilon = \nu m$. Then $\varepsilon = \sum_{i=1}^{4} \varepsilon_i$, $\nu m = \varepsilon_4 + \sum_{i=1}^{3} \nu_i m_i$, and $m = \sum_{i=1}^{3} m_i$. Hence

$$\nu = \frac{\varepsilon_4}{m} + \sum_{i=1}^{3} \left(\frac{m_i}{m}\right) \nu_i.$$

[32]Of course, such an enhancement of aggregate expenditure could be entirely due to price increases.

TABLE 11-1. Demands, Excess Demands, or Supplies of Individual Agents in the Various Markets

Agent	The Market For						
	x	y	ℓ	a_x	a_y	a_β	a_m
γ	$x^t_{\gamma e}$	—	$\ell^t_{x\gamma e} + \ell^t_{y\gamma e} + \ell^t_{\beta\gamma e}$	$a^t_{x\gamma e} - \hat{a}^t_{x\gamma}$	$a^t_{y\gamma e} - \hat{a}^t_{yy}$	$a^t_{\beta\gamma e} - \hat{a}^t_{\beta\gamma}$	$a^t_{m\gamma e} - \hat{a}^t_{m\gamma}$
x	$x^t_e + \hat{x}^t$	y^t_{xe}	ℓ^t_{xe}	Δa^t_{xe}	$a^t_{yxe} - \hat{a}^t_{yx}$	$a^t_{\beta xe} - \hat{a}^t_{\beta x}$	$a^t_{mxe} - \hat{a}^t_{mx}$
y	—	$y^t_{ye}, y^t_e + \hat{y}^t$	ℓ^t_{ye}	$a^t_{xye} - \hat{a}^t_{xy}$	Δa^t_{ye}	$a^t_{\beta ye} - \hat{a}^t_{\beta y}$	$a^t_{mye} - \hat{a}^t_{my}$
β	—	$y^t_{\beta e}$	$\ell^t_{\beta e}$	$a^t_{x\beta e} - \hat{a}^t_{x\beta}$	$a^t_{y\beta e} - \hat{a}^t_{y\beta}$	$\Delta a^t_{\beta e}$	m^t_e as defined in equation (11.4-3)

TABLE 11-2.   Important Parameters in Agent Decision Making

Agent	Parameters Exogenous to the System during Period t	Perceived or Expected and Other Parameters
γ	$\hat{\ell}^t_\gamma, \hat{s}^t_\gamma, \hat{w}^t$	$\bar{p}^t_x, \hat{v}^t_\gamma$, expected q^t_x, q^t_y, q^t_β
x	$\hat{x}^t, \hat{y}^t_x, \hat{s}^t_x, \hat{a}^t_x, \hat{p}^t_x, \hat{w}^t$	$\bar{p}^t_y, \hat{v}^t_x$, expected q^t_y, q^t_β
y	$\hat{y}^t, \hat{y}^t_y, \hat{s}^t_y, \hat{a}^t_y, \hat{p}^t_y, \hat{w}^t$	$\hat{v}^t_y$, expected q^t_x, q^t_β
β	$\hat{y}^t_\beta, \hat{s}^t_\beta, \hat{a}^t_\beta, \hat{p}^t_\beta, \hat{c}^t_\beta, \hat{w}^t, \hat{g}^t, \hat{m}^t, \hat{r}^t$	$\bar{p}^t_y$, expected $q^t_x, q^t_y, \rho^t_x, \rho^t_y$

($\bar{p}^t_x$ and $\bar{p}^t_y$ in period t) and sell what the buyers will take. Such markets, which seldom clear, and hence may produce involuntary inventory
accumulation, have been described in Section 7.2. In the labor market, the wage $\hat{w}^t$ has already been exogenously set, perhaps determined
contractually, leaving the buyers in control of the market quantity and
its distribution if $\hat{w}^t$ is too high and the seller with the corresponding
power if it is too low. The outcome in the money market is partly the
result of the activity in the markets for the IOUs of firms x and y and
the bank, since these markets fix the portfolio held by the bank and
help determine the demand for money by firms and the consumer. The
money market, itself, in which the market price will, in due course,
be seen to be defined as the "risk-free market rate of interest," differs
from other markets in that the demands and supplies in it are demands
and supplies for stocks rather than flows. However, a net change in
the stock demand for money (assuming the velocity of circulation remains fixed) introduces a positive or negative flow demand for money.
Likewise a net change in the stock supply by the bank causes a positive or negative flow supply. Due to the willingness of the bank to
create money endogenously (within the constraint arising from existing reserves) by purchasing the IOUs issued by firms and, if necessary,
through its banking operations, the flow demand for money, limited by
the realization of price and quantity variables in other markets, always
equals the flow supply similarly limited. But this does not mean that
individual consumer and individual firm plans to hold stocks of money
balances are necessarily realized. In both labor and money markets,

then, market clearing is also not the rule.

The activity in the three IOU markets in any period is based on the simultaneous decisions made by the individual agents γ, x, y, and β in that period. These markets operate as follows.[33] The price of an old issue of the IOUs of firm x, say, is determined by the last trade of that issue that takes place. This trade sets the equalized market yields, and hence the market prices, of all previously issued IOUs of firm x. It also defines the required rate of return for new issues. In determining planned acquisitions or sales of commodities, labor time, IOUs, and money balances in period t, each buyer and seller has (possibly incorrect) perceptions or expectations of, among other things, IOU prices. Generally, after making plans (decisions), buyers and sellers come together to attempt to put them into effect. These attempts occur sequentially as different buyers and sellers meet to try to effect trades. In the IOU markets, buyers and sellers look for each other as long as they have not been sufficiently disappointed in their previous encounters to cause them to reconsider their trading plans.[34] A trade of an old issue of an IOU is effected between a particular buyer and seller whenever the buyer's expected price of that IOU is at least as large as the seller's expected price and the buyer's planned purchase quantity of it is no greater than the seller's planned sale quantity. When these conditions obtain, the realized trade price is the seller's (lower) expected price, and the realized trade quantity is the buyer's (lower) planned purchase quantity. If the conditions are not met, then no trade between this particular buyer and seller occurs during the period.

Buyers and sellers meet in a random way during the period. Each time a buyer and seller come together under the requisite conditions, trade takes place and a new price, not necessarily different from the old price, is established. Assume, for simplicity, that no buyer meets the same seller more than once during a given trading period.[35] After all buyers have met all sellers, some trades will have been effected while

---

[33]Markets of this sort have also been discussed in Section 7.2.

[34]It is assumed that such reconsiderations can only take place at the beginning of the next period.

[35]In the present model, there are three IOU markets and four potential participants in each. Hence there are at most six buyer-seller meetings, each of which can result in trades in at most three markets during period t.

others will not. Effected trades mean that plans have, at least in part, been realized. Plans are not even partly realized when the expectations on the part of buyers and sellers are sufficiently out of line so as to violate the conditions ensuring trade. Such failed expectations mean that the affected buyers and sellers revise their perceptions and expectations in making plans for the next period.

New issues of IOUs are handled similarly. If a new issue comes to the market, it will be sold to a particular buyer whenever the buyer's expectation of the required rate of return is no larger than that of the seller (that is, x, y, or β) and the buyer's planned purchase quantity is no greater than the seller's planned sale quantity. If trades occur, the realized-trade required rate of return and the realized-trade quantity are the lower of those respective expectations and plans of the buyer and the seller. Suppose, again for simplicity, that a new issue will not be forthcoming unless there are enough buyers to satisfy the minimum sale requirements of the supplier at his expected required rate of return. Such trades, assuming the issue is forthcoming, not only set the required rate of return on the new issue but also fix the equalized market yields and IOU prices of all outstanding IOUs of the seller until the next transaction involving this seller's IOUs. When there are not enough buyers, the seller's perceptions or expectations have failed and he cannot try again until he reconsiders his plans at the start of the next period. Evidently, as with the commodity, labor, and money markets, and except for the "limited flow demand" and "limited flow supply" in the money market described above, there is likely to be little movement toward market clearing.

In any case, there is a finite sequence of, say, N realized IOU price vectors $\bar{q}^{t^1}, \ldots, \bar{q}^{t^N}$ in every period t emerging from trades involving both old and new issues of IOUs. Here $\bar{q}^{t^n}$ is the vector arising from the nth confrontation of buyers and sellers in period t, and $\bar{q}^{t^N}$ is the final price vector of the period, which also serves as the basis for evaluating portfolios in future plans.[36] Clearly the timing of events as they

---

[36] Of course, N may depend on t, and there is a corresponding vector of quantities traded. Further comments bearing on the size of N appeared in n. 35 on p. 358. It is not necessary that each of the components of the $\bar{q}^{t^n}$ be established simultaneously, only that the elements of sequences of components like $\bar{q}_{x\tau}^{t^1}, \ldots, \bar{q}_{x\tau}^{t^N}$, say, be arranged in their actual order of occurrence over period t. In addition, it is also not necessary

unfold during the period determines, in part, the nature of this sequence. As described, each $\bar{q}^{t^n}$ is such that the market yields on all issues of the IOUs of x, y, or β, respectively, are equalized. In addition, these market yields minus their respective risk premiums,[37] or what may be referred to as *the* risk-free market yields, equalize across x, y, and β. The latter yields, since they are all the same, may be thought of as characterizing the risk-free market yield on IOUs. The risk-free market yield, in turn, consititutes an implicit rate of interest that defines the price, or opportunity cost, of holding money.[38] The realized required rates of return on new issues $(\bar{\rho}_x^t, \bar{\rho}_y^t, \bar{\rho}_\beta^t)$, which figure into the calculation of $(\hat{\rho}_x^{t+1}, \hat{\rho}_y^{t+1}, \hat{\rho}_\beta^{t+1})$ for the next period, are found as the risk-adjusted market yields of the IOUs of x, y, and β.[39]

Note that employing realized IOU prices with other realized price and quantity magnitudes, determined either as indicated above or, in some cases, still to be determined below, the economy's realized money supply $\bar{m}^t$ is calculated from (11.4-3). Evidently, even with all realized magnitudes set, $\bar{m}^t$ may still vary over period t as transactions in the IOU markets involving the bank are effected, that is, as appropriate components of the $\bar{q}^{t^n}$ (if they are present) vary over n. The pattern of variation in $\bar{m}^t$ depends, as does the sequence of IOU prices, on the timing of events determining the order in which potential buyers and sellers of IOUs meet. But the value of $\bar{m}^t$ at the end of the period is necessarily based on $\bar{q}^{t^N}$.

It is interesting to remember in passing that combining the above commodity, labor, and IOU markets (with the other elements as indicated) into a single model as described here captures, in part, the idea of Hicks [2, p. 23] that modern economies contain both "fixprice" and "flexprice" markets. In the present context, the former are the commodity and labor markets where prices, set exogenously or by pro-

---

that there be the same number of trades of each issue of each IOU of x, y, and β.

[37]Risk premiums differ for firms x and y and the bank because (perceived) risk has been assumed to be heterogeneous across them.

[38]This price is distinct from the unit asset value of money, $q_m^t = 1$, employed in earlier analysis.

[39]In this terminology, the originally described market yields are the same as the risk-adjusted market yields. The latter, in turn, are equivalently expressed as sums of the risk-free market yield and appropriate risk premiums.

ducers, remain fixed throughout the period. The latter appear as the IOU markets in which prices continually adjust during the period as buyers and sellers interact.

From the perspective of the economy as a whole, where all agents and markets are interacting with each other, and where inconsistent simultaneous activity in the model has to be resolved into a unique and internally consistent outcome, the operation of the IOU markets clearly does not preclude the possibility that an agent might not obtain sufficient funds from other economic activity to cover his planned purchase IOU quantities at the prices he perceives or expects. To the extent that trades actually take place in IOU markets, realized IOU-price and quantity magnitudes typically depend on, and are internally consistent with, realized price and quantity magnitudes elsewhere. The latter magnitudes, in particular, partly reflect initially planned agent demands and supplies of commodities, labor time, and money balances. But if these initial plans in non-IOU markets are not fully realized at t, then, as indicated, there may be insufficient funds to put all IOU plans into effect. That is, the income or revenue expectations of buyers planning to buy IOUs have failed and these buyers may, as a result, have to withdraw as buyers in some or all of the IOU markets. This is another reason why market clearing in IOU markets may not occur. Similarly, failed revenue expectations may also mean that the actual rates of return earned by the firms and the bank on the money capital invested in them need not equal their corresponding average required rates of return. In such cases, these agents may have to default on the payments due on their debts.[40] A third possibility is that a firm or the bank might not be able to sell new issues of its IOUs at the hoped-for price, and may not, therefore, be able to implement its investment plans. Thus failed expectations in the IOU markets can have reper-

---

[40]As an alternative to default, the firms and the bank may sell new IOUs in order to obtain funds to cover their revenue deficits. Such new capital issues may be possible because of favorable long-term, income-earning prospects. Moreover, with respect to the firms, the central bank may facilitate the commercial bank's acquisition of their new issues by relaxing the reserve requirement. It may also provide the commercial bank with additional funds by purchasing some of that bank's debt. But regardless of whether they default or not, the firms and the commercial bank continue in existence. Recall n. 12 on p. 337.

cussions for the goods and labor markets. In any event, the realized
IOU price and quantity magnitudes and the realized non-IOU price and
quantity magnitudes that go with them, are the outcomes of a coherent
model that are valid only in period t.

With the determination of market prices, the required rates of return on new issues of IOUs, and the traded quantities of IOUs now
described, it remains to consider the extent to which planned individual demands and supplies of goods, labor time, and money balances
are able to come to fruition. This sets, in part, the actual return on the
money capital invested in the two firms and the bank and influences
the future market yields on their IOUs. Subject to certain consistency
requirements introduced momentarily, the quantity variables actually
realized are determined by the short-side trading rule: The market
quantity of any good can be no more than and, indeed, will be exactly
the smaller of the amount that the buyers wish to buy compared to the
amount that the sellers wish to sell. Thus the market quantity of the
consumer good is

$$\bar{x}^t = \min\left[x^t_{\gamma e}, \, x^t_e + \hat{x}^t\right]$$

and that of the intermediate good is

$$\bar{y}^t = \min\left[y^t_{xe} + y^t_{ye} + y^t_{\beta e}, \, y^t_e + \hat{y}^t\right].$$

Generally, as indicated in Section 7.2, if quantity demanded is permitted to be unequal to quantity supplied, as it is here, then when
inequality prevails planned quantities cannot all be realized, and to
obtain unique solutions requires the specification of rationing schemes
that distribute goods bought among buyers when quantities supplied
are too small and goods sold among sellers when quantities supplied are
too large. In the consumer-good market, this problem does not arise
because there is only one buyer and one seller. The rationing scheme
in the durable-good market may be taken to be a simplified priority
queuing system:[41] when $\bar{y}^t < y^t_{xe} + y^t_{ye} + y^t_{\beta e}$, assume the units of the
durable good that are produced are always allocated to the consumer-
good-producing firm first, then to the bank, and finally to the durable-
good-producing firm, and let $\bar{y}^t_x$, $\bar{y}^t_y$, and $\bar{y}^t_\beta$ represent the outcome of

---

[41]Benassy [1, p. 18].

this allocation procedure.[42] When $\bar{y}^t = y_{xe}^t + y_{ye}^t + y_{\beta e}^t$, write $\bar{y}_x^t = y_{xe}^t$, $\bar{y}_y^t = y_{ye}^t$, and $\bar{y}_\beta^t = y_{\beta e}^t$. Thus in all cases $\bar{y}^t = \bar{y}_x^t + \bar{y}_y^t + \bar{y}_\beta^t$.

Similarly, some kind of rationing scheme in the labor market (which it is not necessary to specify) sets the actual quantities of labor bought by the two firms and the bank. This yields realized labor supplies $\bar{\ell}_x^t$, $\bar{\ell}_y^t$, and $\bar{\ell}_\beta^t$, where

$$\bar{\ell}_x^t + \bar{\ell}_y^t + \bar{\ell}_\beta^t = \min \left[\ell_{xe}^t + \ell_{ye}^t + \ell_{\beta e}^t, \ell_{x\gamma e}^t + \ell_{y\gamma e}^t + \ell_{\beta\gamma e}^t \right].$$

Actual money capital requirements, realized earnings, and actual rates of return are calculated by substituting these values into the appropriate equations as described above for the two firms (those for firm y were not actually written down) and the bank. It is not necessary that the actual rates of return equal either each other or the realized required rates of return on new issues during the period. To the extent that they do not, there will be repercussions on all future consumer, firm, and bank decisions.

Observe also that if, by chance, it turned out that at realized prices and quantities, all markets but one cleared so that all plans with respect to those markets were realized, and hence that planned quantity supplied equaled planned quantity demanded in each, it would still not follow that the last (seventh) market would necessarily clear. This is because, contrary to the Walrasian, general equilibrium microeconomic system, things like the consumer's financial resources constraint (11.2-1), the present analogue of the Walrasian budget constraint, need not be satisfied as an equality. In addition, money balances can be both created and destroyed, thus puncturing the airtight circular flow of the Walrasian system that prevents such "leakages."

The striking fact about this construction is that, as suggested above, the consumer, the two firms, and the bank are not always able to buy

---

[42]Alternatively, the highest priority might be only to replace worn-out real capital in the consumer-good-producing firm, with the second priority being the replacement of worn-out real capital in the bank and the third priority to replace worn-out real capital in the durable-good-producing firm. Thereafter the remaining demand of the consumer-good-producing firm, if any, could be satisfied, and what is left of the durable good supply would then be available for net investment in the bank and, finally, in the durable-good-producing firm.

and sell what they want. For example, if supply is greater than demand in the consumer-good market (that is, if $x_e^t + \hat{x}^t > x_{\gamma e}^t$), then, assuming it is able to obtain sufficient labor to produce $x_e^t + \hat{x}^t$, there will be involuntary inventory investment by firm x. This means that the firm's realized earnings and actual rate of return will be less than intended, and compensating adjustments will have to be made in the next period. And, although the possibility is not explored, the firm might not even be able to meet the current contractually required rate of return payments on its debt. Generally, however, in order for the price and quantity magnitudes that emerge above to hold up at t, that is, in order for them to constitute a solution of the simultaneous relations of the model at t regardless of whether all agent plans are fully realized, it must be the case that at these magnitudes the consumer has enough income to purchase at least the stated amounts of IOUs and the consumer good, enough labor is supplied to produce at least the stated outputs and to support the money supply, and both firms and the bank have enough funds to cover at least their labor and portfolio expenses, the required payments on their debts, and their purchases of the intermediate durable input for future use. In other words, with bars denoting realized values (including those defined above), the respective inequalities

$$\bar{p}_x^t \bar{x}^t + \bar{q}^t \cdot \left(\bar{s}_\gamma^t - \hat{s}_\gamma^t \right) \leq \hat{w}^t \left(\bar{\ell}_x^t + \bar{\ell}_y^t + \bar{\ell}_\beta^t \right) + \left(\bar{q}^t \cdot s_\gamma^t \right) \bar{v}_\gamma^t ,$$

$$\bar{x}^t - \hat{x}^t \leq F^{xt}(\hat{y}_x^t, \bar{\ell}_x^t),$$

$$\bar{y}^t - \hat{y}^t \leq F^{yt}(\hat{y}_y^t, \bar{\ell}_y^t),$$

$$\bar{m}^t \leq F^{\beta t}(\bar{\rho}_x^t, \bar{\rho}_y^t, \hat{y}_\beta^t, \bar{\ell}_\beta^t),$$

$$\bar{p}_x^t \bar{x}^t + \left[\left(\bar{q}_y^t, \bar{q}_\beta^t, 1 \right) \cdot \hat{s}_x^t \right] \bar{v}_x \geq \hat{w}^t \bar{\ell}_x^t + \hat{\rho}_x^t \hat{a}_x^t + \bar{p}_y^t \bar{y}_x^t + \left(\bar{q}_y^t, \bar{q}_\beta^t, 1 \right) \cdot \left(\bar{s}_x^t - \hat{s}_x^t \right),$$

$$\bar{p}_y^t \bar{y}^t + \left[\left(\bar{q}_x^t, \bar{q}_\beta^t, 1 \right) \cdot \hat{s}_y^t \right] \bar{v}_y \geq \hat{w}^t \bar{\ell}_y^t + \hat{\rho}_y^t \hat{a}_y^t + \bar{p}_y^t \bar{y}_y^t + \left(\bar{q}_x^t, \bar{q}_\beta^t, 1 \right) \cdot \left(\bar{s}_y^t - \hat{s}_y^t \right),$$

and

$$\frac{\hat{g}^t}{\hat{r}^t} - \hat{m}^t \geq \left[\sum_{\tau=1}^{t} \left(\bar{q}_{x\tau}^t \check{a}_{x\beta\tau}^t - \bar{q}_{x\tau}^t \tilde{a}_{x\beta\tau}^t + \bar{q}_{y\tau}^t \check{a}_{y\beta\tau}^t - \bar{q}_{y\tau}^t \tilde{a}_{y\beta\tau}^t + \bar{q}_{\beta\tau}^t \tilde{a}_{\beta\tau}^t \right) \right]$$

$$- \check{a}_{\beta t} - \left(\bar{q}_x^t \cdot \bar{a}_{x\beta}^t + \bar{q}_y^t \cdot \bar{a}_{y\beta}^t \right) \bar{v}_\beta + \hat{w}^t \bar{\ell}_\beta^t + \hat{\rho}_\beta^t \hat{a}_\beta^t + \bar{p}_y^t \bar{y}_\beta^t$$

have to hold, where all IOU price variables are appropriate components of the vectors of the sequence $\bar{q}^{t^1}, \ldots, \bar{q}^{t^N}$. If not, the model could not furnish an internally consistent outcome, and additional assumptions concerning allocation procedures (that indicate which quantities are scaled back) would have to be introduced to bring the quantity magnitudes into line. Thus the question of the conditions that might be imposed on the functions and parameters of the model (including those defining the Section 4.3-type decision makers) at time t to ensure the model's coherence is both meaningful and important.[43] Formally, it is much the same as the question of the conditions under which equilibrium in a Walrasian microeconomic model exists and is unique. But the answer to this question in the present context has a very different interpretation and significance from what it has in the Walrasian framework because the present model describes kaleidic events in historical time, where all functions and parameters change from period to period, where markets may not clear, and in which the different and possibly inconsistent activities that take place simultaneously are resolved into coherent outcomes by short-side trading rules (and their accompanying rationing schemes) subject to the above inequality constraints.

Assuming that the model, as presented, has an internally consistent and unique solution, that is, is coherent, the price and quantity magnitudes described above represent the outcome of the economic interactions among the consumer, the two firms, and the bank during period t. This outcome influences contemplations of the future and expectations in the next period $t + 1$. It also sets some of the parameter values for that period. Thus, in the case of firm x, for example,

$$\hat{a}_x^{t+1} = \hat{a}_x^t + \Delta \bar{a}_x^t,$$

---

[43]Of course, the satisfaction of the above inequalities only ensures internal consistency. Coherence requires, in addition, the determination, through the short-side trading rules and specified rationing schemes, of a unique outcome.

where $\Delta\bar{a}_x^t$, recall, is the realized net change in the firm's outstanding debt;

$$\hat{y}_x^{t+1} = \hat{y}_x^{*t} + \bar{y}_x^t,$$

where $\hat{y}_x^{*t}$ represents the durable input left over from period t after depreciation is taken into account; and, since firm x is assumed to act on the basis of its estimates, and since the consistency assumption implies it is able to hire at least enough labor to produce realized sales minus inventory,

$$\hat{x}^{t+1} = \hat{x}^t + F^{xt}(\hat{y}_x^t, \bar{\ell}_x^t) - \bar{x}^t. \tag{11.5-1}$$

The new portfolio $\hat{s}_x^{t+1}$ is obtained similarly, and the new average required rate of return on outstanding debt, $\hat{\rho}_x^{t+1}$, is calculated by correcting $\hat{\rho}_x^t$ for buy-backs and averaging in the required rate of return on new issues contractually agreed to in period t. But, of course, due to the kaleidic nature of the economy, no such statement about the determination of the future functions and solution values of the model for period $t + 1$ can be made. Note that even though the desired level of inventory in firm x has been assumed to be zero, (11.5-1) indicates that the firm may not be able to reach this goal. Nevertheless, when planning for period $t + 1$ the firm will, as it did for period t, attempt to adjust output so as to wind up with no inventory. In any case, the continued interaction of γ, x, y, and β in the economy's markets results in a kaleidic sequence of coherent outcomes evolving as time moves on.[44]

Of course, it could happen that, for example, along the kaleidic sequence actually emerging as time passes, quantities are produced and supplied in the consumer-good market persistently in excess of quantity demanded. This, in turn, might imply deteriorating economic conditions and what might be referred to as a "quasi-permanent" underemployment situation. Moreover, the source of the "demand defficiency," if it be so called, could lie in the consumer's decisions with respect to his savings and the allocation of his financial resources between the holding of money balances and the acquisition of IOUs. The possibility of these kinds of outcome sequences is explored further in the context of macroeconomics in the next chapter.

---

[44]It is clear that, due to the absence of both conceptual and structural prerequisites, the sequence so obtained cannot be a temporary equilibrium as described in Section 1.2.

There is an obvious, if still highly simplified, generalization of the present model to many consumers, firms, banks, and commodities. Let each new firm that is added produce its own unique commodity. Expand the number of arguments in firm production functions to allow for more durable and nondurable inputs. Enlarge the dimensionality of consumer decision sets so that each person can purchase more final commodities, buy the IOUs of more firms, and supply additional kinds of labor. Treat the decision sets of the firms and banks similarly. Finally, employ the same consumer, firm, and bank decision mechanisms in this more general context. Then commodity prices are set by firms as before. Nothing is changed in the operation of IOU markets. Short-side trading rules and (more complicated) rationing schemes fix the magnitudes of market and individual quantity variables, and hence firms' and the banks' actual rates of return. And these calculations are repeated for each period of time with new and different functions and parameters.

It is also possible to add a more complete government to the model so that the effects of legislative and executive economic policies could be analyzed in addition to those of the central bank. With respect to central bank policy options in the model as presently constructed, it has already been observed that either increases in $\hat{g}^t$ or decreases in $\hat{r}^t$ expand the potential money supply in period t, and that since $\hat{g}^t$ rises as the commercial bank borrows more funds from the central bank, the latter, in addition to reducing $\hat{r}^t$, could encourage the expansion of $\hat{g}^t$ by lowering the cost to β of borrowing funds. The central bank could also buy the IOUs of x, y, and β in the open market. But, in any case, such policies only increase the potential for monetary creation. Whether or not that potential is realized depends on the activity of the individual agents in the economy. Only if their behavior is such as to call forth additional sales of IOUs to the bank and other transactions that would push the quantity of money beyond the limit currently set by the values of $\hat{g}^t$ and $\hat{r}^t$, would a central bank attempt to expand the money supply be successful. Likewise, the central bank can contract the money supply only when changes in $\hat{g}^t$ and $\hat{r}^t$ lower the money supply limit below that which would otherwise emerge from agent economic activity.

11.6 References

1. Benassy, J. P., *The Economics of Market Disequilibrium* (New York: Academic Press, 1982).

2. Hicks, Sir J., *The Crisis in Keynesian Economics* (New York: Basic Books, 1974).

CHAPTER 12

A Model of the Macroeconomy

Macroeconomics, in contrast with microeconomics, deals with the analysis of aggregate variables. Concepts such as (aggregate) real consumption replace those like an individual's demand for a single good. In particular, macroeconomic inquiry is concerned with explaining the interdependent forces that determine (aggregate) real output, the commodity price level, the (aggregate) level of employment, and the interest rate.[1] Its scope may include an explanation of rates of change in relevant variables, such as inflationary changes in the price level and sustainable rates of real income growth, as well as an examination of the significance and formation of expectations in the context of intertemporal analysis. But such issues of macroeconomic dynamics tend to add layers of conceptual complexity and open wider fields of inquiry than are frequently addressed. To stay within more common boundaries, then, and to keep discussion more manageable, the approach taken here, in its use of a short-run, one-period-at-a-time methodology with each period unique, is framed, substantially, in a "static" environment. Nevertheless, the significance of historical time is still accounted for, and the ensuing discussions of uncertainty, and of decisions in the condition of ignorance that uncertainty bequeaths, still point to the essence

---

[1] As has been the case throughout this book, attention is confined to a closed economy.

of a dynamic analysis.

Moreover, and especially in the context of nonequilibrium analysis, similarities between micro- and macro-analyses remain. The uncertainty facing decision makers created by the presence of historical time and ignorance, and all that that implies for the frequent failure of expectations and plans, has to be accounted for at both levels. Thus micro- and macromodels of general economic reality are models of monetary, kaleidic economies. They are monetary, remember, in that money, providing a refuge from uncertainty and a substitute for knowledge, functions in them not only as a medium of exchange but also as a store of value (n. 1 on p. 331). And they are kaleidic in their acknowledgment of the ability of their exogenously changing surroundings (including perceptional and expectational variation) to dissolve their micro- or macrostructures at any moment (Chapter 8). In addition, both models specify the behavior that is to occur simultaneously in each period, and the relations describing that behavior, as well as their assumed unique solutions, are relevant only for the specified period. Because this simultaneity is constructed in each case to allow for the fact that, typically, some plans are realized while others are not, it becomes of paramount importance to understand something of the nature of the dynamic adjustment processes, alluded to above, that are unleashed by the unfulfilled plans.

These similarities notwithstanding, the possibility still exists that at the macrolevel relations among variables may have a stability over historical time that is lacking at the microlevel. Now it has been argued by Keynes and others that, at the microlevel, judgments about future outcomes made by individual decision makers for use in determining their decisions are often conventions arrived at in the course of their interactions in markets, and that these conventions "do lend an orderedness to the economic pattern of things."[2] Thus the replanning by individuals in response to unrealized earlier plans and failed expectations, even when parameter values and decision functions modulate, may not lead to alterations in their behavior. Nevertheless, because change is always occurring in the economy and its environment, and because it is impossible to know in advance where and how that change

---

[2]Vickers [11, p. 28].

will take place, and what effects it will bring forth, when focusing attention on a single decision maker or a relatively small group of decision makers, the presumption must be that the individual or group will respond with modified behavior. Thus stability of microeconomic relations over time is inappropriate to consider before it occurs.[3] But, when thinking about the economy as a whole, change need not occur everywhere. And, regardless of whether it does or not, variation in one place can cancel out variation in another. The possibility of macroeconomic relations remaining stable across periods of time, then, cannot be dismissed out of hand.

To illustrate this difference in potential stability of relations over time, consider the microeconomic model of the previous chapter. That model accounted for the issuing of new IOUs by firms and the bank in each period t. This meant that new variables representing, among other things, the planned quantities of new IOUs to be issued, had to be introduced at every t and hence that the numbers of variables and the relations of the model incorporating them were necessarily different for period $t+1$, say, than for period t. Therefore, without even considering the possibility of preference, expectation, or technological modification, the stability of these relations across time is out of the question. But at the macrolevel, where the focus is on, say, planned aggregate receipts from the sale of IOUs or the supply of bonds, an offer of sale of a new issue of IOUs is just another offer that would, if the sale went through, increase the receipts from selling IOUs in general, and the increased receipts that this offer represents could be offset by reduced offers and receipts elsewhere. Thus the introduction of new variables and the consequent microlevel transformation that is implied need not register at the macrolevel. Although the macroeconomy is still kaleidic in character, intertemporal stability of macrorelations under certain circumstances is conceivable.

It has already been suggested in Chapter 7 that, with conditions of historical time and ignorance in force, usable aggregate relations for a market (*i.e.*, usable market demand and supply functions) cannot be obtained by summing the relevant microeconomic behavioral rela-

---

[3]Recall the discussion of routine behavior at the end of Section 4.3. See also nn. 17, 18 on pp. 25.

tions over the individual agents who participate in the market. However, suitable market relations could be derived as analogues of the microeconomic relations of single, representative agents. The same argument applies with even more force to macroeconomic relations, and the model developed here proceeds from this perspective.[4] Thus, in spite of the previously described difference of potential for stability across time, it is nevertheless assumed that there is a likeness between the events and the forces determining them at the macrolevel and those at the microlevel. Observe, however, that likeness is not identity, and for macroeconomic purposes it is not necessary to maintain a single all-encompassing model of the microeconomy as the sole underlying microfoundation for the macroeconomic structure. That is, different combinations of micro-units, even overlapping combinations, and different and not necessarily compatible models of them, may serve as the analogical basis for different pieces of the same macroconstruction. Thus, for example, to analyze the production or supply side of the macroeconomy, the behavior of the aggregate of all firms is based, in what follows, on the behavior of a single, representative firm; and, in considering the demand side, the behavior of the aggregate of all firms and banks together, and the aggregate of all consumers, is derived from the behavior of, respectively, a single, representative firm and a single, representative consumer.[5] In addition, to deal with the macrobond market, the behavior of the aggregate of all buyers of IOUs (consumers, firms, and banks) is secured from a single representative decision maker who only buys, while the behavior of the aggregate of all sellers of IOUs obtains from a single representative decision maker who only sells.[6] Moreover, the sources of the behaviors of the aggregates

---

[4]This means, of course, that if there were K micro-units, and if, say, $x_k = h^k(p, m_k)$ were a behavioral relation for unit k, where $k = 1, \ldots, K$, then the macro-analogue $x = H(p, m)$, where $x = \sum_{k=1}^{K} x_k$ and $m = \sum_{k=1}^{K} m_k$, is generally such that

$$H(p, m) \neq \sum_{i=1}^{K} h^k(p, m_k).$$

[5]In particular, the demand-side behavior of all banks is subsumed in the macro-analogue of the demand-side behavior of the representative firm.

[6]Because individual consumers, firms, and banks typically are both buyers and

of consumers, firms, banks, and decision makers are assumed to be the same as those of their corresponding microeconomic analogues. In this way a secure microfoundation for the macrostructure is obtained.

Regardless of the fact that the reduction, by analogy, of the behavior of the general macroeconomy into the behavior of single representative agents already is a considerable simplification, macroeconomic analysis is so coarse that still further simplifying assumptions have to be made. These are introduced where necessary below. One assumption, namely, that there is no government other than a central bank, is made only for convenience and has no substantive impact. The model actually developed is mostly taken from Vickers [12, Pt. 5; and 13] and is traceable, in part, to Weintraub [16, Ch. 2].[7] Before turning attention to it, a general discussion of macroeconomic analysis and some macroeconomic traditions is presented.

12.1 Macroeconomic Traditions

As is true of any theoretical endeavor, in attempting to construct a model of the macroeconomy, it is necessary to have in mind a general vision with respect to which things that are observable in that economy can be framed.[8] Observations, of course, consist of data on aggregate

---

sellers of IOUs, this will require a different underlying microstructure from that employed, as just described, to analyze real output, employment, and the price level.

[7]Although describing a world in which individuals are faced with pervasive uncertainty and ignorance, Vickers' macroeconomic model (and many others like it) still employs, albeit by analogy, relations arising from a notion of imagined profit maximization at all levels of employment that runs contrary to the spirit of the representative firm of Chapter 9 from which the present analogy is taken (*e.g.*, [12, pp. 383-387] and [13, pp. 92-96]). Subsequent argument, then, by drawing on the model of the firm developed in Chapter 9, does not rely on such a permeating use of profit maximization. As a result, the shape of the within-period aggregate supply curve derived below is always linear and can never be strictly convex (see n. 26 on p. 389 below). (In Vickers' context, in spite of diminishing marginal productivity, linearity can still arise but only as a special case [13, pp. 93,95].) Across periods, however, it will be seen that the locus of supply points actually realized by the production side of the macroeconomy may still achieve strict convexity.

[8]Schumpeter [8, pp. 561-562].

variables such as employment, expenditure on goods, the money supply, the level of commodity prices, and the rate of interest. Each period of time, t, yields a single observed vector of such variables. The purpose of constructing a model is to explain these observations in a manner that is faithful to one's vision and, perhaps, to use that explanation to recommend policies. Upon construction, models produce time-paths of values of the same vector of variables as are observed;[9] indeed, the actually observed vectors of variable values are interpreted as falling along a realized time-path generated by the model. In this sense the model is said to explain what is seen.

A model, recall, is coherent if it provides unique hypothetical outcomes for each period that can be used as the basis for explaining actually observed outcomes. An outcome clears markets whenever the components of which it is comprised satisfy the simultaneous equality of planned demand and planned supply in all of the model's markets (and in which the determination of planned demand and supply accounts for all constraints facing individual agents), that is, when it reflects market clearing everywhere. To the extent that macroeconomic constructions incorporate assumptions of market-clearing outcomes, they are explicitly associated with full employment and often implicitly imply an underlying microeconomic Pareto optimality. Whether or not a model is constructed to describe market-clearing outcomes depends on the nature of the builder's vision of reality. Thus, if all observations are perceived in terms of cleared markets, then the model constructed has to contain market-clearing outcomes that are to be identified with what is observed. Based on alternative visions, observations could be thought of, say, as non-market-clearing outcomes that may converge, over time, to market-clearing ones, or they could be taken as outcomes

---

[9]Remember, from Section 1.2, that neoclassical models generate time-paths as solutions of periodic (or differential) equations that start out from specific initial values. These equations remain unchanged from period to period as the time-paths work themselves out through past, present, and future periods. The magnitudes along such time-paths can be either realized or planned but yet to be realized variable values. Alternatively, time-paths in kaleidic economies, as portrayed in Chapters 8 and 11, consist of sequences of realized points whose components are unable to be predicted in advance of their realization. These latter time-paths cannot generally be characterized in advance by single equations or sets of equations because the equations themselves are not stable across time.

having no systematic relation to market-clearing whatsoever. In addition, the multimarket macroeconomy can be understood with respect to outcomes for which only one market, namely, the labor market, does not clear.

Typical approaches to macroeconomic analysis have focused attention on four aggregative markets: goods, labor, bonds, and money. These are, respectively, markets for the single, homogeneous commodity real output, labor measured as number of persons rather than as, in the microeconomic constructions of Chapters 9-11, units of time, bonds or IOUs, and money balances. However, if the main thrust of macro-analysis is to explain the achievement of market-clearing macro-outcomes, then the number of these markets necessary to consider can be reduced to three, two, or even one, depending on the assumptions invoked. For analogously applying to the macro bond and money markets, the fact that an individual's wealth is the sum of the money balances and the value of the bonds he holds, and assuming total wealth to be constant, thereby imposing a "wealth constraint," it follows that the bond market clears if and only if the money market clears. Hence one of these two markets, say the bond market, can be dropped from consideration. Supposing, in addition, that the labor market clears, then application (again by analogy from the microeconomic level) of Walras' law implies that inquiry can concentrate on the mutually determining market-clearing forces in the goods and money markets alone. Finally, use of any nonidentity version of Say's law, which is also drawn from microeconomic considerations and implies that the money market always clears, will reduce analytical necessity to explaining only the determination of market-clearing outcomes in the goods market.

Echoing three of the four broad styles of analysis set out in Chapter 1, at least three broad traditions in the construction of models in macroeconomic analysis can be discerned. In the "equilibrium" tradition, attention focuses on the achievement of market-clearing with respect to all planned quantities as the proper way to approach reality. Every agent is assumed to have complete and perfect knowledge (at least probabilistically) of all past, present, and future outcomes, and the macrosystem arising out of this environment settles, often instantaneously, on a market-clearing equilibrium – an outcome for which, in the absence of parametric modulation, the system is at rest and from

which there is no tendency, over time, to change. Observations necessarily reflect situations in which either all markets have cleared or
the observed values fall along realized time-paths whose variable values are converging to market-clearing, equilibrium values. Along the
time-path generated by a market-clearing equilibrium, since all variable and parameter values remain constant, time itself is irrelevant.
More generally, and as is required in equilibrium analysis, models in
the equilibrium tradition take time to be logical: restarting the system
from the same initial point always reproduces the same time-path as
long as parameter values have remained constant.

The "disequilibrium" tradition is cut from a similar mold except
that observed reality, although in some instances viewed as reaching
for market-clearing equilibrium, may never be seen, in fact, to attain
it. Thus observations are interpreted to lie on realized time-paths that
may or may not converge through time to market-clearing equilibrium
paths. But except for certain, specified imperfections that the system
may eventually correct, knowledge is still, for the remainder, "perfect."
Time, moreover, is still logical. The system may be restarted at any
moment and, if it is, necessarily proceeds down the same converging or
nonconverging path, as long as neither parameters nor initial conditions
have altered.

The third tradition is the "nonequilibrium" tradition of the present
volume in which both perfect knowledge and logical time are fully discarded. As described in earlier chapters, agents in this case know only
a little of past outcomes, hardly anything of present outcomes, and
nothing at all of future ones. In addition, it makes no sense to start the
same macrosystem over and over again because each moment is unique
in history and has its own parameter values, variables, and model associated with it. To explain observations, in other words, may require a
different model in each period. Market-clearing outcomes, though possible, occur only under unusual and coincidental circumstances. And
although some stability of the model's relations over time is possible,
the notion of equilibrium as defined above has no place because the real
world can never actually be at rest.

The macro-analyses of the classical and "new classical" economists
fall squarely in the equilibrium tradition. Both classicals and new classicals look at the economy's markets, in particular the labor market, and

see only market-clearing equilibrium. All unemployment is voluntary, rationally chosen through the maximization of utility by society's members. Walras' law and Say's law are present and the wealth constraint could be interpreted as an implicit analytical component. Furthermore, in the long run for the classicals, and in both short and long runs for the new classicals, money is *neutral*. That is, variation of the economy's nominal money supply does not affect the outcome values, in this circumstance the equilibrium values, of real output, employment, relative commodity prices, and the real rate of interest,[10] but it does cause a (proportional) change in the equilibrium commodity price level. Examination of the macroeconomy can therefore be dichotomized into real and monetary parts. Whereas, due to their assumption of perfect knowledge, expectations are irrelevant to the classicals, the new classicals believe that the expectations of individual agents are endogenous and "rational" in that the errors they make in anticipating outcomes are not systematic. But in either case only real variables are pertinent for an understanding of the economy's markets and for the contemplation of significant macro-aggregates. There is no money illusion. The macroeconomic models constructed by the classicals and new classicals reflect this vision.[11]

By contrast, the Keynes of *The General Theory*, as interpreted by neoclassicals such as Clower and Patinkin, is in the disequilibrium tradition. Writing in the midst of the Great Depression, Keynes saw involuntary unemployment. People wanted work but could not find any. Although Patinkin expressed it in terms of macro-aggregates [6, Ch. 13] and Clower with respect to Walrasian microfoundations [2], both arrived at the same conclusion, namely, that ". . . Keynesian economics is the economics of . . . *dis*equilibrium [*sic*]" [6, p. 235]. Moreover, although Walras' law, Say's law, and the wealth constraint appear, money generally loses its neutrality in the Keynesian system since the demand for nominal money depends, in part, through the liquidity preference function, on the nominal rate of interest. Thus an increase in the nominal money supply would lower the nominal interest rate (unless the

---

[10]The *real* interest rate is the nominal interest rate (or just the interest rate) minus the rate of inflation. In the classical and new classical macroeconomic models, the demand and supply of investable funds depends on the real interest rate.

[11]See Hoover [5, pp. 7-9, 13-16].

economy were caught in a liquidity trap, in which case that interest rate would not change), and could raise or lower the real rate of interest depending on the responsiveness of aggregate demand to changes in the money supply and on the price elasticity of aggregate supply, that is, on the rate of inflation. Dichotomization into real and monetary parts is not appropriate. In addition, expectations play a role, though they are exogenously given.

It is interesting that the neoclassicals as identified by the so-called neoclassical synthesis, along with the monetarists, have one foot in each camp. On the one hand, the neoclassical synthesis uses the Keynesian disequilibrium system when there is unemployment in the labor market arising from downward money-wage rigidity and reverts to a neoclassical representation of the classical equilibrium system where that unemployment disappears and full employment prevails.[12] Walras' law, Say's law (or at least equilibrium in the money market), and the wealth constraint are present, money is nonneutral, and expectations are exogenous. The point at which unemployment ceases to be involuntary and equilibrium obtains is not a matter to be decided by theoretical considerations. One looks at the labor market in the real world and makes a judgment. The monetarist position, on the other hand, is based on a distinction between the long and short runs. In the long run, all markets (including the money and labor markets) clear, money is neutral, and the classical equilibrium vision applies. In the short run, however, money is decidedly not neutral, involuntary unemployment can arise, and the approach is one of disequilibrium.[13] In either case, Walras' law and the wealth constraint are present, although, with respect to the latter, assets in addition to bonds and money are often introduced.[14] To the extent that the monetarists explicitly deal with expectations, they are taken to be exogenous but "adaptive." That is, expectations are subject to systematic error and, depending on the form of the assumed expectations adjustment mechanism, they are changed each period to reflect, in part, the extent of their apparent inaccuracy in the previous period.

---

[12]*Ibid.*, pp. 7-10.

[13]*Ibid.*, pp. 10-12.

[14]*E.g.*, Friedman [4].

In addition, the same Keynes described above as steeped in the disequilibrium tradition can also be, and has been, interpreted as a part of the nonequilibrium tradition.[15] It has further been suggested that the "preclassical" economists, writing during the century before Adam Smith, similarly possessed a nonequilibrium bent.[16] And, were it not for their belief that macroeconomic analysis itself is illegitimate, one could argue that the Austrians should also be included in this category of macroeconomic traditions.[17] In all of these cases, imperfect knowledge and nonlogical time explicitly or implicitly play important roles.

As suggested earlier, the nonequilibrium tradition is also the basis for the macroeconomic model developed here. Due to the presence of historical time and ignorance, the certainty or probabilistic uncertainty (risk) of the equilibrium and disequilibrium traditions is replaced by the nonprobabilistic uncertainty of a kaleidic economy. There is, moreover, no place for Walras' law, Say's law, and a clearing labor market with respect to planned quantities. In addition, money is nonneutral not only because the nominal demand for money depends on the nominal rate of interest (which includes a risk premium) but also because the holding of money deprives producers of the signals they need indicating that investment in durable inputs might be warranted.[18] In other words, consumption expenditures by consumers and investment expenditures by firms both, under normal conditions, send signals through commodity markets that the present purchase of durables for use in future production may be rewarded. Clearly the retaining of money balances deprives producers of those signals and leaves them feeling more in the dark than otherwise about what the future might bring. Not only is there a breakdown in the transmission of signals concerning the future, but since the holders of money balances might not yet know what they will subsequently do with their money balances, the signals to be transmitted might not yet exist. In either case, the very act of holding money as a refuge from uncertainty (or for any other reason)

---

[15]See Shackle [9].

[16]Vickers [10, pp. 295-296].

[17]*Cf*. Hoover [5, pp. 233-234, 236, 239-241, 248-257].

[18]Vickers [12, p. 323]. This is not to say that holding money in and of itself causes unemployment.

creates even more uncertainty. And in this way the presence of money has an impact on the economy's real output and employment. Thus dichotomization as an analytical technique is irrelevant both because money is nonneutral and because of the presence of historical time and ignorance and the kaleidic change it implies.

One further characteristic of the nonequilibrium tradition deserves mention. Because the decision moment is unique in historical time, agents cannot possess enough knowledge for expectations to be adaptive, endogenous, or rational. There is too much ignorance and uncertainty. Rather, expectations, although formulated exogenously at each instant, are nevertheless kaleidic in their possibly turbulent gyrations from moment to moment.

In addition to the general properties of nonequilibrium macroeconomic analysis just described, the specific model developed subsequently has its own peculiarities that further distinguish it from the more standard approaches. For example, the money wage is assumed to be exogenous, the labor supply curve is taken to be perfectly elastic at that money wage, and there is no value of marginal product curve serving as the macro-labor demand curve. (Indeed, there is no labor demand curve at all.) Not surprisingly, this differing assumption content often leads to different analytical conclusions. And such is the case despite the fact that a number of elements employed in the standard approaches are carried over, with suitable contextual modification, into the nonequilibrium framework.

Just as the preclassical nonequilibrium vision gave way to the classical perspective of market-clearing equilibrium and neutral money, so, to a considerable extent, have the Keynesian disequilibrium and neoclassical equilibrium-disequilibrium synthesis approaches lost out to a similar view espoused by the new classicals. While the former transformation emerged from a methodological shift in emphasis to market-clearing equilibrium and a substantive weakness of the preclassical theory of interest,[19] the latter came about, in part, due to the lack of a cogent microfoundation for the Keynesian-neoclassical macroeconomic structures.[20] For purposes of subsequent discussion, the absence of a

---

[19]Vickers [10, pp. 303-305].
[20]Hoover [5, p. 3].

microfoundation in the second case deserves a brief comment. Even though they focus attention in different manners on different phenomena, microeconomic and macroeconomic analyses of the full economy, after all, are still two ways of looking at the same thing. Indeed, many have believed that the whole should equal the sum of its parts.[21] But regardless of whether such specific a belief is warranted, it should be noted that, at least since the days of Adam Smith, a strong tradition of methodological individualism has existed in economics. Emerging quite naturally from this tradition is the thought that there ought to be a reasonable aggregative type of consistency between models of the micro- and macroeconomies, and Keynesian and neoclassical economists early on began to search unsuccessfully for it.[22] With little progress made by 1967, Arrow called the persisting deficiency a "major scandal" [1, p. 734]. But, in light of the Walrasian (general-)equilibrium focus on the search for underpinnings, it is not surprising that satisfactory microfoundations have not yet been found. For even with the proviso that, as is the case in equilibrium analysis, adding across individual units is legitimate, it is still exceedingly difficult, if not impossible, to aggregate microstructures in some consistent way into macrostructures when the former sits firmly in the equilibrium tradition and the latter (or, in the neoclassical case, part of the latter) lies fully in the disequilibrium tradition.[23] Regardless, the problem does not arise in subsequent development due to the close analogical relation between the micro- and macrostructures under consideration.

More precisely, in thinking about the economy's macrobehavior of any period t, prevailing economic institutions that have evolved from prior behavior and previously existing institutions (such as, for example, the nature and operation of markets) are, as is usually the case, taken as given. It follows that the issue of methodological individualism raised with respect to those institutions is irrelevant. For, starting at t, there is not enough time for short-run individual behavior to affect

---

[21]*E.g.*, Samuelson [7, p. 356]. Although it is not necessary to do so, this view of the relation between microeconomic and macroeconomic structures could be derived and explained in terms of the thought forms of philosophical materialism that were referred to in Section 1.1.

[22]Hoover [5, pp. 3,4].

[23]*Cf.* Weintraub [15, pp. 74-75].

current institutions, and, although long-run individual behavior from t on might have an impact, it still cannot explain how behavior before t led to the development of the institutions present in t. However, given existing institutions, the short-run macrorelatons below are, as previously indicated, still "built up" from microrelations, not by aggregation but by analogy. In this sense, then, a secure microfoundation for the macro-analysis is provided, and the relevant requisites of methodological individualism are met.

12.2   The Production Side

To begin construction of the macroeconomic model, imagine that the behavior of the production side of the economy, that is, the behavior of the aggregate of all of the economy's producers, is like the behavior of a single, representative firm whose properties are the same as, say, the firm producing good x (*i.e.*, firm x) described in Chapter 11. Before transposing the latter behavior, by analogy, to the macrolevel, it is useful first to re-examine this microlevel firm to review several previously considered analytical elements and to introduce new ones. In so doing, the relevant equations of Chapters 9 and 11 are reproduced for convenience.

12.2.1   The Microbase

In any period t, recall, firm x has a production function

$$x = F^{xt}(\hat{y}_x^t, \ell_x), \qquad (12.2.1\text{-}1)$$

and estimates the demand function it faces for its output as

$$x + \hat{x}^t = \mathcal{D}_{xe}^t(p_x), \qquad (12.2.1\text{-}2)$$

where x (a scalar) denotes current output produced, $\hat{x}^t \geq 0$ is its current inventory of finished output left over from the previous period, $\hat{y}_x^t > 0$ (also a scalar) is its current stock of durable input, ℓ_x is current labor time employed, and p_x is the price of its output.[24] It should be

---

[24]Remember that the estimated demand function in (12.2.1-2) is neither derived from nor related to individual utility maximization. It will appear subsequently as

borne in mind that the model of the macroeconomy to be established subsequently will be, in accordance with usual analytical convention, a single-good model where the good produced may be allocated to either consumption or investment purposes. In that case, what is designated as $\hat{y}_x^t$ here will be understood to refer to the use, for production purposes in period t, of previously produced output. Assume that F^{xt} is twice continuously differentiable with respect to ℓ_x and that the first derivative, that is, the marginal product, $\partial x/\partial \ell_x > 0$ everywhere. Remember that $\mathcal{D}_{xe}^t$ emerges from an application to the firm of the Section 4.3 model of decision making in ignorance. The firm's desired inventory level is zero, and labor is not required for the carrying of any level of inventory. The inverse of (12.2.1-1) with respect to ℓ_x is written

$$\ell_x = G^{xt}(\hat{y}_x^t, x) \qquad (12.2.1\text{-}3)$$

and that of (12.2.1-2) is

$$p_x = \mathcal{D}_{xe}^{-1^t}(x + \hat{x}^t), \qquad (12.2.1\text{-}4)$$

both defined on suitable domains.

As before, let $\hat{w} > 0$ be the exogenous money wage, $p_y^t > 0$ the durable-good price at moment t (with the bar removed for notational simplicity) as announced by the durable-good-producing firm, $\delta^{xt}(p_y^t) > 0$ firm x's current depreciation charge function, $\hat{a}_x^t > 0$ its current debt, that is, the par value of all previously issued and still outstanding IOUs, and $\hat{\rho}_x^t > 0$ the average required rate of return that must be paid out to the holders of those outstanding IOUs. The firm is assumed to set the price it charges for its output according to a markup formula. If, in period t, it were to determine that price by marking up from its unit labor cost in order to exactly cover, per unit, the labor cost plus its current depreciation charge and the required payments on its outstanding debt, then its markup factor k_x would be defined by the

---

part of the basis for the producers' expected proceeds function at both micro- and macrolevels. In the present formulation, if $\mathcal{D}_{xe}^t(p_x) < \hat{x}^t$ for some value of p_x, so that $x < 0$, then at that price the firm produces no output and is unable to sell all of its inventory. Recall the assumption of Chapters 9 and 11 that, even in this case, the firm remains in existence.

equation[25]

$$\hat{w}\ell_x + \hat{\rho}_x^t \hat{a}_x^t + \delta^{xt}(p_y^t) = k_x \hat{w}\ell_x \qquad (12.2.1\text{-}5)$$

or

$$k_x = 1 + \frac{\hat{\rho}_x^t \hat{a}_x^t + \delta^{xt}(p_y^t)}{\hat{w}\ell_x}. \qquad (12.2.1\text{-}6)$$

As in Section 9.2, with the maintenance of break-even revenue levels, $k_x > 1$,

$$\frac{\partial k_x}{\partial \hat{w}} < 0, \qquad (12.2.1\text{-}7)$$

$$\frac{\partial k_x}{\partial \ell_x} < 0, \qquad (12.2.1\text{-}8)$$

and

$$\frac{\partial^2 k_x}{\partial (\ell_x)^2} > 0.$$

But in actual fact, due to the limitations imposed by historical time and ignorance, firm x has to set its markup factor exogenously at the beginning of the period in anticipation of what might happen during that period. This exogenous markup factor is denoted by $\hat{k}_x$, and it is assumed that $\hat{k}_x > 1$. Of course, $\hat{k}_x$ may change over time and not necessarily in a manner that is consistent with (12.2.1-7) and (12.2.1-8). In any case, assuming the firm plans in the current period to sell all of its inventory plus what it produces, the price the firm charges in period t, namely, p_x^t, is fixed (recall Section 9.2) as the solution of the markup equation

$$p_x = \hat{k}_x \frac{\hat{w}\left[G^{xt}(\hat{y}_x^t, \mathcal{D}_{xe}^t(p_x) - \hat{x}^t)\right]}{\mathcal{D}_{xe}^t(p_x) - \hat{x}^t}, \qquad (12.2.1\text{-}9)$$

and substitution of p_x^t into (12.2.1-2), and the result of that substitution into (12.2.1-3), determines, for period t, the respective estimates, x_e^t and ℓ_{xe}^t, of the output firm x will produce and the input it will employ.

The above variables and equations are the foundation on which three additional relations appropriate to firm x are now constructed. Let

$$z_x = x p_x \qquad (12.2.1\text{-}10)$$

---

[25]To eliminate fractions, both sides of equation (12.2.1-5) have already been multiplied by x.

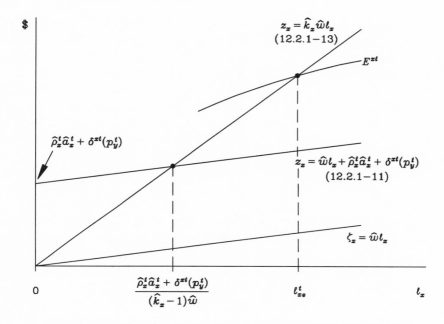

Figure 12-1.   The firm's supply and expected proceeds curves.

symbolize, in general, the money proceeds that the firm obtains from the sale of its output. Different interpretations of z_x, each of which implies a distinct meaning for x, lie at the heart of these three relations. Suppose, first, that z_x in (12.2.1-10) were construed as the money proceeds from the sale of currently produced output required for the firm to exactly cover its labor and depreciation costs and also the obligations on its outstanding debt. Then, as in (12.2.1-5),

$$z_x = \hat{w}\ell_x + \hat{\rho}_x^t \hat{a}_x^t + \delta^{xt}(p_y^t). \qquad (12.2.1\text{-}11)$$

The graph of z_x as a function of ℓ_x is a straight line with slope $\hat{w}$ and vertical intercept $\hat{\rho}_x^t \hat{a}_x^t + \delta^{xt}(p_y^t)$ as shown in Figure 12-1. Note that were the marginal productivity of labor, as derived from the production function (12.2.1-1), assumed to be positive and diminishing, then hypothetical increases in ℓ_x along the graph of (12.2.1-11) would be accompanied by declining increases in x. Furthermore, the value of p_x that would go into z_x according to (12.2.1-10) could still rise, fall, or remain constant with changes in ℓ_x depending on what is necessary to maintain equality between the right-hand sides of (12.2.1-10) and (12.2.1-11). To see what is involved, eliminate z_x from (12.2.1-11) by substituting from (12.2.1-10), solve for p_x, and, recognizing that x depends on ℓ_x according to (12.2.1-1), differentiate with respect to ℓ_x. Thus

$$\frac{\partial p_x}{\partial \ell_x} = \frac{\hat{w}}{x}\left(1 - \frac{\ell_x}{x}\frac{\partial x}{\partial \ell_x}\right) - \frac{\hat{\rho}_x^t \hat{a}_x^t + \delta^{xt}(p_y^t)}{x^2}\left(\frac{\partial x}{\partial \ell_x}\right).$$

Clearly, from Theorem 9.2-13, diminishing marginal productivity implies that the first term to the right of the equals sign is positive. Yet $\partial p_x/\partial \ell_x$ could still be negative (or zero) if the magnitude of the second term is big enough. More generally, regardless of the presence of diminishing marginal productivity, if $(\ell_x/x)(\partial x/\partial \ell_x)$ is sufficiently large, then, as ℓ_x increases along the graph of (12.2.1-11), the firm can afford to reduce the price it charges for its output even as, due to greater sales, it covers exactly its depreciation expenses and the payments required on its outstanding debt. But whether this turns out, in fact, to be possible, or even desirable, depends on the firm's perception of the demand conditions it faces (including both the level of and the elasticity of that demand). At present, however, demand conditions are not yet relevant since concern is only with the possible changes in selling price that will allow the firm to cover all of its costs and debt obligations exactly. And, in this regard, equation (12.2.1-11) defines the sales proceeds necessary to enable the firm to break even, precisely meeting the required obligations on its debt at each level of labor employment. It follows, as shown in (12.2.1-8), that along the graph of (12.2.1-11) the markup factor diminishes as ℓ_x rises. But, in any case, the values of p_x implied as z_x advances on that graph are typically not those chosen by the firm. Rather, the decision values of p_x lie along the firm's supply curve, which is considered next.

The most common notion of the supply curve of the firm employed in microeconomic theory indicates, assuming input prices are given, the quantity of output supplied that corresponds to each possible output price or, equivalently, the output price necessary to call forth from the firm each possible output quantity. Under perfectly competitive Walrasian conditions, of course, that supply curve is the upward sloping portion of the firm's marginal cost curve above mimimum average variable cost. With imperfectly competitive conditions in force, however, but still in the Walrasian context, either the firm does not know the demand curve it faces or, if it does, it reacts to the entire demand curve rather than to any single price value. In either case, the firm's supply curve cannot be defined. By contrast, the following discussion introduces a different concept of supply curve, relevant to non-Walrasian environments of historical time and ignorance, that is definable regardless of the competitive situation in existence. In particular, the supply curve is characterized in proceeds-employment space rather than in the more traditional price-output space. And it describes, in consideration of the firm's supply-side decisions, the proceeds it deems necessary in order to make the employment of each possible quantity of labor hours economically worthwhile.

It might seem, given this new vision of the firm's supply curve, that the break-even line in Figure 12-1, that is, the graph of (12.2.1-11), would qualify as such a curve. For at any level $\ell_x \geq 0$, the firm knows its wage bill and its fixed cost. It therefore knows the proceeds it needs to cover those costs and to meet, exactly, its debt obligations. The proceeds required are shown on the break-even line above each value of ℓ_x, and these proceeds are clearly sufficient to make the employment of ℓ_x worthwhile. But such an interpretation of the supply curve implies, as described above, that as the firm moves along that curve, its markup factor varies. Recall, however, that the model of the firm on which present analysis rests, recognizes the uncertainty that confronts the firm with respect to the demand conditions it faces. (The uncertainty, mentioned in Section 9.2, that surrounds the firm's ability to secure the labor supply it thinks it needs is ignored here since, at the macrolevel, that supply is taken to be perfectly elastic.) That is, the firm is unable to know in advance whether it can sell all its planned output at the price it sets for that output. And in light of this uncertainty, it is assumed that the firm exogenously fixes its markup factor for the entire period. With such a pricing policy in place, the proceeds required to make the employment of ℓ_x labor hours worthwhile within any given period will momentarily be seen to be proportional to the firm's wage bill, and may or may not result in the firm breaking even. Thus the break-even line cannot be the within-period supply curve.

Keeping these ideas in mind, the second additional relation for firm x, the graph of which *is* the firm's supply curve, is found by substituting (12.2.1-2) and (12.2.1-3) into (12.2.1-9) so that

$$p_x = \hat{k}_x \frac{\hat{w}\ell_x}{x},$$

or

$$xp_x = \hat{k}_x \hat{w}\ell_x, \qquad (12.2.1\text{-}12)$$

where $\hat{k}_x \hat{w}\ell_x$ may be taken to be the equivalent of the money proceeds z_x thought by the firm (possibly incorrectly) to be required from the sale of currently produced output to make, given $\hat{k}_x$, the employment of ℓ_x units of labor time worthwhile as just described. Using the same symbol, z_x, from (12.2.1-10), to designate these required proceeds, (12.2.1-12) becomes

$$z_x = \hat{k}_x \hat{w}\ell_x. \qquad (12.2.1\text{-}13)$$

The function characterized by equation (12.2.1-13) will be referred to as the firm's *supply* function. Given $\hat{k}_x$ and $\hat{w}$, the graph of (12.2.1-13), that is, as suggested above, the firm's supply curve is the straight line through the origin with slope $\hat{k}_x\hat{w}$ pictured in Figure 12-1.

It is evident that, since the firm expects to sell all existing inventory and output produced during the period, x in (12.2.1-12) may be thought of, from (12.2.1-1), as a function of ℓ_x. This, of course, is entirely appropriate in light of the fact that (12.2.1-12) reflects only the supply behavior of the firm, independently of what the firm thinks the demand conditons it faces might be like. The firm's estimate of those demand conditions, and the impact of that estimate on its behavior, is accounted for later. Moreover, p_x in (12.2.1-12) varies over the prices the firm thinks it must charge to secure what it believes to be the proceeds it requires as it moves along its supply curve. With respect to the setting of these prices, it should be remembered that, in the approach followed here, it is the ignorance of the demand conditions it confronts that forces the firm to pursue a pricing policy based on an unchanging markup factor, and which thereby implies a supply curve that is linear and runs through the origin. And, as will be seen, this rule of thumb markup procedure provides the basis for the macro-analogue developed subsequently.

It should also be pointed out that because $\hat{k}_x$ and $\hat{w}$ are fixed, even adding an assumption of diminishing marginal productivity of labor, the supply curve is still linear and cannot be strictly convex. That is, as ℓ_x hypothetically rises (and continuing to ignore the firm's perception of the demand conditions set against it), p_x adjusts according to equation (12.2.1-12) so that, taking into account the diminishing marginal productivity, the money proceeds thought by the firm to be required increase proportionately.[26] To argue formally, solve (12.2.1-12) for p_x, recall that x depends on ℓ_x according to (12.2.1-1), and differentiate with respect to ℓ_x to secure

$$\frac{\partial p_x}{\partial \ell_x} = \hat{k}_x \left(\frac{\hat{w}}{x} \right) \left(1 - \frac{\ell_x}{x} \frac{\partial x}{\partial \ell_x} \right), \qquad (12.2.1\text{-}14)$$

where, as before, $\partial x / \partial \ell_x$, assumed to be positive, is the firm's marginal product of labor given $\hat{y}_x^t$. It is easy to show, first, that $\partial p_x / \partial \ell_x = 0$ if and only if (12.2.1-1) takes on a form in which x is proportional to ℓ_x, and, second, that $\partial p_x / \partial \ell_x > 0$ if and only if, again in reference to (12.2.1-1),[27]

$$\frac{\ell_x}{x} \frac{\partial x}{\partial \ell_x} < 1. \qquad (12.2.1\text{-}15)$$

The circumstance of proportionality, or unit elasticity of output, is uninteresting and not pursued here. Of course, $\partial p_x / \partial \ell_x > 0$ is the

---

[26]Were profit maximization on the part of the firm assumed at all levels of employment (recall n. 7 on p. 373), $\hat{k}_x$ could not generally remain constant, and a relation like (12.2.1-9), but with a varying $\hat{k}_x$ reflecting that maximization, would underlie this supply curve, which, in addition to still being upward sloping, would frequently be strictly convex. Indeed, sufficient conditions for such strict convexity have been given by Vickers [13, pp. 92-96]. In the present case, however, except possibly for determining the exogenous markup factor, profit maximization is irrelevant to the operation of the firm (Chapter 9). Indeed, the fact that $\hat{k}_x$ is fixed here generally prevents the firm from fully achieving profit maximization as it moves along its supply curve.

[27]Recall from Theorem 9.2-13 and the discussion following it that (12.2.1-15) is implied by, but does not itself imply, diminishing marginal productivity of labor.

statement that p_x rises as ℓ_x increases along the firm's supply curve. From (12.2.1-14), it is clear that three exogenous elements affect the magnitude and sign of the derivative $\partial p_x/\partial \ell_x$: the marginal product of labor, which depends, in part, on $\hat{y}_x^t$; the markup factor $\hat{k}_x$; and the money wage $\hat{w}$. To the extent that any of $\hat{y}_x^t$, $\hat{k}_x$, and $\hat{w}$ vary, the alterations in p_x that accompany movements along the firm's supply curve will change. But only modulations in $\hat{k}_x$ and $\hat{w}$ will cause the supply curve to shift. In this regard, the impact on $\hat{k}_x$ of changes in the firm's perception of its market power (one aspect of the firm's output-demand conditions alluded to earlier) in which, for example, the firm correctly recognizes that it is able to raise its markup with little effect on sales, is a possibility.

Thus the firm's supply curve indicates the hypothetically perceived proceeds thought, in the circumstance of ignorance and uncertainty that it faces, to be required to make different employment levels economically worthwhile during a given period in which both the markup factor and the money wage remain fixed. Across periods, however, increases in ℓ_x may well be accompanied by revisions in $\hat{k}_x$ and transformations in $\hat{w}$. Through historical time, then, the firm may actually plan to follow a supply path or locus whose points are all drawn from different supply curves. Such a supply locus cannot have a linear shape. Discussion will return to the macroversion of this locus subsequently. It should also be emphasized that the actual outcome of the firm's economic activity, that is, the actual quantity of output it sells, the extent to which its initially projected selling price is actually revised in light of changing perceptions of demand conditions and the effective markup that results, along with the actual profit or rate of return on money capital invested in it, remain to be examined. These issues, too, will be discussed in the construction of the macromodel below.

Returning to the single-period focus, the break-even line determined by (12.2.1-11) and the supply curve (12.2.1-13) evidently intersect where $k_x = \hat{k}_x$ and

$$\ell_x = \frac{\hat{\rho}_x^t \hat{a}_x^t + \delta^{xt}(p_y^t)}{(\hat{k}_x - 1)\hat{w}}. \qquad (12.2.1\text{-}16)$$

Since the right-hand side of (12.2.1-11) is the same as the left-hand side of (12.2.1-5), and since the right-hand sides of (12.2.1-13) and

(12.2.1-5) are identical, these values of k_x and ℓ_x also satisfy (12.2.1-5). Hypothetical movement along the graph of (12.2.1-11) entails a changing value of k_x as described earlier, and each point of this graph could be thought of as intersecting a supply curve having a different value of $\hat{k}_x$. Similarly, each point of the supply curve could be viewed as intersecting a line obtained from (12.2.1-11) with a different intercept $\hat{\rho}_x^t \hat{a}_x^t + \delta^{xt}(p_y^t)$. But it is clear that once the intercept and $\hat{k}_x$ have been specified, only at that value of ℓ_x given by (12.2.1-16) does the markup factor turn out to exactly cover the firm's labor and depreciation costs and all obligations on its outstanding debt. For larger values of ℓ_x, along its supply curve the firm receives proceeds in excess of these operating and debt costs, and its actual rate of return is greater than its required rate of return; for smaller values of ℓ_x, contrary to its expectations, it is unable, out of current revenue, to cover its costs fully, and its actual rate of return falls below its required rate of return. Observe that, upon projecting argument to the macrolevel, movements in historical time along the supply curve, or along a supply locus, which will go with variation in the level of employment, will also imply "movements along" the "aggregate demand curve" defined in the next section.

For purposes of comparison, the wage costs of the firm as a function of ℓ_x, which are represented by the equation $\zeta_x = \hat{w}\ell_x$, are drawn in Figure 12-1 as the lower upward-sloping straight line through the origin. This wage-cost line is obviously parallel to the graph of (12.2.1-11). The vertical distance between the supply and wage-cost lines, depicting the difference between proceeds and labor cost, and expressed as

$$\left(\hat{k}_x - 1\right)\hat{w}\ell_x, \tag{12.2.1-17}$$

for each ℓ_x, widens as ℓ_x increases. Furthermore, the share of the firm's required proceeds going to labor along the supply curve, or

$$\frac{\zeta_x}{z_x} = \frac{1}{\hat{k}_x}, \tag{12.2.1-18}$$

remains fixed in the face of rising values of ℓ_x since $\hat{k}_x$ is constant. To the extent that $\hat{k}_x$ modifies, say, falls (hypothetically or in historical time), with increases in ℓ_x (recall such changes require shifts in the firm's supply curve), the difference between proceeds and labor cost in (12.2.1-17) can increase, decrease, or remain the same, but labor's share in (12.2.1-18) necessarily rises. (Such effects also have important demand-side implications at the macrolevel.) Evidently, changes in $\hat{k}_x$ that come about exogenously, whether or not they are accompanied by changes in ℓ_x, have their own independent effects. Thus, for example, an alteration of the firm's perception of its market power, which raises $\hat{k}_x$, as described in conjunction with (12.2.1-14) above, would certainly, in light of (12.2.1-18), lead to a decline in labor's share.

To obtain the third relation pertaining to firm x that emerges from (12.2.1-1) through (12.2.1-9), think of z_x in (12.2.1-10) as the money proceeds expected from total sales (including sales out of inventories) according to the estimated demand function (12.2.1-2) and expressed, given $\hat{y}_x^t$ and $\hat{x}^t$, as a function of the labor time it employs. That is, x in the version of (12.2.1-10) used here is actually $x + \hat{x}^t$ rather than just x, and

$$z_x = E^{xt}(\ell_x), \qquad (12.2.1\text{-}19)$$

where, combining (12.2.1-1), (12.2.1-4), and the present interpretation of (12.2.1-10),

$$E^{xt}(\ell_x) = \left[F^{xt}(\hat{y}_x^t, \ell_x) + \hat{x}^t\right]\left[\mathcal{D}_{xe}^{-1^t}(F^{xt}(\hat{y}_x^t, \ell_x) + \hat{x}^t)\right],$$

and the parameters $\hat{y}_x^t$ and $\hat{x}^t$ have been subsumed in the functional symbol E^{xt}. Observe that E^{xt} is called the firm's *expected proceeds* function,[28] as distinct from its estimated demand function $\mathcal{D}_{xe}^t$. The graph of E^{xt} from (12.2.1-19), that is, the firm's expected proceeds curve, could have any shape depending on the properties of F^{xt} and $\mathcal{D}_{xe}^t$. It is drawn in Figure 12-1 as upward sloping and strictly concave. Clearly, when the firm's expected money proceeds, determined, in part, from the estimated demand curve lying behind (12.2.1-19), equal the

---

[28]It is more common in the literature to refer to E^{xt}, at least after transformation into macroeconomic terms, as the firm's expected demand function. But this terminology is not used here to avoid confusion with the estimated demand function $\mathcal{D}_{xe}^t$. The present nomenclature will require a further departure from standard usage below in that what the literature calls either the "expected proceeds function" or the "aggregate supply function" will only be described as the latter. Anticipating subsequent argument, that aggregate supply function will be secured as the macro-analogue of the firm's supply function described earlier.

required money proceeds necessary, given $\hat{k}_x$, to support its labor input in (12.2.1-13), equation (12.2.1-12) has to be satisfied. Indeed, the firm would never plan to be anywhere else. But this only means that the firm's production and employment plans are consistent with the application of the markup formula in (12.2.1-9) to determine its output price. Suppose there is exactly one value of ℓ_x consistent with the equality of the money expected proceeds of (12.2.1-19) and (12.2.1-13). Denote it by ℓ_{xe}^t. Thus the firm's expected proceeds and supply curves in Figure 12-1 necessarily intersect at ℓ_{xe}^t.

It ought to be noted, however, that there is nothing to guarantee that the graph of the break-even line (12.2.1-11) also intersects the expected proceeds and supply curves at ℓ_{xe}^t. Should the graph of (12.2.1-11) intersect the supply curve to the right of ℓ_{xe}^t (the opposite of what is pictured in Figure 12-1), then the firm's planned position, ℓ_{xe}^t, will turn out to leave it unable to cover all of its operating and debt costs. The realization of this situation will certainly force the firm to modify subsequent plans.

Observe that, since buyers of the firm's output necessarily face the same price as that which the firm sets (a fact that is implicit in the previous relations), points on the supply and expected proceeds curves above each value of ℓ_x have the same output price p_x associated with them. The corresponding x values from (12.2.1-10) are different because along the supply curve x denotes current output produced, whereas along the expected proceeds curve it represents expected output sales. The difference is the change in inventory that the firm expects with each ℓ_x. Where the two curves intersect, the x values are the same and the change in inventory is zero.[29] This does not mean, however, that p_x remains constant as the firm moves along the expected proceeds and supply curves. Indeed, just the opposite has been demonstrated earlier along the latter in connection with equation (12.2.1-14). Similar calculations provide an equivalent analysis of the same transformations in p_x with respect to movements along the firm's expected proceeds curve.

---

[29]Thus, although the firm's desired total inventory level remains at zero, if the firm actually realized its planned position at the intersection of its supply and expected proceeds curves, it will end period t with the same inventory, namely, $\hat{x}^t$, with which it began.

12.2.2   The Macro-Analogue

Consider, now, the macroeconomic analogue of this model of firm x that is used to represent the joining together of all producers in the economy. Only those of the above equations that are relevant for subsequent discussion are translated into their macroeconomic counterparts. Observe that the micromodel of the firm presented above contains two goods, namely, the output produced by the firm in question and the durable input that it employs in production. In passing to the macrolevel, however, these goods are condensed into one, quantities of the intermediate good (*i.e.*, the durable input) disappearing as a separate variable. The price of the single good that remains becomes the economy's price level. And although the banks do not manufacture this good, the labor they employ is still counted as part of the labor used in its production. Therefore the value of national or aggregate output is the value of the quantity of the good produced. National or aggregate income is the combined value of all labor hired by firms and banks plus all depreciation charges and rate of return payments on outstanding debt. Of course, in realized terms, national income equals the value of national output, as is asserted by the realized versions of the macrorelations described below. Notationally, macrovariables are denoted by capitalizing the microvariables to which they are analogous. Of course, the subscript and superscript x is dropped. Thus, consolidating all of the economy's goods into a single good referred to as "aggregate real output" or just "real output," and thinking of all producers as making up a single firm, let X, L_X, P, and Z be, respectively, aggregate real output, aggregate labor or the number of persons employed in the production of real output (not labor time), the commodity price level (*i.e.*, the unit price of X), and aggregate money proceeds required from the production and sale of, or aggregate expenditure on, real output. Note that $Z = XP$ where, in parallel to the microlevel, X can represent either current real output produced or expected sales of real output. In keeping with tradition, drop the hats and write the exogenous money wage as W and the exogenous markup factor as k.

Denote the number of persons hired in the banking sector by L_β. Clearly, the total amount of labor, L, employed productively in the economy is the sum of L_X and L_β. It follows that $L_X = \Theta L$, where Θ

is the proportion of L engaged in the nonbank sector, and

$$\Theta = \frac{L - L_\beta}{L}.$$

In general, of course, Θ varies with L_β and L. But to keep matters simple in subsequent discussion, it is assumed that Θ is constant within each period of time.[30] Analogously to (12.2.1-1), the macroproduction function may therefore be written as

$$X = \mathcal{F}(L), \qquad (12.2.2\text{-}1)$$

where the parameters Θ and the economy's current stock of durable input are hidden in the functional symbol $\mathcal{F}$. Of course, the supposition of a fixed stock of durable input imposes a short-run character on the model developed below. Denote the first- and second-order derivatives of $\mathcal{F}$ by, respectively, $\mathcal{F}'$ and $\mathcal{F}''$ and assume that $\mathcal{F}'(L) > 0$ and $\mathcal{F}''(L) < 0$ for all $L > 0$. Thus $\mathcal{F}$ is increasing and strictly concave.

There are three additional macroequations of interest. Each is obtained by replacing microvariables in the relevant microequation with their macrocounterparts and by substituting ΘL for L_x. The parameter Θ is then subsumed as part of either the functional symbol E^t or the aggregate-level markup symbol k. Thus the *aggregate* expected proceeds function translates from (12.2.1-19) as[31]

$$Z = E^t(L), \qquad (12.2.2\text{-}2)$$

the *aggregate* supply function obtains from (12.2.1-13) as

$$Z = kWL, \qquad (12.2.2\text{-}3)$$

---

[30]This simplifying assumption implies, of course, that an involuntary reduction in employment in the goods sector will be accompanying by a proportional reduction in employment in the bank sector.

[31]The function $E^t(L)$ is sometimes decomposed to reflect income distribution parameters in a fashion similar to the realized aggregate demand function on the right-hand side of (12.3-10) below. Such a decomposition would yield a more detailed analysis of how the aggregate of all firms might determine the aggregate expected proceeds function. But since this involves considerable repetition of subsequent argument, it is not discussed here.

and the *aggregate* wage bill markup equation,[32] reflecting the equality of
the values for Z in (12.2.2-2) and (12.2.2-3), is secured from (12.2.1-12)
as

$$XP = kWL_e^t, \qquad (12.2.2\text{-}4)$$

where L_e^t is the value of L at which Z in (12.2.2-2) and (12.2.2-3) is
the same.[33] Evidently the values of Z in (12.2.2-2) and (12.2.2-3) are
generally different when $E^t(L) \neq kWL$. It is clear that, given the
perceptions and expectations of the individual firms making up the
macro-aggregate of all firms, the production part of the macroeconomy attempts to achieve L_e^t. In particular, prices are marked up at
L_e^t to secure P in (12.2.2-4) under the assumption that those expectations will be met.[34] Since they are carried over as analogues from
the microbase described above, and since Θ is constant, the relations
of (12.2.2-2) through (12.2.2-4) have the same properties as their microeconomic counterparts. Graphs of (12.2.2-2) and (12.2.2-3) appear
in Figure 12-2. (The curves labeled E^{*t} and H^t in Figure 12-2 will be
referred to later.) Of course, in parallel with the micromodel of firm x,
the slope of the aggregate supply curve is kW. To the extent that k and
W stay fixed, as they are assumed to do within periods, the aggregate
supply curve remains in place. But any alterations across historical
time, such as those discussed earlier, will cause it to shift.[35] In that
case, and as described for the analogous microeconomic firm above, a
nonlinear locus of planned aggregate supply points would be generated

---

[32]$Cf.$ Weintraub [17, p. 22].

[33]It is inferred, by transposition to the macrolevel of a similar property previously
developed in the microeconomic analogue, that, for each value of L, the values of
P underlying $Z = XP$ in (12.2.2-2) and (12.2.2-3) are identical. And, except for
$L = L_e^t$, the accompanying values of X are different at each L.

[34]To calculate this value of P, let φ be that value of Z which, along with L_e^t, simultaneously satisfies (12.2.2-2) and (12.2.2-3). Then, using (12.2.2-1), $P = \varphi/\mathcal{F}(L_e^t)$.

[35]Thus the effect of producers attempting to markup over labor costs to cover
those costs plus depreciation and debt service costs could result in k varying with
L as k_x modified with ℓ_x according to (12.2.1-8). Alternatively, changes in the
composition of aggregate demand (the notion of aggregate demand will be formally
introduced in the next section) could alter the perception and fact of the market
powers of various producers across the economy and cause thereby a different kind of
relation between changes in k and L as suggested at the microlevel in the discussion
following (12.2.1-15).

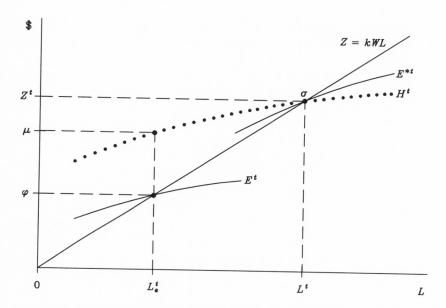

Figure 12-2. Aggregate supply and the expected proceeds curves, and the realized aggregate demand locus.

where each point could lie on a different aggregate supply curve. Furthermore, a sufficient condition for P to increase as L rises along any single aggregate supply curve is given by imposing the macrotranslation of (12.2.1-15) on the macroproduction function (12.2.2-1).

The macro-labor market, where producers attempt to hire the labor upon which their production plans are based, is assumed to have a perfectly elastic supply curve at the exogenous money wage W.[36] Thus producers are able to employ all labor they desire at W. It is neither appropriate nor necessary to specify an aggregate demand curve for labor. (Recall that there is no profit maximization and no value

---

[36]This does not mean that the labor market clears in the sense of fulfilled plans discussed earlier. Individuals may still not be able to supply the labor they plan to supply, *i.e.*, there may still be involuntary unemployment, during the period.

of marginal product curve reflecting the economy's behavioral demand curve for labor.) However, it should be noted that, as a separate unit, the aggregate of all suppliers of labor (and not necessarily the individuals making up that aggregate) is subject to money illusion in the sense that changes in the real wage have no impact on the aggregate amount of labor supplied.

12.3   The Demand Side

The next step is to consider the aggregate of all consumers as depicted by analogy to a single, representative consumer who functions similarly to, for example, person γ of Chapter 11. Recall that, at the microlevel, the decision set facing γ is defined by several constraints, including the following financial resources inequality

$$p_x^t x_\gamma^t + q^t \cdot \left(s_\gamma^t - \hat{s}_\gamma^t \right) \leq \hat{w}^t \left(\ell_{x\gamma}^t + \ell_{y\gamma}^t + \ell_{\beta\gamma}^t \right) + \left(q^t \cdot s_\gamma^t \right) v_\gamma^t, \quad (12.3\text{-}1)$$

where, at time t, p_x^t (again, the bar is removed for notational simplicity) is the price of good x set by the firm producing it, x_γ^t is a quantity of that good demanded by γ, s_γ^t is his currently planned marketable asset portfolio (which includes money), $\hat{s}_\gamma^t \geq 0$ is the portfolio with which he begins the period, q^t is a corresponding vector of perceived or expected asset prices, v_γ^t is the anticipated, per period rate of return on his planned portfolio as a whole, $\hat{w}^t$ is the wage, and $\ell_{x\gamma}^t$, $\ell_{y\gamma}^t$, and $\ell_{\beta\gamma}^t$ are, respectively, quantities of labor time supplied to firms x and y, and the bank β. The generalization of (12.3-1) to many consumer goods, firms, and banks is obvious and need not be discussed here. In addition, p_x^t, $\hat{s}_\gamma^t$, q^t, and $\hat{w}^t$ are parameters for γ. Thus the repeated selection of values of x_γ^t, s_γ^t, $\ell_{x\gamma}^t$, $\ell_{y\gamma}^t$, and $\ell_{\beta\gamma}^t$ by γ as these (and other) parameter values vary (such selections are made through application of the apparatus of Section 4.3 as described in Sections 10.2 and 11.2) defines x_γ^t, s_γ^t, $\ell_{x\gamma}^t$, $\ell_{y\gamma}^t$, and $\ell_{\beta\gamma}^t$ as functions of those parameters. But, although appropriate at the microlevel (for period t only), such functions, in the form in which they would be expressed if so derived, are not suitable as an analogical basis for macro-analysis.

To obtain microeconomic relations that have relevance for the macrolevel, rewrite (12.3-1) as

$$p_x x_\gamma + q \cdot (s_\gamma - \hat{s}_\gamma) \leq \hat{w} \ell_\gamma + (q \cdot s_\gamma) v_\gamma, \qquad (12.3\text{-}2)$$

where the superscripts t have been dropped to simplify notation and

$$\ell_\gamma = \ell_{x\gamma} + \ell_{y\gamma} + \ell_{\beta\gamma}.$$

Now the right-hand side of inequality (12.3-2) reflects two kinds of income for γ, namely, wage and portfolio (or "profit") income. Representing this income as

$$z_\gamma = \hat{w} \ell_\gamma + (q \cdot s_\gamma) v_\gamma, \qquad (12.3\text{-}3)$$

and designating the wage share of it by

$$\theta_\gamma = \frac{w \ell_\gamma}{z_\gamma},$$

(12.3-2) becomes

$$p_x x_\gamma + q \cdot s_\gamma \leq \theta_\gamma z_\gamma + (1 - \theta_\gamma) z_\gamma + q \cdot \hat{s}_\gamma. \qquad (12.3\text{-}4)$$

Note that θ_γ is a distribution parameter, $0 \leq \theta_\gamma \leq 1$, reflecting the share or proportion of γ's anticipated income generated from wages. Taking p_x, q, θ_γ, z_γ, and $\hat{s}_\gamma$ as parameters, and thinking of γ as choosing x_γ and s_γ from the options defined by (12.3-4) and other constraints (recall Section 11.2), repeated use of the model of Sections 10.2 and 11.2 yields the function

$$x_{\gamma e} = h_{\gamma x}^t (p_x, z_\gamma, \theta_\gamma, q \cdot \hat{s}_\gamma),$$

where $x_{\gamma e}$ represents planned purchases, and any remaining parameters from the other constraints are concealed in the functional symbol $h_{\gamma x}^t$. Since, from (12.3-4), $h_{\gamma x}^t$ is homogeneous of degree zero in p_x, z_γ, and q,[37] it follows that person γ's individual "consumption function" takes the form of

$$p_x x_{\gamma e} = p_x h_{\gamma x}^t \left(\frac{z_\gamma}{p_x}, \theta_\gamma, \frac{q \cdot \hat{s}_\gamma}{p_x} \right). \qquad (12.3\text{-}5)$$

---

[37]In the definition of the zero-degree homogeneity of $h_{\gamma x}^t$, multiplication of z_γ by some number κ means multiplication of both $\hat{w}$ and q by κ in (12.3-3).

Clearly, as shown in (12.3-3), z_γ is a function of, in part, ℓ_γ. Equation (12.3-5) is the microeconomic foundation for subsequently writing aggregate (planned) consumption as a function of real income, a distribution parameter, and the real value of assets.[38]

The construction of Section 4.3 is also the present basis for modeling the firms' and the banks' demand for durable inputs or investment. Take firm x of Chapter 11 as the representative micro-unit purchasing durable inputs and denote its planned investment during period t by the scalar variable y_{xe}^t. The decision set out of which a value for y_{xe}^t is selected is defined by a number of parameters, including the price of the durable input p_y^t as announced by the durable-good-producing firm y. (In transposing to the macrolevel, of course, the output of firm x and the durable input employed by firm x will be compressed into a single good, and their associated prices will become identical.) As in the case of consumer γ, the firm's demand for durable input can be expressed as a function of these parameters. In the process of making its decisions, and hence determining the demand function for durable input, firm x sets the price of its output, p_x^t, and estimates its current rate of return, ρ_{xe}^t, and the current output demand function it faces, $x + \hat{x}^t = \mathcal{D}^t(p_x)$, where $\hat{x}^t$ is the inventory with which it began period t. Now ρ_{xe}^t may be viewed as the firm's estimate of its current market yield (that is, the rate of return it would be required to pay on any new IOUs it issues) or its risk-adjusted rate of interest.[39] In addition, substitution of the firm's current price into the estimate of its current demand function provides an estimate of sales of currently produced output x_e^t. Although ρ_{xe}^t and x_e^t are variables in the original model of firm x, they are added here to the list of parameters specified at the point at which the firm makes its decision. Modifying decision making in the original model accordingly, firm x's demand function for durable input can be expressed as

$$y_{xe} = h_{xy}^t(x_e, \rho_{xe}),$$

---

[38] In the present microeconomic framework, since firms do not issue equities, the value of all outstanding IOUs reflects the value of real capital assets. Thus it is not necessary to treat real capital as a distinct asset.

[39] Of course, this estimate of its market yield may turn out to be incorrect. Recall Section 11.5.

where the superscripts t on variables and parameters have been discarded and the remaining parameters not appearing explicitly as arguments of h_{xy}^t are subsumed in the symbolism h_{xy}^t. Therefore firm x's individual "investment function" may be written in the form

$$p_y y_{xe} = p_y h_{xy}^t(x_e, \rho_{xe}).$$ (12.3-6)

Equation (12.3-6), translated to the macrolevel, describes planned investment as a function of real output and the nominal, risk-adjusted, rate of interest.

The macroversions of (12.3-5) and (12.3-6) are, as indicated, the aggregate, but not aggregated, (planned) consumption and (planned) investment functions. Using previous notational conventions, these are written, respectively, as

$$C = C\left(\frac{Z}{P}, \theta, \frac{\mathcal{G}}{P}\right)$$ (12.3-7)

and

$$I = \mathcal{I}(X, i*),$$ (12.3-8)

where C represents aggregate consumption expenditures at current prices, Z aggregate income, $\mathcal{G}$ the nominal (net) value of assets (bonds and money) which depends on the interest rate, $\theta = WL/Z$ the wage or labor's share of aggregate proceeds, I aggregate investment expenditures at current prices, and $i*$ the nominal, risk-adjusted, interest rate.[40] Assume $0 < \theta < 1$. Note that because they arise from independent sources, symbols such as Z and L used above have a different meaning from the same symbols employed in the previous section. For example, Z referred to aggregate proceeds contemplated by firms in Section 12.2, and denotes aggregate income anticipated by consumers in (12.3-7). Similarly, L represents aggregate labor demanded in Section 12.2 and aggregate labor supplied here. But, upon resolution of any macrosystem explicitly including (12.3-7) and (12.3-8), should such a system (which would incorporate the equilibrium methodology avoided

---

[40]By contrast with more traditional analyses in which the consumption function, say, links real consumption to (in part) real income, here the consumption function relates nominal consumption to (again, in part) the same real income.

in the present approach) be of interest, and should a unique solution exist, the solution values of Z and L obtained are, respectively, the same in both usages.[41] Observe that $\mathcal{C}$ and $\mathcal{I}$ are behavioral functions drawn, by analogy, from representative microeconomic units. Although possibly possessing, as argued earlier, more stability across successive periods of historical time than their microeconomic counterparts, they are still subject to all of the vagaries of relations appropriate to models of kaleidic economies.

It is also worth pointing out that in moving from the micro- to the macrocontext, and in replacing the micro p_x with the macro P, the analytical role of the concept of price has undergone a substantive transformation. For at the microlevel, price information provides the consumer, say, with the means by which the relative costs of commodities can be compared to their relative desirability. But, ignoring commodity-asset and intertemporal substitution, in the macroworld there is only one good and hence there can be no relative costs and desirabilities to compare. Instead the price concept, now the price level, allows for the conversion of variables such as nominal income and the nominal value of assets into, respectively, real income and the real value of assets.

Consider, now, realized expenditure and income, Z, at the macrolevel. Analogously to (12.3-3), income can be split into wage income, WL, and nonwage income, $Z - WL$, sometimes called profit income. Let c_w and c_π denote the average propensities to consume out of wage and profit incomes, respectively, where $0 < c_w < 1$, $0 < c_\pi < 1$, and $c_w > c_\pi$. Then realized consumption appears as

$$C = c_w WL + c_\pi(Z - WL). \qquad (12.3\text{-}9)$$

Evidently, the planned consumption function (12.3-7) could also be decomposed to reflect the separation of wage and profit income and, in light of this decomposition, c_w and c_π are seen to both depend[42] on

---

[41]To ensure that a unique solution exists, it would be necessary to assume at least that the sum of all marginal spending propensities, *i.e.*, the total derivative of $\mathcal{C} + \mathcal{I}$ with respect to Z/P, is less than unity. Regardless, this equilibrium-type system is not pursued further.

[42]The relevant decomposition of (12.3-7) is

$$C_w = \mathcal{C}^w\left(\frac{WL}{P}, \theta, \frac{\mathcal{G}}{P}\right),$$

$(Z/P, \theta, \mathcal{G}/P)$. The dependency of c_w and c_π on $\mathcal{G}/P$, of course, introduces the possibility of changes in real or nominal wealth, or wealth effects, as a component of the analysis. Using the distribution parameter $\theta = WL/Z$, (12.3-9) becomes

$$C = c_w \theta Z + c_\pi (1 - \theta) Z.$$

Since, again in realized terms, when the plans of all decision makers with respect to expenditures are effected in a mutually consistent manner, $Z = C + I$ and aggregate expenditure equals aggregate income (both being denoted by Z), it follows that

$$Z = c_w \theta Z + c_\pi (1 - \theta) Z + I, \qquad (12.3\text{-}10)$$

and hence, upon solving for Z,

$$Z = \frac{1}{1 - [\theta c_w + (1 - \theta) c_\pi]} I, \qquad (12.3\text{-}11)$$

where the term to the left of I is the investment multiplier. Observe that

$$\theta c_w + (1 - \theta) c_\pi < \theta c_w + (1 - \theta) c_w = c_w$$

because $c_w > c_\pi$. Hence, since $0 < c_w < 1$, the denominator, and therefore Z, in (12.3-11) is positive.

In general, Z on the left-hand side of the equal sign in (12.3-10) represents realized aggregate expenditure, while Z on the right-hand

$$C_\pi = C^\pi \left(\frac{Z - WL}{P}, \theta, \frac{\mathcal{G}}{P} \right),$$

where the sub- and superscripts w and π symbolize, respectively, consumption out of wage and profit incomes. Since $\theta = WL/Z$ and $(1 - \theta) = (Z - WL)/Z$, it can be shown that

$$c_w = \frac{C_w}{WL} = \frac{1}{\theta Z} C^w \left(\frac{\theta Z}{P}, \theta, \frac{\mathcal{G}}{P} \right),$$

$$c_\pi = \frac{C_\pi}{Z - WL} = \frac{1}{(1 - \theta) Z} C^\pi \left(\frac{(1 - \theta) Z}{P}, \theta, \frac{\mathcal{G}}{P} \right).$$

Therefore the average propensities to consume c_w and c_π both depend on $(Z/P, \theta, \mathcal{G}/P)$. To the extent that profits are retained by firms, profit earners' disposable income, and therefore their consumption expenditure, would be less than otherwise. This would imply a lower value of c_π.

side symbolizes realized aggregate income. But because, with respect to the latter income interpretation, $Z = (WL) + (Z - WL)$, realized aggregate income Z is partly dependent on realized L. Stressing this dependency, equation (12.3-10) is abbreviated to

$$Z = H^t(L), \qquad (12.3\text{-}12)$$

and H^t is referred to as the *realized aggregate* demand function. An illustration of the graph of this function, that is, the realized aggregate demand curve, appears in Figure 12-2. Note that, because this curve is a locus of realized points, to move along it implies crossing over periods of historical time. Thus, with the rapid and substantial change and the consequent instability of structures through time that kaleidic economies entail, it is not possibe to infer any general shape that H^t might have. Nor is it even necessary that the points of the locus fit together to form a continuous curve. Indeed, the only aggregate demand points that can actually be known in any period are those that have been realized by the economy in previous periods, and hence the filling in between those points to form the curve in Figure 12-2, although done for convenience, is necessarily a fiction. That having been said, Figure 12-2 adheres to tradition in that the graph of H^t it contains is drawn with a strictly concave shape.[43]

12.4   Goods and Employment

Although traversing the realized points of the aggregate demand locus necessitates the passage of time, movements along the aggregate supply curve, which is a collection of points valid for a single period (of course, only one of these points can represent actually planned variable values during the period), are hypothetical and involve no change in time. Therefore, when analyzing the simultaneous interaction of both curves and including them, for that purpose, in the same diagram (as is done in Figure 12-2), it is necessary to assume that the supply curve remains

---

[43]Of course, the points of H^t actually thrown up by the economy are a consequence of the interaction of demand-side and production-side forces. Possible reasons why the interaction of these forces might yield points along a strictly concave curve have been given by Vickers [12, pp. 431-434].

constant for whatever time periods a fixed supply curve is needed in the analysis. The more general situation in which the supply curve shifts over time is considered momentarily. The particular assumption relevant to the various circumstances subsequently under consideration (*e.g.*, that the supply curve is variable) is often implicit in the discussions that follow.

Evidently, with respect to goods and labor time, all expectations will be realized and all plans will be fulfilled only when the realized aggregate demand equation (12.3-12), the aggregate expected proceeds equation (12.2.2-2), and the aggregate supply equation (12.2.2-3), and hence (12.2.2-4), are satisfied simultaneously. Such a circumstance occurs for $L = L^t$ and $Z = Z^t$ in Figure 12-2. At this value of L, the aggregate supply ($Z = kWL$), the realized aggregate demand (H^t), and the higher aggregate expected proceeds (E^{*t}) curves[44] intersect at σ, and $\theta = 1/k$. Of course, the last equality means that the markup factor determining the slope of the aggregate supply curve through σ is realized as the reciprocal of the actual magnitude of labor's share. A value for X, namely, X^t, is found by setting $L = L^t$ in (12.2.2-1), and a value for P, or P^t, is secured, as in n. 34 on p. 396, upon substitution of the just-obtained values of Z and X into the equation $Z = XP$. Thus real output, the price level, and the level of employment are determined in period t.[45] But only if firms happen to guess correctly in estimating the demand curves they actually face, firms and banks happen to select an expenditure on durable inputs suitable for the profits with which they end up, and consumers happen to choose the expenditure appropriate to the income they earn, will σ actually obtain in period t. Otherwise, for example, firms and banks might be shooting for and consumers might be expecting L_e^t. In that circumstance, firms are anticipating an expenditure of φ, but, given the income and the particular distribution of it generated at L_e^t, consumers and investors in durable inputs actually spend μ. Thus firms are faced with an unexpectedly large demand for their outputs. Once inventories are exhausted, they can only attempt to meet this extra demand by expanding production,

---

[44]There is no reason for any one of these curves to be parallel to any of the others.

[45]Recall that, as described at the end of Section 12.2, the macro-labor supply function is assumed to be perfectly elastic at the exogenous money wage W. Planned labor demand, then, can always be realized.

raising prices, or both. But with the markup factor and the money wage fixed (*i.e.*, assuming an unchanging supply curve), the extent to which prices can be raised depends, by analogy to the movement of the microfirm along its supply curve as discussed earlier in relation to (12.2.1-14), on the values of k and W and on the marginal product $\mathcal{F}'(L)$. In any case, firms' expectations change, adjustments are made in plans for subsequent periods, and one would expect $L_e^{t+1} > L_e^t$. Similar difficulties could arise as a consequence of failed expectations in the bond market taken up in the next section. Regardless, if the aggregate supply curve remains stable long enough and the aggregate demand points actually brought forth by the economy continue to follow H^t, then the macroeconomy may eventually arrive at σ. But even with curves that are stable over time, whether or not that actually happens depends on particular circumstances that are not explored here.

It should be noted that actual movement of the economy away from L_e^t in Figure 12-2 can only take place through historical time. But it has already been pointed out that in passing from period to period neither k nor W need remain fixed. To illustrate the kinds of things that might happen in that case, consider the situation in which k varies but W is held constant. Place the economy at L_e^t in Figure 12-2, a position that is redrawn in Figure 12-3 with firms attempting to go to Q on the aggregate supply curve $\mathcal{Z}^t$ (the aggregate expected proceeds curve through Q, labeled E^t in Figure 12-2, is not redrawn in Figure 12-3), and consumers and investors actually going to R. (The values of φ and μ and the point σ are the same as in Figure 12-2.) Thus firms discover during period t that, as described above, demand was much larger than they had anticipated. Assume now, as a consequence, that in the next period firms respond in two ways. On the one hand, they revise their estimated demand functions "upward" in such a manner that the new aggregate expected proceeds function, E^{t+1}, passes through, say, R.[46] On the other, they recognize that there are profit opportunities still

---

[46]As a matter of fact, there is no reason why the new aggregate expected proceeds curve should, in general, go through R. Firms might think that some of the unexpectedly large demand for their output is only temporary, or they could conclude that a previously unrecognized structural change will induce an even larger demand in the future. In these cases, the new aggregate expected proceeds curve would lie below or above R, respectively.

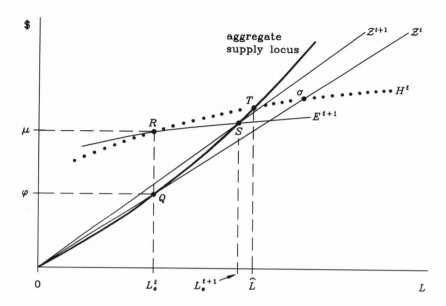

Figure 12–3. Movement along the locus of aggregate supply points.

to be exploited by increasing their markup factors, and in so doing they shift the aggregate supply curve to $\mathcal{Z}^{t+1}$. The production side of the macroeconomy, then, attempts to hire labor magnitude L_e^{t+1} and move to S. Of course, at L_e^{t+1}, with its new level of income and new income distribution, realized aggregate demand in the diagram still turns out to be greater than planned aggregate supply, so the process continues. Clearly the points Q and S are on the locus of aggregate supply points defined earlier.[47] Supposing that the realized aggregate

---

[47]Based on the assumptions made here, the aggregate supply locus would appear to be strictly convex. In general, the shape of the locus over any interval depends on the sign of the derivative $\partial k / \partial L$ over that interval. When $\partial k / \partial L > 0$, the supply curve in Figure 12-3 shifts to the left with increases in L and the locus is strictly convex. Similarly, with $\partial k / \partial L$ negative or zero, the locus is, respectively, strictly concave or linear. Dropping the superscript t and the subscript e on L_e^t

demand points continue to constitute the locus H^t as they arise, the process approaches T at the intersection of the aggregate supply and realized aggregate demand loci. At that point, an aggregate expected proceeds curve and an aggregate supply curve (not shown in Figure 12-3) also intersect the aggregate demand curve as at σ in Figure 12-2. A parallel argument could be constructed under the assumption that the money wage rises with L, with or without increases in k. In this latter case, a larger W implies a greater disposable income at every employment level and, given wage earners' consumption propensities, leads to a higher expected and actual demand expenditure.

Of course, there is nothing to guarantee that σ in Figure 12-2 or T in Figure 12-3 is associated with full employment, that is, with the full realization of all planned labor supply, and hence the clearing of the labor market. Indeed, due to the assumption of a perfectly elastic labor supply curve, L^t in Figure 12-2 or $\hat{L}$ in Figure 12-3 will generally be smaller than that required for full employment. Thus the present model contributes mostly to the understanding of situations of unemployment as opposed to the full-employment equilibrium explained by the classicals and new classicals.

When the producer and bank activities behind the interaction of the aggregate expected proceeds function and aggregate supply function lead to φ in Figure 12-2 or Q in Figure 12-3, and the consumer and producer activities underlying the realized aggregate demand function result in μ or, respectively, R, that is, when the simultaneous behavior of consumers, firms, and banks results in unrealized plans and failed

---

in (12.2.2-4), letting X, P, k, and L all vary (recognizing, in particular, that X changes with L, and P changes with X), differentiating that equation with respect to L, and substituting from the same equation, it can be shown that

$$\frac{\partial k}{\partial L} = \frac{k}{L}\left[\frac{L}{X}\frac{\partial X}{\partial L}\left(1 - \frac{X}{P}\frac{\partial P}{\partial X}\right) - 1\right].$$

Using this relation, sufficient conditions for $\partial k/\partial L$ to be positive, negative, or zero can be obtained. Expressed in the language of the representative firm from which the production side of the present macromodel is, by analogy, drawn, the shape of the supply locus depends on the firm's production function, which fixes the firm analogue of $(L/X)(\partial X/\partial L)$, and its estimate of its demand function, which sets the firm analogue of $(X/P)(\partial P/\partial X)$.

expectations, then the allocation of resources, and hence the values of the microvariables actually emerging, are determined, as in Section 7.2, by short-side trading and market-rationing rules. The completion of this microlevel activity in period t leads to the setting of the micro parameters for period $t + 1$. Thus a sequence of realized values of microeconomic variables emerges. As suggested with respect to the argument illustrated in Figure 12-3, the model of the macroeconomy developed above behaves similarly. Indeed, in the absence of stability of the macrorelations across periods, the macroeconomy mirrors the kaleidic changeabilities of the microeconomy described in Chapter 11.[48] In this regard, it should be noted that the uncertainty giving rise to the economy's kaleidic evolution lies behind the aggregate expected proceeds function and the consumption and investment functions underlying the realized aggregate demand function. In all cases, this uncertainty is accounted for through the approach to decision making in ignorance of Section 4.3 as the models of representative agents are projected, by analogy, to the aggregate level in deriving the various macroeconomic relations. There is no such uncertainty, however, with respect to the aggregate supply function, which remains fixed as long as the parameters that go into the construction of the aggregate-level markup factor k do not change.

Regardless of the stability of macroeconomic relations, comparative static analysis, as argued in Section 5.2, is still both appropriate and useful. By way of illustration, the remainder of this section examines the possible significance for aggregate expenditure Z, employment L, real output X, and the price level P, of an increase in the money wage W. The latter increases have been a notable feature of real world economies in recent times. At any rate, it is clear, starting at σ in Figure 12-2, that an enlargement of W with no change in k causes the aggregate supply curve to rotate counterclockwise around the origin. The realized aggregate demand locus, with I fixed, could move upward depending, in part, on the way in which the rise in W affects c_w and

---

[48]Stability of macrorelations like the aggregate expected proceeds function, should it occur, would tend to hide underlying microeconomic variability. But such macrostructures remain, nevertheless, highly sensitive to expectational alteration that could occur at any moment and therefore still take into account the kaleidic nature of economic reality.

c_π via changes in Z and P working through a realized version of the decomposed consumption function described in n. 42 on p. 402. Such an upward movement turns, that is, on individual decisions leading to higher consumption expenditures out of the wage and profit incomes referable to each employment level. But whether the modification in the realized aggregate demand locus offsets the counterclockwise shift in the aggregate supply curve so that, for example, L^t remains unchanged, cannot be determined without deeper analysis. One possibility is that the higher money wage is not accompanied by a large enough increase in productivity to prevent a rise in the price level and, in light of expenditure revisions, a decline in employment. Thus, in this way, the model provides an explanation of the phenomenon known as "stagflation."

More generally, it is of interest to consider the manner in which changes in the money wage affect the solution values of L and other variables in the system when k (and hence θ) remains fixed.[49]   To keep matters simple, the normally endogenous variables I and $\mathcal{G}$ are also taken to be positive constants. The system itself, then, may be summarized by the four equations[50]

$$Z = c_w WL + c_\pi (Z - WL) + I, \qquad (12.4\text{-}1)$$

$$Z = kWL, \qquad (12.4\text{-}2)$$

$$Z = PX, \qquad (12.4\text{-}3)$$

$$X = \mathcal{F}(L), \qquad (12.4\text{-}4)$$

---

[49]For a different analysis in a related context see Davidson and Smolensky [3, pp. 149-154].

[50]Here the realized aggregate demand relation (12.4-1) is obtained as the combination of (12.3-9) and the equation $Z = C + I$ (it is also equivalent to [12.3-10] and has earlier been abbreviated as $Z = H^t$); the aggregate supply relation (12.4-2) is the same as (12.2.2-3); the definition (12.4-3) is the macrotranslation of (12.2.1-10) from the micro-analogue; and (12.4-4) is the macroproduction function (12.2.2-1). The aggregate expected proceeds relation (12.2.2-2) is redundant (*i.e.*, like the aggregate supply and realized aggregate demand relations, it passes through σ in Figures 12-2 and 12-3) and need not be included.

in the four variables Z, L, X, and P and parameters W, I, $k = 1/\theta$, and $\mathcal{G}$, where c_w and c_π may be viewed as depending on θ, WL, P, and $\mathcal{G}$ as implied in n. 42 on p. 402. The simultaneous solution of this system (assumed to exist) determines the values of Z^t, L^t, X^t, and P^t (as functions of W, I, k, and $\mathcal{G}$) that relate to an intersection of aggregate supply and realized aggregate demand curves such as at σ in Figures 12-2 and 12-3. And the main focus of attention is to determine expressions, and possibly signs, for the partial derivatives $\partial Z^t/\partial W$, $\partial L^t/\partial W$, $\partial X^t/\partial W$, and $\partial P^t/\partial W$. However, it should be borne in mind in the course of subsequent considerations that, even though, for analytical purposes, the system of equations (12.4-1) through (12.4-4) and the parameters I, k, and $\mathcal{G}$ are taken as "given," nothing in a kaleidic, churning world actually remains fixed for very long. The following calculations, then, only suggest possible directions of change that may arise under certain specific circumstances and may never, in fact, have the time, or the absence of additional mediating influences, to fully work themselves out.

Now, before pursuing the comparative statics analysis leading to the determination of expressions for the above derivatives in a systematic way, it is instructive to consider, by itself, the partial derivative $\partial Z^t/\partial W$ from two alternative perspectives. First, using (12.4-2) to eliminate WL in (12.4-1), solving the result for Z, and concentrating on solution values of (12.4-1) through (12.4-4), it follows that

$$Z^t = \frac{k}{(1 - c_\pi)k + c_\pi - c_w} I. \tag{12.4-5}$$

Evidently the difference between (12.3-11) and (12.4-5) is the taking into account of equation (12.4-2), and

$$\frac{k}{(1 - c_\pi)k + c_\pi - c_w}$$

is another expression for the investment multiplier. Of course, (12.4-5) and this latest version of the multiplier could also be secured by substituting $\theta = 1/k$ into (12.3-11). Moreover, it has already been shown in conjunction with (12.3-11) that the investment multiplier is positive. Hence, $Z^t > 0$ since $I > 0$. But from (12.4-5), it is also

clear that the impact on aggregate expenditure of an enlargement of
the money wage, that is, the sign and magnitude of $\partial Z^t/\partial W$, turns on
the effect that that change has on the investment multiplier through
the consumption propensities c_w and c_π. And to the extent that the rise
in W creates modifications in k and $\mathcal{G}$, and alterations in savings that
are absorbed in a new value of I (possibilities ruled out by the above
assumptions), the actual impact on Z^t of the change in the multiplier
might not turn out to be the same as otherwise.

Second, substituting (12.4-2) for Z on the right-hand side of (12.4-
1) and again confining attention to solution values of (12.4-1) through
(12.4-4) yields

$$Z^t = [c_w + (k-1)c_\pi]WL^t + I,$$

and, upon partially differentiating with respect to W (assuming c_w and
c_π are continuously differentiable functions of WL and P),

$$\frac{\partial Z^t}{\partial W} = \left[\frac{\partial c_w}{\partial W} + (k-1)\frac{\partial c_\pi}{\partial W}\right]WL^t + [c_w + (k-1)c_\pi]\frac{\partial(WL^t)}{\partial W}, \quad (12.4\text{-}6)$$

where

$$\frac{\partial c_w}{\partial W} = \frac{\partial c_w}{\partial(WL^t)}\frac{\partial(WL^t)}{\partial W} + \frac{\partial c_w}{\partial P^t}\frac{\partial P^t}{\partial W},$$

$$= \frac{\partial c_w}{\partial(WL^t)}\left[L^t + W\frac{\partial L^t}{\partial W}\right] + \frac{\partial c_w}{\partial P^t}\frac{\partial P^t}{\partial W}, \quad (12.4\text{-}7)$$

and

$$\frac{\partial c_\pi}{\partial W} = \frac{\partial c_\pi}{\partial[(k-1)WL^t]}\frac{\partial[(k-1)WL^t]}{\partial W} + \frac{\partial c_\pi}{\partial P^t}\frac{\partial P^t}{\partial W}$$

$$= \frac{\partial c_\pi}{\partial[(k-1)WL^t]}(k-1)\left[L^t + W\frac{\partial L^t}{\partial W}\right] + \frac{\partial c_\pi}{\partial P^t}\frac{\partial P^t}{\partial W}. \quad (12.4\text{-}8)$$

Observe that the first term to the right of the equal sign in (12.4-6) reflects the change in aggregate spending that arises from the alterations
in c_w and c_π; the second records the change in aggregate spending that
comes about from the variation in the wage bill. It is the combination
of these two components that determines what happens to Z^t as W
rises. For example, it may well happen that an increase in W at any

given employment level, since it enlarges wage income, leads to a higher rate of saving out of that income than might otherwise have occurred (after the effects of any change in P have been taken into account). In that event, $\partial c_w/\partial W < 0$. At the same time, the increase in W, by virtue of its forcing a counterclockwise rotation of the supply curve (k, recall, is assumed fixed), induces a rise in profit income also at each level of L (see [12.2.1-17] in the micro-analogue). Here an expansion in the proportion saved is also conceivable and, should that take place, $\partial c_\pi/\partial W < 0$ too. It follows that the portion of the change in Z^t that arises from modification in the consumption propensities in (12.4-6) is negative. However, that decline in Z^t could be either enhanced or offset depending on the effect on Z^t of the variation in the wage bill. Regardless, the value of $\partial Z^t/\partial W$ in (12.4-6) depends on the values of $\partial L^t/\partial W$ and $\partial P^t/\partial W$. And the only way to determine expressions for all three of these derivatives that are independent of each other is through the aforementioned comparative statics analysis, to which discussion now turns.

It is useful to begin by identifying two terms that will arise in subsequent manipulations. These are as follows:

$$\Upsilon_{WL} = \frac{\partial c_w}{\partial (WL^t)} + (k-1)^2 \frac{\partial c_\pi}{\partial [(k-1)WL^t]}, \qquad (12.4\text{-}9)$$

$$\Upsilon_P = \frac{\partial c_w}{\partial P^t} + (k-1)\frac{\partial c_\pi}{\partial P^t}. \qquad (12.4\text{-}10)$$

The first of these is referred to as the *income* effect since it measures the impact on the consumption propensities of changes in money income. The second, which describes the consequences for the same propensities of variations in the price level, is called the *price* effect. Now if, for both wage and profit earners, consumption is a strictly concave function of money income (or a linear function with positive consumption at zero income), then the partial derivatives to the right of the equal sign in (12.4-9) are negative. If, in addition, the decline in real income that accompanies an increase in the price level forces wage and profit earners to save less to maintain their standard of living, and if this is not offset by the attendant fall in real wealth, then the partial derivatives to the right of the equal sign in (12.4-10) are positive.

Under these conditions, then, the fact that $k > 1$ implies

$$\Upsilon_{WL} < 0 \quad \text{and} \quad \Upsilon_P > 0 \quad\quad (12.4\text{-}11)$$

throughout their domains.

The system under investigation, namely, (12.4-1) through (12.4-4) can be simplified considerably by using (12.4-2) to eliminate Z in (12.4-1) and then substituting first (12.4-3) and then (12.4-4) into (12.4-2). This gives

$$L = \frac{I}{kW - c_w W - (k-1)c_\pi W} \quad\quad (12.4\text{-}12)$$

and

$$kWL = P\mathcal{F}(L). \quad\quad (12.4\text{-}13)$$

Allowing for the variation of c_w and c_π as indicated earlier, (12.4-12) and (12.4-13) is a system of two equations in the two variables L and P. Its simultaneous solution (assumed to exist) yields L^t and P^t as functions of the parameters W, I, $k = 1/\theta$, and $\mathcal{G}$. With L^t and P^t known, Z^t can be secured from either (12.4-1) or (12.4-2) and X^t can be derived from (12.4-3) or (12.4-4). Of course, as described above, the values of L^t, P^t, Z^t, and X^t so obtained are those arising at the intersection of an aggregate supply curve and a realized aggregate demand curve. However, because the form of the production function $\mathcal{F}$, along with the forms of the relations between c_w and WL, $\theta = 1/k$, P, and $\mathcal{G}$, and between c_π and the same variables and parameters, are not specified, exact solution values for L^t, P^t, Z^t, and X^t cannot be determined. Nevertheless, implicit differentiation of (12.4-12) and (12.4-13) will yield expressions for $\partial L^t/\partial W$ and $\partial P^t/\partial W$, and these can be used to obtain expressions for $\partial Z^t/\partial W$ and $\partial X^t/\partial W$.

Proceeding with these latter derivations, multiply both sides of (12.4-12) by $[kW - c_w W - (k-1)c_\pi W]$ and partially differentiate with respect to W to procure

$$k\left[L^t + W\frac{\partial L^t}{\partial W}\right] - c_W\left[L^t + W\frac{\partial L^t}{\partial W}\right] - WL\frac{\partial c_w}{\partial W}$$

$$-(k-1)c_\pi\left[L^t + W\frac{\partial L^t}{\partial W}\right] - (k-1)WL\frac{\partial c_\pi}{\partial W} = 0.$$

Substituting from (12.4-7) and (12.4-8), rearranging terms, and then further substituting from (12.4-9), (12.4-10), and (12.4-12) gives

$$
\left[\frac{I}{L^t} - W^2(L^t)\Upsilon_{WL}\right]\frac{\partial L^t}{\partial W} - W(L^t)\Upsilon_P\frac{\partial P^t}{\partial W}
$$

$$
= -\frac{I}{W} + W(L^t)^2\Upsilon_{WL}. \tag{12.4-14}
$$

Next, partially differentiating (12.4-13) with respect to W, and using (12.4-13) to eliminate the term kW leads to

$$
P^t\left[\mathcal{F}'(L^t) - \frac{\mathcal{F}(L^t)}{L^t}\right]\frac{\partial L^t}{\partial W} + \mathcal{F}(L^t)\frac{\partial P^t}{\partial W} = kL. \tag{12.4-15}
$$

Now (12.4-14) and (12.4-15) constitute a linear system in the variables $\partial L^t/\partial W$ and $\partial P^t/\partial W$ whose matrix of coefficient has the determinantal value

$$
D = \begin{vmatrix} I/L^t - W^2(L^t)\Upsilon_{WL} & -W(L^t)\Upsilon_P \\ P^t\left[\mathcal{F}'(L^t) - \mathcal{F}(L^t)/L^t\right] & \mathcal{F}(L^t) \end{vmatrix},
$$

or, upon expansion,

$$
D = \left[\frac{I}{L^t} - W^2(L^t)\Upsilon_{WL}\right]\mathcal{F}(L^t)
$$

$$
+ \left[\mathcal{F}'(L^t) - \frac{\mathcal{F}(L^t)}{L^t}\right](P^t)W(L^t)\Upsilon_P. \tag{12.4-16}
$$

Assume that $D \neq 0$ everywhere. Then, upon application of Cramer's rule, it is not hard to see that

$$
\frac{\partial L^t}{\partial W} = \frac{1}{D}\left\{\left[-\frac{I}{W} - W(L^t)^2\Upsilon_{WL}\right]\mathcal{F}(L^t) + kW(L^t)^2\Upsilon_P\right\} \tag{12.4-17}
$$

and, after elimination of P^t by substitution from (12.4-13),

$$
\frac{\partial P^t}{\partial W} = \frac{k}{D}\left[I - W^2(L^t)^2\Upsilon_{WL}\right]\frac{L^t}{\mathcal{F}(L^t)}\mathcal{F}'(L^t). \tag{12.4-18}
$$

Finally, partially differentiating (12.4-2) and (12.4-4), respectively, with respect to W,

$$\frac{\partial Z^t}{\partial W} = k \left[L^t + W \frac{\partial L^t}{\partial W} \right], \tag{12.4-19}$$

$$\frac{\partial X^t}{\partial W} = \mathcal{F}'(L^t) \frac{\partial L^t}{\partial W}, \tag{12.4-20}$$

and expressions for $\partial Z^t / \partial W$ and $\partial X^t / \partial W$ can be calculated from (12.4-17).

Consider, now, the signs of the derivatives in (12.4-17) through (12.4-20). According to Theorem 9.2-13, the assumption that $\mathcal{F}''(L) < 0$ for all $L > 0$ implies

$$\mathcal{F}'(L^t) - \frac{\mathcal{F}(L^t)}{L^t} < 0$$

everywhere. But even invoking the conditions described earlier ensuring the inequalities of (12.4-11), namely, that the income effect Υ_{WL} is negative and the price effect Υ_P is positive, D in (12.4-16) contains one positive and one negative term. It follows that the sign of D, and hence those of $\partial L^t / \partial W$, $\partial P^t / \partial W$, $\partial Z^t / \partial W$, and $\partial X^t / \partial W$ cannot generally be determined without further assumptions. In other words, the new intersection of the aggregate supply and realized aggregate demand curves that obtains from a higher money wage depends on the interplay between the income and price effects and the marginal product of labor. In particular, the aggregate expenditure outcome that emerges following the expansion of the money wage is likely to involve a different price-level, real-output breakdown from that which previously existed. But in any case, with (12.4-11) in force (and in light of the assumption that $\mathcal{F}'(L) > 0$ everywhere), the sign of $\partial P^t / \partial W$ is the same as that of D, and the signs of $\partial L^t / \partial W$ and $\partial X^t / \partial W$ are identical.

However, in the special situation in which $\Upsilon_{WL} = \Upsilon_P = 0$ (that is, say, each partial derivative in [12.4-9] and [12.4-10] is zero), the signs of all left-hand derivatives in (12.4-17) through (12.4-20) can be specified. For, upon direct substitution, $D = I\mathcal{F}(L^t)/L^t$ and

$$\frac{\partial L^t}{\partial W} = -\frac{L^t}{W} < 0,$$

$$\frac{\partial P^t}{\partial W} = \frac{k\,(L^t)^2}{[\mathcal{F}(L^t)]^2}\mathcal{F}'(L^t) > 0,$$

$$\frac{\partial Z^t}{\partial W} = 0,$$

and

$$\frac{\partial X^t}{\partial W} = -\frac{L^t}{W}\mathcal{F}'(L^t) < 0.$$

(The conclusion that $\partial Z^t/\partial W = 0$ could also be deduced by substituting into [12.4-6].) The geometric interpretation of these results is as follows: the counterclockwise rotation of the supply curve and the upward shift in the aggregate demand curve caused by the increase in the money wage leads to a new intersection of new curves at which the level of aggregate expenditure is the same as before but the level of employment has declined. Also at the new intersection, real output has been reduced and the price level has gone up.

Finally, dropping the fixity of the level of investment I and the nominal value of assets $\mathcal{G}$, an increase in the money wage, as is implicit in the development of the macro bond and money markets in the next section, has further significance for aggregate expenditure, employment, real output, and the price level in terms of its impact on the money supply, the demand for money, the rate of interest, and central bank monetary policy. For any rise in the price level that might occur as a consequence of an enlarged money wage could tend to expand the transactions demand for money. That, in turn, could put upward pressure on the interest rate and, thereby, reduce the nominal value of assets. Now, conceivably, the higher interest rate might lower investment expenditure, and a decline in the nominal value of assets could lead to a fall in consumption expenditures. Such a fall in consumption expenditure may also result from the decline in the real value of assets induced by the rise in P. But any reduction in expenditure coming from these sources would reduce employment still further and thus constitute an additional stimulus to whatever stagflation is already under way. Moreover, to satisfy the larger demand for money, to preserve the previously existing interest rate, and to prevent the induced reduction in investment expenditure, the central bank may attempt to enlarge the money supply. Should it be successful in avoiding a fall in

investment expenditure and maintaining output and employment levels
at the higher prices, the central bank can be said to have "validated"
the wage and price increases.

12.5   Bonds and Money

There remains to consider the macrodetermination of the rate of interest and the money supply. This is accomplished here through analyses of the macroeconomy's two asset markets, that is, the markets for
bonds or, equivalently, IOUs, and for money.[51] Since there are but
two additional markets in the full macromodel, namely, those for goods
and labor, application, by analogy drawn from the microworld, of the
proposition that the sum of all realized expenditures throughout the
economy, including "expenditure" on money balances, equals the sum
of all realized receipts, including receipts of money balances (a sort of
Walras' law for the single collection of prices and quantities realized in
the economy during each period), market clearing with respect to realized quantities demanded and supplied in any three markets implies
similar market clearing in the fourth. Thus, because market clearing
in realized terms has already been described for the goods and labor
markets, it is only necessary to consider the determination of realized market clearing in one of the asset markets. In either event, the
underlying microeconomic counterparts are a collection of micro-IOU
markets and a micro-money market operating as described in Chapter
11. Commercial banks add to and subtract from the money supply
according to the IOU market demands placed upon them and the other
transactions in which they engage. Firms and banks (not consumers)
issue their own IOUs to raise money capital, and all agents (consumers,
firms, or banks) are permitted to buy and keep the IOUs of any issuing
agent. There is also a central bank, which holds the reserves of the
commercial banks, requires no physical or financial inputs for its operations, and does not issue IOUs to raise money capital. The central
bank sets the fraction of total deposits that the commercial banks are
required to maintain as reserves and is able to loan funds to them and
to buy and sell firm and commercial bank IOUs in the IOU markets.

---

[51]Recall n. 38 on p. 400.

At the macrolevel, the present discussion focuses primarily on the bond market. Thus analysis is mostly concerned with the planned and realized demand and supply of bonds or, equivalently, planned and realized receipts from IOU sales and planned and realized expenditure on IOUs. One approach to setting the microeconomic base out of which the appropriate macroeconomic equations emerge is to recognize that consumers, firms, and commercial banks can be both buyers and sellers of IOUs. Abstracting from this situation, divide each agent into buying and selling "parts" and respectively combine these parts across agents into an aggregate of all IOU buyers and an aggregate of all IOU sellers. Next construct microeconomic models describing how the representative IOU-buying and IOU-selling agents behave (*i.e.*, make their decisions in all possible circumstances). Presumably these models would draw in suitable ways from the models of the consumer, firm, and commercial bank of Chapter 11. The behavioral relations derived from them could then be transformed, by analogy, into macroequations as described and effected above. A similar approach could also be applied to construct the macro-money market, should that be desired. Without pursuing the details of the microeconomic base, subsequent analysis proceeds along these lines. An explanation of the bond market is provided first. Thereafter the implications for the money market are considered.

In a microworld with a single firm x, imagine an IOU-buying agent, $\mathcal{E}$, purchasing the IOUs issued by x.[52] Let $\alpha_{x\mathcal{E}\tau}^t$ be the (net) number of IOUs issued by firm x in period τ that $\mathcal{E}$ plans to buy in period t,[53] and write $q_{x\tau}^t$ for their price in t as perceived or expected by $\mathcal{E}$. With $\tau = 1$ indicating the first (*i.e.*, the earliest) period under consideration, and with $q_{xt}^t = 1$ representing the issue price of current IOUs, set $q_x^t = (q_{x1}^t, \ldots, q_{xt-1}^t, 1)$. Ignoring details, specify a model of decision making in ignorance of the sort developed in Section 4.3 that explains

---

[52]The microeconomic model of the previous chapter contained many firms, each issuing its own IOUs on many different dates. IOUs were thus heterogeneous both with respect to their source and across time. Here, however, there is only one firm issuing IOUs. In the present case, then, IOUs are homogeneous with respect to their source but still heterogeneous across time.

[53]That is, $a_{x\mathcal{E}\tau}^t$ is the difference between what ε plans to hold in period t and his initial holdings at the start of the period. Recall Section 11.2.

the decisions of $\mathcal{E}$ and out of which emerges the behavior functions

$$\alpha^t_{x\mathcal{E}\tau} = h^t_{x\mathcal{E}\tau}(q^t_x), \quad \tau = 1, \ldots, t, \tag{12.5-1}$$

where all other parameters of $\mathcal{E}$'s decision problem are subsumed in $h^t_{x\mathcal{E}\tau}$.

Price determination during period t in the market for IOUs issued by x implies that the prices of old issues of IOUs adjust until the current yields on all outstanding IOUs and new issues of IOUs are equalized. Let i^*_t be $\mathcal{E}$'s perception or expectation of this market yield in period t. Then each $q^t_{x\tau}$, for $\tau = 1, \ldots, t$, can be expressed as a function of i^*_t. Hence the vector q^t_x in (12.5-1) can be replaced by the scalar i^*_t with appropriate modifications in $h^t_{x\mathcal{E}\tau}$. Moreover, planned expenditure by $\mathcal{E}$ on IOUs in period t is therefore found from (12.5-1) as

$$\lambda_{x\mathcal{E}} = B^t_{x\mathcal{E}}(i^*), \tag{12.5-2}$$

where

$$\lambda_{x\mathcal{E}} = \sum_{\tau=1}^{t} \alpha^t_{x\mathcal{E}\tau} q^t_{x\tau},$$

$$B^t_{x\mathcal{E}}(i^*) = \sum_{\tau=1}^{t} h^t_{x\mathcal{E}\tau}(i^*) q_{x\tau},$$

the $h^t_{x\mathcal{E}\tau}$ have been altered so that i^* appears as the argument in place of q^t_x, the dependence of each $q^t_{x\tau}$ on i^* is implicit, and the superscript t on $\lambda_{x\mathcal{E}}$ and subscript t on i^* have been dropped.

A similar construction obtains for the IOU-selling agent, $\aleph$, from an application of the apparatus of Section 4.3 to $\aleph$'s selling-decision problem. This results in a planned IOU sales receipts function

$$\lambda_{x\aleph} = B^t_{x\aleph}(i^*), \tag{12.5-3}$$

where $\lambda_{x\aleph}$ represents the planned receipts from the sale of firm x's IOUs held by $\aleph$, and i^* is $\aleph$'s perception or expectation of the current market yield. Note that the money capital requirements of firms and banks are met by that part of $\lambda_{x\aleph}$ arising from the sale of new issues of IOUs. Of course, the i^* in (12.5-2) is not the same as the i^* in (12.5-3): the former is the representative buying agent's perception of the risk-adjusted interest rate, while the latter is the generally different perception of the same variable value on the part of representative selling agent.

To transform (12.5-2) and (12.5-3) into their macrocounterparts which emerge, by analogy, from the unspecified micromodels explaining the behavior of $\mathcal{E}$ and $\aleph$, requires only the replacement of the appropriate microvariables and functions in these equations. Thus, substituting Λ for λ, and $\mathcal{B}^t$ for B^t, leaving i^* as it is, and dropping the subscript x, (12.5-2) and (12.5-3) become, respectively,

$$\Lambda_\mathcal{E} = \mathcal{B}_\mathcal{E}^t(i^*) \tag{12.5-4}$$

and

$$\Lambda_\aleph = \mathcal{B}_\aleph^t(i^*). \tag{12.5-5}$$

Observe that (12.5-4) and (12.5-5) represent, respectively, the macro demand and supply functions for bonds expressed in terms of expenditure on bonds. To the extent that failed expectations occur in the micro-IOU markets as individual buyers and sellers sequentially interact (recall Section 11.5), these relations cannot be stable during period t. Although the plans of micro-agents cannot generally be revised until the start of period $t+1$, the behavior of the aggregates of all IOU buyers and IOU sellers (*i.e.*, the behavior of the respective, representative agents) still has to be adjusted to reflect plans as they fall through because the nominal value of assets, $\mathcal{G}$, in the consumption function (12.3-7) varies as the perceived values of i^* modify, and this wealth effect, in turn, affects (12.5-4) and (12.5-5). At the end of period t, after all transactions that are going to occur have taken place, the functions $\mathcal{B}_\mathcal{E}^t$ and $\mathcal{B}_\aleph^t$ that emerge have to be consistent with what has actually happened. Furthermore, since realized demand is always equated to realized supply in the bond market, the realized values of $\Lambda_\mathcal{E}$ and $\Lambda_\aleph$ have to be equal, and $\mathcal{E}$'s and $\aleph$'s perception or expectation of the current market yield have to be identical to the realized market yield. Thus, at the end of period t, the supply and demand functions reflecting "plans" relating to bonds may be described by (12.5-4) and (12.5-5) with the subscripts $\mathcal{E}$ and $\aleph$ on Λ dropped and bars placed over $\mathcal{B}_\mathcal{E}^t$ and $\mathcal{B}_\aleph^t$, that is, by the system

$$\Lambda = \bar{\mathcal{B}}^t_{\mathcal{E}}(i^*),$$

$$\Lambda = \bar{\mathcal{B}}^t_{\aleph}(i^*),$$

(12.5-6)

where, in a highly restricted kind of market clearing, the simultaneous solution of (12.5-6) determines, for period t, the unique realized expenditure on bonds and the unique realized market yield i^{*t}. As in Section 11.5, the latter is actually the risk-adjusted market yield. Observe that, as suggested above, the parameters concealed in the functional symbols $\bar{\mathcal{B}}^t_{\mathcal{E}}$ and $\bar{\mathcal{B}}^t_{\aleph}$ are likely to include things like P that depend on what is happening in the remainder of the macroeconomy of equations (12.3-8) and (12.4-1) through (12.4-4). Similarly, as was suggested earlier, the variables in these latter equations explicitly or implicitly depend on i^*. But the ways in which P, X, Z, and L, on the one hand, and i^*, on the other, interact are not considered here.[54] In any case, (12.3-8), (12.4-1) through (12.4-4), plus some appropriate relation (also not to be explored here) between i^* and the nominal value of assets $\mathcal{G}$ all have to be solved simultaneously to determine the full solution values for the macrosystem at each t. And, as long as these macroeconomic constructions are not stable over time, the functions and parameters they contain, together with the macroeconomic outcomes that they generate, will continually be transformed across periods in a manner similar to that discussed at the start of the previous section.

The macro-money market is modeled quite similarly to the money market of the microeconomy analyzed in Section 11.5. On the one hand, there is the limited flow demand for money always equal to the limited flow supply due to the willingness of the commercial banks to create and destroy money through purchases and sales of IOUs and other banking operations. On the other hand are the planned demands and planned supplies of the stock of money that may or may not be realized. All of the flow and stock demand, and part of the flow and stock supply, arise in conjunction with the portfolio decisions made by the economy's agents. The remainder of the flow and stock supply is determined by central bank open-market operations. The money

---

[54]This interaction, of course, defines expressions for partial derivatives (assuming they exist) like $\partial i^{*t}/\partial W$.

supply, then, has both an endogenous and an exogenous component. As in the microeconomic case, the risk-adjusted market yield determined in the bond market minus a risk premium is the risk-free market yield. And the risk-free market yield, i^t, is the rate of interest in period t or, due to the market clearing of realized quantities in the goods, labor, and bond markets, the price of (or opportunity cost of holding) money. Thus $i^{*t} - i^t$ is the risk premium.

It has been suggested here and in Chapter 11 that the central bank can influence microeconomic outcomes in at least three ways: by changing the reserve requirement of commercial banks, by changing the rate at which these banks can borrow reserves from the central bank and so encourage the commercial banks thereby to alter the reserves they have available for making loans, and through open-market operations or the buying and selling of firm and commercial bank IOUs in the IOU markets. Clearly all of these central bank options translate into the macroeconomic world described here. To the extent that each impacts on the demand or supply of bonds, the risk-adjusted market yield determined in the bond market is affected. But the second option has a further effect that has not yet been considered. For the rate at which the commercial banks are able to borrow from the central bank, frequently referred to as the *discount* rate, can also be thought of as the actual risk-free market yield or rate of interest i^t. On this view, then, the central bank sets i^t and is able to exert some influence through the bond market over i^{*t}. Moreover, the risk premium $i^{*t} - i^t$ becomes the commercial banks' "markup factor" over cost, which fixes the interest they receive on their current loans and therefore determines their current profitability.[55]

Because the money supply is partly endogenous in the model developed here, the classical, new classical, and monetarist proposition that the direction of causality between changes in the money supply and similarly directed changes in the price level runs only from the former to the latter need no longer be so. Certainly the central bank can still attempt to, say, enlarge the money supply through buying IOUs on the open market, lowering the discount rate, or lowering the reserve requirement. And, to the extent that the demand for goods is thereby

---

[55]See Vickers [14].

increased, the price level may rise.[56] But causality may also go in the opposite direction; that is, a change in the price level could result in a change in the money supply. For example, as described at the end of the previous section, a rise in W could lead to a larger value of P. Were X and the overall velocity of circulation of money (n. 31 on p. 355) to remain constant, then the demand for money would have to increase to finance the purchase of X at the higher prices. And this could bring forth a higher interest rate, an expanded money supply, or both.

In any case, the money supply (*i.e.*, the total money stock) actually realized in the economy during any period t may, upon specification of the relevant parameter values, be calculated either from the appropriate, although unspecified, equations representing the macro-money market or from the stock of money in period $t - 1$ and the change in that stock in period t implied by the aggregate of realized spending on goods, labor, and bonds. Alternatively, the same result would obtain upon substitution of the proper realized variable values into the relevant generalized version of equation (11.4-3) in the micromodel of Chapter 11 that allows for many consumers, firms, and banks. Moreover, it is clear that the other variable values realized during period t in such a suitably generalized micromodel must necessarily, when correctly summed, be identical to the associated macrovariable values realized in that period.[57] And this is so even though the macrorelations are analogues rather than sums of their microeconomic counterparts. Evidently, the present macroeconomic construction provides a different vision of the same underlying reality than the microeconomic models, such as that of Chapter 11, from which, by analogy, it springs.

Finally, it should be remembered that in the course of constructing the present macromodel, a number of structural relations involving

---

[56]Note, however, that the classical equation of exchange asserting, in its most restrictive form, that variations in the price level are proportional to alterations in the money supply, is not relevant in the present model because, due to the nonneutrality of money and wealth effects, changes in the money supply are likely to force modifications in real output, the overall velocity of circulation (n. 31 on p. 355) via asset portfolio adjustments, and their ratio.

[57]That is, coherent aggregation of realized variable values is an actual fact after those variable values have been realized. But, as indicated in Chapter 7, there is no way to describe analytically that aggregation in terms of appropriate behavioral functions of unrealized variables before hand.

important decision-based variables have been specified, and that, at every stage, the significant feature of these relations lies in the qualitative or causal interdependencies that are represented in them. No thoughts suggesting or implying that such relations necessarily assume unchanging functional forms are entertained. Indeed, the spirit of the macromodel developed here places much heavier weight on the likely instability through time of whatever decision-reflecting relations are introduced rather than on the constancy across time of any particular form in which those relations are postulated.

12.6   References

1. Arrow, K. J., "Samuelson Collected," *Journal of Political Economy* 75 (1967), pp. 730-737.

2. Clower, R. W., "The Keynesian Counter-Revolution: A Theoretical Appraisal," in *The Theory of Interest Rates*, F. H. Hahn and F. P. R. Brechling, eds. (London: Macmillan, 1965), pp. 103-125.

3. Davidson, P., and E. Smolensky, *Aggregate Supply and Demand Analysis* (New York: Harper and Row, 1964).

4. Friedman, M., "The Quantity Theory of Money – A Restatement," in *Studies in the Quantity Theory of Money,* M. Friedman, ed. (Chicago: University of Chicago Press, 1956), pp. 3-21.

5. Hoover, K. D., *The New Classical Macroeconomics* (Oxford: Basil Blackwell, 1988).

6. Patinkin, D., *Money, Interest, and Prices* (Evanston: Row Peterson, 1956).

7. Samuelson, P. A., *Economics*, 11th ed. (New York: McGraw-Hill, 1980).

8. Schumpeter, J. A., *History of Economic Analysis* (New York: Oxford University Press, 1954).

9. Shackle, G. L. S., "Keynes and Today's Establishment in Economic Theory: A View," *Journal of Economic Literature* 11 (1973), pp. 516-519.

10. Vickers, D., *Studies in the Theory of Money, 1690-1776* (Philadelphia: Chilton, 1959).

11. ———, *Financial Markets in the Capitalist Process* (Philadelphia: University of Pennsylvania Press, 1978).

12. ———, *Money, Banking, and the Macroeconomy* (Englewood Cliffs: Prentice-Hall, 1985).

13. ———, "Aggregate Supply and the Producers's Expected Demand Curve: Performance and Change in the Macroeconomy," *Journal of Post Keynesian Economics* 10 (1987-88), pp. 84-104.

14. ———, "The Monetary and the Real: Sectoral Interdependence and Market Outcomes," in *Post-Keynesian Economic Theory*, P. Wells, ed. (Boston: Kluwer, 1995), pp. 49-72.

15. Weintraub, E. R., *Microfoundations* (Cambridge: Cambridge University Press, 1979).

16. Weintraub, S., *An Approach to the Theory of Income Distribution* (Philadelphia: Chilton, 1958).

17. ———, *A Keynesian Theory of Employment, Growth, and Income Distribution* (Philadelphia: Chilton, 1966).

PART IV

Theory and Observation

CHAPTER 13

History

It is commonplace that history has an impact on present behavior. Events such as the discovery of America, the Industrial Revolution, the two World Wars and, most recently, the decline of communism and the collapse of the Soviet empire have each, in their turn, changed lives in such a way as to make a reversion to pre-existing worlds impossible. One would have expected, then, that the outgrowth of historical effects, or the consequences of values that variables have taken on in the past, would, as a matter of course, be explicitly accounted for in economic analysis. But it is only recently that the importance of making a place for history in analytical thinking has begun to be recognized by economists. To illustrate the nature of that acknowledgment, Georgescu-Roegen [8] has argued that an individual's demand for goods might depend on his past experience. In particular, temporary price and (or) income changes causing a reallocation of purchases could, as a result of his experience with the new purchases, bring about a permanent change in his preferences. Even with the old prices and income restored, then, the individual would not return to his original position. And Phelps [12, pp. xxii, 77-80] has suggested that the natural rate of unemployment depends, in an analogous manner, on the history of unemployment actually experienced in moving from one steady state to another.[1] Indeed, according to Georgescu-Roegen [9, p. 126], history is so significant in arriving at understandings of economic happenings that

---

[1]Further examples in the areas of industrial organization, international trade, and labor economics are surveyed by Franz [7, pp. 115-121].

This chapter is reproduced, with considerable additions, corrections, and other modifications, from my "Some Notes on the Role of History and the Definition of Hysteresis and Related Concepts in Economic Analysis," *Journal of Post Keynesian Economics* 15 (1993), pp. 323-345.

". . . no search for a complete description of . . . [such] phenomena can avoid . . . [it]."

By this time, it should be abundantly clear that Georgescu-Roegen's admonition is one of the pillars on which nonequilibrium analysis rests. For, in point of fact, previous discussion has made repeated reference, both explicitly and implicitly, to the prominence of history in the understanding of economic reality that nonequilibrium analysis constructs. The present chapter explores several aspects of the role of history in building explanation in greater detail.

Now, the importance of history in the contemplation of economic matters notwithstanding, it is still the case that ". . . the past itself cannot have influence upon the present over and above the influence that is mediated by the traces left by the past in the present."[2] Present behavior, that is to say, is determined by present decisions based on present relationships among present variables and parameters, even though the present relationships and present parameter values might have emerged, in part, from history. The crucial question concerns the manner in which the "traces left by the past" are manifested, or thought to be manifested, in the present.

In the mainstream of contemporary economics, with its equilibrium or disequilibrium approach and its assumptions of logical time and perfect knowledge, the notion of hysteresis has been introduced to conceptualize these traces of the past in connection with the variable values produced by an economic system. In a typical approach, hysteresis is said to be present if, as described in the example of the consumer above, the removal of a temporary change imposed on a system does not restore the variables determined by that system to their original values.[3] One common way to incorporate temporary change in an economic system is to build into its texture the possibility of random shocks. In such a case, then, hysteresis arises when the variable values created by the system depend, in addition to its relations and parameters, on the history of the shocks.

But it turns out that this definition does not exactly capture the same idea as what could be referred to as its "practical" version as

---

[2]Elster [3, p. 373 (italics removed)].
[3]Cross and Hutchinson [2, p. 3].

applied to, say, a first-order, linear, periodic equation that contains a shock term within its structure. For, although hysteresis is usually said to be present with respect to the latter when the equation possesses a "unit root,"[4] the existence of the unit root is not the only circumstance in which the variable values produced by that equation are colored by the values of past shocks.[5] Thus the meaning of hysteresis and the manner in which history affects variable values under conditions of logical time and perfect knowledge is not yet completely understood.

To use as a foil against which to compare and contrast, this chapter begins with an exploration of these and related notions as they arise in the more traditional settings of equilibrium and disequilibrium analysis that incorporate logical time and perfect knowledge. In particular, Section 13.1 investigates the role of history in systems of periodic equations with random shocks in great detail and then defines two concepts of hysteresis in that framework. To keep matters simple, only a single first-order, linear equation is studied.[6] While doing so, a comparison to the notion of hysteresis in the physical sciences and engineering is made, the possibility of "removing" the effects of history by "differencing" is entertained, and the ideas of integrated and cointegrated variables are briefly discussed. Readers interested in avoiding mathematical details may omit the proofs of Theorems 13.1-8, 13.1-10, and 13.1-11, along with the last quarter of the section starting, roughly, at equation (13.1-15).

With the foil in place, Section 13.2 then resets the environment in which the concepts of hysteresis are characterized and the impact of history is felt by substituting the historical time and ignorance requirements of nonequilibrium analysis in place of the logical time and perfect knowledge foundations upon which typical systems of periodic equations rest. In addition, clearly, and as described and illustrated in earlier chapters, the periodic equations themselves, at least in their standard interpretations, have to be discarded in favor of different kinds

---

[4]*E.g.*, Franz [7, p. 110] or Wyplosz [16, p. 124].

[5]This fact may lie at the heart of Flemming's confessed uncertainty about ". . . whether a temporary effect as well as a permanent effect qualifies as hysteresis" [5, p. ix].

[6]Thus, in particular, hysteresis in nonlinear, periodic equations and in differential equations is ignored.

of systems. But the result is a much simpler and more natural way of thinking about hysteresis and history in economic analysis. It is more natural because actual history occurs in historical – not logical – time, and it is simpler because additional structure in the form of shocks and their properties does not have to be introduced to account for the impact of that history.

13.1 Hysteresis from a Traditional Vantage Point

Suppose x_t, where $t = 0, 1, 2, \ldots$, is a real, scalar variable, and let ε_t be independent, scalar, random variables whose expected values, $E(\varepsilon_t) = 0$, and variances, $var(\varepsilon_t) = \sigma^2$, for $t = 1, 2, \ldots$. Consider the first-order, linear, periodic equation

$$x_t = \alpha x_{t-1} + \varepsilon_t, \tag{13.1-1}$$

where $\alpha \neq 0$ is a real number and $t = 1, 2, \ldots$. With the initial value x_0 specified, the solution or time path of (13.1-1) is given by

$$x_t = \alpha^t x_0 + \sum_{n=1}^{t} \alpha^{t-n} \varepsilon_n \tag{13.1-2}$$

for $t = 1, 2, \ldots$. Thus the past history of shocks, that is, the values of $\varepsilon_1, \ldots, \varepsilon_{t-1}$, plus the value of the present shock ε_t, affect the value of x_t, for all $t \geq 1$, regardless of the value of α.

Now consider the *first differences* $\Delta x_t = x_t - x_{t-1}$ for $t \geq 1$. Upon substitution from (13.1-2), the time path of first differences determined by (13.1-1) is seen to be

$$\Delta x_t = (\alpha - 1)\left(\alpha^{t-1} x_0 + \sum_{n=1}^{t-1} \alpha^{t-1-n} \varepsilon_n \right) + \varepsilon_t, \tag{13.1-3}$$

where $t = 1, 2, \ldots$. It follows that, for any $t \geq 1$, the past history of shocks affects Δx_t as long as $\alpha \neq 1$. When $\alpha = 1$, equation (13.1-3) reduces to $\Delta x_t = \varepsilon_t$ and, for all t, Δx_t depends only on the shock at time t.

Recall, from Section 1.2, that a time path is stationary whenever there exists a real number $\bar{x}$ such that $x_t = \bar{x}$, for all t. Supposing $\varepsilon_t = \bar{\varepsilon}$, for $t = 1, 2, \ldots$, every stationary time path of (13.1-1) must meet the condition that

$$\bar{x} - \alpha\bar{x} = \bar{\varepsilon}.$$

A value of α that satisfies this equation is called a *root*. Provided that the equation does not have a *unit* root, that is, as long as $\alpha \neq 1$, the stationary path is uniquely determined from

$$\bar{x} = \frac{\bar{\varepsilon}}{1 - \alpha}.$$

Otherwise, in the unit-root situation, when $\alpha = 1$, no unique stationary path can exist. Indeed, with $\alpha = 1$ and $\varepsilon_t = \bar{\varepsilon} = 0$, for $t = 1, 2, \ldots$, equation (13.1-1) becomes $x_t = x_{t-1}$, and every value of x_0 defines a stationary path. In the general case in which the conditions $x_t = \bar{x}$ and $\varepsilon_t = \bar{\varepsilon}$ for all t are not imposed, if $\alpha = 1$, then equation (13.1-1) is still said to have a unit root. Hence the presence of a unit root in that equation eliminates history from the determination of the first differences Δx_t in (13.1-3) but, as a consequence of (13.1-2), does not remove history as a determining factor of x_t.

Note also that if a constant $\beta \neq 0$ were added to (13.1-1), so that

$$x_t = \alpha x_{t-1} + \beta + \varepsilon_t \qquad (13.1\text{-}4)$$

for $t = 1, 2, \ldots$, then in the unit-root case, (13.1-2) would become

$$x_t = x_0 + t\beta + \sum_{n=1}^{t} \varepsilon_n. \qquad (13.1\text{-}5)$$

Here the term $x_0 + t\beta$ represents a linear trend around which x_t moves depending on the sums of past and present shocks.

Consider next the random variable

$$\xi_t = \sum_{n=1}^{t} \alpha^{t-n} \varepsilon_n,$$

which identifies, in part (since it also includes the present shock ε_t), the impact of the history of past shocks on x_t in (13.1-2) for each t. It will be convenient in subsequent discussion to refer to ξ_t as recording the impact of the history of past shocks on x_t alone, without reference to the presence of ε_t. This, however, is an abbreviated reference only and does not signify the removal of the term ε_t from ξ_t. Because, by assumption, the ε_n are independently distributed random variables with means $E(\varepsilon_n) = 0$ and $\text{var}(\varepsilon_n) = \sigma^2$, it can be shown that $E(\xi_t) = 0$ and

$$\text{var}(\xi_t) = \sigma^2\left(\sum_{n=1}^{t} \alpha^{2(t-n)}\right) = \sigma^2\left(\frac{1 - \alpha^{2t}}{1 - \alpha^2}\right), \qquad (13.1\text{-}6)$$

where $t = 1, 2, \ldots$. Hence

$$\lim_{t \to \infty} E(\xi_t) = 0$$

for all real α and

$$\lim_{t \to \infty} \text{var}(\xi_t) = \begin{cases} \sigma^2/(1 - \alpha), & 0 < |\alpha| < 1, \\ \infty, & |\alpha| \geq 1. \end{cases} \qquad (13.1\text{-}7)$$

Moreover, from (13.1-2), $E(x_t) = \alpha^t x_0$ and $\text{var}(x_t) = \text{var}(\xi_t)$. Therefore, in any future period t, although neither the size of "past" shocks nor their weights in (13.1-2) effect the expected value of x_t, the weights still influence the variance. When $0 < |\alpha| < 1$, however, the impact of the weights on $\text{var}(x_t)$ is finite for each t and limited (bounded) as $t \to \infty$.

But of much greater significance is the probability (written P) that ξ_t or the impact of shock history on x_t in (13.1-2) remains bounded as t becomes large. Assertions concerning this probability are contained in the following three propositions.

Theorem 13.1-8. *Let $0 < |\alpha| < 1$. Then for any real number δ, where $0 < \delta < 1$, there exists another real number b, where $0 < b < \infty$, such that*

$$P(|\xi_t| < b) \geq 1 - \delta$$

for all $t = 1, 2, \ldots$.

Proof:
By Chebychev's inequality[7] in conjunction with (13.1-6),

$$P(|\xi_t| \ge b) \le \frac{\sigma^2}{b^2}\left(\frac{1 - \alpha^{2t}}{1 - \alpha^2}\right) \qquad (13.1\text{-}9)$$

for any $b > 0$ and any $t > 0$. Now let δ be given such that $0 < \delta < 1$. Set

$$b = \left[\frac{\sigma^2}{\delta(1 - \alpha^2)}\right]^{\frac{1}{2}}.$$

Then substituting this value for b into (13.1-9) and noting that $0 < |\alpha| < 1$ gives, for $t > 0$,

$$P(|\xi_t| \ge b) \le \delta(1 - \alpha^{2t}) < \delta.$$

Therefore

$$P(|\xi_t| < b) \ge 1 - \delta$$

for all $t = 1, 2, \dots$.

Q.E.D.

In other words, and in the sense described by the theorem, for any t, the probability that ξ_t or the impact of history on x_t in (13.1-2) is bounded, where the bound is independent of t, can be made as close to unity as desired.

Theorem 13.1-10. *Let $\alpha = 1$ and suppose, in addition to the previous assumption that they are independently distributed with zero means and the same finite variance, that the ε_n are identically distributed for every n. Then for any $b > 0$,*

$$\lim_{t \to \infty} P(|\xi_t| \le b) = 0.$$

---

[7]*E.g.*, Chung [1, p. 48].

Proof:

With $\alpha = 1$ and $t = 1, 2, \ldots$, $E(\xi_t) = 0$ as before and, using the middle expression in (13.1-6), $\mathrm{var}(\xi_t) = t\sigma^2$. Since the ξ_t are independently and identically distributed, the Central Limit Theorem[8] implies that the distribution of

$$Z_t = \frac{\xi_t}{\sigma\sqrt{t}}$$

is asymptotically normal with mean zero and variance one. Denote the limiting random variable by Z.

Now let $t_0 > 1$ be fixed and consider any $b > 0$. Then, for all $t \geq t_0$,

$$P(|\xi_t| \leq b) = P\left(Z_t \leq \frac{b}{\sigma\sqrt{t}}\right) \leq P\left(Z_t \leq \frac{b}{\sigma\sqrt{t_0}}\right).$$

Hence, since Z is normally distributed with mean zero and variance one,

$$\lim_{t\to\infty} \sup\ P(|\xi_t| \leq b) \leq P\left(Z \leq \frac{b}{\sigma\sqrt{t_0}}\right) = \frac{1}{\sqrt{2\pi}} \int_{-b/\sigma\sqrt{t_0}}^{b/\sigma\sqrt{t_0}} e^{-z^2/2}\, dz.$$

By choosing t_0 large, the integral on the right becomes small, establishing the conclusion of the theorem.

Q.E.D.

Theorem 13.1-11. *Let $|\alpha| > 1$ or $\alpha = -1$, and suppose, in addition to the assumption that they are independently distributed with the same zero mean and the same finite variance, that the ε_n are all normally distributed with that zero mean and variance σ^2. Then, for any $b > 0$,*

$$\lim_{t\to\infty} P(|\xi_t| \leq b) = 0.$$

Proof:

Since, for $n = 1, 2, \ldots$, the ε_n are independently and normally distributed with mean zero and variance σ^2, it follows[9] that ξ_t is normally

---

[8] *Ibid.*, pp. 169-170.

[9] *E.g.*, Wilks [15, p. 158].

distributed with mean zero and variance s^2 where, as in (13.1-6),

$$s^2 = \text{var}(\xi_t) = \sigma^2 \left(\frac{1 - \alpha^{2t}}{1 - \alpha^2} \right).$$

Hence

$$P(|\xi_t| \leq b) = \frac{1}{s\sqrt{2\pi}} \int_{-b}^{b} e^{-\zeta^2/2s^2} \, d\zeta.$$

Making the change of variable $y = \zeta/s$, this becomes

$$P(|\xi_t| \leq b) = \frac{1}{\sqrt{2\pi}} \int_{-b/s}^{b/s} e^{-y^2/2} \, dy,$$

which approaches zero as $t \to \infty$ because, in light of (13.1-7) with $|\alpha| \geq 1$, $s \to \infty$ as $t \to \infty$.

Q.E.D.

Theorems 13.1-10 and 13.1-11 assert that, under their respective hypotheses, the probability that shock history has a bounded impact on x_t in (13.1-2) approaches zero as t becomes large. These and previous results describe the manner in which the history of past shocks affects the time path of x_t as generated by the first-order, linear, periodic equation (13.1-1). Clearly, past shocks have influence over x_t no matter what the value of α. (It has been assumed, recall, that $\alpha \neq 0$.) Only with respect to the time-path of first differences (13.1-3), and only in the unit-root case, does history lose its impact on the present.

Consider, then, the notion of hysteresis in terms of the periodic equation (13.1-1). If hysteresis were characterized, as suggested earlier, as a situation in which the removal of each shock ε_n in the period immediately after it is introduced, a phenomenon that occurs for all shocks ε_n as described in (13.1-2), does not restore the variable x_t to its original value, then equation (13.1-1) would exhibit hysteresis for all nonzero values of α. For, given $\hat{n}$, setting $\varepsilon_n = 0$ where $n \neq \hat{n}$ in (13.1-2),

$$x_t = \alpha^t x_0 + \alpha^{t-\hat{n}} \varepsilon_{\hat{n}}$$

for all $t \geq \hat{n}$. Hence, as long as t remains finite, the term $\alpha^{t-\hat{n}} \varepsilon_{\hat{n}}$, that is, the effect of the shock in period $\hat{n}$, is always present. Asserting that (13.1-1) exhibits hysteresis in the sense described above, then, does not distinguish one manifestation of (13.1-1) from any other. Hysteresis is present in (13.1-1) for all $\alpha \neq 0$ because the past history of shocks irreversibly influences all "present" and "future" values of x_t for all $\alpha \neq 0$, that is, the concept of hysteresis is synonymous with the general idea that traces of the past color the present. Refer to this notion as *general* hysteresis. Evidently general hysteresis arises in both long-run and short-run contexts. Observe, however, that if $|\alpha| < 1$, then the impact of $\varepsilon_{\hat{n}}$ becomes smaller as t increases and, in the limit, it vanishes. This suggests that a more specific notion of hysteresis could be identified in the long run as one that excludes such a case. More precisely, define *specific* (long-run) hysteresis as a situation in which the effects of past shocks do not approach zero as $t \rightarrow \infty$. Note that the existence of specific hysteresis always implies the presence of general hysteresis in the long run but not conversely.

Clearly, under the proposed definition, the first-order, linear, periodic equation (13.1-1) exhibits specific hysteresis when $|\alpha| \geq 1$. That is, the influence of each nonzero shock ε_n is "permanent" in the sense that it does not die out as t becomes large. Moreover, in this situation, the value of $|\alpha|$ can serve as a measure of the specific hysteresis in (13.1-1): the larger $|\alpha|$, the greater the effect of each nonzero ε_n as t, where $t \geq n$, increases, and the more hysteresis, or the stronger the effect of shock history on x_t. In the special unit-root case where $\alpha = 1$, equation (13.1-1) may be said to exhibit *minimal* (specific) hysteresis.

As suggested at the outset, the term "hysteresis" has been employed in the economics literature to mean both general and minimal specific hysteresis. The situation in which $0 < \alpha < 1$, a special case of general (but not specific) hysteresis, has also been referred to as "persistence."[10] In addition, other phrases, such as, for example, "partial hysteresis" and "pure hysteresis," either represent, or may be interpreted as representing, the circumstances analogous to those in which $0 < \alpha < 1$ and $\alpha = 1$, respectively.[11]

It is interesting that the notion of hysteresis, as it arises in the physical sciences and engineering, has a rather distinct flavor from that

---

[10]*E.g.*, Franz [6, p. 94] and Wyplosz [16, pp. 124-126].

[11]Such an interpretation of partial and pure hysteresis is consistent with the usage of Layard, Nickell, and Jackman [10, pp. 336,374,375].

associated with its typical appearances in economics described above. Interpret ε_t as representing the amount of a "force" applied to an object (the force will continue to be referred to as a shock below) and interpret x_t to be the object's (quantitative) response.[12] Rather than being subject to random variation, suppose ε_t and x_t vary cyclically over time according to respective functions that depend on t. Then eliminating t from the latter relations (assuming it can be done), yields a separate relation between ε_t and x_t, which is independent of t, and whose graph in ε-x space (the subscripts t are dropped here since they are no longer of any significance) comprises one or more "hysteretic loops."[13] Conversely, a given hysteretic loop (such as points on the unit circle in the example of n. 13 at the bottom of this page) may often be decomposed into dynamic relations that cyclically determine ε_t and x_t as functions of t. In either case, as time moves on, the cyclical behavior of ε_t and x_t generates movement along the hysteretic loop or loops. This is illustrated in Figure 13-1 in which it is assumed that t rises through the (not necessarily successive) values $t^0 < t^1 < t^2 < t^3 < t^4$, and the coordinates of the points in the ε-x plane labeled $t^0, \ldots, t^4$ are the values of (ε_t, x_t) found from the dynamic relations at those values of t. The diagram also supposes that there is only one loop and at some $t^5 > t^4$, $(\varepsilon_{t^5}, x_{t^5}) = (\varepsilon_{t^0}, x_{t^0})$. Hysteresis is present in the sense that increasing the shock from, say, ε_{t^0} to ε_{t^1}, so as to move from $t = t^0$ to $t = t^1$, increases x_t from $x_{t^0} = 0$ to $x_{t^1} > 0$, but then removing the increase in the shock to go back to $\varepsilon_{t^2} = \varepsilon_{t^0}$ does not return x_t to $x_{t^0} = 0$, but changes it instead to $x_{t^2} > 0$. In this way the past history of shocks influences the value of x_t and a form of general hysteresis is present.

In addition to the above, there are also highly specialized conditions under which equation (13.1-1) or (13.1-2) may be viewed as defining a hysteretic loop. To illustrate, take $\alpha = 1$ and assume that the behavior of ε_t and x_t over time is nonrandom and may be expressed as functions of t according to Table 13-1, where $\varepsilon_t = \varepsilon_{t+8}$ and $x_t = x_{t+8}$, for all t. Then (13.1-1) and (13.1-2) are satisfied and the hysteretic loop derived from the functions in Table 13-1 appears as the points labeled $t = 0$,

---

[12]See, for example, Lazan [11, pp. 16-19].
[13]For example, if $\varepsilon_t = \sin t$ and $x_t = \cos t$, then eliminating t gives $(\varepsilon_t)^2 + (x_t)^2 = 1$, and the points (ε_t, x_t) of the single loop so obtained lie on the unit circle.

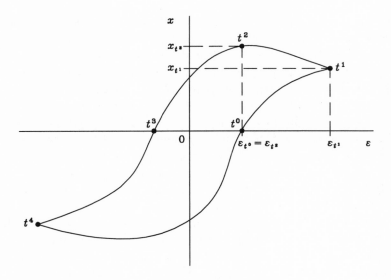

Figure 13–1.   Movement along a hysteretic loop

$t = 1, \ldots, t = 8$ in Figure 13-2. But even so it is clear that the physical science and engineering concept of hysteresis, like that examined in the milieu of historical time and ignorance in the next section, is generally set in a quite different environment, with a different formal structure, than the economist's standard notions, which, in the present discussion, are framed in the context of (13.1-1) with ε_t as a random variable.

Return now to that latter context. As an application of the ideas developed here, it is worth observing that the typical characterizations of integrated and cointegrated variables may be interpreted as implicitly incorporating an assumption of minimal hysteresis. Before defining these notions, it is first necessary to introduce the following concept: remembering that the variance of ε_t has been assumed finite, the random variable ε_t is called *stationary*[14] if and only if its distribution does not depend on t. Thus the ε_t in (13.1-1) are stationary provided that,

---

[14]See, for example, Stock and Watson [13, p. 149n].

TABLE 13-1. Illustration of Equations (13.1-1) and (13.1-2) with Nonrandom ϵ_t

t	x_t	ϵ_t
0	0	–
1	1	1
2	3	2
3	4	1
4	4	0
5	3	-1
6	1	-2
7	0	-1
8	0	0

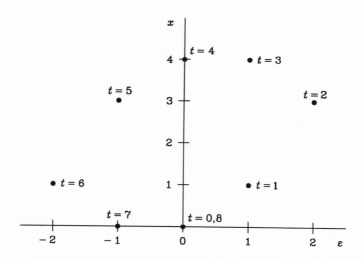

Figure 13-2. Hysteretic loop generated by (13.1-1).

in addition to being independent (as hypothesized at the outset), they are also identically distributed. Now, the variable x_t is referred to as *integrated of order one*[15] whenever x_t is nonstationary and

$$\Delta x_t = \beta + \varepsilon_t, \qquad (13.1\text{-}12)$$

where $E(\varepsilon_t) = 0$, $\text{var}(\varepsilon_t) = \sigma^2$, and ε_t is stationary, for $t = 1, 2, \ldots$. Evidently, adding the constant β to (13.1-1) as in (13.1-4), assuming minimal hysteresis ($\alpha = 1$), and supposing, in addition to earlier assumptions, that the ε_t are identically distributed yields equation (13.1-12) with the properties required of ε_t in that equation intact. Therefore, under these conditions, x_t in (13.1-1) is integrated of order one and x_t moves about the trend $x_0 + t\beta$ as described in (13.1-5). Using (13.1-4) as its underlying structure, then, x_t is integrated of order one if minimal hysteresis is present or, equivalently, if the effects of past shocks, that is, its history, can be removed by taking first differences.

Of course, some equations will require differencing more than once to eliminate the history of past shocks. For example, consider the second-order, linear, periodic equation obtained by replacing x_t and x_{t-1} by, respectively, Δx_t and Δx_{t-1} in (13.1-1):

$$x_t = (\alpha + 1)x_{t-1} - \alpha x_{t-2} + \varepsilon_t, \qquad (13.1\text{-}13)$$

where $t = 2, 3, \ldots$. Then the solution of (13.1-13) will include the history of past shocks, as does the solution of the equation secured upon returning to first differences in (13.1-13), namely,

$$\Delta x_t = \alpha \Delta x_{t-1} + \varepsilon_t.$$

Analogously to (13.1-1) and (13.1-2), the solution of the latter, given x_0 and x_1, is

$$\Delta x_t = \alpha^{t-1}\Delta x_1 + \sum_{n=2}^{t} \alpha^{t-n}\varepsilon_n \qquad (13.1\text{-}14)$$

for $t = 2, 3, \ldots$. Continuing the analogy by taking *second differences*, that is, letting $\Delta^2 x_t = \Delta x_t - \Delta x_{t-1}$, for $t \geq 2$, and substituting from (13.1-14),

$$\Delta^2 x_t = (\alpha - 1)\left(\alpha^{t-2}\Delta x_1 + \sum_{n=2}^{t-1} \alpha^{t-1-n}\varepsilon_n\right) + \varepsilon_t,$$

---

[15] *Ibid.*, p. 151n.

where $t = 2, 3, \ldots$. Thus the impact of past shocks on x_t in (13.1-13) can only be removed by going to second differences and setting $\alpha = 1$. Note, however, that since the solution of (13.1-13) contains the terms $(A_{nt} + 1)\varepsilon_n$, for $n = 1, \ldots, t$, where A_{nt} is a polynomial in α that depends on t, there is no value of α such that the influence of each ε_n on x_t dies out as $t \to \infty$. Under the above definitions, then, equation (13.1-13) exhibits both general and specific hysteresis.

In general, kth-*order differences* are given by $\Delta^k x_t = \Delta^{k-1} x_t - \Delta^{k-1} x_{t-1}$, where $t = k, k+1, \ldots$. By repeatedly replacing first x_t and x_{t-1} in (13.1-1) by Δx_t and Δx_{t-1}, then x_t, x_{t-1}, and x_{t-2} in (13.1-10) by $\Delta^2 x_t$, $\Delta^2 x_{t-1}$ and $\Delta^2 x_{t-2}$, and so on, a kth-order, linear, periodic equation can be built up in which the history of past shocks is eliminated only upon taking differences up to order k to secure the equations

$$\Delta^k x_t = (\alpha - 1)\left(\alpha^{t-k}\Delta^{k-1} x_{k-1} + \sum_{n=k}^{t-1} \alpha^{t-1-n}\varepsilon_n\right) + \varepsilon_t,$$

for all $t \geq k$, and requiring $\alpha = 1$. It is clear, however, that the removal of history in this way is only possible in highly specialized circumstances such as those relations built up from (13.1-1) described here. Most periodic equations (linear or otherwise) will not, in general, permit it. And practically all such equations will exhibit both general and specific hysteresis.

Nevertheless, for the case in which the kth-order, linear, periodic equation is constructed from (13.1-1) as set forth above, integrated variables of higher orders may be defined. Thus x_t is *integrated of order* k when it must be differenced k times to obtain an equation analogous to (13.1-12), that is,

$$\Delta^k x_t = \beta + \varepsilon_t,$$

where $E(\varepsilon_t) = 0$, $\text{var}(\varepsilon_t) = \sigma^2$, ε_t is stationary, and $t = k, k+1, \ldots$.[16] Evidently the structural requirements underlying this notion even when $k = 1$ are, as identified above, rather severe.

Return, again, to the first-order, linear, periodic equation as it appears in (13.1-4) with a trend. To discuss the idea of cointegrated variables, it will be useful to introduce two preliminary lemmas. The

---

[16] *Ibid.*

first is quite obvious and its proof is omitted. Let ε_t and η_t be independently, nonidentically distributed random variables such that

$$E(\varepsilon_t) = 0, \quad \mathrm{var}\,(\varepsilon_t) = \sigma_\varepsilon^2,$$

$$E(\eta_t) = 0, \quad \mathrm{var}\,(\eta_t) = \sigma_\eta^2, \tag{13.1-15}$$

for $t = 1, 2, \ldots.$ Take u and v to be arbitrary real numbers.

Lemma 13.1-16. *If ε_t and η_t are stationary for all t, then so is $u\varepsilon_t + v\eta_t$.*

Lemma 13.1-17. *If x_t is integrated of order one, and η_t is stationary for all t, then $ux_t + v\eta_t$ is also integrated of order one.*

Proof:
Since x_t is integrated of order one,

$$\Delta x_t = \beta + \varepsilon_t,$$

where $E(\varepsilon_t) = 0$, $\mathrm{var}\,(\varepsilon_t) = \sigma_\varepsilon^2$, and ε_t is stationary for all t. Hence

$$\Delta(ux_t + v\eta_t) = u\Delta x_t + v\Delta\eta_t = u\beta + u\varepsilon_t + v[\eta_t - \eta_{t-1}].$$

Observe that $u\beta$ is a constant term, and $u\varepsilon_t + v[\eta_t - \eta_{t-1}]$ is a random variable for which

$$E(u\varepsilon_t + v[\eta_t - \eta_{t-1}]) = uE(\varepsilon_t) + v[E(\eta_t) - E(\eta_{t-1})] = 0$$

and

$$\mathrm{var}\,(u\varepsilon_t + v[\eta_t - \eta_{t-1}]) = u^2\mathrm{var}\,(\varepsilon_t) + v^2[\mathrm{var}\,(\eta_t) - \mathrm{var}\,(\eta_{t-1})],$$

$$= u^2\sigma_e^2 + 2v^2\sigma_\eta^2,$$

thus satisfying the implicit requirement for stationarity that $\mathrm{var}\,(u\varepsilon_t + v[\eta_t - \eta_{t-1}])$ be finite. Moreover, since ε_t, η_t, and η_{t-1} are all stationary, by invoking Lemma 13.1-16 twice, so are $\eta_t - \eta_{t-1}$ and, hence, $u\varepsilon_t + v[\eta_t - \eta_{t-1}]$. Therefore x_t is integrated of order one.

Q.E.D.

Consider two variables x_t and y_t. If x_t and y_t are both integrated of order one, and if there exist real numbers u and v such that $ux_t + vy_t$ is stationary for all t, then x_t and y_t are said to be *cointegrated*.[17] To illustrate, suppose x_0 is given and

$$x_t = x_{t-1} + \beta + \varepsilon_t,$$

$$y_t = \gamma(x_{t-1} + \beta) + \eta_t,$$

$$(13.1\text{-}18)$$

where ε_t and η_t, for $t = 1, 2, \ldots$, are stationary with means and variances as indicated in (13.1-15), and $\gamma \neq 0$ and β are real numbers. Then x_t is integrated of order one. Since it is a linear combination of $(x_{t-1} + \beta)$, which is integrated of order one (Lemma 13.1-17 with $u = v = 1$ and $\eta_t = \beta$ for all t), and η_t, which is stationary, y_t is also integrated of order one by Lemma 13.1-17. Furthermore, for all t and any u,

$$ux_t - \frac{u}{\gamma} y_t = u\varepsilon_t - \frac{u}{\gamma} \eta_t \qquad (13.1\text{-}19)$$

is stationary since ε_t and η_t are stationary (Lemma 13.1-16). Therefore, in this case, x_t and y_t are cointegrated.

Note that the solution of (13.1-18) is given by

$$x_t = x_0 + t\beta + \sum_{n=1}^{t} \varepsilon_n, \qquad (13.1\text{-}20)$$

$$y_t = \gamma \left[x_0 + (t-1)\beta + \sum_{n=1}^{t-1} \varepsilon_n \right] + \eta_t, \qquad (13.1\text{-}21)$$

where $t = 1, 2, \ldots$. Clearly η_t is a temporary disturbance. Unlike the ε_n, it has no lasting effect on either x_t or y_t. Past shock history in this example, which, excluding ε_t, is the same for both x_t and y_t, is removed from them by first differencing, that is,

$$\Delta x_t = \beta + \varepsilon_t \qquad \text{and} \qquad \Delta y_t = \gamma\beta + \gamma\varepsilon_{t-1} + \eta_t$$

for all t, and from linear combinations of them according to (13.1-19). (Observe that even with the presence of $\gamma\varepsilon_{t-1}$ in Δy_t shock history is still eliminated because Δy_t is defined in terms of periods t and $t - 1$.)

---

[17]*Ibid.*, p. 164.

In general, random variables that are stationary tend, since their variances are finite, to stay "close" to their means. Integrated variables of order one, which remain near their trends – not their means – can vary much more, since their variances, that is, the variance of ξ_t, become large as $t \to \infty$, but their first differences, being stationary, cannot. If these integrated variables are also cointegrated, then when they move around they do so together. In other words, cointegration implies a long-run relation between them. With respect to (13.1-18), and as suggested by (13.1-20) and (13.1-21), that long-run relation is

$$x_t = \frac{1}{\gamma} y_t$$

for all t. The deviations from that relation, namely, $x_t - [1/\gamma]y_t$ as calculated from (13.1-19) with $u = 1$, are stationary and, depending on $\text{var}\,(\varepsilon_t - [1/\gamma]\eta)_t$, cannot diverge too far from the mean deviation

$$E\left(\varepsilon_t - \frac{1}{\gamma}\eta_t\right) = E(\varepsilon_t) - \frac{1}{\gamma}E(\eta_t) = 0.$$

It should be pointed out that the notion of cointegrated variables can be extended to distinguish between variables that are cointegrated of various orders[18] and, in addition, has found application in econometric analysis.[19] But as with integrated variables, there is considerable structural intricacy underlying the idea of cointegration in any form. However, these structural complexities, upon which the notions of general and specific hysteresis are also based, disappear when the analytical context is transformed into the nonequilibrium-analytic realm of historical time and ignorance. Although the ideas of integrated and cointegrated variables loose their meaning and importance in such a framework, the hysteresis concepts do not. It is to this alternative approach, then, that attention now turns.

---

[18]*E.g.*, Engle and Granger [4, p. 253].
[19]*E.g.*, Stock and Watson [13, pp. 165-167].

13.2 Hysteresis in Historical Time and Ignorance

Periodic equations such as (13.1-1) and (13.1-4), which include formulations that are intended to encapsulate human behavior, generally require the presumptions that time is logical and knowledge is perfect. The significance of the latter requirements has been heretofore discussed at length. On the one hand, logical time describes only the sequencing of events through time as abstracted from the experiencing of those events. One may move back and forth through logical time, much as a machine or equation can be restarted over and over again from an initial position. On the other, knowledge is perfect in the sense that all behavior encapsulated by the equation is known to be completely described by that equation except for the error ε_t whose probability distribution is fully known. But, as has been implicitly suggested at various points in earlier chapters, when time is historical and ignorance prevails, equations like (13.1-1) and (13.1-4), to the extent they carry over, appear in this altered environment with a different meaning and significance. In particular, these equations, which may not last intact from one period to the next, are unable to project behavior into an unknown future; nor do they reflect enough knowledge to view the ε_t in terms of probability. Moreover, in arriving at the start of period t, history has determined, in part, individuals' epistemic statuses, the characteristics of each decision to be made and the decision moment each individual faces, and the institutional environment in which individuals operate. History, that is to say, brings individuals and the economy up to the point at which the next stage, that of period t, is set to emerge. In this way the traces of the past enter the present, and history has an impact on present behavior.

To illustrate, consider an investigation of the following sort: suppose, to keep things simple, there is only one variable, x_t, whose value is required to be explained for each period t. Suppose also that there is only one parameter, θ_t, that is fixed at the start of period t by what has happened in period $t - 1$, and that θ_t is thought to figure into the determination of x_t. Then, in general, to explain a sequence of outcomes, say, $x_1, \ldots, x_T$, a different model involving θ_t and x_t would be built for

each $t = 1, \ldots, T$. Moreover, the model for period t, say, would determine not only x_t but also θ_{t+1} for the next period, and the relations of
the model in period t might further influence, in some manner, those of
the model for period $t + 1$. Thus θ_t and the relations in period t explicitly inject traces of the past into the present, and x_t depends critically
on what has gone before. With respect to this particular illustration,
then, past history directly and continually colors the present.

In the special case in which the investigator arrives, with hindsight,
at the judgment that sufficient stability over past periods $t = 1, \ldots, T$
makes it reasonable to employ a single model as in Section 6.2,[20] having
a single, unchanging set of relations for all of those periods, to explain
a collection of already observed outcomes $x_1, \ldots, x_T$, or, in particular, that evidence from the past does not support rejection of the idea
that one model might suffice to illuminate the past, it follows, since x_t
depends on θ_t, and θ_t, in turn, depends on x_{t-1}, that functions such as

$$x_t = f^t(x_{t-1}, x_{t-2}, \ldots, x_0),$$

where x_0 is a parameter and $t = 1, \ldots, T$, are implied. All functions f^t
are generated by the fixed relations of the model according to a single
rule that is dictated by those relations. One possible specification of
the f^t in "stochastic" form might be (13.1-1), namely,

$$x_t = \alpha x_{t-1} + \varepsilon_t, \tag{13.2-1}$$

or its solution (13.1-2), that is,

$$x_t = \alpha^t x_0 + \sum_{n=1}^{t} \alpha^{t-n} \varepsilon_n, \tag{13.2-2}$$

where $t = 1, \ldots, T$, α is an unrestricted real number, and the ε_t are
error terms. But in the context of historical time and ignorance, these
equations need to be interpreted with care. First, the ε_n are not random
variables with associated probability distribution or density functions.
(Probabilities, remember, cannot exist.) Second, for (13.2-1) and (13.2-
2) to be meaningful, assumptions to the effect that the ε_n are nonsys-
tematic and, on average, small, have to be introduced. Otherwise, the

---

[20]Recall also the discussion of Section 1.5.

case in which $\alpha = 0$ in (13.2-1), implying that x_t is unrelated to x_{t-1}, could not be ruled out. Under such assumptions, moreover, α could be estimated with nonprobabilistic curve-fitting techniques.[21] Third, since the unexpected may occur, events might transpire at, say, the end of period T (the collapse of the Soviet empire is a dramatic example), that shatter the investigator's initial judgment of stability from period $t = 1$ onward. Generally, then, the presumption is that, with the addition of period $T + 1$ to the analytical time frame, a new system of relations, different from that used for periods $t = 1, \ldots, T$ to determine each x_t from each θ_t, would be required to explain the determination of x_{T+1} from θ_{T+1} (of course, θ_{T+1} still emerges from what actually happened in period T), and hence the relation (13.2-1) (and [13.2-2]) would break down. Even if (13.2-1) were later judged (with hindsight) to have remained in force through period $T + 1$, the presumption remains that the value of α relevant to periods $1, \ldots, T$ would be different from that appropriate to periods $1, \ldots, T + 1$. It therefore makes no sense to ask if $\alpha^{t-n}\varepsilon_n$ approaches zero as $t \to \infty$ because, with t rising above T, even if (13.2-1) were to hold up, sooner or later the value of α would change. Thus the value of α cannot be used as an indicator of specific hysteresis.

Regardless, the fact that, as indicated above, the past continually influences the present, still points to the pervasive general and specific hysteresis existing in all models of this sort. As historical time moves on, history is created period by period. To model behavior in, say, period t, is to explain the history of that period. Thus general hysteresis obtains in both long-run and short-run settings because, as reflected in the changing models from one period to the next, the steady alterations in the epistemic statuses and decision opportunities of individuals as they learn of and experience new things, and the unremitting evolution of society's institutions do not permit a return to an earlier state. And the existence, in the long run, of specific hysteresis is assured in the sense that many historical events (*e.g.*, the collapse of the Soviet empire) are so significant that, even though they cannot be explicitly accounted for in advance, their impact on the changing models and

---

[21]The problem of estimation under conditions of historical time and ignorance is considered briefly in Section 14.3.

outcomes can never completely die out. Evidently these notions of
hysteresis are visualized without a concept of time that, contrary to
the historical process, is reversible; without abstract shocks, ε_t, that
need to have certain probabilistic properties; and without requiring
equations like (13.1-1) and (13.1-4) that define explicit and unchanging
structures. The simpler and more natural way to conceive of hysteresis in economic analysis, then, is in the context of historical time and
ignorance.

It is also clear that long-run relations, such as those implicit between
cointegrated variables, are generally not relevant under conditions of
historical time and ignorance. For long-run relations are founded upon
behavioral patterns that are stable through historical time. While it is
possible, with hindsight, to observe such patterns, the presumption is
necessarily one of instability. And, in any case, there is never enough
knowledge in the present to project, with any degree of certainty, a previously stable pattern into the future. Thus long-run analysis, insofar
as it focuses on a future position toward which things gravitate, is not
viable when historical time and ignorance are taken into account.[22] Under these conditions, where a system advances at any particular point
in time depends on the path it has taken up to that point. Where
it subsequently proceeds cannot be said to be influenced by where it
is being pulled or pushed according to particular equations of motion
because those equations, as they propel variable values into the future,
cannot, in reality, be specified or known. Indeed, such equations might
not, in reality, even exist. The occurrence of the unexpected and the
kaleidic change it implies produces a unique history that is unrecogniz-
able before its time. Therefore, it is only the short-run approach that is
useful in explaining the events constituting the history that is created
from period to period; and that approach is likely to require changing
analytical structures as historical time passes.

13.3   References

1. Chung, K. L., *A Course in Probability Theory*, 2nd. ed. (New
York: Academic Press, 1974).

---

[22]See Vickers [14].

2. Cross, R., and H. Hutchinson, "Hysteresis Effects and Unemployment: an Outline," in *Unemployment, Hysteresis and the Natural Rate Hypothesis*, R. Cross, ed. (Oxford: Basil Blackwell, 1988), pp. 3-7.

3. Elster, J., "A Note on Hysteresis in the Social Sciences," *Synthese* 33 (1976), pp. 371-391.

4. Engle, R. F., and C. W. J. Granger, "Co-Integration and Error Correction: Representation, Estimation, and Testing," *Econometrica* 55 (1987), pp. 251-276.

5. Flemming, J., "Hysteresis and Unemployment," in *Unemployment, Hysteresis and the Natural Rate Hypothesis*, R. Cross, ed. (Oxford: Basil Blackwell, 1988), pp. ix-xi.

6. Franz, W., "Hysteresis, Persistence, and the NAIRU: An Empirical Analysis for the Federal Republic of Germany," in *The Fight Against Unemployment*, R. Layard and L. Calmfors, eds. (Cambridge: MIT Press, 1987), pp. 91-122.

7. ———, "Hysteresis in Economic Relationships: An Overview," *Empirical Economics* 15 (1990), pp. 109-125.

8. Georgescu-Roegen, N., "The Theory of Choice and the Constancy of Economic Laws," *Quarterly Journal of Economics* 64 (1950), pp. 125-138.

9. ———, *The Entropy Law and the Economic Process* (Cambridge: Harvard University Press, 1971).

10. Layard, R., S. Nickel, and R. Jackman, *Unemployment* (Oxford: Oxford University Press, 1991).

11. Lazan, B. J., *Damping of Materials and Members in Structural Mechanics* (Oxford: Pergamon, 1968).

12. Phelps, E. S., *Inflation Policy and Unemployment Theory* (New York: Norton, 1972).

13. Stock, J. H., and M. W. Watson, "Variable Trends in Economic Time Series," *Journal of Economic Perspectives* 2, no. 3 (Summer 1988), pp. 147-174.

14. Vickers, D., "The Long Run and the Short," Bateman Memorial Lecture, Department of Economics, University of Western Australia (Perth), 1991.

15. Wilks, S. S., *Mathematical Statistics* (New York: Wiley, 1962).

16. Wyplos, C., "Comments," in *The Fight Against Unemployment,* R. Layard and L. Calmfors, eds. (Cambridge: MIT Press, 1987), pp. 123-131.

CHAPTER 14

Empirical Analysis

Empirical analysis is the employment of observed facts to shed light on a particular problem. It involves, in general, the gathering of appropriate data, the organizing and summarizing of that data, and the interpretation of the results of the organizing and summarizing process in reference to the issues raised by the original problem. The data may be numerical in character or consist of collections of verbal descriptions. (The previous chapter interpreted such data in terms of history.) In either case, the techniques for organizing and summarizing are similar.[1]

Although the problems to which empirical analyses are addressed can spring from a variety of sources, many arise in connection with theoretical models. Theoretical models, after all, are traditionally built, as pointed out in Chapter 1, to explain what is seen and (or) to predict future events. Such models usually come under the umbrella of equilibrium or disequilibrium analysis and may metaphorically be taken to approximate the generating mechanism that determines, subject to error, the observations. From this perspective, the observations themselves are often interpreted, with respect to the argument of Sections 1.2 and 1.3, as approximating the solution points of static models consisting of simultaneous equations[2] or as approximately lying along equilibrium or nonequilibrium paths produced by dynamic models containing dif-

---

[1]See Katzner [2, Chs. 12,13].

[2]Single-equation models such as, for example, the Cobb-Douglas production function, are special cases in which all observations (that is, in the Cobb-Douglas example, all observations of inputs and outputs) approximately satisfy the equation.

This chapter is reproduced, with considerable additions, corrections, and other modifications, from my "The Role of Empirical Analysis in the Investigation of Situations Involving Ignorance and Historical Time," *Eastern Economic Journal* 17 (1991), pp. 297-303.

ferential or periodic equations. In other words, models are viewed as approximating an underlying real structure, and observations are regarded as approximating the solution values or time-paths of models.[3]

Most empirical analyses today are set in a context in which the relevant data are numerical in character and are explained, as described above, by a theoretical model and error. In addition, it is frequently assumed that the error has its own generating mechanism, and that this latter mechanism is based on a law of probability. The purposes of these empirical analyses often include one or more of the following overlapping goals: describing the observed phenomenon, estimating or fitting particular functional forms to the data, predicting future observations, testing specific theoretical hypotheses in particular, and empirical confirmation or falsification of theoretical constructions in general.

Difficulties arise, however, when examining, from the nonequilibrium perspective of this volume, situations in which time is viewed as historical, and human ignorance is confronted in a significant way. Historical time, remember, has the quality that each moment of it is attached to a distinctive history and is, therefore, unique. This uniqueness generally precludes the possibility of replication of decision situations and repeated contemplations of the same future economic outcomes. Ignorance is a fact of humanity which comes about because of man's limited ability to know certain things. Recognizing both historical time and human ignorance in a given economic situation produces an uncertainty that renders the assumption of a probabilistic error-generating mechanism for that situation untenable. Nor can theoretical models have the same explanatory meaning in the presence of this uncertainty. The formulation of probability functions and the standard interpretations of the theoretical models of equilibrium and disequilibrium analysis simply presume more information than is available. It follows, then, that empirical analysis under conditions of historical time and ignorance has a rather different flavor from that which it possesses

---

[3]It is possible, in the first instance, that the model actually developed is a quantitative "approximation" of an underlying qualitative structure and, in the second, that quantitative observations actually "approximate" qualitative solutions or dynamic time-paths. With respect to the latter, Katzner [2, Ch. 5] describes methods for obtaining nonquantifiable solutions and time-paths from, respectively, systems of simultaneous static and periodic equations involving nonquantified variables.

when these elements are absent.

This final chapter is primarily concerned with the role and nature of empirical analysis in the simultaneous presence of both ignorance and historical time. To set the stage, it begins (Section 14.1) with a brief summary of previous discussion that re-creates some of the characteristics of the historical-time environments in which ignorance appears, and part of the analytical structure developed earlier that may be employed in those environments. It then proceeds to a discussion of the nature of empirical analysis in such situations: Section 14.2 first identifies a few of the traditional kinds of investigations that have to be discarded, and Section 14.3 presents several illustrations of the sort of empirical analysis that can still be undertaken. The chapter (and book) ends with some general concluding remarks in Section 14.4.

14.1 A Partial Recapitulation of Preceding Argument

All actual, economic events in our world take place in historical time. The latter notion of time, as opposed to logical time, is unidirectional and irreversible. Every moment (or period) of historical time is unique with the particular occurrences of that moment emerging from a singular historical past. The distinctive history that each moment carries necessarily imparts its own peculiar knowledge, and this knowledge may be perceived differently by different people. When considered in their relevance for economic decisions and behavior, successive moments in historical time bring with them their own special institutional structures and environments and their own totality and distribution of resource endowments. They also come with their own distinguishing implications for perceptions of the future possibilities that time, at each moment, conceals from view. Historical time can never be started over again as in, for example, the ordinary stability analysis of a Walrasian system, because it is impossible for history to repeat itself without change.[4] A model that is constructed at a given moment and

---

[4]History may, on occasion, give the impression of repetition (recall nn. 17, 18 on p. 25 and the discussion of routine decisions at the end of Section 4.3). But on closer

that recognizes historical time, then, whether employed by an actor in the making of a decision, or by an outside investigator studying those decisions, because it acknowledges the uniqueness of each moment of decision or analysis, generally diverges from all other models having the same purpose but constructed at other moments.

In the environments of present concern, ignorance arises, in part, because time is historical and reality is overwhelmingly complicated. As historical time passes, the present separates the past from the future. Only the present and the past, however, are capable of observation and description. By looking at present and past events, both the decision maker and the investigator can gain perceptions of what is presently happening and what has previously occurred. These perceptions may find expression in the form of a theoretical model explaining that which is and was seen. But it is important to recognize that perceptions are only perceptions, and no more. They are fraught with errors and gaps. The same is true of intellections and knowledge. The world is just too complex to be able to know and to understand everything. Moreover, as suggested above, knowledge, intellections, and perceptions are unique to each individual: everyone thinks different thoughts and knows different things. Thus the decision maker and the investigator always remain partially ignorant of the past. Even after all information available about prior events is taken into account, after all imaginable inferences are drawn, at least a kernel of impenetrable ignorance remains. And this ignorance cannot be assumed away in the formulation of a probabilistic event-generating mechanism or in the standard application of a theoretical model because the decision maker and the investigator have no idea of what they do not know.

Matters are even worse with respect to the future. Because the future cannot be known until it has arrived, neither the decision maker nor the investigator is able to obtain much information about coming events. Knowledge of natural laws and knowledge of human intentions is hardly knowledge of future economic happenings. In Shackle's words [5, p. 3], "What does not yet exist, can not now be known." Nor do human beings have the capacity to see novelty in advance. Even the totality of all possibilities is unknowable. The unexpected can and

---

inspection of details, such impressions often turn out to have been illusory.

does occur. Thus the decision maker and the investigator are in real ignorance about the future. But this does not mean that, based on their error-prone and incomplete perceptions of the present and the past, they cannot guess and imagine possible future contingencies. And such guesses and imaginings may serve as the basis for decisions and analyses in the present as well as for speculations about future eventualities.[5] In this way the decision maker attempts, borrowing from Keynes [3, p. 155], ". . . to defeat the dark forces of time and ignorance which envelop . . . [the] future."

Clearly, then, the decision maker and the investigator come upon at each moment or period of, respectively, decision and analysis with a unique background and with unique thoughts derived from that background. The setting in which the decision maker decides and the investigator analyzes is also unique with its own characteristics and history. In other words, the decision maker and the investigator have their own perceptions of the moment with regard to history, their own perspectives of the moment concerning the things that they take as given, and their own epistemic abilities of the moment to bring to bear on the issue at hand. The same background, the same setting, and the same decision or analytical opportunity can never occur again.

The existence of a residual ignorance of the present and the past and of a more pervasive ignorance of the future mean that the decision maker and the investigator are confronted by uncertainty in the carrying out of their respective activities. Although knowledge removes some (but never all) uncertainty about the present and past, since (as noted above) no knowledge of the future is ever available, the future is always uncertain. To use the idea of probability to describe present, past, or future events (or errors), however, is to assume, from the vantage point adopted in previous chapters, certain knowledge about those events (recall, in particular, Section 2.4). Furthermore, the knowledge that the assumption of probability requires rests, in certain respects, on the possibility of replication. Now probability is clearly a relevant and useful idea in analyzing, say, the drawing of red and white balls

---

[5]It is interesting to note that in this context Shackle [4, p. 13] defines expectations as "imagination constrained to congruity with what seems in some degree possible. . . ."

from an urn because one may draw from the urn over and over again, and the mechanism that generates the outcome of each draw has a stable and unchanging structure. Knowledge of that structure, then, may be obtained from repeated drawings. But in the context of economic decision making, because the existence of ignorance precludes the possession of knowledge of future outcomes and sufficient knowledge about the present and the past, and because historical time rules out replication (since it implies an inability to hold other things equal or constant through time), the application of probability by the decision maker or investigator in dealing with uncertainty has to be dropped.

In constructing a model for a given period in the past (which may come up to and include the present), the investigator (or the decision maker who is investigating prior history for purposes of making a decision in the present) can begin much as if he were exploring a situation in which ignorance did not exist. A differential or periodic equation model could be developed and investigated, and one of its time-paths could be associated (exactly or approximately) with observed reality for the period. If, for example, the investigator were studying the behavior of a decision maker, then the investigator might say that the decision maker behaved "as if" his behavior were determined according to the investigator's model. Then, by extending the model beyond the intended period, the investigator could examine some of the possibilities that might transpire at subsequent dates. However, as described in Section 13.2 and elsewhere, it must be understood that once the time period for the initial explanation is enlarged, the investigator is actually examining a different person (decision maker) in a different world. There may, of course, be similarities between the two worlds and two decision makers, or a "stability" over time that links them together. Nevertheless, the general presumption remains that it would be necessary to construct a separate model or explanation of the behavior of the "new" or changed person and that this model would not be the same as the original. In addition, as time passes, the investigator may have more information available for his study, his own background may have changed, and the environment in which he is doing his study may have modified. For these reasons, too, the model he now builds to explain what he sees may well be different from the original. In particular, when exploring a historical process or the movement and change of a phenomenon over time from some date in history to the present, as time moves on to reveal the unpredictable novelty that weaves itself into the tapestry of life, the model explaining that phenomenon must necessarily undergo significant alteration.

One kind of model that an investigator might employ to explain individual economic behavior is the model of decision making in ignorance built up in Section 4.3. In this model, remember, the decision maker faces certain specified choice options (objects of choice) and, in thinking about them, imagines an incomplete collection of states of the world that might emerge along with his selection of any one option. Although the residual hypothesis (defined, recall, as the unknowable class of all remaining states that the decision maker is unable to imagine and symbolically represented as the null set) is not an element of this latter collection, it is still a subset of it. Since the decision maker is assumed to define a potential surprise function over all subsets of the collection of imagined states of the world, it follows that potential surprise is characterized for both imaginable and unimaginable states (Section 2.2). Specifically, the potential surprise of a subset A is the surprise the decision maker imagines now that he would experience in the future were a state in A actually to occur. This potential surprise function is translated into potential surprise density functions, one for each choice option, defined over the incomplete collection of imagined states expressed in terms of utility values or outcomes with respect to that option. And using the density function, it is legitimate to speak of the potential surprise of a single utility outcome. Although similar in certain features, potential surprise and potential surprise density functions are generally distinct in both conception and in their attendant characteristics from probability and probability density functions. A full exposition of their differing axiomatic foundations was provided in Chapters 2 and 3.

The decision maker is also assumed to define, for each choice option, an attractiveness function over the collection of all pairs consisting of a utility outcome and the potential surprise value identified with that outcome. The attractiveness function serves to order these pairs according to the extent to which they stand out in the decision maker's mind and secure his attention. It is taken to have sufficient properties so as to permit its maximization subject to the potential surprise density function associated with the same choice option. Under the assumptions of the model, there are actually two maximizing pairs, the focus gain and focus loss, and these serve to characterize that option. Finally, decisions are made among the various choice options by comparing, according to a decision index devised by the decision maker, the focus gain and focus loss that characterize each. It is clear in this model that the collection of choice options, the imagined states of the world that emerge from them, the potential surprise and potential surprise density functions, the attractiveness function, and the decision index all depend on the moment (or period) of historical time at which the decision is made, and on the nature and epistemic status of the decision maker at that moment. Different decision makers, obviously, or the same decision maker at different moments of historical time, would be expected to make different decisions.

The historical time and ignorance environment in which this model is set implies, among other things, that it is not possible to obtain traditional market-level and macroeconomic-type behavioral functions by first applying the model to each of a collection of individuals to secure their individual behavioral functions and then aggregating across them. This is because the behavioral functions of each individual have that individual's perceptions of market prices as independent variables, not the prices actually existing in the markets, and the functions themselves reflect only the individuals' plans and expectations, which are likely to fail or remain unfulfilled. Thus, in the case of market analysis, say, the standard approach involving the equilibration of demand and supply is underspecified and can no longer be employed and, in its place, the use of market analogues of individual behavioral functions, price-setting by sellers, or pairwise bargaining by individual buyers and sellers has been suggested.

Another implication of the analytical incorporation of historical time and ignorance into economic models is that the simultaneous activity of individuals in those models produces kaleidic sequences of events that have no relation whatsoever to the notion of equilibrium. The passage of historical time brings new epistemic statuses, new situations, and new opportunities to individuals. And as expectations continually fail out of individuals' ignorance, and as plans are continually revised to overcome those failures, new models generating new behavioral functions continually emerge to meet the continually changing circumstances. In general, all explanations of behavior taking place across historical time have to reflect the necessity of discarding the model built for any one moment or period in order to construct a model for the next. Such explanations, moreover, must also recognize that where the economic world is today depends on where it has been in the past; and that where it is going tomorrow, although emerging from where it is today, cannot be known in advance. The models of the firm, the consumer, the microeconomy, and the macroeconomy developed in Part III above rest on these ideas.

14.2 What Cannot Be Done

In discussing the role of empirical analysis under conditions of historical time and ignorance, it may be helpful to start by identifying some kinds of inquiry that, although legitimate in the world to which probability relates, are not possible when ignorance is present. Perhaps the most obvious of these is probabilistic prediction. Such prediction requires the use of a theoretical model and past data to discern trends probabilistically and then the extrapolation and projection of those trends into the future. One way to do this when using a static, simultaneous equations model is to estimate the coefficients of the model's reduced-form equations from the data. Predictions of future values of the dependent variables are obtained from these estimated equations by projecting values of the independent variables over the future period under consideration. But in order to execute any such procedure in a way that is faithful to the traditional probabilistic methodology, it is necessary to know, first, that the model describing yesterday is valid for tomorrow (in particular, that novelty will not appear), and, second, the probabilistic law governing error. Such knowledge, although obtainable, as indicated above, when studying, for example, the drawing of red and white balls from an urn, does not exist for the decision maker and investigator dealing with economic phenomena in historical time and with ignorance depicted in Section 14.1 and elsewhere. Their uncertainty about the past, present, and future, then, completely rules out any possibility of probabilistic prediction.

A second line of inquiry that has to be abandoned in the presence of historical time and ignorance is the determination of whether a particular decision made by an actor under study turns out to be "correct" in light of the outcome that follows it.[6] For situations in which the notion of probability is applicable, to be able to judge the correctness of a previous decision usually requires that the forces determining the outcome, given the decision, are accurately described by a known probability density function, and that both the density function itself, as well as the criteria of judgement, have not changed from the time of decision to the time of outcome. In this setting the correct decision is often one that maximizes the expected value of the criteria of judgment. The reason why evaluations of correctness cannot be undertaken when time is historical and ignorance exists is because decisions rest on information about the present and the past, and on contemplations of the choice options and their possibile future effects as they are envisaged at the decision date. Outcomes are determined independently by unknowable events that occur in the future. Since there is no causal link between choice options and future events that can actually be known to the decision maker (though such causal links do exist and may be imagined), and since the criteria of judgment need not remain fixed, the idea that he is able to make correct or incorrect decisions has no relevance for evaluations of the outcome of the decision process. In time, the decision maker can certainly come to regret his decision. But, although the possibility of regret can be contemplated in advance, there is no way for him to anticipate the fact of its occurrence at the moment of decision.[7]

With hindsight, of course, the decision maker may conclude that some decisions would have produced better results than others. These conclusions, however, are speculations only. For looking back, a model covering the period during which the decision was made and the outcome emerged could be constructed, and the decision itself could be judged in terms of that model. But it is not possible to assert, even in the context of that model, that an alternative decision would definitely have been better. To establish such an assertion would necessitate

---

[6]See Vickers [6, p. 50].

[7]*Ibid.*, p. 55.

returning in time to the point of decision, inserting the decision alternative in place of the original decision, and watching to see what different forms of newness would arise and how the outcome would be affected. Therefore, even if the criteria for evaluating decisions remains the same, because time is irreversible and replication impossible, evaluations of decisions with respect to outcomes can only be highly informal and conjectural.

It might be thought that in analyzing, in the framework of historical time and ignorance, an issue that has already been considered in the context of logical time and perfect knowledge through the use of probabilistic techniques, the replacement of probability functions with potential surprise functions could prove useful. Empirical analysis could then focus on discovering the actual potential surprise or potential surprise density counterparts to the analogous probability or probability density functions for the problem at hand. Although, as will be argued momentarily, such replacement is not helpful in rescuing probabilistic statistical analysis from its probability environment, it should be noted here that the empirical determination by an outsider of an individual's potential surprise or potential surprise density function (which might be employed in place of corresponding probability functions) from observed data of the present and past is a third line of inquiry drawn from the context of probability (viz., the empirical discovery of probability and probability density functions) that becomes invalid upon translation into a world of historical time and ignorance. (Recall that in the decision model of Section 4.3, the decision maker possesses a potential surprise function over subsets of imagined states of the world that is translated into potential surprise density functions, one for each choice option, defined with respect to utility outcomes. Alternatively, an investigator could also have such functions in mind when thinking about the error that might arise in postulating a relation among certain variables.) The reason why a potential surprise function, say, cannot be so determined is because, as pointed out above, there can be no causal link knowable to the decision maker or the investigator between present and past data, on the one hand, and speculations about the future on the other. At least three factors contribute to the unknowability of this link: first, as indicated in n. 10 on p. 48, to say, based on knowledge of the present and past, that the surprise one currently anticipates feeling were a state of the world in some subset A to occur in the future (or, in other words, that the potential surprise of A) is s', does not mean that if a state in A actually appears one will, in fact, feel s'. By the time the state in A comes to pass (if, indeed, it actually does), things will have changed, and a modified epistemic status might lead one to feel, say, $s'' \neq s'$. Second, a person's potential surprise function is a very personal matter. Present and past data, along with the perception of historical trends that may be suggested by them, are three of many things that go into its making. Also included are personal experiences; psychological elements such as habits, biases, and the emotional state of the individual; political and social pressures coming from colleagues; and even how well the individual is feeling when he is calculating potential surprise values. To pass from all of these things to the potential surprise function involves an unexplainable leap in the mind of the individual from the partially perceived present and past to an independently generated and unknowable future. The individual, himself, cannot say how he does it. Third, the elements that go into the construction of his potential surprise function, along with the process of construction itself, change from moment to moment as historical time moves on. Thus, for example, in the course of making a decision, the perceptions and other subjective inputs that the decision maker brings to bear may modify. Hence the potential surprise function that the decision maker employs at the moment of decision can be quite different from that which he would have had if his perceptions and other subjective inputs had remained as they were when he first began thinking about the decision he should make. In general, then, although the individual is perfectly capable of stating what his potential surprise function is, an outsider is unable to reconstitute it by observing the present and the past.

The last inappropriate line of inquiry to be described here (potentially derived by analogy to probabilistic analysis) is the use of distributional techniques to analyze data. Because replication is impossible, any statistical method of analysis that relies on the idea of repeated sampling from a distribution has to be discarded. In particular, standard statistical (inferential) sampling procedures such as hypothesis testing, estimation, and determining confidence intervals can no longer be used. Even if the probability distribution upon which these methods rest were replaced by a potential surprise distribution, the methods themselves would still not hold up because the notion that each element of data is taken from the same distribution, that is, the notion that repeated observations are produced by an event-generating mechanism that is unchanging over (historical) time, lies at the core of each sampling procedure.

14.3 What Can Be Done

With all of these limitations on empirical analysis under conditions of historical time and ignorance, what role can empirical inquiry play in helping to understand situations in which both ignorance and historical time are present? There are at least three possibilities. The first role is to describe history, that is, to collect and summarize historical data. The gathered data can be in either verbal or numerical form, and summaries of the latter kind of data can be expressed in terms of means and variances, quantitative trends, tendencies, and patterns, and so on, as long as these summary numbers are not interpreted in reference to (*e.g.*, as moments of) probability distributions. (Verbal data, too, can often be "summarized" in similar numerical form. For example, one way to condense verbal data that characterizes the nature of past investment projects is to use in its place the average number of times investment projects undertaken in a particular area have turned out to be profitable). Of course, in addition to the aid it affords in understanding various phenomena, the description of historical data – numerical or otherwise – often contributes, as has previously been suggested, to the formation of imagination and potential surprise in the process of decision making.

When the data are quantified, one may even, as indicated in Section 13.2, "estimate" the parameters of equations in the context of historical description. Suppose, at a previous moment or over a previous period of time, an investigator (or decision maker) observes a scatter of data that seems to suggest a linear relation between two variables. Such a scatter can arise in time-series or cross-sectional form. For, just as an investigator might come to the judgment that, as described in Section 13.2, a single, fixed model reasonably explains the past behavior of one individual over several moments or periods of time, so might he, in another instance, conclude that a single, fixed model reasonably explains the past behavior of several individuals at one moment or period of time.[8] In either case, the investigator can certainly fit a straight line to the scatter by minimizing the sum of squared residuals. This, by itself, is a nondistributional approach to estimating the parameters of the relation because it does not require the assumption that the residuals follow a law of probability. Of course, the estimates so obtained (which are properly called "least squares" estimates) cannot be examined to determine if they are "best, linear, and unbiased" since these latter properties have meaning only when a probability distribution is present. In any case, the fitted line can be taken by the investigator to be part of his perception of the history of the two variables.

The second use of empirical analysis by an investigator (or, again, a decision maker) facing ignorance in the context of historical time is as the springboard for nonprobabilistic predictions. Nonprobabilistic predictions are derived from the trends, tendencies, patterns, and estimated equations developed to describe history by projecting them into the future[9] without any presumptions concerning probability distributions. As such, these predictions may be employed to guide the investigator's understandings of possible future observations of the phenomena under scrutiny.

The third role for empirical analysis in situations of historical time and ignorance is the nonstatistical, empirical falsification and corroboration of theoretical propositions and models for specific periods of history. The degree to which a model, say, is consistent with historical fact can be investigated by informally comparing the model and its properties to the actual history of the period – verbal or numerical. Of course, as has been argued in Section 6.1, behavioral functions cannot, in general, be so checked against the observed data generated by a single individual because they are not usually functions of observed variables, and even if they were only a single point on each function could ever be observed. Nevertheless, as suggested by the discussion of Chapter 6 and Section 13.2, to the extent that (under appropriate and special conditions) the same model may be used to describe be-

---

[8]Recall the discussion at the start of Section 6.2.

[9]See Hutchison [1, p. 21].

havior over more than one period or across more than one individual, the possibility of confronting that model, or certain of its parts, with observed data arises. And even the general case, in which the model is presumed to modify from period to period and from person to person, the investigator can still, as indicated in the introduction to Chapter 6, question the actors to see if it has, or has had, any relevance for what they do.

These three roles for empirical analysis are very important both to be able to understand and to take action (*i.e.*, make decisions) in historical-time situations of ignorance. Clearly, the main goal of the scholar is comprehension, that is, explanation of the observed world, including behavior, action, and events in it. And comprehension is not complete without both theoretical and empirical analysis. Moreover, if an individual bases actions or decisions on prior events or, as in the decision-making scheme of Section 4.3, on imagined future states of the world (which depend, in part, on prior events), then empirical descriptions of history are crucial to his decision making. For they are the only source for the development of his perceptions of the past, and these perceptions figure significantly in the formulation of any potential surprise function that he uses.

14.4 Conclusion

Preceding chapters and sections have been concerned with economic inquiry when historical time and ignorance are taken fully into account. Because, in the nonequilibrium-analytic approach adopted here, certain, rather common, investigative perspectives and techniques can no longer be employed, because, that is, both theory construction and empirical exploration have to be recast in different hues, the present volume has largely focused on the issue of what economic investigation might look like under these conditions. What kind of structure could it have? What characteristics would it take on? As has been seen, these questions have many facets and may be considered in a variety of ways: It is now clear, for example, that Walrasian- or general-equilibrium-type analysis is not relevant to understanding a world with historical time and ignorance, and that, instead, simultaneity has to be understood in the context of kaleidic change. In addition, to the extent that the "partial equilibrium" approach of Marshall (who, as pointed out earlier, seemed to be aware of the problems of both historical time and ignorance) can be modified so as to avoid the notion of equilibrium and related concepts, it is capable of handling the particularities that historical time and ignorance introduce. But regardless of whether the perspective is one of simultaneous activity, or individual or market behavior, the use of abstraction in the analysis of historical time and ignorance phenomena remains, as abundantly illustrated in earlier argument, an appropriate means for building explanation and understanding,[10] although, of course, history necessarily takes on a more significant role.

The comparison of the nature of the analytical structures developed on previous pages to those of traditional general equilibrium and partial equilibrium analyses is worth pursuing. First, in a general equilibrium model the questions of the existence, uniqueness, and stability of equilibria are important because, among other things, an affirmative resolution of them demonstrates internal consistency and determinateness, and permits the interpretation of the actual time-path followed by the economy in the real world in terms of equilibrium in the model (Section 1.2). But, of course, in the models of Part III, there can be no equilibrium. Nevertheless, it is still necessary that these latter models produce unique variable values at each moment or period of time since the unique variable values are to be identified, as in general equilibrium analysis, with the observations of those variable values taken during corresponding moments or periods. In this way, the model is said to explain what has been seen. Thus, in the environment of historical time and ignorance emphasized in the present volume, the existence and uniqueness questions pertaining to any model are only queries about the internal consistency and determinateness of that model. The relation to equilibrium of the variable values produced by the model, and the interpretation of reality with respect to that equilibrium, have no relevance or significance at all.

Second, in the typical general or partial equilibrium approaches, "welfare" analysis has prominence because it establishes the senses in

---

[10]Hutchison has discussed a similar issue [1, Ch. 4].

which the equilibria of general equilibrium models, or the activity explained by partial equilibrium models, are efficient or desirable. Thus, under traditional assumptions, including those that imply the stability of equilibrium paths, one can conclude, for example, that the "invisible hand" of perfectly competitive market activity eventually leads the economy to an outcome that is both predictable in advance and beneficial to society. However, in the models of, say, the micro- and macroeconomies of, respectively, Chapters 11 and 12, because it would require knowledge of an unknowable future, there is no way to tell where either economy is going. All that can be done is to explain how these economies came to be where they are and to describe some future directions they may take. Be that as it may, one might still ask if there is any criterion or method for discovering whether the position in which either economy has arrived, or their possible future positions, are efficient or desirable. This question has been raised, albeit only superficially, in the context of two-person, two-commodity exchange in Section 8.1. More generally, perhaps a welfare function could be developed that, although it would modify with the passage of historical time, could still shed light on these issues. Similar problems arise at the levels of the individual and the isolated market. In any event, these matters have not been pursued seriously here.

Third, and last, in customary general equilibrium analysis, or in standard partial equilibrium analysis, the effects of government policies can be considered by introducing into, respectively, an appropriate general equilibrium model or partial equilibrium model, parameters over which the government exercises control, and asking how changes in the values of those parameters alter the equilibrium position achieved by the model. Although something similar could be and, however briefly (Chapters 11 and 12), was investigated in the context of nonequilibrium analysis, it is not possible to ascertain in general the impact of changes in the values of the control parameters on the future variable values determined by a model. This is because both the functions of the model, as well as the current values of its other parameters, would be expected to modify before the effects of the government policy, that is, the consequences of the changes in the government-controlled parameters, could work themselves out. Nevertheless, as was implicit in the approach taken in Chapters 11 and 12, the *possible* effects of the government policies, assuming no change in functions and other parameters, could still be examined in terms of comparative statics analysis.

An additional tack for policy activity to pursue arises from the fact, described at length in earlier chapters, that in a kaleidic economy the plans of decision makers may be inconsistent with each other, and those inconsistencies may be thought to lead to, for example, situations of high unemployment, inflation, or both. Now, as described previously, when decision makers discover the effects of such inconsistencies in their inablilty to fulfill completely, or even partially, their plans, they set about reworking them. The question arises, then, of whether, under appropriate conditions, policies might be adopted having the objective of inducing decision makers to reformulate their plans in a manner that, it would be hoped, would lead to a wider and more rapid convergence of plans in the future and, thereby, to a higher attainable level of general economic well-being.

There are a number of obvious areas in which the scope for such policy initiatives is clear. To begin with, a necessity for industrial restructuring can arise from variation in the pattern of consumer expenditures, technological change, or alteration of the composition or level of government expenditure brought about by political activities and events. When one or more of these transformations occurs, policies that provide fiscal incentives like investment tax allowances, tax breaks for research and development, and needed infrastructure may help to speed up the necessary restructuring. Furthermore, to stimulate economic growth, or to respond to the investment requirements emerging from significant technological change, it might be thought desirable to put pressure on consumer spending and saving habits to raise the aggregate level of savings. Policies that could succeed in accomplishing the latter include the provision of new forms, like IRAs, in which savings can be held, and the modification of existing inheritance tax laws. And, finally, at the macrolevel, monetary, fiscal, and incomes policies may be invoked to counter the unwanted extremes of the business cycle and promote growth.

It should also be noted that in all cases, the knowledge basis upon which policymakers have to rely in determining policy is similar in many respects to that available to private decision makers. For in an environment of historical time and ignorance, policymakers, like private decision makers, possess only incomplete, if not inaccurate, knowledge of the past and present, and no knowledge at all of the future. Policymakers, after all, are human too, and face the abyss of ignorance along with everyone else. But in the same way that private decision makers can, say, spell out the possible effects of possible choices and be guided by trends in arriving at decisions, so can policymakers, as suggested above, use similar techniques to make policies. Of course, in light of the kaleidic swiftness with which change can occur, and in view of the unknowability of future effects that change might produce, it is evident that a high degree of flexibility is called for. Thus the presence of historical time and ignorance does not imply the nonexistence of effective economic policy. For, as has just been seen, there is both a scope for such policy as well as a knowledge basis from which it can be drawn. The present discussion, however, is only a brief introduction to policy analysis. Clearly there is much room for further investigation in this area too.

Another important matter that has not been explored fully here is the application of the methods and techniques of inquiry developed in earlier chapters to the examination of so-called "applied" problems. Typically, and very generally, an investigation of such a problem would involve the construction of a highly particularized model to suit a very special circumstance. The kaleidic sequence of variable values emanating from that model as it is transformed across historical time would often be fitted to observed variable values, and the role of history in the context of the problem would be considered. In this regard, however, it is not necessary (nor is it necessary in general) to focus only on variable values that can be measured on ordinal, cardinal, or ratio scales. Since it is possible to construct, manipulate, and empirically investigate models involving nonquantified variables, analysis of the unmeasured or unmeasurable need not be dismissed out of hand.[11]

By way of illustration, a number of specific quantitative and qualitative applications, some developed more completely than others, have been presented on previous pages. These include an explanation of the "observed" fact that a person's proportion of savings out of current income tends to rise with his age (Secton 6.2); the derivation of simple

---

[11]See Katzner [2].

decision rules that are usable in real situations (Section 6.3); the interpretation of the (qualitative) scenario approach to decision making at
Shell International, and Franklin's (qualitative) advise on decision making in terms of the elements of Section 4.3's model of decision making
in ignorance (Section 6.3); and, as mentioned above, several propositions analyzing the possible effects of certain government policies on
the micro- and macroeconomies (Chapters 11 and 12). Such illustrations convey an idea of the kinds of applications that are possible. But,
of course, they are only a beginning. Moreover, it is clear that the
potential for developing applications in general is unlimited. For just
as traditional models have been and continue to be applied, say, to explain time-series or cross-sectional data in the context of logical time
and perfect knowledge, so the discussion of Section 6.2 shows that models set in environments of historical time and ignorance are capable of
being built and applied to explain, or provide alternative explanations
of, the same kind of data.

The vision of our economic world emerging from analyses, such as
those elaborated in this volume, that account for historical time and
ignorance is evidently quite different from the Walrasian vision underlying much of contemporary economic thought. That Walrasian vision
consists of consumers engaged in self-interested behavior given their
preferences and endowments, firms engaged in self-interested behavior given their technologies and capital stocks, and the simultaneous,
seemingly chaotic, interaction of those consumers and firms in markets
that produces coherent, well-defined outcomes that may be evaluated
and among which society may choose. It is an image that resonates
with the strong undercurrent of individualism in Western thought and
culture. The vision emanating from Part III above, however, although
encapsulating self-interested behavior on the part of consumers (subject to preferences and endowments) and firms (subject to technologies
and capital stocks), although permitting the evaluation of the possible
future outcomes it furnishes, and although clearly reflecting the tenets
of Western individualism, does not provide a well-defined collection of
outcomes from which selections by society can be made. Indeed, it
cannot. And any attempt to do so would prove illusory. For no sooner
would society attempt to put a such a "choice" into effect than the
model determining the collection of outcomes from which society just

chose could change, and the choice it just made might no longer seem relevant and might not even be available. Thus visions of economic reality that account for historical time and ignorance are in accordance with explanations of the past and present, and possible scenarios of what might come, but they are incompatible with the idea that the future course of economic progress can be selected.

14.5 References

1. Hutchison, T. W., *Knowledge and Ignorance in Economics* (Oxford: Basil Blackwell, 1977).

2. Katzner, D. W., *Analysis without Measurement* (Cambridge: Cambridge University Press, 1983).

3. Keynes, J. M., *The General Theory of Employment Interest and Money* (London: Macmillan, 1936).

4. Shackle, G. L. S., *Decision Order and Time in Human Affairs*, 2nd ed. (Cambridge: Cambridge University Press, 1969).

5. ———, *Epistemics and Economics* (Cambridge: Cambridge University Press, 1972).

6. Vickers, D., "Time, Ignorance, Surprise, and Economic Decisions: A Comment on Williams and Findlay's 'Risk and the Role of Failed Expectations in an Uncertain World,'" *Journal of Post Keynesian Economics* 9 (1986-87), pp. 48-57.

Index